Fine WoodWorking® TECHNIQUES 2

Fine
WoodWorking
TECHNIQUES 2

Selected by the Editors
of Fine Woodworking magazine

The Taunton Press
Newtown, Connecticut

Typeface: Compugraphic Garamond and Univers
Paper: Mead Offset Enamel 70 lb.
Printer: Connecticut Printers, Bloomfield, Conn.
Binder: Haddon Craftsmen, Scranton, Pa.

The Taunton Press, Inc.
52 Church Hill Rd.
Box 355
Newtown, Connecticut 06470

CONTENTS

Introduction vii

WOOD

Chain-Saw Lumbering 2
Getting Lumber 7
Measuring Moisture 8
Lumber Grading 10
Cleaving Wood 13
Knife Checks in Veneer 17

SHOP AND TOOLS

Dust-Collection System 22
Small Workbench 25
Tool Cabinets 26
Holding the Work 28
Methods of Work 31
Basic Blacksmithing 32
Whetstones 36
Sharpening 38
Wooden Clamps 42
A Dowel Maker 45
Methods of Work 48
Scratch Beader 50
Two Tools 51
Sawing by Hand 52
Circular Saws 56
Methods of Work 60
End-Boring Jig 62
Scale Models 63
Basic Machine Maintenance 64

CABINETMAKING

Preparation of Stock 70
Pencil Gauges 75
Triangle Marking 76
Drawers 78
Methods of Work 82
Drawer Bottoms 83
Routed Edge Joint 86
Tambours 88
Shaped Tambours 94
Of the Cylinder Desk and Book-Case 95
Methods of Work 96
Louvered Doors 96
Entry Doors 98
The Right Way to Hang a Door 102
Hanging a Door 103
A Two-Way Hinge 105
Designing for Dining 106
Wooden Clockworks 110

CONTENTS

TURNING AND CARVING

Spindle Turning....................................120
Methods of Work...................................124
Small Turned Boxes.................................125
Turning Spalted Wood..............................128
Laminated Turnings.................................134
Rings from Wedges.................................135
Staved Cones......................................139
Laminated Bowls...................................140
The Flageolet.....................................142
Methods of Work...................................144
Aztec Drum.......................................144
Carving Lab......................................146
Chain-Saw Carving.................................148
Methods of Work...................................152
Relief Carving....................................152
Ball and Claw Feet................................156
Cockleshell.......................................158

BENDING AND VENEERING

Steam Bending....................................162
Hot-Pipe Bending.................................168
Hammer Veneering.................................172
Leather on Wood..................................175
Cutting Corners...................................178
Parsons Tables....................................180

FINISHING

Stains, Dyes and Pigments.........................186
Methods of Work...................................188
Notes on Finishing................................188
Methods of Work...................................192
Sanding...193
Tung Oil..196

Index...198

Credits...200

INTRODUCTION

There are many "right" ways to do a job in woodworking. Though issues ranging from the best way to cut a mortise-and-tenon joint to the best way to screw pieces of wood together often are debated with fervor by equally skilled craftsmen, in the end the results are the only judge. The articles in this book, compiled from issues of *Fine Woodworking* magazine published between Fall 1977 (#8) and Fall 1978 (#13), bring you a variety of successful methods practiced by skilled woodworkers, and also give you a look at the results.

Many aspects of the craft are covered. Have you ever wondered how bentwood furniture parts are made, or how the ribs for boats are formed? Bill Keyser, professor of woodworking and furniture design at Rochester Institute of Technology, describes his steam-bending equipment and techniques. Are you curious about the rich, lustrous surfaces achieved by old-time wood finishers? Master finisher George Frank reveals some of his secrets, methods developed during 50 years in the trade in Paris and New York. Are you dismayed over the high cost of hardwood? Chain-saw lumbering, as described by Robert Sperber, designer and builder of a chain-saw mill, might be the answer.

Other articles in this collection tell about building tool cabinets and a small workbench, preparing your stock, making drawers and tambours, turning spalted wood, carving ball-and-claw feet and constructing entry doors. How to hang a door? Tage Frid, professor of woodworking and furniture design at Rhode Island School of Design, tells you the "right" way, and Willis Ryan III, who has been hanging doors for 15 years, tells *his* "right" way. In woodworking, there is always more to learn.

As in *Fine Woodworking Techniques 1*, a compilation of articles from the first seven issues of *Fine Woodworking*, each article in this second volume is reprinted in full. Where reference is made to another article reprinted in this volume, the text has been amended to reflect the new page numbers. Interspersed throughout the articles are selections from the magazine's Methods of Work column, a forum where readers exchange information on tools, jigs and tricks they've devised at the bench. In many cases, the methods were written in response to the longer articles, and provide hints on some detail of a technique or on another way to do the job. We hope that the format of this book and the methods and techniques presented will enhance your work and make the process more rewarding.

Chain-saw Lumbering

Cut your wood where it falls

by Robert Sperber

I am a woodworker and have always been turned off by the "supermarket" approach to buying wood. In more and more places we must call up and order so many board feet of one kind of wood or another. We have no opportunity to choose a log and tell the mill just how we would like it cut. We can't even pick through a stack. The wood is banded together and we must take what we get. It has always seemed to me that the best way to avoid this situation would be to saw the log myself. Slicing through a log and taking that first peek inside is a great thrill and a wonderful source of inspiration.

The answer that I found is the portable chain-saw mill. It is the only solution that the individual craftsman can afford. In a few days of hard work I can cut enough wood to pay for the mill. The cutting is done by a saw chain specially ground for ripping (see page 5). Power is provided by one or two large chain-saw engines, with horizontal rollers guiding the cutting bar. There is no need to move the log; it can be cut wherever it has fallen. Rather than the log moving through the mill, as at a sawmill, the operator pulls this mill through the log.

Portable mills have been available for years, although little attention has been paid to them. Many knowledgeable people believe that the portable mill is too slow to be practical. But using the proper procedures, power units and a sharp ripping chain, a well-designed mill will move along at up to 10 sq. ft. a minute, cutting efficiently and well.

Most of the wood I have cut has been either from dead trees or trees that were going to be taken down for some other reason. People are willing to give away a dead tree rather than see it rot. Once the tree has been felled, I must decide where to crosscut it into logs. There is no set rule for this: it depends upon one's needs and interests. You may want to include the crotches, which a commercial mill would cut out and discard. Some of the most interesting patterns are hidden away inside the crotches, and they may be well worth keeping, if the wood is to be used for furniture or turning. The tree is then bucked up into separate logs, and the first one to be cut is rolled to a position that takes advantage of its features. For example, if the log is oval in cross section, placing the long

Author, right, and Edgar Anderson (page 7) mill lumber in woods. Two-man chain-saw mill cuts up to a 36-in. wide board from ¼ in. to 15 in. thick. Four horizontal rollers can be adjusted up and down.

Distance between cutting bar and rollers shows on scale on vertical rod. Mill with two chain-saw engines weighs about 75 lbs.; ear protection is essential.

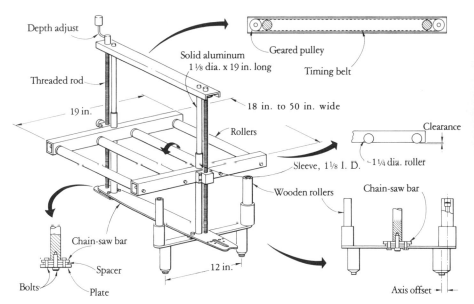

Depth adjust

Threaded rod

19 in.

Solid aluminum
1 ⅛ dia. x 19 in. long

18 in. to 50 in. wide

Rollers

Geared pulley

Timing belt

Clearance

Sleeve, 1 ⅛ I. D.

1 ¼ dia. roller

Wooden rollers

Chain-saw bar

Chain-saw bar

Spacer

Bolts

Plate

12 in.

Axis offset

Diagram at left shows principal parts of Sperber's mill. Diagram below shows how home-built slabbing rail guides first cut. Emery-faced vee blocks, detail photo above, are nailed near ends of log, then clamped to rail. Cross-braces are set below rail's surface so clamps don't interfere with rollers.

diameter horizontally yields the widest boards. A knot or crotch in the horizontal plane results in a flame pattern on the board. To get the best pattern from the crotch, the cut should go through both centers on the same pass.

Since a log is irregular, a slabbing rail is used to guide the first cut. This rail, flat on its top edge, ensures that the cut will also be flat. The rail is placed on top of the log and secured by two wooden blocks nailed into the log at either end, with the nails going into the wood about 3/4 in. The rail is then clamped to the blocks with two adjustable clamps.

Next, the distance from the top of the rail to where the first cut is to be made is measured, and the mill is set to that dimension. One must be sure that this first cut will clear the nails holding the wooden blocks. The mill is then placed with its horizontal rollers resting on the rail and pulled through the log. It is very important on this first cut to keep the rollers flat on the rail and not allow them to tip to one side. This is not difficult, but some attention must be paid to it.

After the first cut, there is no need to use the slabbing rail, because the mill can roll directly on the flat top surface of the wood. The mill is now set and locked at the desired thickness. For the cabinetmaker 5/4, 6/4 and 8/4 are generally the most useful; for the turner, slabs four or five inches thick might be desirable. The carver might want slabs as thick as 10 inches.

Next the mill is placed on the log and pulled through. As the mill cuts, there is a tremendous amount of side force, which pulls the left-hand engine in toward the log. This pulls the vertical rollers firmly against the log but allows the mill to roll forward. With both front and rear vertical rollers firmly against the log, the mill sits at the slight angle at which it will cut best. As the mill moves along the log, the vertical rollers encounter bumps and depressions. By changing the angle, the side force can be shifted from the front to the back rollers, allowing the mill to move smoothly past these obstacles.

At the end of the log, the mill is pivoted around on the rear vertical roller to complete the cut. This keeps the front vertical roller from rolling off the end of the log, and also keeps the plank from falling onto the cutting bar until the very last second. At this point the bar is almost through the wood and cannot be trapped under the plank. Only when very thick planks are being cut is it necessary to drive a wedge into the kerf to support the plank as it is freed.

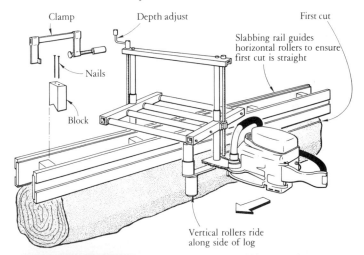

Clamp

Depth adjust

First cut

Slabbing rail guides horizontal rollers to ensure first cut is straight

Nails

Block

Vertical rollers ride along side of log

With slabbing rail (end view) in place, first cut is begun.

Chain-sawn lumber is stickered and sheltered to dry in air.

With ends of log resting on vee-cut blocks, Sperber makes bottom cut using one-engine chain-saw mill. Side force generated by engine pulls front and rear vertical rollers against the log. Mill advances at slight angle, at which it cuts best. At end of cut, mill pivots on rear roller as cutting bar swings free.

When making 2x4's or quartersawing, dividing cut stops a few inches short of log end. Then cut is wedged open and mill backed out, to permit 90° rotation of log for next series of cuts. For quartersawing, dividing cut is the first cut, and is made with slabbing rail.

After 90° rotation of log and first cut on top (with slabbing rail), log is square on three sides. Now groups of 2x4's can be sliced off, and separated later. By changing the mill settings, most construction lumber can be cut easily.

When the log has been cut down to a slab about 4 in. thick, it must be lifted up to prevent the lower vertical rollers from jamming into the ground. By the time a log is that small, it is light enough to lift and place a wooden block under each end. I use two 8-in. high blocks with a vee-cut in the top. Then the final cuts can be made.

Flatsawing is only one of the possible uses for the portable chain-saw mill. Sawing construction lumber is another. Anything from 2x4's to 15-in. x 15-in. beams can easily be cut. The length depends only on the length of the slabbing rail.

To square a beam or make 2x4's, the slabbing rail is set on the log, as in flatsawing, and the first cut is taken. Next a bottom cut is made (top photo). The log now has two parallel surfaces. If a squared beam is desired, no other cut will be made until the log has been rotated; or if it is to be cut into a number of smaller beams, it is divided into the desired dimensions (4 in., for 2x4's). These dividing cuts should stop about 2 in. short of the end of the log and, with the kerf wedged, the mill should then be backed out of the cut. This allows the log to stay in one piece so that the perpendicular cuts can be made. The log is now rotated 90° and the slabbing rail is once again set up and a top cut is made. Next the mill is set at 2 in. (for 2x4's) and pairs or groups of 2x4's are sliced off, to be separated later. When squaring a beam, once the log has been rotated 90°, a top cut is taken using the slabbing rail and a bottom cut is made to complete the beam.

To quartersaw a log, attach the slabbing rail and cut through the *center* of the log, stopping short of the end and backing out the mill, as in making dimension lumber. Then rotate the log 90°, reposition the slabbing rail and again cut through the center, this time all the way through. Place the halves of the log on the ground, curved side down, and make a top cut. Then split each half in two, leaving the log in quarters. Each quarter is propped up on blocks so that one flat face is horizontal and one vertical. Then make a cut, rotate the log 90° so the other flat face is horizontal, cut, rotate back 90°, cut, and so on. Because of all this manipulation, quartersawing is time-consuming. Unless you begin with a very large log, the boards will be so narrow that quartersawing will not be worthwhile.

The chain-saw mill is safer than the conventional chain saw. Since the chain is always engaged in the log, there is no kickback; if the chain breaks, it simply falls off the sprocket and is trapped in the log. A modern chain saw does not vibrate much, but milling is still a noisy and dusty operation. I always wear goggles and ear protection. I advise wearing a dust mask, particularly if you are working on the side of the mill where the rollers are. Pulling the mill through the log is relatively easy, but positioning the logs and hauling your lumber will wear you out. Chain-saw milling is hot, dusty work. At the end of the day you will be weary and grimy, but you will also have the satisfaction of beginning your woodworking where it should begin, with the tree.

[Editor's note: The mills shown in this article were designed, built, and are now being marketed by the author at Sperber Tool Works, Inc., Box 1224, West Caldwell, N. J. 07006. The 36-in. mill attachment sells for about $500, and for about $1,300 complete with two chain-saw engines. The cost of the small mill is about $450 and $850, without and with engine. Portable chain-saw mills are also made by Granberg Industries, Inc., 200 S. Garrard Blvd., Richmond, Calif. 94804 (pictures on page 6), by Haddon Tools, 4719 West Route 120, McHenry, Ill. 60050, and by Sears.]

Rip Chain

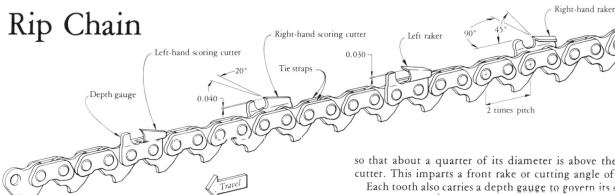

Depth gauge · Left-hand scoring cutter · 20° · 0.040 · Tie straps · Right-hand scoring cutter · 0.030 · Left raker · 90° · 45° · Right-hand raker · 2 times pitch · Travel

Ripping chain is the key to the chain-saw mill. The chain is designed to allow the fastest possible feed when cutting into end grain, parallel to the fibers of the tree. Chain-saw manufacturers don't make it—it is converted from crosscut chain by manufacturers of portable mills.

Logically, for fast cutting, one wants as many cutters in the wood as possible all the time. But the resistance of end grain is so great that too many cutters just overload the engine and the mill jams. The correct balance depends on the type of wood, size of log and power available. I use the Stihl 075 AV engine (6.7 cu. in., direct drive)—one engine in hardwood up to 12 in. diameter and softwood to 18 in., two engines in larger logs. If a portable mill is underpowered, the chain jams constantly and the work becomes slow and aggravating.

To reduce cutting resistance, skip chain is used. Two tie straps separate each cutter, rather than one tie strap as in ordinary chain. I use chain with .404 pitch, which is the distance between the center of one rivet and the rivet after next, divided by two. Furthermore, the chain consists of alternating pairs of right-hand and left-hand scoring cutters and pairs of raking cutters. As the chain speeds around the bar, a pair of narrow scoring cutters first severs the fibers by cutting a groove at the edges of the kerf. Then a pair of wide, chisel-style, flat-top rakers removes the bulk of the wood. This combination maintains highest chain speed, low vibration, and consequently a fast feed.

As in the diagram, the front edge of the scorers is ground at 20° from a line perpendicular to the face of the sawbar, while the rakers are ground square, at 0°. Rip chain is no more difficult to sharpen than ordinary crosscut chain. The most common mistake is waiting too long between sharpenings—I sharpen at least twice during a day of milling lumber. It's very important to sharpen the cutters uniformly. If one is a little too high it will be overworked, the feed will be slow and the chain may break. It's easy to allow the cutters on one side of the chain to become longer than those on the other side. Then the chain will pull to that side and erode the groove in the sawbar. Soon the chain is traveling so loosely that it flops around as it cuts, leaving the wood rough. I guard against this by checking cutter length with a caliper. If the chain is properly maintained, the surface of the wood will be as smooth as that left by the best circular mill.

Using a sharpening jig ensures accurate cutter angles and lengths. When I am out in the field I use a hand file, but for no more than two sharpenings before using the jig again. The jig shown at right does a fine job without removing the chain from the bar, and it costs about $18. For about $42 the same jig can be fitted with an electric motor and a grinding stone instead of a file. The electric version is faster, more accurate and worth the extra money. With either method, the file or stone should be set

so that about a quarter of its diameter is above the top of the cutter. This imparts a front rake or cutting angle of about 45°.

Each tooth also carries a depth gauge to govern its cut, and the scorers must cut deeper than the rakers. I set the depth gauge on the scorers .040 in. below the cutting edge of the tooth, and on the rakers .030 in. below the edge. Sharpening jigs are supposed to file or grind the gauges to the proper setting, but I find that a flat file used freehand and checked with an auto ignition feeler gauge does the best job. Be sure the front edge of the depth gauge remains rounded so it can't grab in the wood.

If you are going to use a portable chain-saw mill, you must be able to sharpen the chain yourself. It is impractical to send the chain out from the woods two or three times a day for sharpening, at $10 each time. A hand or electric jig will do at least as good a job as a saw shop. Once you get the hang of it, a 9-ft. chain takes about 15 minutes to make razor sharp. —R. S.

Cutting angle of 45° is obtained by setting grinding stone so that one-quarter of its diameter is above cutter top.

Granberg's sharpening jig, about $18, files chain while on bar.

Tools and techniques for milling logs where they fall are ingenious and varied. Above left, Granberg's Mini-Mill chain-saw attachment for vertical cutting (about $50); right, Granberg's two-man Alaskan mill ($350 to $450, depending on size; chain saws not included). Left, Australian machine for cutting eucalyptus logs into railroad ties. The operator straddles the log and steers the whirling blade through the wood, with one wheel on either side of the log. Very few of these tie-cutters still exist; their use is now prohibited for obvious safety reasons. Below left, wedge-splitting slabs off a large chunk. Below right, pit sawing in Honduran forest: two-man teams rip logs into boards to transport to market. Top man raises saw and follows cutting line; bottom man powers downward cut and gets face full of sawdust.

Getting Lumber

Take log to mill, or mill to log

by Joyce and Edgar Anderson

When we started making furniture in the 1950s we could select individual boards from 10-ft. high stacks at the country's largest importer of rare woods. Two men with a forklift truck were willing to pull out from the bottom of the pile two 4-in. x 14-in. x 20-ft. Honduras mahogany planks, or to select one board each of paldao, East Indian rosewood, grenadilla and zebrawood. We could select a 5-ft. diameter walnut log from 20 logs sitting in the yard. It would be cut to our order, air-dried, kiln-dried, planed and delivered ready for use. It was very satisfactory and we would have continued to supply our needs from the lumberyard if our supplier had not started selling in 1,000-board-foot banded lots, discouraging the purchase of smaller, mixed-wood orders.

At that time we were also cutting trees on our property for building our house and studio. With the help of our little bulldozer we towed logs to a ramp and rolled them onto our 1-1/2-ton truck for a trip to the sawmill four miles away. Days later, when the logs had been cut into boards, we trucked them home and stacked them outside until we needed them. Walnut and cherry were further dried inside to become the wall paneling and cabinets. Over the years nearby mills went out of business. We no longer owned a bulldozer and truck, but trees continued to be offered to us so we hired a loader and truck to take logs to a mill 30 miles away. Only trees with very good potential could justify the great expense of hauling.

We learned that the sawyer had very different criteria from ours in judging a "good" tree. His first question was whether we were bringing a backyard or fence-row tree, likely to contain buried metal. Fence-row trees need careful scrutiny. We have found bullets, bolts, rocks, concrete and old socks deeply buried in the wood. Inside a cherry tree, we found a maple board studded with nails, presumably the remains of a tree house. Although such found objects can damage expensive equipment, they can also produce beautiful wood. The blue stain from an embedded hammock hook can extend several feet along the grain and give special interest to an otherwise bland oak plank.

Because transporting a large tree section is so difficult, we have greeted eagerly the other approach of bringing the sawmill to the log. All the lumber we have acquired in the past year has been cut with the portable chain-saw mill. We are convinced this is the most practical way of all to obtain boards from individual trees. The chain-saw rig has proved such popular entertainment that people frequently call to offer their own or their friends' trees. Sometimes the tree owner helps operate the mill and shares in the lumber. Or the owner asks for a couple of pieces from the tree and we do all the cutting. We never take a good live tree that is functioning well where it stands. We have not paid money for any of the trees we have acquired.

We became familiar with an interesting ancestor of the chain-saw mill while working on a craft development program in Honduras. A two-man handsaw 10 ft. long was used in a pit-saw operation, with the logs supported on a log trestle 8 ft. off the ground. The top sawyer pulls up and guides the saw while his helper below pulls down. It is a primitive but fast and accurate way to make lumber. We have also extracted usable wood from trees by rail splitting, wedge splitting, freehand chain sawing and bandsawing.

It is almost impossible to compare the cost of FAS (firsts and seconds, the top grade) kiln-dried lumber from the lumberyard to the cost of green, log-run boards at the sawmill, or to the cost of fresh-sawn planks cut with the chain-saw mill. Some of the factors are not calculable in dollars and cents. And with green lumber one must include the time spent building foundations for the lumber pile, then stacking and stickering the boards.

Costs vary widely from area to area, and the figures below are from people we deal with in northern New Jersey. In the lumberyard, kiln-dried FAS 4/4 red oak now runs about $0.90 per board foot; KD #3 common runs about $0.35. Black walnut is between $1.90 and $2.40 for KD FAS 4/4 and about $3.50 for 4-in. FAS. In some very large yards there is a minimum order (1,000 BF or $500). In others there may be a price difference of $0.15 per BF for quantity increments of under 100 BF, under 1,000 BF, and over 1,000 BF. There may be a surcharge of about 25% to select individual boards.

From the local sawmill, the range is about $0.30 to $0.50 per BF for log-run oak; drier, wider and sometimes thicker pieces command the higher prices. Walnut ranges from $0.75 to $2.00, also depending on dryness and width. Board quality at most mills is not good. It is best to pick up boards as soon as possible after they are cut, to ensure straight planks.

Some mills will also custom-cut trees brought to them. On small orders prices may range from $15 to $20 per hour, and on larger orders from $0.05 to $0.15 per BF. It is unwise to pay an hourly rate if one is not familiar with the integrity of the sawyer and the quality of his machinery; we usually arrange to pay by the board foot. Loading and trucking logs to the mill, and the boards home again, may add considerably to the cost.

The portable sawmill involves a different kind of expenditure: the initial cost of the equipment and the running costs of gasoline and maintenance. The other costs involve time. In one minute, two people operating a double-ended mill can cut approximately six to eight sq. ft. of any domestic hardwood. It takes about a day for two people to slab an average-sized tree. For each day of cutting the chain needs about two sharpenings. In two days two people have cut about 1,300 BF of 6/4 poplar, 700 BF of 6x8's and some firewood. This is about 28 man-hours to cut about 1,200 sq. ft. of wood. Board thickness makes no difference in cutting time.

It seems that over the years we have been devoting more time and physical effort, with less outlay of money, to the business of acquiring lumber. We wonder if some year soon we may find ourselves planting a tree farm.

_____

Joyce and Edgar Anderson, designer/craftsmen for 26 years, give a summer lumbering course at Peters Valley, N. J. Edgar "Shorty" Anderson teaches at Philadelphia College of Art.

Measuring Moisture

Portable meters prevent guesswork and grief

by R. Bruce Hoadley

Problems that result from using wood at the wrong moisture content continue to be among the most common frustrations and failures plaguing the woodworker. Many of the symptoms are all too familiar—warp or dimensional change in parts, opened glue joints, raised grain, end checks, finish imperfections—all because the moisture content of the stock was inappropriate.

Perhaps the excuses are also quite familiar. The job just had to get started and there simply was no time to allow the material to come to equilibrium in the shop. Or, the boards were bought from a dealer's bin; the oven-drying of samples just wasn't possible. Such woes can be avoided by using modern moisture meters, which give immediate and highly accurate readings. These magical little meters use the electrical properties of wood, and their development has followed the usual trend in electronics toward portable and miniature units with simplified operation. A wide range of models is now available to suit virtually every situation, from the hobbyist's use to production operations, in the shop or in the field.

For typical woodworking applications two principal types of meters are available. One is based on the direct-current electrical resistance of the wood and involves driving small, pin-type electrodes into the wood surface; the other uses the dielectric properties of the wood and requires only surface contact of the meter with the board.

The resistance meter takes advantage of the fact that moisture is an excellent conductor of electricity but dry wood is an effective electrical insulator. The meter itself is simply a specialized ohmmeter which measures electrical resistance. The piece of wood is arranged as an element in an electrical circuit by driving the two pin electrodes into it. The current (usually supplied by a battery) flows from one electrode through the wood to the other, then back through the ohmmeter. Actually, by simply driving pairs of nails into a piece of wood for electrodes and taking resistance measurements with a standard ohmmeter, readings could be obtained that would indicate relative moisture content. Perhaps some useful values could be obtained this way, but resistance varies non-uniformly with moisture content and a mass of data would have to be accumulated to make a useful and versatile meter. Commercially manufactured meters have the meter scale printed directly in percent moisture content instead of ohms of resistance. Because electricity follows the path of least resistance, the wettest layer of wood penetrated by the electrodes will be measured. For boards that dry normally, a drying gradient usually develops from the wetter core to the drier surface with an average moisture content about 1/5 or 1/4 the board thickness from the surface. Thus for 1-in. lumber, the pins should penetrate only 1/4 in. to measure average moisture content. In the smallest models, the electrodes are a pair of pins extending from one end of the unit, which can be pushed into the wood by hand. More commonly the electrode pins are mounted in a separate handle, attached by plug-in cord to the meter box. Electrodes of various lengths, up to 2 in. or more, are available for measuring thick material so the same meter can be used for thin veneer and heavy planks. Electrodes should be inserted so current flow is parallel to the grain. Electrical resistance is greater across the grain than parallel to it, although the difference is minor at lower moisture-content levels.

Meters using the dielectric properties of wood have a surface electrode array which generates a radio-frequency field that extends for a prescribed distance when placed against the wood. Some meters measure the power-loss effect which varies according to moisture content, whereas others respond to changes in electrical capacitance. Different models have electrodes designed for field penetration to various depths. Field penetration to about half the stock thickness is usual. Where moisture content is uneven, a more or less average reading will be given.

Green wood may have an extremely high moisture content, but woodworkers are most concerned with moisture measurement of seasoned stock. Depending on geographic location, air-dried wood will reach moisture equilibrium levels in the 12% to 15% range. For interior products, stock must usually be kiln-dried or conditioned to the 6% to 8% range. Fortunately, the electrical properties of wood are most consistent at moisture levels below fiber saturation (25% to 30%), the range of most interest to woodworkers. Dielectric meters can indicate moisture contents down to zero. The electrical resistance of wood becomes extreme at low moisture contents, limiting the lower end of the range of resistance meters to about 5% or 6%. More elaborate meters sometimes have scales extending to 60% or 80% moisture content; however, electrical properties are less consistent above fiber saturation so readings in this range must be considered approximate.

Moisture meters usually give scale readings of percent moisture content that are correct for certain typical species at room temperature. Instruction manuals give correction factors for other species and different temperatures. Since density has little effect on electrical resistance, the species corrections are usually less than two percentage points for resistance meters; correction factors may be greater with power-loss meters. Resistance readings must also be corrected about one percentage point for every 20° F departure from the calibration standard. With dielectric meters the correction is more complicated, but is well explained in the instruction manuals. For anyone using meters under regular conditions—with one or a few common species and always at room temperature—correction factors either are not applicable or become routine.

The values obtained with a resistance meter can be expected to agree within one-half a percentage point with those obtained by oven-testing for samples in the 6% to 12% range; within one point in the 12% to 20% moisture-content range, and within two percentage points in the range from 20% to fiber saturation.

It is important to appreciate that a meter in good condition will faithfully and accurately measure the electrical properties of the wood being sampled. The operator must understand the vagaries of wood moisture and interpret accordingly. For example, a new owner of a meter might discover a variation of two or three percentage points up and down a given board. The common reaction is, ''the meter is only accurate to within three percent'' or, ''it gives variable readings.'' But in fact the meter is properly measuring moisture variations that exist in the board. Thus one must measure average or typical areas of boards to avoid the ends or cross-grain around knots, which dry most rapidly.

Each type of meter has its strengths and weaknesses. Resistance meters have the disadvantage of leaving small pinholes wherever the electrodes were inserted, which might be unacceptable in exposed furniture parts, gunstocks and the like. On the other hand, a given meter can be used with a variety of electrodes in a wide range of situations. Resistance meters with a 6% to 30% range are available down to pocket size, with both built-in short pin electrodes and separate cord-attached electrodes, for about $150. Radio-frequency power-loss meters in compact hand-held models, with electrodes for one-inch field penetration and scaled from 0 to 25% moisture content, cost about $400. Their distinct advantage is the ability to take readings without marring surfaces, thereby allowing measurements of completed items, even after the finish has been applied. These meters are extremely quick to use, but are less versatile because a given electrode style works only for a particular area and depth of field.

The actual dollar value of moisture measurement is very difficult to assess. It should be given serious thought, however, as it is most commonly underestimated. Many woodworkers buy machinery costing hundreds of dollars to attain close dimensional tolerances that are later lost when parts shrink or swell because there was no way of measuring moisture. What is the real cost of a solid cherry dining table that is ruined because of the errant moisture content of just one edge-glued board in its top?

Nobody would buy meat without knowing the grade, or a used car without the mileage, and nobody should buy lumber without knowing its dryness. Yet some lumber dealers sell millions of board feet a year and don't own a moisture meter. A relatively tiny investment would allow them to provide this valuable service to their customers.

[Author's note: For more about moisture meters, see *Electric Moisture Meters for Wood* by William L. James (U. S. Forest Products Lab. Gen. Tech. Rpt. FPL-6, 1975), available from the Superintendent of Documents, U. S. Govt. Printing Office, Washington, D. C. Portable moisture meters are made by Delmhorst Instrument Co., 607 Cedar St., Boonton, N. J. 07005; Moisture Register Co., 1510 W. Chestnut St., Alhambra, Calif. 91802; Electrodyne Inc., 2126 Adams St., Milwaukie, Ore. 97222; and Valley Products and Design, Box 396, Milford, Pa. 18337.]

Electrode array of dielectric meter, left, generates radio-frequency field when pressed against face of board, right. Strip arrays for edge measurement are also available.

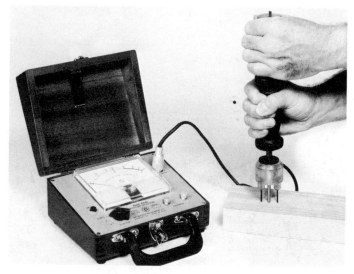

Pin electrodes of resistance meter are pushed into board, parallel to grain. Center pin gauges penetration.

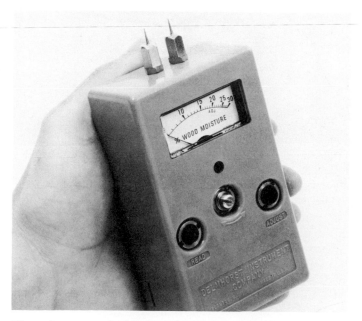

Electrodes are attached to case of pocket-size resistance meter.

Lumber Grading
A guide for the perplexed

by William W. Rice

Typical grade stamps of the Western Wood Products Association (top: Douglas fir, sugar pine) and the Northeastern Lumber Manufacturers Association (right: Eastern white pine, balsam fir). Stamps indicate the association mark, the species, the mill, the grade and sometimes the relative dryness.

When I hear a woodworker exclaim, "How can that board be a Select? It has a knot as big as your fist!" I sympathize with his frustration. But I also know that he, like many, is confused about commercial lumber grading. A bewildering assortment of grades confronts the buyer. There are different standards for hardwoods and for softwoods, and the rules make exceptions for certain species like walnut.

Lumber grading is a way of evaluating the usable lumber in a board. It takes into account the number, size and degree of defects, and the number and size of clear pieces that will remain when the defects are cut away. But not every project needs a perfect board 12 ft. long. Once a cabinetmaker learns his way through the intricacies of the grading system, he will be able to select the most suitable lumber for the job at hand. He may well find that he can cut the size pieces he needs from No. 1 Common as well as he could from Firsts and Seconds—at considerable saving.

As far back as the early 1700s the need for classifying lumber by grades was recognized. Originally, appearance was the primary requisite, but with increased knowledge about wood properties and methods of utilization, lumber grades now also take into account strength characteristics and yield potential. Modern lumber-grading rules provide standards for the manufacture of the same product by different mills. They also serve as common specifications both buyer and seller can use to determine that full value is received and sold.

In the United States, the American Lumber Standards Committee (ALSC) of the Department of Commerce is responsible for general establishment and administration of lumber grades. Application and enforcement of specific grading rules are the responsibility of various lumber inspection associations. For example, the California Redwood Association has jurisdiction over member mills and dealers handling redwood, and the Western Wood Products Association monitors the standards for several West Coast species, including ponderosa pine and Douglas fir. Some other associations are the Southern Pine Inspection Bureau, the Northeastern Lumber Manufacturers Association and the National Hardwood Lumber Association. Altogether there are about 15 associations that oversee the grading of wood products; each is represented on the American Lumber Standards Committee and all operate under its certification. Grading rules are voluntary standards set by the lumber industry through the ALSC, not dictated by the government.

Lumber grading is judging the surface quality of boards with respect to established standards, which are different for softwoods and hardwoods. Softwoods are graded from the best face, usually as surfaced material, and it is assumed that the piece will be used as is, without further manufacturing. Select and Common softwood boards are graded for appearance from the best face, while dimension lumber and timbers are graded for strength by inspecting all four surfaces, with the poorest surface determining the grade. Hardwoods are graded in the rough, from the poor face, and it is assumed that each board will be cut into clear-face parts. Softwoods are generally grade-stamped, hardwoods are not. Both softwood and hardwood grading rules describe the poorest piece permitted in each grade. Softwood Select and Common grades specify a moisture level of 15% or less. There is no moisture-content rule for hardwoods, and generally grading is done while the lumber is green, unless buyer and seller make special arrangements.

Softwood grading

Softwood species most often used for cabinetry and furniture are Eastern white pine and the western pines: sugar, Idaho white, ponderosa and lodgepole. Other species used include Douglas fir, Englemann spruce, Sitka spruce and Western larch. Eastern white pine is graded under the rules of the Northeastern Lumber Manufacturers Association (NELMA). The others are graded under the rules of the Western Wood Products Association (WWPA) and/or West Coast Lumber Inspection Bureau (WCLB). Upper grades are designated Select or Finish and usually are further separated by the letters B, C, and D to indicate descending quality. The exception to the rule is Idaho white pine (IWP), which carries the grade names Supreme, Choice, and Quality in place of B Select, C Select and D Select respectively.

Lower lumber grades are called Commons, and quality within this category is designated by the numbers, 1, 2, 3, 4, 5—with the highest number assigned to the lowest grade. But Idaho white pine Commons carry the names Colonial, Sterling, Standard, Utility and Industrial, with Colonial corresponding to 1 Common, and so on.

While grade descriptions may vary slightly from one softwood association to another, in general each grade describes the type, size and number of defects permitted in the worst board in that grade. For example, the WWPA grade of B and Better Select (B & BTR) for all species permits on the best face: light stain (blue or brown) over not more than 10% of the face; small ($\frac{1}{32}$ in. deep by 4 in. long) season checks, one at each end of the board or 3 or 4 if away from the ends; very light torn grain ($\frac{1}{64}$ in. by 3 in.); two sound, tight pin knots ($\frac{1}{2}$ in. dia.) *or* slight traces of pitch *or* a very small pitch pocket ($\frac{1}{16}$ in. by 3 in.); very slight cup ($\frac{1}{16}$ in. in an 8-in. wide board); very light crook ($\frac{1}{4}$ in. in an 8-in. by 12-ft. board). In addition to the above, the poor face may have wane (bark) $\frac{1}{4}$ the thickness by $\frac{1}{6}$ the length of the piece.

As another example, a Premium (No. 2 Common) Eastern white pine board graded under NELMA rules could contain on the best face: medium surface checks ($\frac{1}{32}$ in. by 10 in.);

Bill Rice, 56, teaches lumber grading in the wood science and technology department at the University of Massachusetts.

red knots (2¾-in. dia. in 8-in. wide boards); sound pith; medium pitch (⅙ the width by ⅓ the length of the piece); short splits; medium stain (not affecting a paint finish); one knothole (½-in. dia. in a 6-in. wide board); one ¼-in. wormhole for every 6 lineal feet of board. The poor face could have all that plus wane ½ the thickness by ¼ the width by ¼ the length of the board.

At first glance the reader might think that anything goes as far as defects in a board. In practice the grader exercises judgment about the number allowed and seldom, if ever, do all the permitted defects occur in a single board. In fact, there may be some pieces in a pile that would make the next higher grade except for one unacceptable defect. For example, a perfectly clear board with too much wane on the reverse face grades as C Select instead of B, or a No. 3 Common board misses the No. 2 Common grade because of one oversize knot. The softwood grade is stamped on each piece when it leaves the mill, although retail lumber dealers often cut long boards into shorter lengths and in the process lose the stamp. Inspection by the association quality-control people ensures that the grade is correct on at least 95% of the pieces.

Hardwood grading

Except for specialty grades such as Factory and Shop or Furniture (NELMA), softwood grading depends on the grader's experience and good judgment and assumes lumber use in full widths and lengths. In contrast, hardwood grading is based on the assumption that the boards will be cut into furniture parts ranging from 2 ft. to 7 ft. long, and that each part should have a clear face. The grade of individual boards is related to the yield of clear parts as determined by a mathematical system called the Cutting Unit Method. In addition, hardwoods are always graded from the poor face.

While there are rules similar to softwood rules for grading hardwood timbers and framing, they are seldom applied commercially. For this reason hardwood grades are usually considered to be furniture grades. There is only one association, the National Hardwood Lumber Association (NHLA), responsible for the grading of native hardwoods as well as many imported foreign and tropical species. Hardwood grading rules define standard requirements for all hardwood species and, in addition, spell out modifications that apply to individual woods. A cabinetmaker who understands the general rules will usually be able to purchase any hardwood species on grade without major problems. An exception might be walnut which, because of the decreasing size of the available trees, has required a number of adjustments.

The standard grades assigned to hardwoods are Firsts, Seconds, Selects, Numbers 1, 2, 3A and 3B Common, and Sound Wormy. Firsts and Seconds are usually combined into the one grade of Firsts And Seconds (FAS). Sound Wormy is essentially No. 1 Common with an allowance for wormholes. As with softwood grades, the more defects in a board, the lower the grade. However, in grading hardwoods the concern is for the yield of clear material, not the number of defects.

A grader spends only 10 or 15 seconds inspecting each hardwood board. In that time, he determines its width, length and surface measure (area in square feet); selects the poor face; visualizes a series of clear face cuttings on the surface; determines the percent of clear material available; and assigns a grade based on board size, number of cuttings, percent of clear area and defect or species restrictions.

The heart of this grading operation is the determination of clear material available and this is done by the Cutting Unit Method. A cutting is a portion of the board that can be obtained by crosscutting, ripping, or both. A cutting must be

MINIMUM GRADE REQUIREMENTS FOR HARDWOODS

Grade	Minimum Board Size width	length	Conversion Factor (% clear face)	Minimum Size of Cuttings	Maximum Number of Cuttings for Board SM
Firsts	6"	8'-16'	11xSM (91⅔%)	4"x5' or 3"x7'	1 for SM 4'-9' 2 for SM 10'-14' 3 for SM 15' or more
Seconds	6"	8'-16'	10xSM (81⅔%)	4"x5' or 3"x7'	1 for SM 4'-7' 2 for SM 8'-11' 3 for SM 12'-15' 4 for SM 16' or more
Selects	4"	6'-16'	11xSM (91⅔%) 10xSM (83⅓%)	4"x5' or 3"x7'	1 for SM 2'-3' 1 for SM 4'-7' 2 for SM 8'-11' 3 for SM 12'-15' 4 for SM 16' or more
No. 1 Common	3"	4'-16'	9xSM (75%) 8xSM (66⅔%)	4"x2' or 3"x3'	1 for SM 2' 1 for SM 3'-4' 2 for SM 5'-7' 3 for SM 8'-10' 4 for SM 11'-13' 5 for SM 14' or more
No. 2 Common	3"	4'-16'	6xSM (50%)	3" x 2'	1 for SM 2'-3' 2 for SM 4'-5' 3 for SM 6'-7' 4 for SM 8'-9' 5 for SM 10'-11' 6 for SM 12'-13' 7 for SM 14' or more

The chart gives the minimum requirements a board must meet to merit a particular grade. In general, a high-grade board is relatively long and wide and a high percentage of its area is free of defect. The clear lumber in a high-grade board must be obtainable in relatively few and large cuttings.

To grade a board, first note its dimensions—they will eliminate some grades immediately. For example, a board that is only 5 in. wide cannot be a First or Second. Next, note the board's surface measure (SM)—its area expressed in square feet. Mentally lay out the largest clear cuttings that could be obtained by straight ripping and crosscuts, and measure each cutting in inches of width and feet of length (cutting units). Then total the number of cutting units available, and count the number of cuttings necessary to obtain the total. The last two columns give the minimum size of a cutting and the maximum number of cuttings allowed for each grade.

The percentage of clear face required for each grade can be found by dividing the number of cutting units by the area of the board, but instead, lumber graders use a conversion factor, which is given in the third column of the table. The surface measure of the board multiplied by the conversion factor gives the minimum number of cutting units required for the grade.

For example, the smallest board that can be a First is 6 in. wide and 8 ft. long, or 4 ft. surface measure. If this board were perfect, it would contain 48 cutting units. It must contain its surface measure times the conversion factor of 11, or 44 cutting units, to be graded a First. This much clear lumber must be obtainable in one cutting.

The two examples that follow show how lumber is graded. The diagrams were derived from real boards, but the defects that determined the grade were too small to reproduce photographically.

parallel to the edges of the board. Further, a cutting must be clear of all defects on one face and it must be of a certain minimum size, depending on the grade to be assigned to the board. Based on the surface area of the board, each grade specifies the maximum number of cuttings that can be used in determining the grade. Note that grading does not consider the thickness of the board, only the surface area. The grader visualizes the various cuttings, but does not actually make the sawcuts. How the buyer ultimately cuts the board may not coincide with the grader's visualization. What is important is that the yield of clear material is mathematically available in specified cuttings and therefore anyone check-grading the inspector should arrive at the same grade.

The mathematics of the Cutting Unit Method are relatively

EXAMPLE 1: RED OAK BOARD

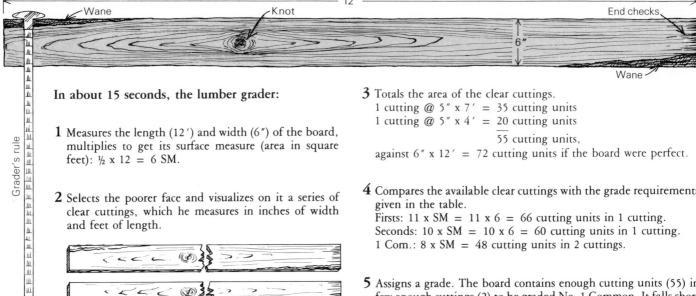

In about 15 seconds, the lumber grader:

1 Measures the length (12') and width (6") of the board, multiplies to get its surface measure (area in square feet): ½ x 12 = 6 SM.

2 Selects the poorer face and visualizes on it a series of clear cuttings, which he measures in inches of width and feet of length.

Board's poor face, above, has wane (bark) along edges; good face, below, is relatively clear.

3 Totals the area of the clear cuttings.
1 cutting @ 5" x 7' = 35 cutting units
1 cutting @ 5" x 4' = 20 cutting units
                      ———
                      55 cutting units,
against 6" x 12' = 72 cutting units if the board were perfect.

4 Compares the available clear cuttings with the grade requirements given in the table.
Firsts: 11 x SM = 11 x 6 = 66 cutting units in 1 cutting.
Seconds: 10 x SM = 10 x 6 = 60 cutting units in 1 cutting.
1 Com.: 8 x SM = 48 cutting units in 2 cuttings.

5 Assigns a grade. The board contains enough cutting units (55) in few enough cuttings (2) to be graded No. 1 Common. It falls short of meeting the requirements for Seconds because it lacks 5 cutting units and because 2 cuttings were necessary to obtain the units available. This grade was determined from the poor face of the board. If the good face could meet the grade of Seconds, the proper grade would become Select. Select is a special grade, generally used for parts or items that show on one face only. But if the good face of the board grades no higher than No. 1 Common, then the poor face determines its grade.

1 cutting, 5" wide x 4' long   1 cutting, 5" wide x 7' long

EXAMPLE 2: WALNUT BOARD

Board size: 2" x 8" x 12'

Surface measure (SM): $\frac{8" \times 12'}{12}$ = 8 sq. ft.

Available clear stock:
    1 cutting 4" x 4' = 16 cutting units
    1 cutting 4" x 4¼' = 17 cutting units
    1 cutting 3" x 3' = 9 cutting units
    1 cutting 4" x 5½' = 22 cutting units
    1 cutting 4" x 5' = 20 cutting units
Total: 5 cuttings with 84 cutting units

Grade requirements (from table):
    Firsts: 11 x SM = 11 x 8 = 88 cutting units in 2 cuttings
    Seconds: 10 x SM = 10 x 8 = 80 cutting units in 2 cuttings
    1 Com.:   8 x SM =   8 x 8 = 64 cutting units in 3 cuttings
    2 Com.:   6 x SM =   6 x 8 = 48 cutting units in 4 cuttings
Modification for walnut: 1 Common standard, unlimited number of cuttings.

Under standard rules (as for oak), this board would grade as excellent No. 2 Common, with 75 units in four cuttings. (Since only four cuttings are permitted for No. 2 Common, the smallest cutting, 9 cutting units, is not included in the total.) But because a modification to the rules allows an unlimited number of cuttings for walnut, the grade of the board is No. 1 Common.

(Poor face shown)

1 cutting, 4" wide x 4' long   1 cutting, 4" wide x 4¼' long   1 cutting, 3" wide x 3' long

split   1 cutting, 4" wide x 5½' long   1 cutting, 4" wide by 5' long   12" split

(Boards are not drawn to scale)

simple. It is a matter of calculating the number of cutting units available and comparing the total to the number required for a given grade. A cutting unit is a portion of clear lumber one inch wide and one foot long. Thus the number of cutting units in each clear portion is determined by multiplying its width in inches by its length in feet. When calculating the total yield of clear material, only those cutting units making up the surface of the clear-face cuttings may be counted. There may be additional cutting units in the board, but in areas too small for furniture cuttings, and thus not available for grade computation. Within each grade there is some leeway because the rules describe the poorest pieces—thus there are both borderline and "good" boards. A good No. 2 Common would be just shy of the total cutting units it would need to qualify as a No. 1 Common. The table lists the requirements for determining standard grades.

As can be seen from the table and the two examples, hardwood grading can be detailed and quite exacting. Grading is a 100% inspection procedure, but in a given pile of lumber an experienced grader can accurately judge whether most boards contain the proper percentage of clear area in the allowable size and number of cuttings without using the complete method. However, for a borderline board he will go through all the necessary measurements and calculations, if the lumber value warrants the effort.

Grading and the woodworker

Although grading rules are of particular use to furniture manufacturers, they can also guide the cabinetmaker in selecting lumber. In sum, Firsts and Seconds are relatively clear boards of good widths and lengths. They yield on the average, 80% to 90% clear material, depending on cutting requirements, and the pieces will be good on both sides. Select boards are about 80% clear on one face and of good widths and lengths. They are often used for items that show only one side. No. 1 Common is probably the best all-around grade, considering both yield (about 65%) and price. This grade can include some long (over 4 ft.) cuttings. If most of your cabinet parts are 16 in. to 4 ft. long, consider the economy of No. 2 Common. Often the grade yield of 50% can be exceeded, especially if the parts are glued into assemblies.

A cabinetmaker who wants to use graded lumber should visit a lumber supplier and look over the available stock in the various grades to become familiar with the typical array of defects (and their spacing) that is permitted. Look for grade stamps on softwoods so you will know you are getting what you are paying for. But most important, try to associate the character and size of the cabinet (or parts) with the appearance of the lumber. Then select the grade that will permit you to cut out the parts with the least waste. Not all parts need to be blemish-free; in fact, defects more often than not add character and interest. The lower grades are less expensive, but figure the waste before buying on price alone. □

AUTHOR'S NOTE: Lumber-grading rules can be obtained from the following associations:

National Hardwood Lumber Assn., 332 S. Michigan Ave., Chicago, Ill. 60604 (*Rules for Measurement of Hardwood and Cypress Lumber,* $2.00).

Northeastern Lumber Manufacturers Assn., 4 Fundy Rd., Falmouth, Maine 04105 (*Grading Rules for Northeastern Lumber,* $2.00).

Western Wood Products Assn., 1500 Yeon Bldg., Portland, Ore. 97204 (*Grading Rules for Western Lumber,* no cost).

Cleaving Wood
Froe follows long fibers

by Drew Langsner

Many craftsmen today have little, if any, experience with the ancient practice of cleaving. Yet before factory-made saws became widespread, cleaving and hewing with an ax were the primary means of reducing wood in size or dividing it into smaller pieces. In cleaving, a tree trunk is split lengthwise into halves, then quarters and sometimes eighths or sixteenths, depending on the diameter of the log and the intended use of the wood. The resulting pie-shaped pieces are squared with a drawknife, then cleaved along tangents to the annual rings with a froe or knife into halves, quarters and so on. These tools allow the use of leverage to follow the grain, rather than a straight line, which a saw must do.

Cleaving has advantages over sawing. Because cleaved material follows the long fibers, it is much stronger than wood sawn by hand or machine. With cleaving, there is no sawdust, but more waste. Cleaved wood will take and hold bends better than sawn wood. And cleaving is faster than hand-sawing.

The crudest examples of cleaving are fence posts and rails, especially black-locust posts and oak rails, which are renowned for their strength and durability. At the other extreme are fine, yet very durable, baskets, woven from splints of white oak, ash, willow or hazel. Other traditional uses of cleft (or "rived") wood include shingles, wall lathing, tool handles, bucket staves, special dowels, "tree-nails" (pegs used in timber-frame buildings), ladder rungs, agricultural implements and small boat ribbing. The technique of cleaving also lends itself to carving projects and chairmaking.

Equipment

Cleaving requires a few basic tools. A peavey or cant hook is useful for maneuvering logs more than 1 ft. in diameter. A 6-lb. to 16-lb. wedging maul ("go-devil") or a sledge hammer, a heavy wooden cudgel, two or three iron wedges (a narrow timber wedge is handy), two wooden "gluts" (large wooden wedges) and a hatchet are useful for splitting the log longitudinally. Gluts are easily hewn from any straight-grained hardwood, usually saplings or limbs of hickory or oak. The beveled sides should be flat. Chamfer the edge around the head to prevent premature fraying. Gluts should be seasoned about one month before being put to use, lest they split and fray too easily. Gluts can be driven with a sledge or go-devil, but will last much longer when pounded by a wooden cudgel. A "brake," or hardwood crotch, holds the wood when the smaller sections are cleaved with a froe and froe club.

The design and workmanship of the froe are critical to its effective cleaving. A froe blade should be 6 in. to 10 in. long, and at least ⅜ in. thick. The cross section of a good froe has a narrow angled edge formed by slightly convex tapered sides beveled the full width of the blade. The back (striking) edge should be nicely rounded to minimize wear on the froe club. Froe eyes are forged or welded shut. The orifice must be

Cleaving: With an iron wedge driven into the end of a white oak log (top left), wedges are leap-frogged along the cleft. Two 3-in. gluts and a dogwood cudgel complete the split (bottom left). Then quarters are cleaved into eighths with a pair of wedges and a 10-lb. go-devil (above). Note the splitting brake at left, propped up by crossed saplings.

smooth. Froes with a tapered eye use a swollen handle, not unlike an adze or mattock haft. These seem to work loose just as easily as round eyes with parallel sides. The handle should be 1½ to 2 times as long as the blade. It may be any stout hardwood, cleaved of course, then well seasoned before fitting. A small wooden wedge should be dabbed with glue and driven into a slot sawn across the end grain.

I have found that a long narrow club is most convenient for cleaving with a froe. A short fat club tends to be in the way. Froe clubs are made from almost any dense hardwood. I've used apple, hickory, dogwood and oak. Clubs made from green saplings and limbs generally check. To avoid checks, use a quarter section from a larger tree. The club (which is unavoidably expendable) should be seasoned a few weeks so that its surface hardens before it is used.

Woods
You can cleave a fairly wide range of deciduous and coniferous woods. For work that requires strong or tough materials, select oak, hickory, ash or locust. White oak makes fine

splints and is used in many bending applications. Most other eastern oaks cleave nicely, except for maul oak and swamp white oak, both of which are almost impossible to split. Hickory, of course, is famous for toughness and ability to take impact, but it is rather stringy and sometimes hard to work (especially when seasoned). Ash is lighter and very nice to split. Locust cleaves easily, but the grain usually warbles, resulting in distorted splints that are "foxy" (uneven or brittle). Beech was preferred by English chair bodgers, the itinerant woodsmen/turners who traditionally made legs and rungs for Windsor chairs.

Among the softwoods, one can choose from pine, hemlock, cedar and redwood. Very fine-grained pine makes superior bucket staves, and sometimes excellent shingles. Hemlock cleaves very easily, though the grain may twist or warp. Its main use is tobacco sticks and tomato stakes. Cedar and redwood may be cleaved into shingles, or made into long-lasting fence posts and rails.

Short bolts of many other woods, such as apple, linden, walnut, dogwood and holly can be cleaved into chunks for

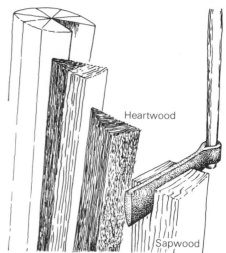

A froe is driven into the wood with a mallet, then worked along the long fibers by leverage. Long pieces of wood may be supported in a brake (far left); short chunks can rest on a stump (left). The diagram shows the cleaving sequence for basket splints. Heartwood is usually discarded; squared-off sapwood is split into halves, quarters, eighths and sometimes sixteenths. A froe makes the first cuts; finer splits are made with a knife.

carving, and bowl and spoon-making. Hazel is traditionally used for bucket hooping and basket materials. Willow rods make nice baskets, too. Until the blight, chestnut was often cleaved for fence posts and shingles.

Felling a tree

When choosing timber for cleaving, select straight-standing trees that are free of knots, scars, twists or other irregularities. White oaks for basket splints should be 5 in. to 8 in. in diameter, with minimal taper at the butt end. Trees with evenly spaced annual rings are preferred, but you can know this only if you have already taken other trees from the same site.

A large body of folklore suggests the ideal time of year, phase of the moon, and prevailing wind conditions for felling. A compilation of all this advice quickly leads to contradictions. My experience in felling trees at various times throughout the year has led to no conclusions whatsoever. I have cut white oaks for basketry that were of the same age and that grew side by side—I found one beautiful to work and the other only mediocre. In general, I recommend cutting trees for cleaving as near as possible to the time when the wood will be worked or used. Oak shingles, for instance, should be rived out and installed green; seasoned shingles may warp or split while being nailed. An exception would be where well-seasoned material is needed, such as for bucket staves, in which case the wood should be bucked and cleaved into quarter or eighth sections whenever possible.

For reasons of esthetics and conservation I prefer to fell timber as close as possible (almost flush) to the forest floor. Discard the lowermost section of stump if it's tapered or punky. Buck the log into bolts. Length depends on intended use: from 20 in. for shingles to 10 ft. for fence rails.

Cleaving the log

Using a wedge and maul, score a radial line from the central pith to the bark. If the wood is already cracked, you must follow along the cleft, because it's impossible to control cleaving once the integrity of the annual rings is broken. I begin by driving a wide, flat timber wedge into the end grain, but one can use a regular splitting wedge. In either case, the first wedge will open a cleft along the bark.

Insert a splitting wedge and drive it within an inch of its head. The cleft will lengthen as the wedge is pounded into place. Place another wedge into the cleft where it's ⅜ in. to ⅝ in. wide. Again, drive to within an inch of the head. Leapfrog the wedges one past the other until the end of the log is reached. Occasionally a wedge will stick in place. Tapping the sides of the head to the left and right will usually free it.

At this point small or easily cleaved logs simply break apart. Tougher logs require a pair of gluts. When inserting a glut try to find a place free of cross fibers. More gluts are ruined when the leading edge intersects cross fibers than by damage caused by pounding. Leapfrog gluts from one end to another, as with iron wedges.

If the log still isn't halved, roll it over and look for any incipient cracks on the reverse side. Sometimes it's necessary to clear off bark with a hatchet before any fissures are located. Drive wedges or gluts into the back side. The log should divide into halves, although it may be necessary to sever stubborn cross fibers with the hatchet. I prefer to do this kind of hatchet work two-handed. Be careful not to strike implanted iron wedges.

Follow the same procedure for cleaving quarter sections and eighths, if the bolts are still too heavy to haul to the shop. Green worked wood should be left in sections that are as large as possible, because small segments dry out much faster. Big sections, however, check more as they dry. Wood should be removed from the forest floor. Many species are subject to invasion and attack by fungi and insects. Ambrosia beetles infest and ruin oak felled in the spring and summer.

The next step is cleaving the radial sections. Most craftsmen hold the wood in place with a brake, a narrow crotch from the trunk or branch of almost any suitably shaped hardwood. The brake may be lashed to posts driven in the ground. Or lay the big end across a log and support the legs with two saplings placed opposite each other, each one running beneath the near leg and above the far leg. The saplings work against each other, and the device is surprisingly rigid and self-supporting. Insert the wood into the brake. Place the froe crosswise at the approximate half-way point, or along the division of sapwood and heartwood. Strike with the club. Once the blade is in, rotate the handle downwards. One may have to strike the protruding blade again but usually the cleft opens and the froe is simply slid downwards. With tough wood I sometimes hold the split open by placing a stick into the wide end of the cleft. If the cleft starts to run out (divide unevenly to one side) rotate the piece 180° and continue to work from the other side. For thinner pieces, subdivide each bolt in half until you reach the required thickness. Attempts to cleave into uneven pieces, such as thirds, will usually fail. One can sometimes save a wild split by reversing the wood and starting again from the other end. The splits should meet, but it may be necessary to separate the two halves with a knife or hatchet.

Basket splints

White oak splints for basketry should be made promptly after the tree is felled. If this cannot be done, submerge the bole under water, but use as soon as possible. Five to six feet is about the maximum length for fine cleaving and weaving basketry. Cleave radial sections 1 in. to 2 in. wide. Split off the heartwood. Remove the bark with a drawknife, and shape to a square or rectangular cross section. Cleave in halves and quarters tangent to the annual rings. Once the wood is reduced to a thickness of about ½ in., it becomes possible to use a knife rather than the more awkward froe. To start, work the knife across a corner of the end grain, or tap in with a light mallet. Twist (rotate) the knife to open the cleft. As soon as possible, insert both thumbs into the cleft and place the second joint of your index fingers externally just below the cleft. Begin to pull the splint apart by using successive knuckles as a fulcrum while pulling your thumbs away from each other. This process requires a "feel" that comes with practice. If the splint starts to run out on one side, pull down and harder on the other side. Sometimes the wood fibers must be pared with a knife to keep the splint running evenly.

Good white oak will cleave to less than 1/16-in. thickness. The splints may be smoothed with a spokeshave, scraper or penknife. They are sorted and tied in bundles, and may be stored until needed.

Shingles

Shingles may be split from conifers (especially cedar, redwood and some pines) or hardwoods (generally red oaks). The tree diameter can be as little as 12 in., but 24 in. or more is much better. In any case, the wood must be straight-grained and free of knots and other imperfections. First crosscut into bolts of desired length, usually 18 in. to 24 in. There are several methods of proceeding. Swiss shinglemakers often use fine-grained 12-in. pines. They halve and quarter the bolts, then split off the heartwood and thin pie-shaped segments on the sides, to form a square bolt, which is usually split into halves, quarters and eighths.

With a larger hardwood bolt, the circumference can be divided into equal segments (3½ in. is excellent), then split into halves, quarters, and then the smaller sections. Any wavy or twisted heartwood is discarded. If the resulting segment is

Top left: White oak stick supported by brake lashed to two posts is worked into basket splints. Then thin splints are held between the knees and further divided. A small knife opens the cleft (top right), then the pieces are pulled apart by inserting the thumbs into the cleft and sliding the fingers down the outside (bottom).

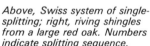
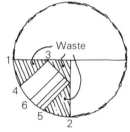
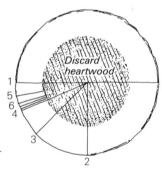

Above, Swiss system of single-splitting; right, riving shingles from a large red oak. Numbers indicate splitting sequence.

more than 5 in. wide, it is split in half. Each squarish section is split into 16 shingles.

In either case, the individual shingles are split across the annual rings. Parallel split shingles will warp unacceptably. Place the froe in the exact center of each segment, or it will run out, resulting in uneven shingles and too much waste. Most shinglemakers use a brake to hold their wood in place, but in Switzerland a leather knee pad is used to hold the material against a knee-high bench. Most shingles need dressing out—curves and bumps must be smoothed before installation. Smoothing is usually done on a shaving horse, using a sharp drawknife. The shingles should be tied into very tight bundles (use a vise to press them together) if they are not installed immediately. □

Drew Langsner, of Marshall, N.C., apprenticed with a Swiss cooper. His most recent book is Country Woodcraft *(Rodale Press, Emmaus, Pa.).*

Knife Checks in Veneer

How they are formed, how to cope with them

by Bruce Hoadley

When considering veneer and its quality, we usually think only of characteristics such as species, thickness and figure, or defects such as knots, stain or pitch streaks. Beyond that, veneer is veneer. But of most serious concern should be knife checks. These are parallel-to-grain fracture planes produced in the veneer at the time of its manufacture and which may go unnoticed, only to cause agonizing problems later. Because they are probably the most common cause of checks in the finished surfaces of veneered work, the woodworker should understand what these knife checks are, how they are formed, how to detect them and how to cope with them.

Sawn veneer does not have these checks, but today most veneer is knife-cut by peeling (rotary cutting) or slicing. In either method, the basic cutting action is similar. A knife sharpened to an angle approaching 0° would distort the wood structure the least, but would, of course, break too easily. Veneer-cutting knives are therefore sharpened to an angle of about 21°—a compromise between a small angle that would minimize distortion of the wood structure and a blunt angle that would minimize knife breakage. This means that as the knife separates the veneer from the flitch, the separated layer of wood is severely bent, and stresses build up in the region near the knife edge. When the strength of the wood is exceeded, the stress is relieved by failure, and the plane of failure thus formed is called a knife check, or lathe check. This bending and breaking cycle is repeated as cutting continues, so each layer of veneer has checks at fairly regular intervals.

The side of the veneer that was against the knife and has knife checks penetrating into its surface is called the loose side, or open face. The other side is called the tight side, or closed face.

To prevent knife checks, lathes and slicers are equipped with a pressure bar or nosebar, a solid bar or roller that bears against the veneer as it is being cut. Its pressure holds the cell structure together in the region where checks usually develop. Too much pressure crushes the cell structure of the veneer, so there is a theoretical optimum opening between the knife and the pressure bar that produces the highest-quality veneer. Experience has shown that checks can be minimized or eliminated when the distance between the pressure bar and the knife is 80% to 90% of the thickness of the cut.

The terms tightness and looseness refer to the relative depth of knife checks. In producing veneer without nosebar pressure, tightness is improved by cutting lower-density species of wood, by heating the wood, and by thin cuts.

Anatomical features of the species being cut are also related to checking. If structural planes of weakness—such as the large rays of oak or the earlywood layer in ring-porous hardwoods—coincide with the probable plane of check formation, the checks will be worse. Diffuse-porous hardwoods with fine, well-distributed rays are more likely to yield tight, uniform veneer.

The tightness of veneer can be assessed in a number of ways. Surface roughness or corrugation (especially of the loose side) is commonly associated with checking. Veneer having any suggestion of a washboard surface is probably loosely cut.

Manually flexing the veneer will help you see the checks. In addition, the veneer will feel stiffer when flexed to close the checks, but will feel more limp when the checks are flexed open. Tightly cut veneer will flex about as easily both ways, so if you can't tell, it's probably cut well.

In some woodworking applications, it is critical to know the

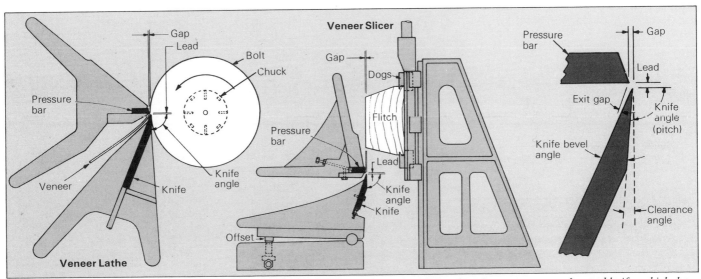

Softwoods for plywood are rotary-cut with a veneer lathe, left, while hardwood veneers are usually sliced, center. The diagram at right shows the relationships between pressure bar and knife, which determine the quality of the veneer.

With nosebar retracted, left, veneer checks seriously as it curls over the knife. A little nosebar pressure, center, reduces the amount of checking. When the nosebar pressure approaches 15% to 20% of the veneer thickness, right, checks are nearly eliminated.

actual depth of the checks. This can be determined by staining with an alcohol or spirit solution of dye such as machinists' layout dye, then beveling the veneer. Cut sample strips of veneer from the ends of sheets and stain them liberally on both sides, keeping the stain away from end grain. Allow to dry thoroughly, then glue or cement the veneer onto blocks of scrap wood. When the glue is set, bevel the veneer with a fine sander disc, or with a sharp chisel or knife. The relative depth of the checks will be apparent across the bevel.

The consequences of knife checks should be quite obvious. The most common problem is parallel-to-grain cracks in the finish on veneered surfaces—nearly always traceable to knife checks. This problem is especially aggravating because it is usually a delayed reaction, appearing months or years after the piece is finished. A surface may be flawless at completion, but the normal shrinking and swelling of the wood in response to seasonal humidity fluctuation cause hidden knife checks to migrate to the surface and through the finish itself.

This problem is second only to delamination as a cause of the bad reputation veneered products have undeservedly acquired. One frequently sees it when softwood structural plywood such as Douglas fir is used for finished or painted surfaces. Structural plywood is designed to carry stresses parallel to the grain direction of its plies, and this capability is little affected by knife checks. Apparently, little serious effort is made to control tightness of veneer in manufacturing commercial softwood plywood. Plywood manufactured with surfaces of medium or high-density impregnated paper overlay (designated M.D.O. and H.D.O.) is best where smooth painted surfaces are needed. Large lumberyards usually stock M.D.O. plywood, which is routinely used for outdoor signs and similar products.

End-grain plywood surfaces may also reveal finish defects caused by knife checks. This is especially common when moisture loss results in excessive shrinkage stress.

Another visual effect of knife checks is bleed-through of glue, which shows up as a series of evenly spaced lines on the veneered surface. This is especially apparent in light-colored woods such as maple or birch sapwood.

In woodworking, veneer should routinely be inspected for tightness. Checks penetrating no more than 25% of the thickness of the veneer can be tolerated under most circumstances. When laying up veneer, spread the loose side with glue. With luck, the glue will penetrate the checks and perhaps glue them closed. It may help to lay the veneer over a slightly convex surface so the checks will be open to the glue. (This will also ensure that the tight side is the exposed face on surface plies.) Care must then be taken not to sand through the tight side of the veneer. I have seen countless situations where veneer surfaces have been sanded right down to expose the knife checks—and the glue in them.

Bookmatched surfaces are a predicament, because the veneers must be placed with alternate open and closed faces up. In such cases, it is important to have relatively tight veneer to ensure uniformity. You may have seen bookmatched patterns in which the finish quality alternated with each piece of veneer, a consequence of knife checks.

Lathe-check troubles are not limited to visual surface effects. Critical mechanical problems may also result. Most typical is some form of rolling shear developed when plywood is stressed in the form of a beam over a short span, so that high

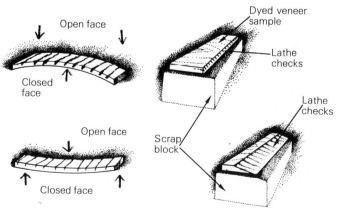

Loosely cut veneer feels more limp when the checks are flexed open, stiffer when the checks are closed. To gauge check depth, dye both sides of a sample and glue it to scrap wood. Bevel the veneer and compare the dye penetration to the bevel length.

This maple veneer is so loose that the surface is corrugated.

Core veneers in fir plywood are usually checked.

Left, checks broke through paint on fir plywood in a year. Baltic-birch panel, right, was smooth when finished with Deft two years ago.

levels of horizontal shear are developed. If the shear coincides with the direction of stress that opens the checks, rolling shear failure may result. The edges of plywood panels "broomed" over in this manner are often misinterpreted as "delamination," which erroneously implies glue failure.

I do not have any specific recommendations for finishing veneer that has knife checks. I think a finish that would provide the best moisture barrier and thus reduce dimensional variation would be best. Also, if the checks were on the surface, any finish that would seal them shut would help. A fin-

Bruce Hoadley is professor of wood science and technology at the University of Massachusetts, Amherst. He wrote his doctoral dissertation on veneer cutting.

ish like linseed oil would have little to offer. A low-viscosity lacquer or varnish in multiple coats might work best.

On the whole, most hardwood cabinet veneer produced by reputable mills is cut with adequate production quality control to ensure reasonable tightness. But beware of "clearance" sales or "closeouts," because loose veneer is hardly a bargain at any price. The best guideline is to buy veneer from reputable dealers and know how to detect, and cope with, the occasional loose veneer. □

EDITOR'S NOTE: Impregnated paper overlay for plywood is available in roll form, usually in 52-in. widths. It has no grain direction and is often glued down as crossbanding when veneering over plywood or chipboard. One brand is "Yorkite," manufactured by NVF Co. of Yorkland, Del.

This simple cutting experiment will help you understand how knife checks develop and affect veneer.

1 *Crosscut four to six 1-in. sections from the end of a plank of medium or low-density wood with even grain (e.g., eastern white pine, basswood).*

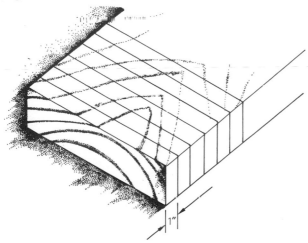

2 *Immerse the wood in water for several days. (The idea is to bring the wood back to the fiber-saturation point. If you start with green wood, the soaking is unnecessary.)*

3 *When ready to cut, heat half the pieces to near boiling while still immersed. Allow at least an hour for the pieces to heat through.*

4 *Clamp a cold piece in a wood vise, side grain up.*

5 *Using a block plane with the throat opened up and the iron set for a thick cut (¹⁄₁₆ in.), plane across the grain a ribbon of wood from the 1-in. face. Your "shaving" will be a strip of veneer.*

"Veneer"

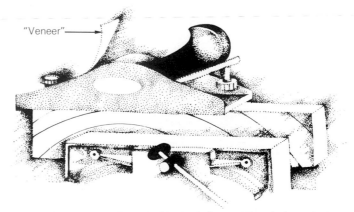

In cutting, you will probably feel the regular clickety feeling of the cyclic knife checking. Since your plane does not have a nosebar, your "veneer" will probably have lots of knife checks. Experiment with different thicknesses of cut and with the hot pieces. Notice how much tighter the veneer is when you cut it thinner. Or when hot wood is cut. Can you readily recognize the "open" and "closed" faces in every strip?

SHOP AND TOOLS

Dust Collection System
Damper-controlled setup keeps basement shop clean

by Doyle Johnson

Opening the damper slide starts the collector.

One problem confronting all woodworkers is how to combat the dust generated by power tools. My shop is in the basement of my home, and my concern over the mess and health and fire hazards led me to design a dust-collection system for my stationary power tools. I wanted the system to be conveniently located at each tool so no time would be wasted in moving hoses or cords. Therefore I installed permanent piping to the machines with a positive shut-off damper at each, so that the collector would run at full capacity at the operating tool.

In designing and installing a system like this, keep the collector as close as possible to the tools. Use as much pipe and as little hose as you can, to reduce resistance and make the system more efficient. To ensure compatibility, locate sources for all the components before you start construction.

I chose a ½-hp cast aluminum industrial collector (model 50) manufactured by the Cincinnati Fan and Ventilator Co., 5345 Creek Rd., Cincinnati, Ohio 45242. The specifications of this model are 110 volt, 450 cfm, 7-in. static pressure, 9150 fpm velocity using a 3-in. hose, with a noise level of 73 db. The collector retails for about $245. The unit has a totally enclosed fan-cooled motor and is suitable for outdoor installation. It is designed to fit a 20-gal. or 24-gal. waste can, but I

modified a 55-gal. drum with a removable top to accept it. Since the collector is weatherproof, I put it outside to eliminate the chore of carrying the refuse up the stairs, to save space and to get the noise out of the shop. I covered the dust-filter bag with a trash-can liner with the bottom removed to keep it dry. The unit was in service through last winter and survived about 84 in. of snowfall without any problem. I plan to build a small louvered enclosure with doors for it, to muffle the noise and reduce the chance of theft.

I decided on 3-in. schedule 30 (thin-walled) PVC drainage pipe instead of metal vent pipe to reduce the noise and to take advantage of a larger choice of fittings. The smooth sweeping bends of the plastic pipe prevent material from settling out as it passes a drop to another machine. Because of building codes, schedule 30 PVC pipe may not be available in some areas, but it costs about 40% less than the heavier schedule 40 pipe. Schedule 30 pipe costs $6 for 10 feet. Fittings cost a dollar or two each.

PVC pipe can easily be cut on a radial arm saw and can be permanently joined with solvent cement. But I found the joints airtight without cement, and I can remove the pipe if I ever want to rearrange my tools. Duct tape can be used if a joint is suspicious. I secured the pipe to the building with perforated plumber's tape.

After looking through several catalogs, I couldn't find a suitable damper. I could have used standard dampers and wired the system to a wall switch, but instead I designed one of maple and sheet metal, with control contacts to start the collector when any damper is opened. Felt seals make a positive seal on the sheet metal slide. I started with two pieces of maple long enough for all the dampers I needed; the drawing gives the dimensions and steps involved.

Each damper needs two contacts for operating the control relay. They are made of .025-in. brass shim stock. Lay out the contacts on flat stock and drill the holes. Then cut and bend them to shape as shown in the drawing. Smooth the edges and curved end for good electrical contact with the slide. These contacts are suitable only for low-voltage applications.

To assemble the damper, place the slide between a set of damper bodies and bolt together using ³⁄₁₆-in. by 3-in. screws. Attach the mounting brackets, tighten the bolts and check for smooth operation of the slide. Next place the unit in the vise, insert one of the seals and push it against the slide until it seats evenly. Hold in this position and drill holes to secure the seal with #8 x 1-in. self-tapping screws. Repeat the procedure for the opposite side. The seals should fit into the damper bodies snugly. If the hole is too large, a wrap or two of 1-in. masking tape around the PVC will tighten the fit. Af-

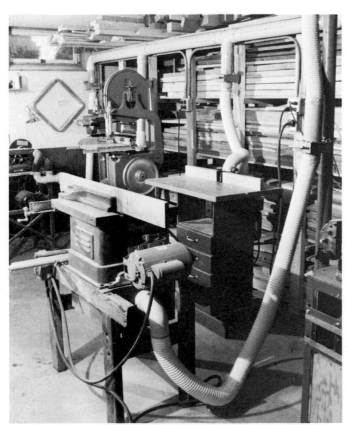

Overhead piping and vertical hoses do not interfere with machines. Dampers are conveniently close to each tool.

Doyle Johnson, 43, of Crown Point, Ind., is electrical supervisor for a steel company. An avid woodworker, his green lumber supply competes with his wife's car for garage space.

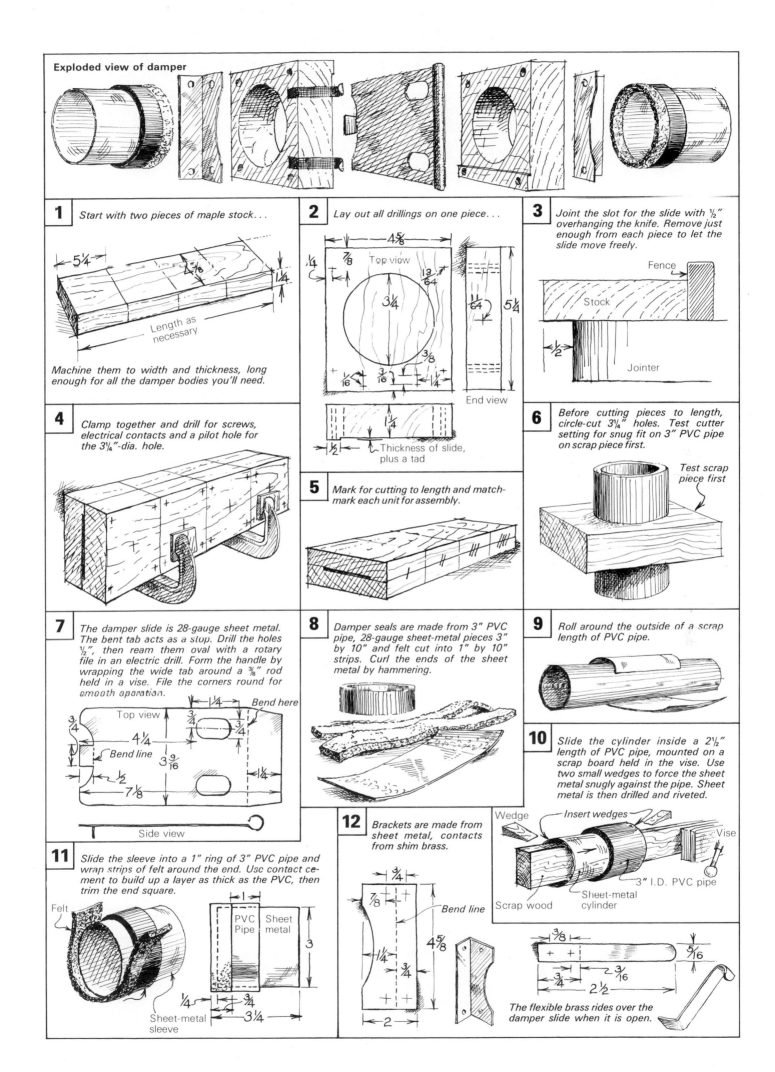

Exploded view of damper

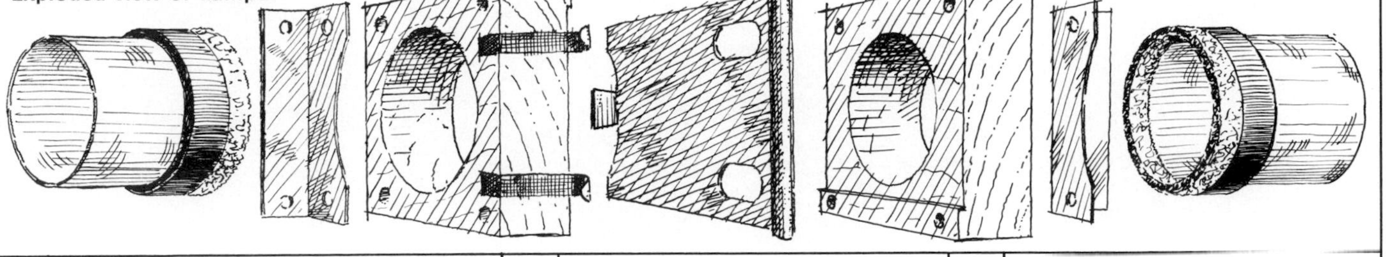

1 *Start with two pieces of maple stock...*

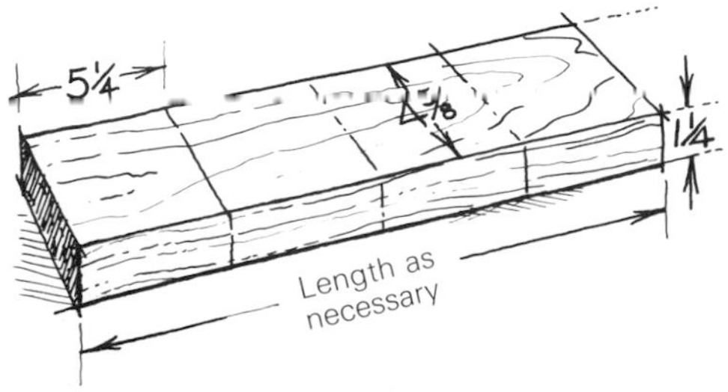
5¼
4⅝
1¼
Length as necessary

Machine them to width and thickness, long enough for all the damper bodies you'll need.

2 *Lay out all drillings on one piece...*

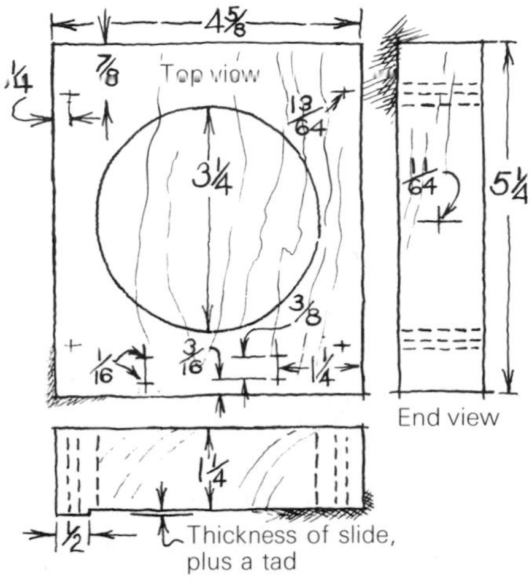
4⅝
¼
⅞
Top view
13/64
3¼
⅜
1/16
3/16
¼
11/64
5¼
End view
1¼
½
Thickness of slide, plus a tad

3 *Joint the slot for the slide with ½" overhanging the knife. Remove just enough from each piece to let the slide move freely.*

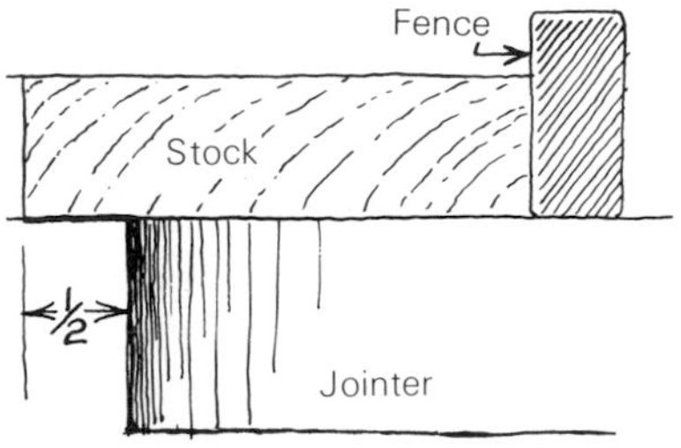
Fence
Stock
½
Jointer

4 *Clamp together and drill for screws, electrical contacts and a pilot hole for the 3¼"-dia. hole.*

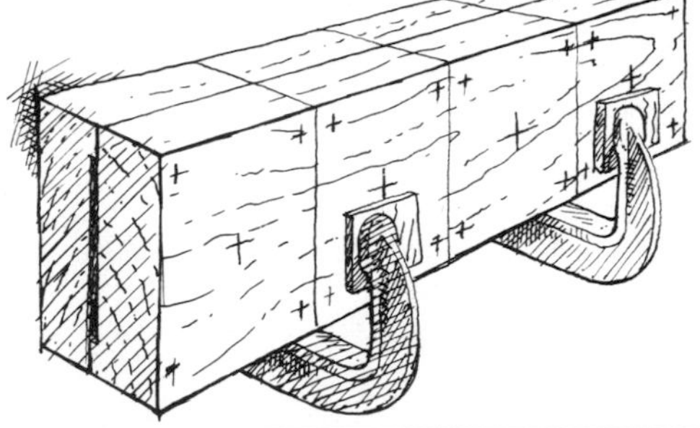

5 *Mark for cutting to length and match-mark each unit for assembly.*

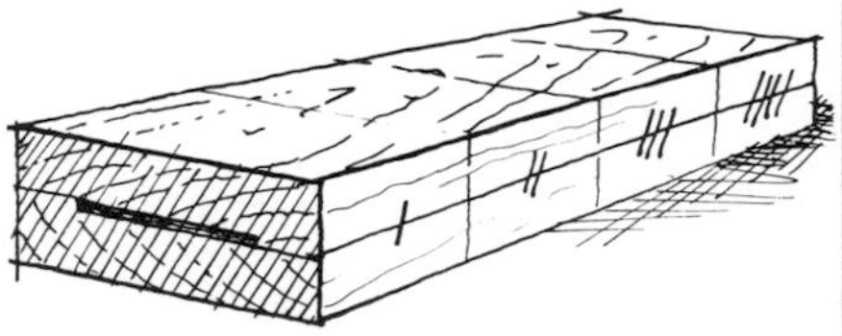

6 *Before cutting pieces to length, circle-cut 3¼" holes. Test cutter setting for snug fit on 3" PVC pipe on scrap piece first.*

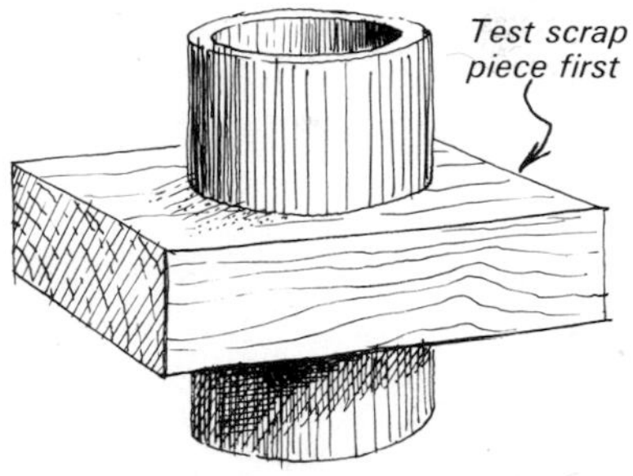
Test scrap piece first

7 *The damper slide is 28-gauge sheet metal. The bent tab acts as a stop. Drill the holes ½", then ream them oval with a rotary file in an electric drill. Form the handle by wrapping the wide tab around a ⅜" rod held in a vise. File the corners round for smooth operation.*

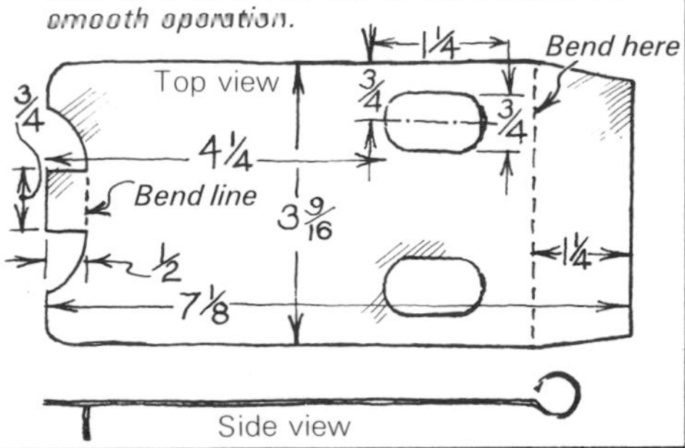
1¼
Bend here
Top view
¾
¾
¾
4¼
Bend line
3 9/16
½
1¼
7⅛
Side view

8 *Damper seals are made from 3" PVC pipe, 28-gauge sheet-metal pieces 3" by 10" and felt cut into 1" by 10" strips. Curl the ends of the sheet metal by hammering.*

9 *Roll around the outside of a scrap length of PVC pipe.*

10 *Slide the cylinder inside a 2½" length of PVC pipe, mounted on a scrap board held in the vise. Use two small wedges to force the sheet metal snugly against the pipe. Sheet metal is then drilled and riveted.*

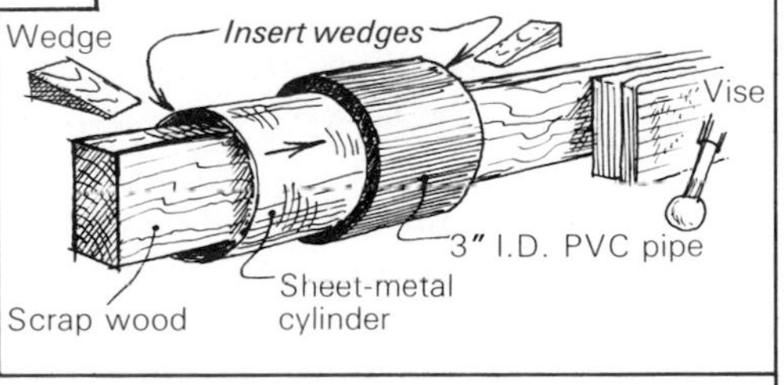
Wedge
Insert wedges
Vise
3" I.D. PVC pipe
Scrap wood
Sheet-metal cylinder

11 *Slide the sleeve into a 1" ring of 3" PVC pipe and wrap strips of felt around the end. Use contact cement to build up a layer as thick as the PVC, then trim the end square.*

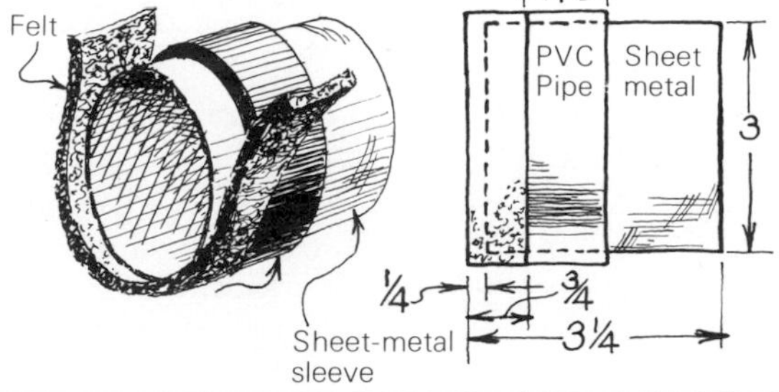
Felt
1
PVC Pipe
Sheet metal
3
¼
¾
3¼
Sheet-metal sleeve

12 *Brackets are made from sheet metal, contacts from shim brass.*

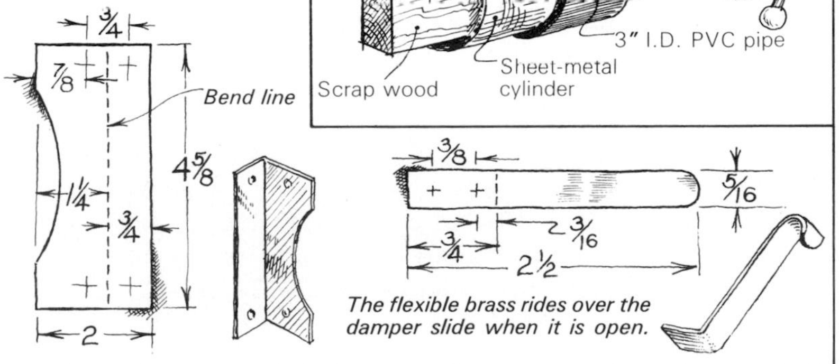
¾
⅞
Bend line
1¼
4⅝
¾
2
⅜
5/16
3/16
¾
2½

The flexible brass rides over the damper slide when it is open.

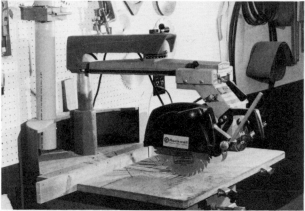
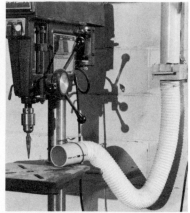

Collector mounted outdoors on 55-gal. drum, left, is connected to machinery inside shop in various ways. Center, semicircular catcher of ¼-in. Masonite and ½-in. plywood funnels debris from radial arm saw into the pipe about 1 in. above catcher bottom. Blade-guard pick-up could also be built. Saw, used mainly for crosscutting, is tight against wall; more space would permit deeper catcher with bottom pick-up. Right, suction hose attached to short pipe is clamped to drill-press column. Damper links hose to overhead pipes.

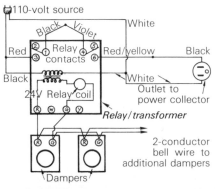

Shaper setup, above, has 45° PVC elbow with sheet-metal sleeve inside. A ⅜-in. threaded rod, bent L-shaped and clamped to elbow with plumber's tape, secures hose to table. Sheet metal closes off area behind cutter. Hose unit swings away to change cutters. Wiring for dust-collection system is diagrammed at left.

Band-saw take-off, far left, is in bottom of sealed-off lower blade guard. Hose is long enough to rest guard on floor while changing blades. Left, table-saw take-off is through a hole in drawer where blade throws sawdust. Hose detaches for vacuuming shop floor. On belt and disc sander, right, system connects to dust pick-ups for shop vacuum.

ter assembly, a small bead of silicone sealer or gutter sealant between seal and body will prevent leakage. This allows the damper to be taken apart if the seals ever need replacement.

The contacts are now attached with #6 x ½-in. sheet-metal screws. Adjust the wipe on the contacts by bending the curved tip up or down to meet the slide. Close the slide and move from side to side; if the contact touches the metal, adjust or trim the contact slightly. Lubricate the slide where the contacts ride by rubbing with a soft lead pencil or graphite-based lubricant to reduce friction and ensure good contact.

For controlling the power to the collector, I selected a 24-volt switching relay/transformer, the kind that controls furnace blowers for air conditioning. The 24-volt circuit is safe to connect to the damper contacts with ordinary doorbell wire. I bought a Sears Model #541.9211D, rated at ¾ hp, 110 volts, for about $15. Its relay controls power to a weather-proof receptacle at the collector. I have enough capacity on the shop lighting circuit to operate the collector system and have it connected so it works only when the lights are on.

I anchored the dampers in easy reach from each machine and ran 3-in. hose to the machine itself. Since hose similar to the 5-ft. length furnished with the collector cost almost $2/ft., I used 3-in. clothes-dryer vent hose at $.60/ft., which has proved satisfactory. To link the hose to a pipe, one of the sleeves like those on the dampers works fine. To go into a hub on a fitting, just put a short piece of pipe over the sleeve. The metal sleeve protrudes 1½ in. on each side of the damper, which allows connection of 3-in. pipe or hose. To secure the hose I used a double wrap of #14 AWG wire twisted tightly.

In adapting my machines for dust collection, I found that each presented its own problems. The objective is to get maximum air flow around the cutter and into the collector, and I devised solutions (shown above) with that in mind.

I have about $325 invested in my dust-collecting system and am satisfied with its performance. To further illustrate the capacity of this unit, I co-own a 12-in. thickness planer with a brother and have it in his shop. We made and installed a collector hood, connected the collector to it with a 5-ft. length of 4-in. hose and found that it does a beautiful job of collecting shavings while planing 12-in. boards. The only problem is that the 55-gal. drum is jammed full in a matter of minutes.   □

Small Workbench
A simple and versatile design

by R. Bruce Hoadley

Wet sand anchors outdoor bench.

Everyone knows a workbench should be rugged and massive, "the bigger the better." But some years ago I set out to build a firm yet semi-portable stand for teaching and demonstrating. The little workbench that eventually evolved is now an indispensable part of my workshop. At first glance it looks like a traditional sculpture stand, and one might hastily conclude that it is too small, too frail and too tippy to be of general use to the woodworker—it simply doesn't look like a workbench. However, it does offer some noteworthy advantages.

First, it is tall. Most benches are 36 in. high or lower, but many—if not most—hand operations are more comfortable at a higher level. For me (I'm 6 ft.), a 42-in. bench makes all those little jobs like letting in an escutcheon plate, carving out a fan, or cutting a dovetail, much easier.

For woodcarving, a top surface of 12 in. by 12 in. is ideal: small enough to work all around, yet large enough to handle a sizable sculpture. For general woodworking the dimensions can be increased to about 16 in. by 18 in. (as shown). Getting much larger subtracts more than it adds.

Making the top in two halves minimizes warping. High-density hardwoods such as oak, birch, maple and beech about 1½ in. thick are suitable. A one-piece top of 1-in. hardwood plywood might also do nicely. Cross support cleats should also be hardwood and the top should be fastened with heavy wood screws, lag screws or carriage bolts. Be sure fasteners are well counterbored below the surface. On my first model I set the screws flush with the surface and frequently hit them with carving chisels until I finally set them deeper.

The dimensions given here are only suggestions and can be modified for each person's specific needs.

The key feature of the top is plenty of clamping edges all around. The middle area has holes to stick C-clamps or quick-set clamps up through. Making the top surface in two halves with an ample slot down the middle adds to this versatility. A carving screw can be put anywhere along the slot, or the slot can be widened in places for clamps. Any number of holes or recesses can be added to accommodate your favorite vise, bench stop or holddown.

A vertical apron on one side might be bothersome to the carver, but helpful to the cabinetmaker for clamping stock to work on edges. Put rows of holes in the apron for support pegs.

The base frame must be stable and rigid, and 2x4's or similar lumber will do nicely. Splaying the legs adds stability but is not absolutely necessary. I try to make the frame with as much unobstructed interior space as possible and with a bottom shelf as low as possible for piling weight on. The first bench I built is at home, and I weigh it down with bricks and stones because I happen to have them: bricks in the cellar shop, stones when I move the bench to the garage or backyard to carve in the summer. Lead would be ideal ballast.

Behind our little summer house on Cape Cod, my favorite carving place, I have another bench, built from wood recycled from the town dump. I enclosed the entire bottom assembly with plywood and once it was set in location, filled it with sand for ballast. Then I slowly poured in as much water as the sand would absorb. The bench has been in place for four years and is now settled in rock solid. Occasionally I water it. A plastic trash bag keeps the top dry when the bench is not in use.

At the laboratory where I work, I have a third bench, as a teaching aid and for research setups. To weigh it down, we pile the base with assorted scrap metal.

This mini-bench will never replace traditional workbenches, but it might well be a good first bench for the woodworker with limited space. Once you've built and used such a bench, complete with your favorite accessories and modifications, you'll understand why it's the "teacher's pet." □

R. Bruce Hoadley, a carver, is a wood technologist at the University of Massachusetts and a contributing editor of Fine Woodworking.

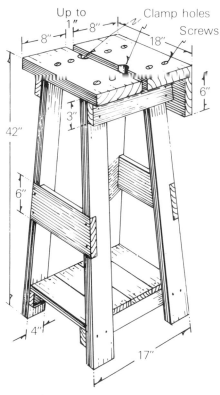

Up to 1" Clamp holes Screws 8" 8" 18" 42" 6" 3" 6" 4" 17"

Mini-bench with typical dimensions: Base frame of 2x4's supports hardwood top.

Tool Cabinets
Removable trays are the heart of them

by Tage Frid

Why bother making a tool cabinet when a crate with shelves nailed in would hold the tools? I believe if a person wants to make a living as a woodworker and furniture designer, a well-designed and executed tool cabinet is very important. It's a pleasure to have a beautiful tool cabinet, where the tools are properly arranged and easy to find. And when a potential customer comes into the shop and sees a nice cabinet, half of the selling job is done right there.

For a cabinetmaker, a cabinet for tools is more practical than a tool chest like carpenters use. Usually a cabinetmaker does most of his work in the shop, while a carpenter has to move his tools from job to job and many times must use the tool chest as a workbench. Also, there is less wasted space in a cabinet, and because you can make it open from the front it is easy to arrange and get at the tools you need.

Most of my graduate students design and make a tool cabinet as their first project. They find it a difficult piece to design because every inch has to be used, but at the same time it has to be flexible, handy and easy to rearrange as you add new tools or replace old ones. The photos shown here are all of cabinets made by my students.

The drawing below is not a working drawing and the joints are left up to you—it is just an idea of how I would make a tool cabinet if I needed a new one. I prefer trays that slide out instead of drawers or shelves because I can take the one that holds chisels out of the cabinet, work with them at the bench, then put them back in the tray and return it to the cabinet. The same goes for screwdrivers and all my other small tools—each kind of tool has its own removable tray.

I wouldn't make the height of the cabinet any less than 40 in. if I wanted to have a bowsaw hanging inside the door, and in that case I wouldn't make any grooves in the door.

Personally, I would have the bowsaw hanging on the outside and use small shelves in the door grooves for storage of small tools. If you aren't going to hang saws inside the door, the height isn't that critical.

Through the years, I've found that 15 in. is the best depth for the cabinet, not counting the door, which should be another 4 in. This is deep enough for nearly everything, including heavy tools. The width, 30 in., is necessary so the jointer plane, slicks and other large tools can fit in the upper part, which can be an open shelf or a drawer.

I make the sides of the trays out of hardwood—use whatever joint you like at the corners—with a bottom of ¼-in. plywood. The grooves in the sides of the cabinet of course are ¼ in. by ¼ in., so the plywood can easily slide in and out. The space between the grooves is 1½ in., which makes the cabinet very flexible—the trays can be 1½ in. apart, or 3 in., or 4½ in. and so on, depending on whether they are used for chisels, planes or whatever. The center divider should be in the exact center of the cabinet, so both sides are the same width, in this case 13½ in., and all the trays and shelves are interchangeable. Remember that the plywood bottom of the tray slides into the groove and add ½ in., making the bottoms 14 in. wide. Inside the sides of the trays it is a good idea to make some vertical ¼-in. grooves for removable partitions. Part of the front of each tray is cut down for a handle, and to make it easy to see what's inside. If the cabinet is made out of solid wood, make the trays ⅜ in. shorter than the cabinet is deep, in case the wood shrinks. ☐

Tage Frid, professor of woodworking and furniture design at Rhode Island School of Design, is a contributing editor and regular columnist for Fine Woodworking *magazine.*

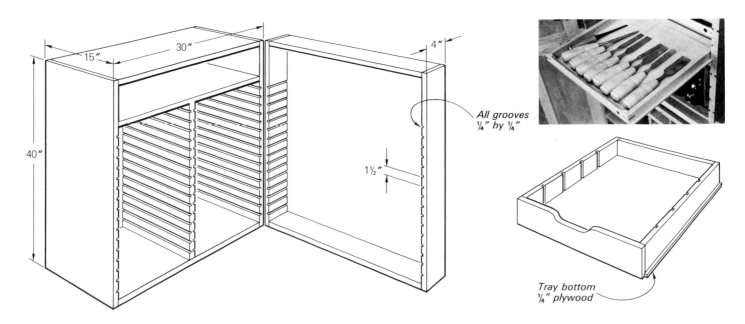

All grooves ¼″ by ¼″

Tray bottom ¼″ plywood

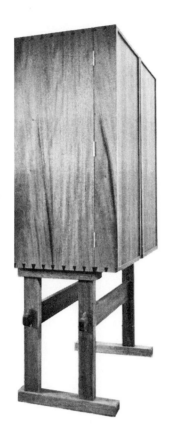

John Dunnigan's tool cabinet (41 in. by 34 in. by 19 in.; base is 24 in. high) is solid mahogany, with plywood door panels veneered in fiddleback mahogany. The inside of the door is 3¼ in. deep. One door holds saws; the other has adjustable shelves with holes and slots for screwdrivers and carving tools. The shelves are 14 in. deep and adjustable in height.

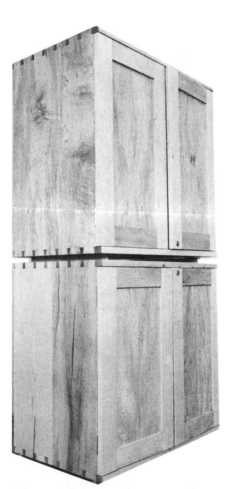

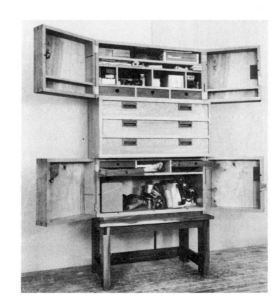

Above and center, these two cabinets (each 32 in. by 32 in. by 19 in.) by Douglas Hale can either stack on top of each other, or sit or hang individually. The doors are a flat frame-and-panel, and hold a few flat tools such as squares or small saws. The detail photo, opposite page, shows how the trays work.

Above and left, solid-oak cabinet by Richard Gallo is 48 in. by 32 in. by 19 in., with 18-in. high base. Stretcher at back makes space underneath usable for storage. Doors, 3 in. deep, have adjustable shelves; three large central drawers hold planes and saws. Lower cabinet was designed for electrical tools.

Holding the Work
Shaving horse and low bench

by John D. Alexander, Jr.

EDITOR'S NOTE: The post-and-rung chair at right is one of the basic seats that for centuries has kept Western man off the ground. It is light, rugged and beautiful. The vertical posts are white oak, the horizontal rungs and the back slats are hickory, and the seat is woven from the supple inner bark of the hickory tree. The chair is not hard to make, when you know how. It is explained in *Make a Chair from a Tree: An Introduction to Working Green Wood*, by John D. Alexander, Jr. (The Taunton Press, Inc., Box 355, Newtown, Conn. 06470, 1978. $7.95, paperback, 128 pp.).

The key to making a post-and-rung chair is working the wood green, as it comes off the tree. Green wood is relatively easy to cut, bore, shave and shape. As it dries, it hardens and shrinks. In chairmaking, the posts are shaped green, dried a little, then mortised to accept the rungs, which also are shaped green. But the rungs are well dried, then tenoned a hair oversize. When the tenons are driven home, they take on moisture from the post wood, expand tightly in their mortises, and then the whole joint dries to equilibrium with the atmosphere. It shrinks tightly together. A few further subleties—the post mortises interlock, the tenons are shouldered, notched and flattened for a dovetail effect and the grain direction of all the parts is carefully orchestrated—make a joint that just won't come apart.

Alexander is a Baltimore lawyer who has spent the last dozen years investigating old tools and chairs and figuring out how they were used and made. This article is taken from his chapter on working surfaces and holding devices. For more on splitting green wood into usable pieces, see "Cleaving Wood," p. 13.

A chopping block is necessary. In the woods, use the stump of the tree you are harvesting. The stump, cut off immediately above the roots, makes a good block for the shop. Its flared, curved wood is not good for much else. Tall and short blocks, side by side, make it easy to hew out long back posts, because they can be shifted from one block to the other. A white oak, elm, locust or catalpa block will last outdoors for a long while, but use whatever is available. Work in a cleared area, with no one in the plane of travel of the hatchet head.

You need a low workbench and a shaving horse, although the shaving horse can be modified to serve as both. I'll describe the low bench first. The standard cabinetmaker's bench is not as useful for chairmaking as a bench that is low, narrow and heavy—a bench that can be moved, sat upon and battered.

The body of a low bench is a heavy slab. Split a slab between three and five feet long out of heavy hardwood. White oak is best both for weight and for resistance to weathering. Work while the wood is still wet. Make the slab anywhere between two and five inches thick and between nine and sixteen inches wide. The bench should be low enough and narrow enough to be straddled comfortably, either standing or sitting. When you sit astride the bench, your legs should be comfortable. Fixed dimensions are not important—make the

bench fit yourself and your task. You will spend a lot of time at this bench, so design it carefully. The important thing is a flat top. If no logs are available, use heavy planks or 2x4s glued face-to-face.

The bench posts taper up into the bench surface. It is easier to cut and adjust them if the posts come right through the slab. If you don't have a tapered reamer for making conical mortises in the slab, tapered rectilineal mortises and tenons chopped out of the green wood with a heavy chisel will also do a good job. Don't permanently secure the posts in the slab because they will swell and shrink throughout the life of the bench. If the movement of the wood makes the posts project above the slab, trim them off. If they become loose, drive a wedge alongside them.

Make the posts from wood that isn't good enough for chairs. Taper them to fit the tapered mortises. Drive them home. Building the bench is a good introduction to wet woodworking in general and to post and slab construction in particular. You will learn how to hew, chisel and bore wet wood. Almost no mistake is fatal with this bench. The harder you pound on it, the tighter it will become.

When moving the bench, be careful that one of the heavy posts doesn't fall out and smash your foot. I wasn't. I have never taken the time to put in stretchers.

What you have made is the ancestor of the common Wind-

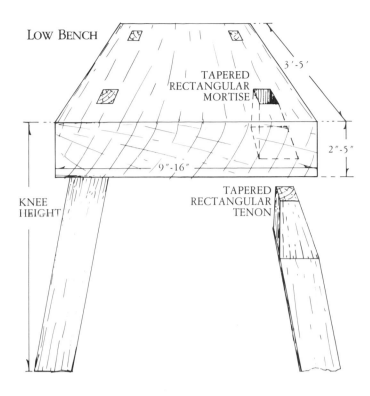

LOW BENCH

TAPERED
RECTANGULAR
MORTISE

3'-5'

2"-5"

9"-16"

KNEE
HEIGHT

TAPERED
RECTANGULAR
TENON

The low bench should be heavy and about knee height, so it can be locked between the knees whether the maker is sitting or standing. It is made of split green wood or from scrap lumber. Tapered pegs driven into round holes in the bench, right, hold work for boring or mortising. A wedge locks the pieces in place.

sor chair. Your bench (also called mare, horse, buck or trestle) allows you to align your body with your work. The bench puts the work at your waist rather than at your chest. You can sit down at and on your work, which is a big help. Once you are sitting on the bench or standing astride it, locking it between your knees, you, the work and the bench become one mechanical system—if you can secure the work to the slab.

To secure work for boring or mortising, drive three or four square tapered pegs into round holes in the bench. Lay sticks between the pegs and lock them in place with a wooden wedge or wedges. Space the holes and pegs so that posts can be held down singly and in matching pairs. The simplicity of this holding system was hard to accept until I tried it. It was the last method I tried.

You can also use screws as holding devices. Wooden screws of 7/8-in. or 1-in. diameter are more than strong enough. Because permanent handles get in the way, make the screws with large heads and drill holes through them. You'll always

have rung rejects (factory seconds) lying around to put into the holes for handles.

Hold-down yokes are fastened to the bench top by boring a hole through the middle of the slab to accept the wooden screw bolt. I don't tap vertical holes in the bench, but use a wooden screw bolt from above the slab and a wooden lever nut from below. A deep-engagement pipe clamp also works, with the pipe running through a hole in the bench and the screw beneath the bench. Run the pipe up through a hole in the hold-down yoke and screw a threaded pipe flange or sleeve on the top end. Protect your tools by covering with wood any metal projecting above the bench so metal doesn't strike metal.

I use the English style of shaving horse, also called a bodger's bench, cooper's shaving bench or shaving brake. It holds posts, rungs and slats for drawknifing and shaving. The crossbar on the horse securely locks the workpiece in place. The shaving horse is a perfect holding device: The harder you

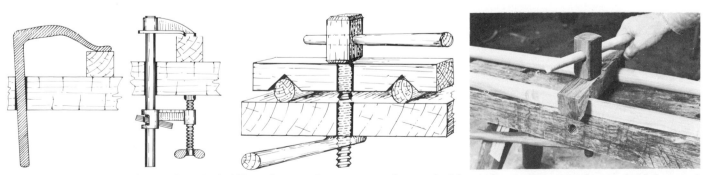

More holding systems (left to right): the holdfast, the pipe clamp, the hold-down yoke. A holdfast works by spring action. A tap at its knee jams it against the sides of a hole in the bench. A pipe clamp can be run through a hole and tightened underneath the bench, but

cap the metal with wood to protect tool edges. A hold-down yoke will secure matching posts side by side. It is tightened by a square-headed wooden screw fitting loosely through the bench into a wooden lever nut below.

pull the tool toward you, the harder your feet push the lever arms away from you. The crossbar is thus forced down on the workpiece.

The horse design I use allows more adjustment than some versions, and it makes the horse adaptable for various tasks. My horse has two horizontal parallel beams, like a lathe, rather than a solid slab. The work surface is nailed (with deeply countersunk nails) to a tiller that fits between the beams. Pegs driven through the sides of the beams and the tiller adjust the surface to any angle or height. I made my shaving horse from scrap hardwood lumber. White oak is excellent, but almost any wood will do. Of course you can split the parts out of green wood.

The shaving horse crossbar is square in cross section. Its round ends friction-fit into the side lever bars. Thus the crossbar can rotate and will always seat squarely on the work. One surface of the bar is notched to hold square-sectioned sticks corner up.

Shaving-horse dimensions depend on the worker. The height and size of the bench should allow the worker's heels to rest on the ground while his toes touch the lever foot bar.

To make a shaving horse double as a low bench, mount a heavy plank on the beams. You'll find a separate low bench a help, but you can get started without one. If you make both a horse and a bench, or two benches, make them the same height, so they can double as sawhorses or be used to hold larger pieces of work laid across them.

Because the work surface is adjustable, the shaving horse has a variety of other uses. I hold sharpening stones or tools with it: both my hands are free to control sharpening pressure and angle.

Take time to make a tool box or rack. Tools get lost easily, and edges become nicked and ruined in the mess. The rack must be easy to move from one work area or bench to another. I have a rack made of sticks with tapered ends (conical tenons) jammed into mortises that are bored and taper-reamed through post-wood rejects. The rack is bound together by a toggle rope. A twist or two on the rope adjusts for dimension and design changes.

Now we are ready to make a chair. ☐

SHAVING HORSE

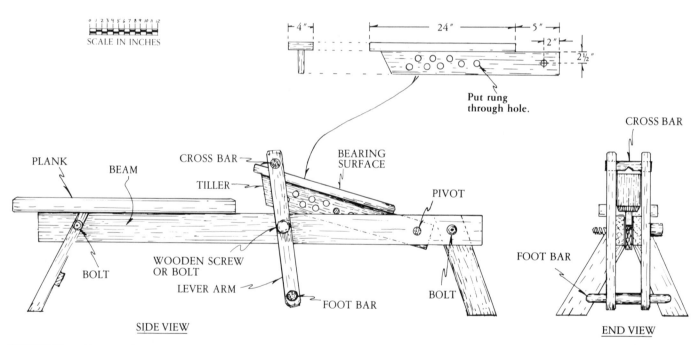

This style of shaving horse is light enough to be toted into the woods for drawknifing split sticks right where the tree is felled.

A post-and-rung tool rack can be made quickly from spare and rejected chair parts, bound together with a toggle rope.

Methods of Work

Leg vise

For years I have admired in museums and photographs those sturdy, simple contraptions I call leg vises. They are mounted at one end of a bench, in front of and parallel to its front leg, and are as high as the top of the bench. This type of vise was prevalent in old woodshops both in this country and abroad. A day at a bench equipped with one and you begin to understand its previous popularity and question its present scarcity.

This vise can be adjusted to hold at various angles and gains much of its holding power from simple leverage. It is capable of holding much larger pieces of wood, both in width and thickness, than most commercial bench vises can. Because the bottom of the front jaw is on the floor and the rear jaw is the bench itself, it is quite stable (or as stable as your bench) and will withstand great abuse from pounding. With the addition of a few holes and a peg or two in the other front leg, you can support long boards on edge. Hardware can be had for about $20 from well-stocked tool suppliers such as Woodcraft Supply Corp., 313 Montvale Ave., Woburn, Mass. 01801. But for less than half that price you can have a leg vise with features that standard bench screws don't allow.

You will need a piece of wood about 3½ in. by 3½ in. by the height of your bench, a pipe-clamp or bar-clamp fixture, a piece of pine 1 in. by 4 in. by 12 in., a dowel, a couple of wood screws and a few hand tools. For wood I've used common 4/4 fir, but anything you have will work. Softwoods can be fitted with hardwood faces at the inside top for better wear. The lower adjustment shown in the diagram works the same as the second screw on a handscrew works. It enables you to keep the vise faces parallel, or at the angles you need. The hole in the upper part of the vise must be elliptical to allow for changes in the relationship of the pipe to the jaw. These changes take place only vertically, so the width of the

ellipse should match the outside diameter of the pipe, usually ¾ in. I bore two holes at 75° off horizontal, intersecting at the center of the wood. This gives a round hole in the center of the piece and ellipses at the outer edges. Cutting two parallel holes also works but is sloppy.

With this bar-clamp system, you get quick action by releasing the bar at the stationary fixture behind the bench leg. Simply pushing closes the vise on whatever is in it. A quick short twist of the crank and all is secure.

—*Craig Schoppe, Arlington, Vt.*

Bench clamp

My clamping device extends the top of a small workbench in limited-floorspace workshops. It can be used in conjunction with a tail vise on the opposite end of the bench or alone with dog holes drilled on line with the clamp-head device.

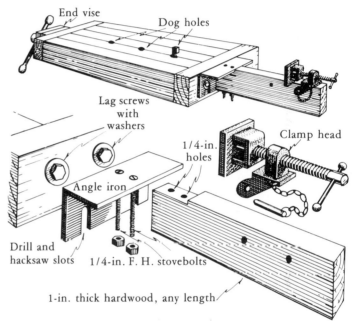

The Record brand clamp head can be bought from Silvo Hardware, 107-109 Walnut St., Philadelphia, Pa. 19106.

My unit was constructed with 3-in. angle iron 6 in. long with the slots drilled and hacksawed 1 in. from either end. The ⅜-in. x 4-in. lag screws were driven through the slots into the end of my workbench so that the angle iron is flush with the top. Tightening and loosening the lag screws facilitates rapid installation and removal. Wooden bars of various lengths are handy for different projects.

—*Robert Bessmer, Averill Park, N.Y.*

Glass scraper

Microscope slides work very well as scrapers, particularly in tight places like the interiors of small boxes, or drawers. When the edge is fresh, they cut beautifully, and though they lose the edge faster than a metal scraper, they are disposable and don't require the time spent on resharpening. I've found that so-called petrographic slides (27mm x 46mm) are sturdier than biological slides (25mm x 75mm). One supplier (of many) is Buehler, Ltd., 2120 Greenwood St., Evanston, Ill., 60204. The order number is 40-8000-001 for 1 gross, price $7.00.

—*John Reid, Amherst, Mass.*

Basic Blacksmithing

What a woodworker needs to forge tools

by Ray Larsen

Author files weld on shell auger.

The furniture maker ruins a mahogany table base while trying to cut a deep mortise in it. He is using the wrong chisel because the right one has been out of stock for eight months. The instrument maker applies pressure to the shell auger buried deep in the boxwood clamped in front of him. The bit snaps in his hand. The turner walks from his lathe, shaking his head. A poorly designed gouge has just ripped through the tulipwood bowl he's been working on all day. The sculptor lays down his mallet and puts his work aside in frustration. He can't get the effect he wants, although he's tried every tool in the catalog.

Such incidents, all too common in woodworking, have led to a resurgence of interest in hand forging high-quality tools, at least those special tools unavailable from even the best supply houses. This has developed a number of skilled blacksmiths able to produce special tools of the highest quality, and woodworkers need only avail themselves of their services. In addition, a growing number of serious woodworkers are taking up blacksmithing themselves. They are discovering that with a little perseverance they can forge their own tools.

It takes a substantial investment to set up a forge and a substantial block of time to locate equipment and learn the necessary skills. Each woodworker should ask himself how serious his need is for special, high-quality tools before deciding to make them. The devoted craftsman will quickly resent the time taken from his first love to produce tools he really doesn't need.

Once a woodworker learns blacksmithing, he never again need worry about tools breaking, or not holding an edge, or ruining the work. Less time struggling with tools means more time producing high-quality work. And the most exotic tools are readily available. Need a special shape for turning the inside of a box? It's there for the making. Many woodworkers find that a tool especially designed for a job enables them to produce pieces others can't, or to produce them faster or more economically. The right tool for the job means superior work.

After the initial investment, the blacksmith-woodworker saves time and money; others must wait until special tools become available, or run around searching them out, or pay the relatively high cost of having them made by a specialist. The woodworker who can make tools can also repair and modify them. A chipped screwdriver is reshaped at a fraction of the cost of replacing it; an old parting tool is reworked to turn a special configuration. In addition, the blacksmith-

Ray Larsen, 37, of Hanover, Mass., is a professional blacksmith who makes high-quality tools on special order through Woodcraft Supply Corp.

woodworker can also forge special pulls, latches, hinges and other hard-to-find hardware. This ability is especially important to specialists in antique reproductions.

Equipment

I began blacksmithing with a homemade forge, two borrowed pairs of tongs, a $35 anvil and a beat-up grindstone. Most serious woodworkers already have several pieces of equipment essential to toolmaking, including a good grinding wheel or other sharpening system, high-quality bench honing equipment and a heavy-duty drill press. But additional equipment is required, including a forge, anvil, tongs, hammers, punches and chisels, fullers and hardies, swages, vise and quench tub. Start with a few pieces of equipment and master them before buying more.

The heart of the blacksmith shop is the forge, in which a blast of air applied to a coal, coke or charcoal fire heats steel to the elevated temperatures required for forging. There are many sizes and styles, from big, permanent types costing well over $1,200 to small, portable types found in junkyards and secondhand shops for $50 to $200 depending on size, quality and the buyer's ability to bargain. The thrifty craftsman can make a forge using a discarded barbecue grill for the bed and the guts of an old vacuum cleaner or hair dryer for the blower.

Forging generates soot, smoke and dust that must be vented away from clean areas of the shop. I recommend buying a hooded, ventable forge over an open type for this reason. Some manufacturers have substituted stamped metal for cast iron in recent years, but cast iron remains best for the job because of its superior fire-resistant properties. Cranking the blower by hand may be romantic, but it isn't as efficient or as easily managed as an electric one. Buffalo Forge Co., Buffalo, N. Y., and Champion Blower & Forge, Inc., Roselle, Ill., are respected forge manufacturers.

Do not use the forge without first lining it with a suitable refractory, a non-metallic, ceramic material with heat-resisting properties that protects the forge bed from burning out. It comes in many forms but a powdered type, Kast-Set, made by A. P. Green Refractories Co., Mexico, Mo., is excellent; it is mixed with water like cement and cast in place. Such refractory will protect the forge and greatly extend its life at minimum cost (less than $20 for approximately a two-year supply).

If the forge is the heart of the blacksmith shop, the anvil is its soul. No other single piece of equipment (save perhaps a favorite hammer) inspires blacksmiths to such heights of enthusiasm and such depths of despair. Like forges, anvils come in a wide variety of types, styles and sizes, from new but

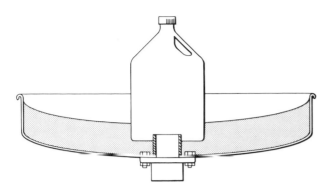

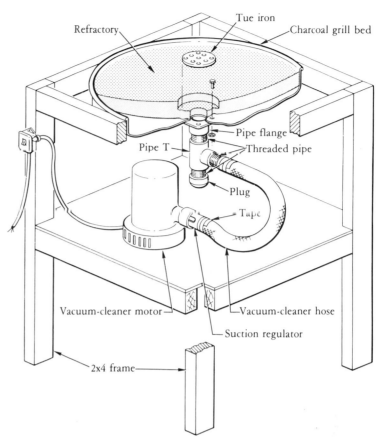

Refractory
Tue iron
Charcoal grill bed
Pipe flange
Pipe T
Threaded pipe
Plug
Tape
Vacuum-cleaner motor
Vacuum-cleaner hose
Suction regulator
2x4 frame

A serviceable forge can be constructed from readily available materials. The bed is built from a new or used stamped metal outdoor grill. A hooded type (not shown here) makes essential venting easier. Or a hood can be made from sheet metal and a stovepipe. The factory-made tubular legs are discarded in favor of a heavy-duty 2x4 frame with braced 2x4 legs. The bed should be at workbench height. The center hole in the bed is enlarged to accept a 2-in. pipe flange; a T-fitting introduces air blast and a plug is loosely fitted beneath for ash clean-out. A vacuum-cleaner or hair-dryer motor with heating element removed is affixed to the frame; the blower outlet is linked to the T-fitting with vacuum-cleaner or hair-dryer hose. Adjustable clamps and duct tape ensure an airtight fit. A vacuum-cleaner suction regulator or similar device regulates the blast. Refractory is troweled around a suitable form, such as a plastic bleach bottle with 2-in. pipe inserted through its bottom, placed over the center hole (as above). A tue iron cut from heavy-gauge sheet metal and drilled or punched is laid over the 2-in. blast opening in the bed.

expensive all-steel types available from such supply houses as Centaur Forge Ltd., Burlington, Wis., (about $200 for a 125-pound size) to traditional, steel-faced types available from secondhand dealers for $75 and up. The anvil should be mounted on a heavy tree stump.

When selecting an anvil, look for a smooth, flat face and unflawed horn. Use a steel straightedge to spot valleys. The quality of the work depends to a great extent on the condition of the anvil. Don't buy a used one with badly chipped edges on the face, a sure sign of misuse over the years. And don't buy an anvil whose steel face is separating from its cast or wrought-iron base. Improper welding of face to body is a clue to inferior manufacture. Two respected brands are Peter Wright and Hay-Budden; both companies are out of business but their anvils may be purchased through dealers or at junkyards.

Anvils come in many sizes, but the 125 to 150 lb. range is good for toolmaking. Anything smaller is too light to stand up to tool steels, while heavier anvils are too expensive and hard to transport. Before buying, strike the face moderately with a hammer. A good ring and strong bounce are signs of a strong, well-made anvil. Avoid limp clunkers.

Tongs, the long-handled tools used to hold steel while it is heated and forged, come in a bewildering range of sizes and styles. Early trade manuals, such as *Hand Forging* by Thomas F. Googerty (Popular Mechanics Co., Chicago, Ill.), suggest making one's own as a good way to learn the blacksmith's craft. There is a great deal of sense in that. But because tongs are readily available at junk shops and flea markets for as little as 50 cents, it is easier for the woodworker to buy them—at least at the outset. Pick a few simple sizes and shapes and purchase more pairs as needed.

There also are hundreds of new and used blacksmith, me-

chanic, farrier and other hammers on the market these days and each blacksmith has favorites (my own are an odd, one-pound cross-peen type that I use for delicate finish work and an old electric sharpening hammer that is excellent for hammering in blade edges). Start simply with several ball-peen and mechanic's hammers ranging from one to three pounds and fill in with special types as required. Buy only the highest quality (Sears' Craftsman mechanic's hammers are excellent).

Punches and chisels are special long or handled types which come in hot and cold versions for punching and cutting heated or unheated steel. They are available used from supply houses such as Centaur or manufacturers such as Diamond Tool and Horseshoe Co., Duluth, Minn. Prices vary. As with tongs and hammers, buy a few simple ones and fill in as requirements dictate.

Fullers and hardies fit in the hardie or square hole at the heel of most anvils. Fullers are used to draw steel, hardies to cut it. The metal is heated to forging temperature, then placed over the tool and struck with a hammer. Start with a few simple types from reputable supply houses or manufacturers and supplement as needed. Expect to pay about $10 each.

Swages come in two types. Bottom swages fit into the hardie hole and come in various round, square and other shapes. They permit the toolmaker to hammer hot steel to a desired configuration. Sets consist of matched bottom and top swages. The bottom fits in the hardie hole, and the top is handled like a hammer. Hot steel is held between the two and the top swage is struck with a hammer. This procedure generally requires a helper.

Supply houses stock only a limited number of swages. Secondhand shops, junkyards and tool dealers specializing in blacksmith equipment are better sources. Expect to pay $5 and up apiece. An alternative to buying a large number of swages is the swage block, a large block of cast steel with a variety of shapes on its four sides. The block is fitted to a special stand or placed on a heavy stump in the same manner as an anvil. Swage blocks, unfortunately, are expensive new and extremely rare used.

A good machinist's vise is satisfactory for the beginning toolmaker but he should consider buying a blacksmith's type as soon as possible. This vise has a steel leg that sets into the floor of the shop. The leg dissipates the shock of hammering steel in the vise. New blacksmith's vises are expensive compared to readily available used ones. Pay about $50 for one with five-inch jaws in very good condition.

Finally, a reservoir of water is essential for quenching tools. A large, galvanized washtub will do. Half a whiskey barrel is better.

Fuel

Some blacksmiths in England prefer coke for forging. Blacksmiths at Old Sturbridge Village in Sturbridge, Mass., use charcoal for authenticity. But the rest of us use "blacksmith coal," a soft, low-sulfur type especially suited for forge work. Blacksmith coal is available from Centaur and other supply houses but these are expensive sources. Try phoning a coal supplier in your area. Most dealers know who sells blacksmith coal and will quickly suggest a source. Buy 200 pounds

(less than $10 worth) to start. Pick it up at the yard—it's cheaper that way.

Steel

Domestic and overseas producers make a wide range of steels suitable for woodworking tools. New steel is preferable to used because the toolmaker knows what to expect when working it and can select the right type for the job. No matter how good the smith is at identifying used steel, there is always an element of risk in forging it. Because of producer restrictions on minimum order sizes, woodworkers will have to rely on local service centers or warehouses for the small amounts they require. If in doubt, select a company that advertises itself as a member of the Steel Service Center Institute (SSCI), an organization of highly reputable steel suppliers. Two basic families of steel are used in toolmaking: carbon and specialty.

Carbon steel is the single largest type of steel produced in this country and comes in many grades. There are two good reasons for using carbon steel: It costs considerably less than specialty steel, and it comes in many toolmaking shapes not readily available in specialty steels. Prices of carbon steels vary, depending on market conditions.

The amount of carbon determines the steel's hardenability and ability to do work. Only the high-carbon steels are of concern to the woodworker, those types whose carbon content exceeds 0.50%. High-carbon steel ranges from American Iron and Steel Institute (AISI) classification 1055 (containing

Author at work. Note rack of tongs by the forge and hardies mounted in slips around base of anvil, a 350-lb. Hay Budden.

Below, fuller in hardie hole of anvil speeds drawing down steel. Bottom, swage block gives steel round or gouge-like shape.

Spark patterns
identify steels

Medium-carbon steel: Some exploding or bursting sparks. Some sparking around periphery of wheel.

Low-carbon steel: Streamers thrown from wheel are straight, light straw in color. Some small amount of sparking.

High-carbon steel: Considerable bursting, sparking around wheel. Gold/white color.

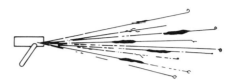

Cast iron (not forgeable): Short, thin, brick-red streamers. Very slight sparking.

High-speed tool steel: Similar to high-carbon steel but with fine explosions. Reddish streamers. No sparking around wheel.

Wrought iron (inappropriate for blades): Very similar to low-carbon steel. Long yellow streamers. Practically no sparking.

0.55% carbon) to AISI classification 1095 (containing 0.95% carbon).

Decent, general-purpose tools can be forged from AISI 1055 steel, but its use is not strongly recommended. A smith forging high-carbon steels should work with the highest grades, 1085 and above. If these are unavailable, move up to a specialty steel rather than down to a lesser grade. High-carbon steel is recommended for screwdrivers, chisels, turning chisels and gouges, plane irons and carving tools.

Most of the specialty steels used in toolmaking are tool steels. They are expensive, some more than $3 a pound. Configuration is limited and finding small quantities can be a problem. They do make excellent tools, however. Commonly used types:

AISI W2 is a high-quality, water-hardening tool steel. As with high-carbon steel, it relies on carbon content (up to 1.40%, depending on producer) for hardness. Use it for tools that must hold an exceptional edge.

AISI O1 is a low-alloy, oil-hardening tool steel. It will not harden to quite the same degree as W2, but is easier to forge, harden and temper. Use it as an alternative to W2 where shape presents heat-treating problems.

AISI D2 is a high-carbon, high-chromium, air-hardening steel. Some cutlers consider it the best material for long, thin blades. It is especially good for bench knives and similar tools.

AISI S5, an oil-quenched, silicon-manganese tool steel specially designed for shock resistance, is difficult to forge but unsurpassed for tools subject to high impact. It makes excellent cold chisels.

AISI M2 is a molybdenum-type tool steel. Smiths report that it makes excellent planer and shaper knives.

AISI 44OC Stainless is a high-carbon steel favored by most blade makers where exposure to the elements is a major consideration. It relies on high chromium content for its corrosion resistance. It will not hold as fine an edge as W2.

Used or recycled steel is attractive because it is cheap and some woodworkers may want to try it. Look for a scrap yard specializing in identified grades of high-carbon and specialty steels. These yards charge a premium, but knowing the exact qualities of the steel is worth it. Toolmakers can also rework certain steel implements manufactured from known types of high-carbon steel. Some typical items and the AISI steel they are made from:

Plow discs, plowshares and harrow discs, 1080; hay-rake

teeth, 1095; leaf springs, 1085 to 1095; mower blades, 1055 to 1085; clutch discs, 1060 to 1070; and most heavy coil springs, 1095.

Toolmakers can apply the grinding wheel or spark test to steels of unknown composition. Steel is put in contact with a rotating grinding wheel and the resulting spark pattern is studied for clues to the nature of the steel.

Technique

There is no substitute for experience and woodworkers interested in making their own tools should seek training from an experienced smith. Most local smiths are willing to work out arrangements for instruction and forge time. In addition, several colleges and universities offer courses in blacksmithing and farriery (horseshoeing). Reading also is helpful and the following bibliography offers several excellent starting points.

The Making of Tools and *The Modern Blacksmith*, both by Alexander G. Weygers (Van Nostrand Reinhold Co., 450 W. 33rd St., New York; $4.95 each, paperback). Weygers, a sculptor, began making his own tools when he became dissatisfied with available types. His suggestions for setting up shop economically, improvising equipment and using secondary materials are particularly good.

Blacksmithing for the Home Craftsman by Joe Pehoski (Stuhr Museum, Grand Island, Nebr.; $1.75, paperback). Pehoski is a working smith who believes in plain speaking and his book is packed with good advice. His troubleshooting section is especially useful.

Blacksmiths' and Farriers' Tools at Shelburne Museum by H. R. Bradley Smith (Shelburne Museum, Inc., Shelburne, Vt.; $5.00 paperback). To understand blacksmiths' tools is to gain insight into the subtlest techniques for using them. This is the best available book on tools.

The Blacksmith's Craft (Council for Small Industries in Rural Areas [CoSIRA], 11 Cowley Street, London, SWIP 3NA; $3.50 hardcover). Absolutely the finest book available on the techniques of blacksmithing for the beginner.

Drake's Modern Blacksmithing and Horseshoeing by J. G. Holstrom (Drake Publishers, Inc., New York; $4.95 hardcover). Holstrom is disarmingly folksy but his book contains a great deal of down-to-earth advice.

The Art of Blacksmithing by Alex W. Bealer (Funk & Wagnalls Publishing Co., Inc., New York; $12.45 hardcover). This book has come in for criticism in some circles for occasional inaccuracies and oversimplifications but still contains a wealth of good information.

Decorative and Sculptural Ironwork by Dona Z. Meilach (Crown Publishers, Inc., New York; $7.95 paperback). An excellent survey of the latest work and techniques of the country's best smiths.

Blacksmith's Manual Illustrated by J. W. Lillico (The Technical Press Ltd., London; $7.75 hardcover). An excellent advanced course in smithing with special emphasis on large, complex forgings.

Whetstones
How novaculite is quarried and finished

by William G. Wing

*Ben diverse maner of whetstones,
and some neden water and some neden oyle
for-to whette.*
—from a work by John De Trevisa, 1398

Whetstones have been around a while, as the 600-year-old quotation from De Trevisa suggests. Stone tools were among the things that got people to come down from the trees and start acting like people. This isn't meant to suggest whetstones are quite that old, because stone cutting tools got their edges mostly by chipping and flaking. But even before metal tools were made, some edges were obtained by abrasion—by rubbing the edges on harder stones. When metal tools did come in, abrasion was absolutely necessary.

The constant problem in abrasives, though, is the trade-off between speed and smoothness. The brilliant insight that led to forming the abrasive in the shape of a wheel, the grindstone, gave speed but left a rough edge on the tool or weapon—all right for hacking off someone's head but not good for careful slicing. A "fine" edge could be produced only by final rubbing on something harder and smoother than the grindstone. This was the process that came to be know as whetting or honing. The fact that both words are among the few that have stayed alive and healthy from Old English shows how basic the operation is.

Workmen in every region had to find the best whetstones they could. When farmers pioneered into the wilderness of America, their survival depended on good cutting edges on axes and scythes. One can imagine them moving westward, testing any likely-looking rock on their axes. They picked up a lot of advice from the Indians who, as Stone Age people, knew a lot more about rocks than the newcomers did.

This is the way—by reports from Indians—that pioneers in central Arkansas learned of quarries producing superior white, almost translucent, spear and arrow points. There were Indian quarries in the Ouchita Mountains near the valley filled with hot springs (known today, appropriately, as Hot Springs). The rock was quarried in open pits, by fires built against outcrops, which were then cracked off by being doused with cold water. Some of the pits were so deep it was obvious that mining had been going on for a long time.

How quickly this hard rock was put to use as a whetstone is not recorded. It was early, though—a letter written in 1818 says that 200 pounds of whetstones, priced at $2 a pound, had been shipped out by flatboats on the Ouchita River the previous year. (The Ouchita runs into the Red River, which empties into the Mississippi.)

Hard Arkansas (pronounced "Ar-kan-zus") stones, and a softer variety that picked up the name Washita (from Ouchita), developed a market on the East Coast and in Europe but did not rise to the top quickly. A host of whetstone varieties were available in the last century: Ayr stone, snake stone, Charnley Forest stone, Norway ragstone, Cutler's greenstone, and so on. Remember that interest went

far beyond the workshop—until the disposable razor blade was invented, every man had the choice of raising whiskers or learning how to keep an edge on a razor. Turkey stone, which was mined somewhere in Asia Minor, finished in Marseilles and shipped by the ton into America, set the standard of excellence. Eventually, though, it was superseded by Arkansas stones, of the mineral novaculite.

With such a background, with so many kinds of stones available, with a planet composed mostly of stone, why have Arkansas stones, from one little patch of hillside near Hot Springs, established themselves as the standard of excellence? To find out, I seized a chance to visit the leading manufacturer of Arkansas whetstones last summer.

The Hiram A. Smith Whetstone Co., Inc., is located on the fringe of the suburbs of Hot Springs. It is said to account for about 70% of the production of Arkansas whetstones, and it is now being run by the fourth generation of Smiths. James A. Smith, the president, is named after his great-grandfather, who got the family into the whetstone business because the land he had acquired for real-estate speculation happened to include the best of the stone deposits.

Until 1964, the company simply mined and shipped raw stone for finishing overseas. Smith's father, Hiram, began developing lapidary knowledge of his own. He developed a stone-cutting saw, essentially a flat steel disc about two feet in diameter. Small industrial diamonds—"sweepings"—were glued along the rims. The saw was mounted overhead, like a radial arm saw, but the operator pushed the stone through the saw while it was bathed with a stream of cooling and lubricating oil. In 1976, the Smiths built an integrated plant and now have about 75 employees and all the business they can handle. "I guess we sell about 100,000 stones a month," Smith said. Most are sold under other companies' labels.

Raw stones are found in the quarries within about 30 feet of the surface. Holes from four to eight feet deep are drilled in the rock with jackhammers, and then filled with explosives. Dynamite can't be used because it shatters the rock; instead, a low-density explosive, which goes "whoomp," is tamped into the 1¾-inch dia. holes. After the blast, every broken piece of rock is examined by an expert, who taps the rocks with a dressing hammer. More than two-thirds of the broken rocks are rejected and thrown on the waste pile. The rest, mostly in sizes slightly larger than the human head, are scooped up into a truck and carried a few miles to the plant.

The first process is cutting each piece of stone into its optimum size. The slabber has a sharp eye for chitchat (rubbish stone), quartz lines, sand deposits and short cracks, and he tosses away about half of the stone that has been brought in from the quarries as below standard. He then decides how to cut each of the remaining stones to obtain the longest possible pieces from each. The hope is to get 20-in. lengths, but novaculite is a much-fractured rock and such long pieces are

Bill Wing, of Englewood, N.J., is a writer and an amateur woodcarver.

rare. Next, dicers cut the slabs into standard widths, ranging from wide hones to pocket sharpeners. Then the stones are cut to standard lengths by clippers. The aim at each step is to produce a stone of the highest possible value.

After being cut, the stones are finished. From 200 to 300 stones are "lapped," or polished, at a time as they ride on a revolving iron plate covered with industrial grit. Polishing continues by lapping the stones with increasingly fine grits. Edge bevels are ground by hand on abrasive wheels. At the same time that these flat whetstones are cut and polished, files are cut and hand-finished in a variety of cross sections.

After finishing, the stones are assessed once more and about a fourth of them are discarded. The arithmetic doesn't quite work out, but Smith says that of all the rock quarried only about 5% gets to market. The surviving stones are then graded into four categories of hardness.

The softest and coarsest grade is called Washita, sometimes called calico stone in the old days because of its very showy grain and colors. This grade will produce an edge most quickly, but not an edge of the finest quality. The second grade up the scale of hardness is called soft Arkansas. This, a greyish and sometimes mottled stone, is described by Smith as the best general-purpose grade—that is, the best compromise between speed of sharpening and quality of edge. The next grade is hard Arkansas, a clear white stone said to be the best for the final polishing of an already sharp edge. Finally, at the top of the ladder, is black hard Arkansas, which Smith's catalog describes as the "supreme ultimate." Blacks, which range in color from ebony to dark grey, are for specialists, those who need to touch up an already extremely sharp edge. Because black novaculite is rare and hardly ever occurs in long pieces, its price is correspondingly high.

After grading, some stones are glued together in combinations of grades, some are glued on paddles or blocks and some are fitted into sets. The standard flat whetstone goes into a lacquered red-cedar box; the label under which it is to be sold is then stamped in gold on the cover. Smith no longer makes the boxes, but buys them under contract. (Smith has the best of both worlds with the red cedar. Its red and cream streaks make the boxes look exotic and expensive. Actually, the wood is readily available locally, since little cedar trees cover northern Arkansas and southern Missouri.)

Smith talks candidly about the fact that his company's control of its raw supplies and its insistence on selling only first-quality stones enable it to maintain fairly high prices. The chief reason for downgrading a stone from first to second-class quality is the presence in the novaculite of small pockets of a softer material, called sand pits. Seconds will sharpen an edge just as well as firsts, Smith says, unless the pits are so big they snag the blade. If you can find them, they cost only a quarter as much as firsts. But since quality is the essential reason for owning an Arkansas whetstone, and since they last so long that the initial price is amortized over a long period, there is little reason for buying anything except a first-class stone. Natural stones last longer than industrial ones, not because they are harder, but because the bonding agent that holds together the particles in manmade stone breaks down.

Insistence on quality also stems from the fact that Arkansas stones were hurt badly in the past when the market was flooded with bad stones. L. S. Griswold, a geologist who in 1890 wrote the only comprehensive work on Arkansas stones, told how inferior stones were passed off as first quality.

Blocks of novaculite blasted out of a quarry at the Hiram A. Smith Whetstone Co., Hot Springs, Ark. Only about 5% of the novaculite quarried will become finished whetstones.

Raw Washita stone has been halved on diamond-edged steel wheel.

Stones are lapped, or polished, on a grit-covered iron plate.

37

Often, they were polished with pumice because the powder filled and concealed defects. Smith says bad stones are still being sold; some of them are not novaculite at all but a softer mineral called tripoli.

How, then, can you judge a good stone in the marketplace? Smith said the customer's best procedure is to rely on the reputation of the company selling the stone. Also, he said, a good stone looks good. Griswold said almost the same thing in his book: "Good stones seldom have a poor finish." Check the edges and sides to see if they have been ground true. Griswold also recommends things that wouldn't be tolerated today: testing for defects with a knife point and scratching the surface with your fingernails. (If you can scratch it, the stone is soft; if your nails come off, it's hard.)

To use the stones, Smith advocates standard sharpening techniques. He is not a purist about lubricant: Use a little oil,

he says, but if you don't have oil, use water. When customers complain the stones won't sharpen, invariably, Smith says, they are not using enough muscle. After use, he recommends washing the stone with soap and water, and then drying it.

Novaculite is a form of quartz, and it is almost pure silica. Technically, novaculite is a kind of chert, which is similar to flint. It is composed of a dense mass of crystals that range in size from one to ten microns (a micron is a thousandth of a millimeter). No matter how smooth the stones feel, they can be seen through a microscope to be covered with protrusions that scratch away metal. The crystals are interspersed with spaces (pores) that seem to play a role in sharpening, too, because they hold the oil.

Jim Smith says the stones work so well because they "polish while they sharpen." This brings us around to the vagueness of sharpening terms, which need to be sorted out. All the

(to top of next page)

Sharpening

A sampling of techniques and tips

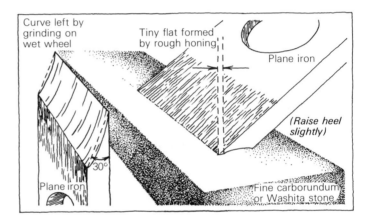

*E*veryone agrees that precise, efficient woodworking is impossible without properly sharpened tools, but there are probably as many ways to get a keen edge as there are practicing craftsmen. The bewildered novice is confronted by a vast array of sharpening equipment and advice, and as the following confirms, there are no absolutes, only preferred ways. Some of the writers are professional woodworkers; others, informed amateurs. All describe what works for them.

The cutting edge

Three steps form the cutting edge: wet grinding, rough honing and fine honing. I feel strongly that dry grinding on any wheel will damage the hardness of the blade edge. Even if you watch carefully and cool the metal in water after each pass, can you definitely say that you have not removed the temper on the terminal .001 in. of the blade, where the edge is actually formed? It seems ridiculous to me to dry-grind a blade and then to use a hard Arkansas stone or to strop the edge afterward. The first cut will dull the edge, and the tool will never cut as well as it would have had it been wet-ground. I even use wet grinding for metal lathe bits and feel it makes a difference. Your blade was carefully heat-treated for a purpose. Don't ruin it.

I use a wet wheel, either manmade or natural, grit from 40 to 100, and turning in either direction to remove the surplus metal, form the edge angle and facilitate resharpening. Edge angles will vary from 2° for a straightedge razor, which is never ground, to 90° for scrapers used to form barrel channels in rifle stocks. My acute-angle block plane, (the only metal plane I use) is ground to around 20° but cuts with the angle up, so blade angle is about 32°. My other planes are about 30°, with 35° for wood chisels. Planer knives are ground to about 30°. Knives should have angles close to 40° but should seldom be ground, with kitchen knives the one exception. No knife should ever show grind or hone marks on the flat of the

blade, but should be tipped well up away from the stone in honing. Scissors and tin snips are ground around 85°.

After grinding, wire edges are removed by rough honing to prepare for the final edge. Many woodworkers abhor a wire edge; instead, welcome it, for after you acquire proficiency, you are only 20 seconds or so away from a shaving edge. Your aim in rough honing is to form a narrow flat (a micro-bevel) along the front edge, using a fairly fine carborundum or Washita stone with thin oil for cutting fluid. I use diesel fuel with a bit of crankcase drainings added. Oil alone is too thick for fast cutting. Set the blade on the stone with both heel and toe touching, raise the heel slightly and lock your wrists to hold that angle. Give the blade a dozen or so strokes, either reciprocating or figure eight, holding the angle constant. Check to see if you have formed a narrow flat; if so, turn the blade over. With the blade flat on the stone, make one stroke toward the edge to remove the wire edge now formed.

The next few strokes are the ones that produce a fine edge with a minimum of effort. Position the blade on the stone, raise the heel as before, and make one stroke toward the edge. Now turn the blade over and make another single stroke with the blade flat on the stone toward the blade edge. Rotating the blade with each stroke, make six or eight single strokes toward the cutting edge on alternate sides of the blade, and you should have a shaving edge. If not, go back to rough honing and try again. From the fine wire edge to the shaving edge takes 5 to 10 seconds if properly done. If you wish, you may repeat the rough and fine honing on an Arkansas stone and/or use a leather strop, but I feel the blade processes of sharpening—grinding, whetting, honing, stropping and polishing—remove metal from an edge by abrasion. All the way down the line to buffing with jeweler's rouge, or stropping on the heel of the hand, the purpose is to get the saw teeth on the edge smaller and smaller. The term "polishing" can be confusing, but in the case of edge tools, "polish" means to produce a bright surface finish by abrasion. The key is always the size of the scratches produced on the edge of the tool.

An 1876 book on grindstones makes it clear: "If we were to examine the surface of a tool that has just been removed from a grindstone, under the lens of a powerful microscope, it would appear as if it were like the rough surface of a field which has been recently scarified with some implement which formed alternate ridges and furrows. . .(the edge) seems to be formed of a system of minute teeth rather than to consist of a smooth edge." The tool, therefore, is ground and polished with finer and finer grit "to reduce the serrature." An Arkansas geologist gave the same sort of explanation. There is no magic in novaculite, he said. The scratches always can be seen through a microscope, no matter how small they are. The fine edge comes from the regularity of the size of the individual crystals in the Arkansas whetstone.

There is also no magic, the geologist said, in the fact that novaculite is mined only in this one spot. The Hot Springs region of Arkansas is interesting geologically, as evidenced by the hot springs, and the fact that it is one of the two best places in the country to find rock crystal, and the fact that Arkansas—alone among the fifty states—has a diamond mine. But other regions are interesting geologically, too, and there is no reason for believing commercial deposits of novaculite will not turn up somewhere else. □

---

fresh from the fine honing will be as sharp as a stropped blade that has made a couple of cuts in hardwood, and you will have wasted the extra time. I realize that in woodcarving, especially in softwoods, a stropped edge may be required, but this is seldom true for planes and chisels. A blade properly fine-honed will shave hair from your arm and will smoothly cut a hard pine knot or rock maple.

To resharpen, repeat the second and third steps until the blade has worn enough to need lengthy honing, with a wide flat on the edge. One could skip the grinding and sharpen solely with the oilstone, but grinding makes it easier and quicker. Another test for sharpness is drawing your thumbnail along the edge with light pressure. If the pull is even along the edge, the blade is sharp. Or hold it in a good light and look for a bright line or spot. If you see one, that part is dull, for a sharp edge is invisible. Check for the wire edge in rough honing by drawing the ball of your thumb along the flat of the blade and out over the edge. If you do not feel the wire edge, it needs more honing.

—*W.A. Haughey, Burlington, Colo.*

Grinding and honing

Many techniques will produce a keen edge; those described here were acquired from a craftsman with over 50 years at the bench. They work well for me. To grind the bevel of a chisel or plane iron preparatory to honing, a good first step is to mark a square edge on the flat side of the blade (with a felt-tip pen, grinding ink or a glasscutter's diamond) as a guideline for the edge. I prefer to mount a ¾-in. by 6-in. medium carborundum grindstone on the lathe, for two reasons. First, the tool rest offers a large and firm bearing surface on which to steady the blade, a real boon for accuracy. Second, low speeds on the order of 1200-1500 rpm can be used, with less danger of drawing the temper. However, grinding on the lathe with an unshielded stone does pose some safety risk, and should be done cautiously and only at low speeds. Patience is a real asset because trying to remove too much steel too fast will draw the temper of the best tool. The slower the better. Never allow a blade to become too hot to hold while grinding; quench frequently in cold water. Do not use oil on the grindstone because it may cause deterioration and crumbling. I check the angle frequently with a protractor bevel; on plane irons, I use an angle of 24° for soft-

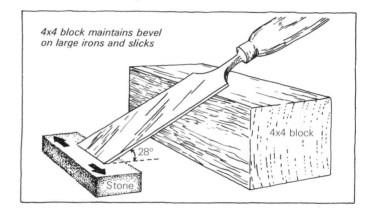

4x4 block maintains bevel on large irons and slicks

4x4 block

28°

Stone

woods, 28° for hardwoods. The blade is passed rapidly and evenly from side to side at the proper angle over the width of the blade until the guideline is reached. Allowing the blade to remain stationary for too long generates heat and usually causes an uneven grind. As a final step, I touch the bevel lightly to the side of the grindstone to take off any high spots.

After grinding to the proper bevel, I remove most of the burr with several heavy strokes on a coarse oilstone with the bevel and the flat side. Then I set to work with a fine India (artificial) stone, using a light penetrating oil. Special oils are sold for honing but I have found those used to free up rusty bolts, such as Liquid Wrench, work just as well. At this point, the woodworker is often advised to rock the iron in a figure-eight movement, holding the heel of the bevel slightly off the stone, in the direction of front to back. I feel this is wrong for several reasons. It is very difficult to maintain a constant acute angle, which is crucial for a keen edge; it produces inequalities over the width of the edge; it causes hollowing of the stone, it is laborious and inefficient. I place the entire bevel absolutely flat on the stone and hone with a constant side-to-side movement, keeping the edge of the iron parallel to the long axis of the stone. I traverse the full length of the stone, changing positions every several strokes, continuing until a highly polished, nearly mirror surface is obtained. Then I reverse the iron and hone the flat side in the same fashion, keeping the entire surface flat on the stone. Honing the flat side of the iron will remove most of the burr, leaving a fine burr on the bevel side. Then I reverse the iron and hone on the bevel, side to side, keeping the bevel absolutely flat on the surface of the stone. Several cycles of alternate honing of bevel and flat side are needed to remove the burr, each cycle shorter as the burr becomes finer. By the time the burr is nearly gone the edge should be keen, and the surface of the bevel mirror-like. The polished surface, however, is irrelevant. The important thing is the edge. A keen edge, when directly illuminated, will not reflect light.

The experienced woodworker uses generous amounts of oil, wiping it off as soon as it becomes black and applying fresh oil. Allowing the porous surface to become glazed will surely ruin a stone. When honing the flat side of the iron, keeping it flat on the stone is mandatory. Honing large plane irons and chisels, such as slicks, can become tiresome. A convenient guide can be made with a heavy block of wood such as a 4x4. Lay the block parallel to the stone and place the bevel on the stone. Move the block toward the stone until the iron rests on the long edge of the block, keeping the bevel flat on the stone. If the block and the stone stay parallel, the angle will be constant and the cutting edge square.

Using an inexpensive artificial stone as above, a satisfactory edge can be obtained, at least for rough work. However, a small white Arkansas stone is a good investment and will produce a fine razor edge. I use it in exactly the same way as the fine India. Only a small amount of honing on the Arkansas should be required for a proper edge.

These techniques do not produce a secondary bevel, or "micro-bevel." This is a personal preference. I feel if the blade is properly ground for its intended purpose in the first place, a micro-bevel isn't necessary. For example, I prefer to have extra plane irons ground for hard and soft woods. I find it harder to produce a razor edge with a secondary bevel because the angle is more difficult to regulate. However, the techniques can be modified during the later stages to produce a secondary bevel if desired. One must keep the heel of the bevel the same distance above the stone during each stroke, though, or the edge will not be keen.

The final stage consists of stropping the bevel and flat side with a piece of leather dressed with jeweler's rouge. The latter can be purchased from jeweler or craftsman supply houses in the form of a bar that is rubbed on the leather. Glue the leather to a block of wood. Strop in the same manner as honing, with the bevel and flat side flat on the leather surface. The edge should not be stropped directly or it will be blunted. The result should be a bevel with a gleaming surface like an old-fashioned razor and a super-fine edge.

—*Daniel A. Symonds, Towson, Md.*

Which way to hone?

When honing on a flat stone, some workers advise moving the tool in a figure eight, some in a straight line back and forth, and some from side to side. I've always been confused by these various instructions, since it seems to me that one way should have something to recommend it over the others. Although I don't have any scientific evidence, logic tells me always to work the tool back and forth over the stone with the cutting edge perpendicular to the direction of honing.

The edge of a tool is a narrow wedge, and most of its work is done by the last few microns of metal. Grinding and honing polish the metal by making smaller and smaller scratches in it. What looks mirror bright to the unaided eye is, under the microscope, an uneven terrain of ridges and gullies. On a tool honed my way, the ridges and gullies run off the edge,

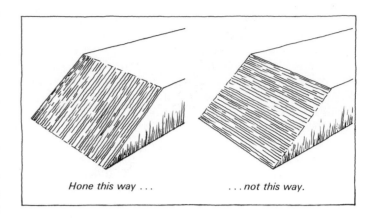
Hone this way . . .   . . . not this way.

which is made up of tiny points supported by a relatively broad base of metal. But on a tool honed the other way, the scratches are parallel to the cutting edge. This seems liable to weaken the very edge you have worked so hard to create. It may break right off in a long sliver of metal, dull after the first cut. So when we have a choice, we should sharpen and hone in the way that leaves these microscopic scratches parallel to the direction of cutting.

—*R. Bruce Hoadley, Amherst, Mass.*

Brush and buff

Over the years I have collected a drawerful of stones, strops and hones. However, I now get along with almost no use of any of them. Instead I sharpen everything (except saws) on a grinder, a wire brush, and a coarse buff. First I shape the tool on the grinder until a wire edge appears, dipping the tool in water more and more frequently as the grinding gets close to the edge. Because the sharpening process is so simple and so little trouble, I feel free to experiment with long bevels, skew chisels, etc., for special purposes. Next I knock off the wire edge on the rotary wire brush. The last step is to charge the buff, which runs at about 2100 rpm, with white emery and proceed to polish the edge. I buff for a short time on the wrong side of chisels to cut off any wire edge that might come with working on the right side. I can shave with anything I sharpen. At the slightest sign of dullness, the tool goes back to the buffing wheel for a few seconds. The buffing wheel is not only faster than the oilstone but also cleaner.

—*John Owen, Isaacs Harbor, N.S.*

Resurfacing stones

Usually, stones become hollow due to long use, but even a new stone may not be really flat. Lack of honing oil can clog or glaze a stone so badly that no amount of rubbing your edge tools on it will have much effect. My early attempts with machine surface-grinding old stones on a silicone-carbide wheel produced a totally useless, glass-smooth surface.

In a short evening I flattened my remaining stones and unglazed the others (eight stones in all) by lapping them. The method is simple: Just pour some kerosene onto a piece of plate glass, sprinkle on about a tablespoon of 60-grit carborundum powder and start rubbing. As the kerosene dries out, add more. When the powder no longer "bites," sprinkle on another spoonful. Rub over the whole surface of the glass to avoid wearing hollows in it. Very fine stones such as Washita or hard Arkansas may be too rough after this treatment, but another minute of lapping on the other side of the glass with kerosene and 220 wet-or-dry silicone-carbide paper removes the roughness. After that, the stone should hone better than ever. Keep on lapping once in a while to prevent your stones from getting hollow again.

—*Rich Baldinger, Schenectady, N.Y.*

Hand grinder

I learned to sharpen tools on a conventional motorized grinder, went over to the sandstone water-trough variety and was finally converted to a hand grinder. The hand grinder does the job well without any chance of ruining the tool and gives a lot of sensitive control over the result. You don't have to worry about the stone disintegrating or softening if kept in water continuously, and it doesn't wear unevenly or crumble. The pronounced hollow grind makes honing a snap. One develops more of a direct, personal relationship with one's tools when they are ground this way, and this probably has a subtle effect on workmanship as well. And a hand grinder is about one-quarter the price of motorized types.

My grinder has a 1:20 ratio. It is model #1107 from Gustav Kunz, 30 Hannover-Wulfel, Volgerstrasse 9m, West Germany. Woodcraft Supply, 313 Montvale Ave., Woburn, Mass. 01801, and Silvo Hardware Company, 107-109 Walnut St., Philadelphia, Pa. 19106, sell something similar.

I have kept the wheel the grinder comes with, though I discarded the stock tool holder. I also added a few washers to eliminate the disengagement feature of the crank handle.

It was especially bothersome to use a clamp and to have to readjust the tool rest each time, so I glued and screwed a block underneath the mounting board for clamping in my end vise. The rest itself is fastened to the board by two bolts equipped with large butterfly nuts or wing nuts. The heads of these bolts lie countersunk in two slots in the mounting board, so adjusting the rest is a matter of positioning it properly and tightening the nuts. Once made, the adjustment remains when you take the grinder off the bench. When the wheel diameter changes with wear (mine lost 5 mm in two years) or if the angle need be changed (I grind both chisels and plane blades at 26°), a wedge can easily be inserted between the rest and the base. When set up this way, the grinder is always ready for use at a moment's notice.

My tool rest has an optional sliding fence that holds the blades at precisely 90° to the edge of the wheel. Making a slider like this is easy. Most builder's supply stores and hardware stores sell anodized aluminum channel. One length of channel having a base measurement of ⅜ in. and one measuring ⅜ in. between the legs are needed, about 12 in. of the former and 6 in. of the latter. Cut a rabbet in the tool rest slightly deeper than the combined height of the 12-in. piece plus the thickness of the wall of the 6-in. piece. The rabbet should be as wide as the width of the 6-in. channel plus ⅛ in., or about 9/16 in. With wood screws, fasten the long piece, open side up, to the rest. Leave about ⅛ in. between it and the rabbet wall. Bandsaw all but ⅛ in. off the legs on the shorter channel and fasten it to the fence with 4/40 screws. Clearance is important here. Be sure to center the screwheads in the channel. The fence may be made of 3/32-in. plastic, aluminum or brass sheet. Double up on the thickness at the fence edge—use epoxy, first abrading the surfaces. My knob is 2 in. long, held from underneath by two deeply countersunk woodscrews.

The edges of the channels may need breaking or adjusting to permit free sliding. To ensure that the fence edge lies at precisely 90° to the channel guides, hold an accurate try-square against the inset channel and adjust the fence edge to meet its blade exactly. To use this tool rest, turn the wheel toward you with the right hand, while the blade is held lightly against the slider by the thumb of the left. The index finger holds the blade down flat against the surface of the rest and the three remaining fingers rest on the left side of the knob. The index finger also feeds the blade into the rotating wheel as the hand moves back and forth. □

—*Alan Marks, Pacific Grove, Calif.*

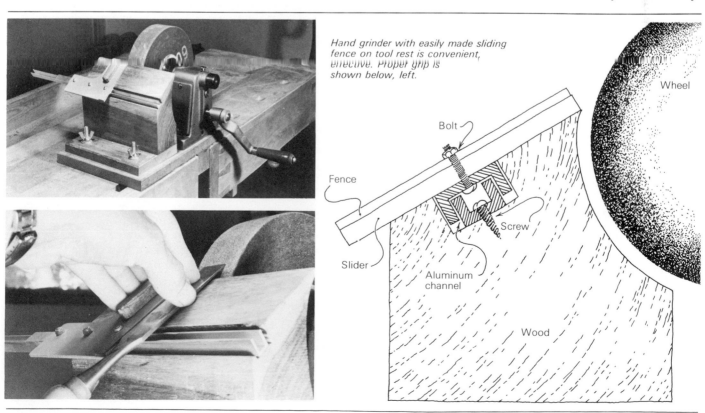

Hand grinder with easily made sliding fence on tool rest is convenient, effective. Proper grip is shown below, left.

Wheel

Bolt

Fence

Screw

Slider

Aluminum channel

Wood

Wooden Clamps

They're strong, handsome and cheap to make

by Richard Showalter

Author's tub of clamps.

During the six years I've been making my living as a woodworker, I've lived in a small town in Oregon, fifty miles from the closest city. The markets for the expensive children's toys I make are still farther away and it became obvious very early that shipping and packing were going to be an important part of making my livelihood. I became interested in using wooden screws (*Fine Woodworking*, Spring '77) as a way to make my work collapsible and more easily shipped. I bought a wooden threading tool and began making my own screws. They did everything I had hoped in making my work more portable and added to the value of the toy as well.

The most important spin-off has been the manufacture of wooden clamps. My shop is now equipped with a wonderful variety of them. They are fitted to my own hand, suited to my particular needs and esthetically pleasing to me by virtue of their materials and because they were fashioned in my own shop. The financial benefits are not to be despised either—it would cost hundreds of dollars to duplicate the number and range of clamps now at my disposal.

The scale you work on will determine the size clamps you need. If you want to make clamps corresponding to Jorgenson hand screws in the 8-in. to 12-in. range and want to buy only one threading set, the best size is 7/8 in. This makes a screw

heavy enough to handle the strains of most applications, but still slender enough to be in proportion to a comfortable handle. One-inch screws make the clamp a little clumsy and the extra strength seems unnecessary. Wooden screws rarely strip. Most hand-screw clamps fail—when they do—by breaking at the center hole in the unthreaded jaw. If you work on a smaller scale, making instruments or doing similar, delicate work, the 1/2-in. and 3/8-in. sizes will make little hand-screw clamps as well as luthier's clamps.

Clamp jaws may be made from nearly any hardwood. (I've even made acceptable clamps using yew, technically a softwood but a very dense and springy one.) Clamp jaws flex considerably in use and should be free of knots, bark inclusions and wind shakes. The slightest fault will be magnified by the stress of use.

The finished width of the jaw should be at least double the diameter of the screw. A clamp using 1/2-in. screws should have jaws at least 1 in. wide. Jaws should be as thick as or slightly thicker than they are wide. These tolerances are critical for large clamps. Obviously, adding more width and thickness increases the strength of the clamp, but in the larger sizes also increases the weight and clumsiness of the tool and ruins its feel. In the smaller sizes bulking up the measure-

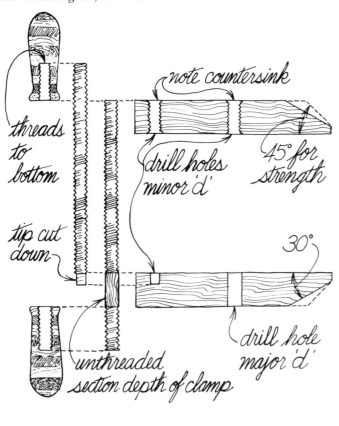

Wooden hand screws may be made in almost any size, with jaws and handles shaped to fit particular types of work.

ments can provide a valuable safety margin and does not make them too clumsy.

Surfaces of jaw stock should be square and parallel. Clamp the jaws together during drilling so the surfaces will mate when the clamp is finished. Holes should be drilled with a drill press or doweling jig. Any skew to these holes will cause the finished clamp to bind in a way that cannot be corrected. The middle hole should be centered from end to end of the clamp. A 12-in. jaw will have its middle screw 6 in. from either end. The rear hole should center 1 in. from the back edge of the jaw in large clamps, 3/4 in. in smaller ones.

Because the tap raises a small curl of wood as it enters and leaves the stock, I use a Forstner bit 1/8 in. larger than the hole I'm drilling and drill a countersink 1/8 in. deep in the top surface of the clamp jaw that will be threaded. (The other jaw is not threaded.) I then use the proper-size bit to drill the two holes to be tapped, stopping the bit when the point breaks through. Using the breakout hole as a guide, I switch back to the larger bit and drill the same 1/8-in. deep hole on the opposite surface. The same result may be achieved by leaving the stock 1/8 in. oversize and planing or jointing to dimension after it has been tapped.

Holes in the piece of jaw stock that is not tapped should be located by allowing the point of the bit—remember, the jaws are clamped together—to break through. The middle hole in the untapped jaw should be drilled the same diameter as the screw, e.g., a 1-in. hole for a 1-in. screw. The rear hole in the unthreaded jaw should extend one-third of the way through the piece of stock, and should be the same diameter as the hole in the threaded jaw before it's tapped, e.g., for a 1-in. screw the hole is 7/8 in. If this hole is too shallow the clamp

Holes in upper jaw are countersunk with Forstner bit before drilling through and tapping. Rear hole in lower jaw is blind.

falls apart in use; if it's too deep the clamp will be weak.

I put a 30° slope on the front of the jaws. If you are going to use your clamps to apply very heavy pressure most of the time, the angle should be increased to 45°. This extra material in the nose makes the clamp stronger. It is amazing how such a small change in dimensions will affect the clamp's feel.

I plane or joint a bevel on the two upper edges of each jaw, but this is cosmetic. In use clamps are often laid in piles and banged around, and the bevel keeps them from looking chewed up quite so soon.

No sandpaper, by the way, should be used on any piece until after it is completely threaded. Small pieces of abrasive will cling to the work and dull thread cutters. Although they

Threading Tools

A user's evaluation

I presently have taps and screwboxes (*Fine Woodworking*, Spring '77) in 1/2-in., 3/4-in. and 1-in. sizes. The best commercially available threading tools I've found are made in West Germany (there is no brand name on them) and were formerly sold by Woodcraft Supply. Woodcraft has since begun manufacturing its own version of this tool in this country. My 3/4-in. tool is a Woodcraft product but I like the West German one better because its screwbox handle is fixed to the box with a full-length metal tang, headed over at the end. The Woodcraft handle is attached to the screwbox by a coarse screw threaded into end grain—a poor woodworking practice. The handle constantly unscrews itself in use if you are left-handed, as I am.

The most serious fault of the Woodcraft tool is that the screwbox cuts only a fair thread. The West German tools I have leave a small portion of the original dowel surface intact at the crown of the thread; the Woodcraft tool brings the thread to a sharp crown that makes the threads very delicate.

Frog Tool in Chicago still carries the West German imports and I would advise buying from them.

Marples, which ordinarily makes excellent tools, markets a threading set whose 1/2-in. model I found unsatisfactory. The die consists of a wooden box with a metal cutter, the traditional way in which this tool has been made. The tap is cast metal, not machined tool steel. The thread it cuts is sharply crowned and overfine, with too many threads to the inch. The only way I found to make it produce any sort of screw was to cut the wood off to length as it emerged from the box. This inefficient procedure limits the number of things that may be done with the tool. The Marples tap is also very fragile. (My difficulty with this tool is not unique. I spoke with a high-school shop teacher who had purchased the Marples sets in all sizes and was unable to make them perform as they should.)

Brookstone Co. markets a threading set in three sizes, made by Conover Woodcraft of Parkman, Ohio. This is almost an excellent tool. Both tap and screwbox produce a clean thread and the tools are attractively priced. But at three inches the shank of the tap is simply too short.

Finding adequate doweling can be almost as difficult as finding a satisfactory screw set. Stanley used to market a hand-cranked dowel maker, and expensive lathe-powered tools are still available. Commercially available doweling is usually birch or hard maple and very seldom truly round. Variations in moisture content during manufacture and storage often produce doweling that is oval in cross section. For the same reason, much doweling is not straight either. Always check doweling for straightness, piece by piece, before buying it.

Woodcraft Supply sells sizing blocks for doweling that consist of a piece of tempered tool steel with accurately sized circular holes. Doweling is driven through them with a mallet to remove excess stock and bring it back to round. These blocks do not include sizes over 1/2 in., however. I have made sizing blocks for larger sizes by detempering a piece of automobile leaf spring and having a machine shop drill appropriate holes, countersunk on the underside. If you do this, have two holes drilled for each size, one the exact size and one 1/32 in. smaller. The reason for this is that the West German tap and screwbox are made on metric lathes that only approximate U. S. sizes. The "1-in." tool, for example, is made for 2.5-cm doweling. A true inch is 2.54 cm. The undersized holes allow you to make appropriate adjustments. Also drill two small holes in the plate so you can fasten it to a bench top. And don't forget to retemper the metal. —*R. S.*

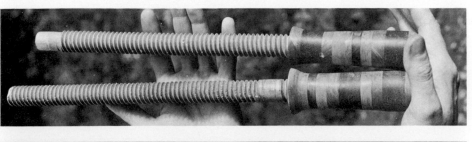

handle blank —

hole threaded through half of blank before the last sections are glued on

Handle blank is laminated as in drawing at right. Rear screw, top and enlargement, has shaped tip to fit blind hole in jaw. Middle screw is longer of the two, is unthreaded near handle where it passes through lower jaw, and its handle has substantial flange where it bears against jaw.

can be sharpened again, extreme care must be used to make the tools perform properly and you will wish to do it as seldom as possible.

The two holes in the threaded jaw should be tapped next. The tap needs to be backed off one-quarter of a turn every two turns to break the chip and help keep the nose clear of impacted shavings. The tap should turn freely, without much resistance. If the tap becomes difficult to turn, removed stock is probably packing up in its nose. It should be backed out and the chips and shavings removed. For this purpose I use a heavy piece of Bakelite plastic that I have sharpened to a point. A copper or brass rod about 4 in. long and sharpened to a long point will work well too. Steel should not be used; sometimes considerable force is necessary to clear chips from the nose hole and it is easy to slip and damage the cutters. Packing is worst in threading blind holes where there is no place for removed stock to go but the bottom of the hole.

If you find yourself using all your strength to turn the tap, something is wrong. The tap should be backed out and the trouble located. I keep a small lump of beeswax on my bench and after tapping the first hole in a piece of work I run the beeswax over the tap. Friction makes the tap warm, and the beeswax flows on nicely and eases the work. I then stick a small piece of rag or cotton in each tapped hole and drip Danish oil into it until it is saturated. Remove the rag in an hour or so, after the thread is thoroughly soaked. It is not uncommon in use for some glue to drip on the wooden screws. If a drip gets inadvertently turned into the tapped hole in the jaw while the clamp is being adjusted, the oil will keep it from adhering and freezing the clamp. Danish oil also strengthens the threads. If you try your clamp while the oil is wet it will make an ear-splitting squeal with every turn. The squeal disappears as soon as the oil is dry.

After the initial tapping, even with a well-sharpened tap, stresses in the wood and compression caused by the tapping process cause the sides of the hole to expand slightly over a period of two or three days. This can make the screws bind. It is not critical in hand-screw clamps, which can always be taken apart and retapped, but in other applications—C-clamps and bar clamps where the tool cannot be taken apart after assembly—stock should be set aside and retapped after a few days. Take care to start the tap in the same track as

for the first threading. Only a very small amount of material will be removed in the second tapping but it will make a great difference in how smoothly the finished tool will turn. If the clamp still binds, rethreading the screw will help.

The jaws of the clamp can be scraped or sanded to final surface finish. I oil and wax my clamps. Besides making them more attractive, wax keeps glue drips from sticking.

Screws should be made from dense, close-grained wood that is free from knots. I've successfully used beech, cherry, pear, apple, dogwood, black walnut, yew and myrtle. I own an antique clamp that has ash screws, but I've had poor results with both ash and oak, though these woods tap well and make good clamp jaws. I have successfully used oak stock taken from root balls rather than the trunks of trees.

There are two methods of making screws and their handles. The standard way is to turn both handle and screw from one piece. I don't have a lathe so I make handles and screws separately. The only difference is that in the lathe-turned method the rear screw cannot be threaded all the way to the shoulder of the handle—it has to be slightly longer to compensate.

Because taps cannot be used in end grain, I laminate handle blocks by alternating blocks of wood according to grain, sometimes as many as seven or eight for each handle. This is a good use for scraps. I laminate half the length of the handle at a time, drill it through and tap it, then glue on three or four blocks to finish the blank. This allows the screw to bottom out in the hole made for it. If the handle is glued together completely and then tapped, the screw will not fit in the portion of the hole left unthreaded by the nose of the tap. This void in the handle will be weak.

When I first started making clamps I drilled a hole the diameter of my screw stock in my handle, inserted the unthreaded end of the middle dowel with a liberal dose of glue and put another, smaller dowel across the handle to secure it. This didn't work because the middle handle undergoes great stress. All of these original handles eventually broke their pins and glue joints and had to be redone in the way I am describing.

I turn handles by removing the appropriate tap from its handle, chucking it in the drill press and screwing the blank onto the tap. With the drill press running, I shape and finish them free-hand with a Surform and sandpaper. The handle of the middle screw should have a good flange of very hard wood at the bottom, where it will bear against the clamp jaw. This flange should be at least 1/8 in. wide all around and well-supported. The handle above it shouldn't be thinned too drastically. The rear handle is under much less stress and need have no flange. Of course very nice handles can be made without turning—simply cut them into hexagonal shapes.

The two screws that fit into the handles aren't identical. The middle screw should have an unthreaded section the depth of the unthreaded jaw. If this section is threaded the clamp jaw tries to ride down the spiral when the clamp is turned two-handed, and it gives a galloping effect to what should be a smooth rotation. If your doweling is accurately sized you will have to scrape or sand this unthreaded portion to get it to fit the hole and turn smoothly.

The tip of the rear screw should also be sanded or shaped to fit its socket in the unthreaded jaw. Shallow grooves showing the bottom of the threads should still be there when the fit is proper. The accuracy of the fit in these holes makes the difference between a sloppy and a tight clamp.

On large clamps I make the screws long enough to open the jaws 9 in. I rarely use the clamp opened this far because flex in the center screw cuts down on the pressure that may be applied. Occasionally, however, it has been nice to have this

A Dowel Maker

by Trevor Robinson

Because commercial dowels are made only in birch, beech or maple, and large diameters are expensive or hard to get, it is useful to be able to make your own with the simple tool shown here. Properly sharpened and set, the tool turns easily around a square length of hardwood, cutting it smooth and round in a single pass.

The body of the tool is made from a block of hardwood about 2-3/4 in. square and 7-1/2 in. long. First locate and bore a hole the diameter of the desired dowel. Then on the lathe a conical depression is turned to meet the hole so that about an inch of cylindrical bore remains. For a 1-in. dowel, the mouth of the cone is 2-1/8 in. wide; for other dimensions the cone should allow the square of wood to enter about 1/2 in. before it encounters the cutter. This means that the large diameter of the cone is about twice the small diameter. The next step is to drill the holes for the four screws that will fasten the two sections together. By drilling them before sawing the block; alignment is automatic. Two saw cuts separate the clamping section from the main block. Mating channels are then chiseled along the inner faces of the two pieces to hold the cutting blade, which is just a saw kerf thicker than the resulting channel. Thus the cone remains smooth, and the screws hold the blade tightly.

Blades can be made from old files. The file should first be annealed by heating red-hot and cooling slowly. Then a suitable length can be cut off and shaped. Before the final sharpening the cutter should be retempered by heating red-hot, quenching, and reheating to 475° F (light-orange oxidation color) before the last quench (*Fine Woodworking*, Fall '76).

The position of the cutter is very important for getting a smooth dowel. The heel end of the cutting edge should just graze the surface of the finished diameter so that the dowel is a snug fit as it comes through. Waxing the bore will make it go more easily. The square of wood to be cut should be just slightly larger than the diameter of the dowel—about 1-1/16 in. square for a 1-in. dowel. It helps to chamfer off the four corners at the leading end of the piece to get it started without splintering. Then the wood can be held vertically in a vise and the tool turned without forcing it down. With a sharp, properly positioned blade the weight of the tool is enough to keep it moving along the wood.

Dowel maker, top, is made of one block of wood cut into two parts, bottom. Note rounded heel of cutter—it just grazes finished dowel.

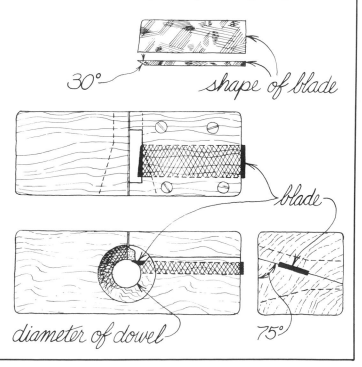

30°

shape of blade

blade

diameter of dowel

75°

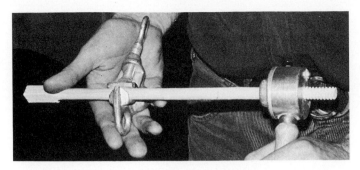

Modified tubing cutter propels dowel through German screwbox.

capacity. If you make both screws 14 in. long from handle flange to tip, you can shorten them until they feel right.

When threading doweling, you can insert it in a bench vise and turn the die round and round the dowel. If the wood you are using is brittle or of small diameter, however, the dowel may twist, cracking the threads. If this happens, hand-hold the dowel and turn the die around it. The flex then takes place in your wrist. Large doweling, 3/4-in. diameter and up, can be hand-held successfully without undue fatigue. Smaller sizes are difficult to grip and your hands are liable to cramp. I have modified a small tubing cutter by removing the cutting wheel and reshaping the bottom jaw into a doweling holder to help thread small screws.

To glue screws to the handles, drip glue into the hole; don't coat the screws with it. If possible, try not to get any glue on the threads in the upper half of the hole. Most of the holding is done by the threads on the screws; the glue is only to keep them from turning off the handles. Too much glue can cause the screw to freeze before it seats because frictional heat rapidly sets the glue. Turn the handles on slowly and evenly without stopping until you feel them seat. It is best to turn the screws in dry first and mark them when they are fully seated. This allows you to stop when you should. The screw provides a lot of mechanical advantage and it is easy to pop the end off the handle. Too much glue and this mechanical

advantage can produce a hydraulic effect, causing the end to come off or the sides to rupture.

The design of the C-clamp I am about to describe is from an article in *USSR* magazine describing a contemporary Soviet woodworker's shop. I've seen a similar clamp in a 17th-century print of a French cabinetmaker's shop.

Wooden C-clamps are bulkier than their metal counterparts and because of the center brace look deeper than they should to someone used to metal clamps. The center brace in the Russian clamp was made from a piece of brass rod threaded for a nut at either end. I use a wooden brace because I have a suitable small threading set.

The three parts of the clamp body are held together by mortise and tenon joints. If you are using a wooden screw for the center brace, make up the upper and lower jaws of the clamp body first and thread the holes. Screw the small-diameter dowel through the holes and then measure for the long piece that will form the spine of the clamp. If you are using a metal rod, all three pieces may be made at the same time, to arbitrary measurements. With a metal rod it is possible to draw the rod down to the dimensions of the clamp; with a wooden rod, clearance in the mating threads can result in play of 1/16 in. in the length of the spine piece.

The threaded hole in the clamp jaw that will receive the main screw should be made slightly less than 90° to the axis of the jaw. Two or three degrees is enough. There is a certain amount of spring in the clamp that, because wood is flexible, cannot be eliminated. If the hole is drilled at the logical 90° angle, the clamp will spring under pressure and tend to slide off the work. This is true not only for the C-clamp but for wooden bar clamps as well.

Handles for these clamps can be made in either of the ways described earlier.

Since the hole in the upper jaw will not be accessible when the clamp is assembled, all C-clamp parts should be set aside for two or three days and the upper jaw hole rethreaded. The screw assembly should be attached to the upper jaw before gluing the spine and lower jaw to this piece.

assemble handle, screw, and upper jaw before gluing to spine and lower jaw

C-clamp

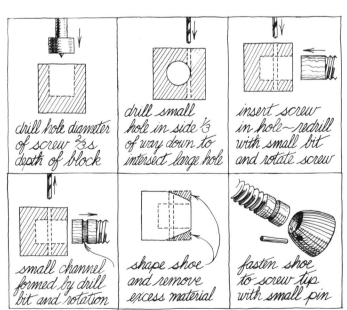

drill hole diameter of screw ⅔s depth of block

drill small hole in side ⅓ of way down to intersect large hole

insert screw in hole—redrill with small bit and rotate screw

small channel formed by drill bit and rotation

shape shoe and remove excess material

fasten shoe to screw tip with small pin

Basic C-clamp, left, can be fitted with freely turning wooden shoe, above. Shoe is made of toughest available wood—author starts with square chunk of hardwood root and drills across the grain, not into end grain. Shoe will break if tip of screw isn't cut truly square. For delicate work, surface shoe with scrap of leather.

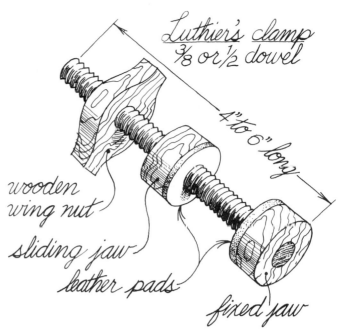

Screws of C-clamp, top, and bar clamp are slanted to allow for flex.

Bar clamps, because they must adjust to material of greatly varying widths, cannot have a center brace. Consequently, they must be more massive. The jaw of the clamp that takes the screw is fixed and heavily made. Again, depress the angle of the screw hole a few degrees from square to allow for spring. The adjustable jaw of the bar clamp should also be slanted a few degrees for the same reason. The bar that secures the adjustable jaw of the clamp can be made from iron or 1/8-in. sheet brass cut to shape and bent with heat.

Luthier's clamps can be made using 1/2-in. or 3/8-in. threaded dowel. The wooden wing nut shown in the drawing

above has numerous applications in clamps and other kinds of woodworking using wooden screws.

Gang clamps for marquetry should be easy to make using the protective tip described for the C-clamp, although this application is outside my personal experience.

By making threaded holes in the tips of the jaws of a standard hand-screw clamp you can increase its possible applications. Different mandrels can be made to screw into the tips, to produce deep engagement clamps or clamps specially tailored to shaped work.

The action of wooden clamps, like all wooden machinery, improves with time. Small mechanical irregularities wear to accommodate one another and the combination of wax, oil, heat and pressure forms bearing surfaces like glass.

I have described the assembly of a single clamp. Obviously it will always be a more efficient use of drill and saw setups to make a number at once. I have a box under my bench where I save likely pieces of material. When it begins to overflow I take a day off and make a batch of clamps. I try to make clamps using all the woods that pass through my shop. This allows me to show wood samples to visitors and it keeps a variety of wood in front of me. The choice of wood for a piece I am making is often suggested by the clamps I am using.

Once you have been through the process you will find you can make five or ten clamps a day without much difficulty.

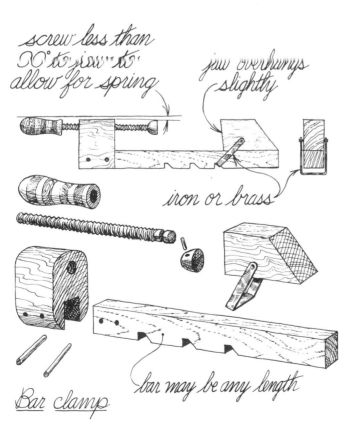

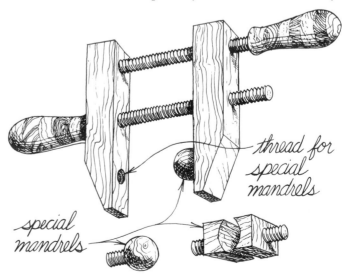

Threads in end grain

When tapping wooden threads with a homemade or commercial steel tap, good clean threads can be gotten only when tapping perpendicular to the grain of the wood. It sometimes is necessary to tap directly into end grain, as in a turning, in which case the threads will be torn out. However, the tap can be sharpened so that the wood fibers on the inside surface of the pilot hole are cut before the root of the thread, thus not tearing out the whole thread. The tap will also work just as well when tapping perpendicular to the grain.

Looking at the end view of the tap, it is filed so that the angle of the two cutting edges is sloped back from the radial position. This could be anywhere from 40° to 50°. A 45° file can be used to rough-form the inside bevel of the cutter. The edge can then be finished with a small slip stone.

—*William Stockhausen, Northville, Mich.*

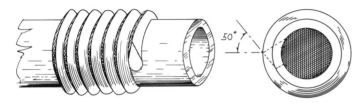

Gluing table

A most functional and sturdy gluing table can be made of angle irons bolted to a wooden base. Dressers, tabletops and wide boards for beds are easily glued up using such a table. The construction allows easy application of clamps, and the specially notched board at the back even holds bar clamps erect and up against the underside of the boards while you align and level them with one hand and crank the clamp with the other. If the vertical face of the angle iron is too narrow, it must be built up to make room for easy placement of clamps, since at least one will go on the underside of the board. Glue dribbles can be easily cleaned off the irons with a few smacks of a hammer after they've dried.

—*James B. Small, Jr., Newville, Pa.*

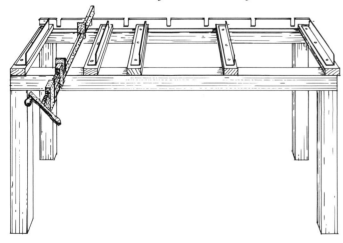

Storing clamps

Instead of piling all your clamps into a tub as if they were to be thrown out with the trash, you can easily make a rack to store them. Lay your wood clamps on a piece of ¾-in. ply-

wood and determine the placement of the hangers by marking the space between adjusting screws and jaws. Hangers are made from 2x4 stock cut to a loose fit between adjusting screws and glued into snug holes in the plywood at 90° to the base. You can make a rack for *C*-clamps in the same way, but set in the hanger parts at 80° rather than 90°; for large *C*-clamps, use 2x6 stock. A free-standing clamp tree can be made from 2x4 stock. —*Everett Traylor, Bettendorf, Iowa*

Sizing

When cutting threads in end grain, an aid to preventing tearout that will give clean-running threads is to size the wood. After drilling the hole in the end grain (or any surface), coat the hole with a watery glue (polyvinyl acetate, plastic resin, etc.) thin enough to penetrate the fibers. Less tear-out will occur during the tapping. Afterward, apply more coats of sizing to harden the wood further. Sizing so applied increases the toughness of any running or bearing surface.

Another use of sizing is to raise the grain. Before the final sanding, apply a thin wash coat of sizing. Avoid thermoplastic adhesives (the white and yellow glues) because they soften with friction and load up abrasive paper. Brown glue such as Borden's or Weldwood plastic resin sand and harden the wood especially well. Another way to raise the grain is with thin shellac or lacquer. When it dries, the sizing keeps the wood fibers and grain raised so they can be sanded away. If a better surface is not immediately noticed, the improvement may well be apparent after several months of humidity fluctuation. —*C.B. Oliver, Durham, N.H.*

Lag-screw tap

For occasional use, an ordinary 2-in. lag screw can be made into an effective wood tap in smaller sizes. Use a triangular file to notch the bolt along about 1 in. Tilt the file in order to get more rake on the cutting edge.

—*Jim Richey, Houston, Tex.*

Gluing frame

I found I did not have a really flat gluing surface and had to improvise one. I used an old window frame to set up my pipe clamps for gluing up solid wood panels. The trick is to keep the clamps parallel and in the same plane, to make sure the panels have no glued-in twist or wind. After notching the frame to accept about half the diameter of the two pipes, place winding sticks across them fore and aft and sight across the top of the sticks to spot any variation from parallel. If there is a variation, simply deepen the one notch necessary to bring the pipes into line.

Once you have trued this setup, don't move it, because the surface on which it is next placed may vary and change the parallelism. When gluing the boards together, place the good side down and use one or two clamps across the top of the boards to even out the pressure. Always use scrap strips between the clamp jaws and the wood to distribute pressure and avoid marks. —*Duane Waskow, Marion, Iowa*

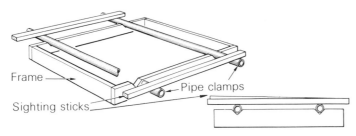

Frame

Sighting sticks

Pipe clamps

Clamping with bedsprings

Old bedsprings make excellent and cheap clamps for hard-to-clamp jobs, such as clamping veneer on curved surfaces. They can also be used for small solid wood patches. Springs can be cut to different sizes, then bent to put pressure in the exact spot needed. A piece of Saran wrap and a block of wood placed over the veneer will give more even clamping pressure, without marring the work. A caution: Bedspring clamps can suddenly spring off, if wrongly placed.
 —*Robert S. Friedensen, Winston-Salem, N.C.*

Clamping a scarf joint

A scarf joint can be clamped securely as shown: After spreading the glue, tack the pieces to be joined with pin brads (#16/18) cut to ¼ in. long. Then sandwich the pieces between wedges made of soft, wet wood. While one C-clamp applies pressure directly on the surfaces to be joined, two others hold the wedges in position. —*Price G. Schulte, St. Louis, Mo.*

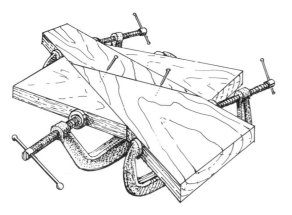

Clamping boxes

Clamping and squaring large box pieces can be a problem. The pressure of the clamps often pulls the piece out of square at the critical moment of final tightening. The first hint is ob-

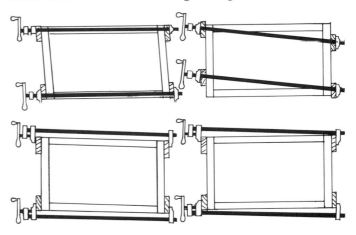

vious but often forgotten: Get all the parts ready to glue and assemble, have all your clamps extended to the length you will need, and tape your softwood clamping blocks either to the work or to the clamp faces before applying any glue. Proper preparation saves precious time.

After assembling, tighten opposing clamps in small increments. When the pieces are just snug, measure the diagonals for squareness. A folding rule with a slide extension is indispensible here. If the work is out of square, move the clamps slightly to oppose the pull, i.e., make the clamps pull more parallel to the longer diagonal. A very small movement will make a lot of difference.

This process becomes much more complicated if all four sides of the rectangle are open and being glued at once. But I have clamped together a post-and-rail crib with all four sides openwork and no top or bottom. Using eight clamps, I pulled it square in all directions at once. A final hint, which most know: Don't wipe the glue. It will be much easier to chip it off the surface than to sand it out of the pores later.
 —*George Pilling, Springville, Calif.*

Picture-frame clamp

This is my no-cost solution for clamping a picture frame: Clamp all four pieces at once with a length of nylon cord. Measure the outside perimeter of the frame and tie a non-slip knot so the cord will just fit around. Then use four or more scrap blocks between the cord and the frame to stretch the cord tight and draw up the joints. Pieces of cardboard or leather folded over the corners prevent the cord from digging in. If the frame twists when tensioned, place a weighted piece of plywood on top—after you have tested the squareness of the frame. (Try the procedure dry first, to spot bad joints.) On narrow frames, use eight blocks, all located near the corners. With white glue, heavy clamping pressure is not required to make a solid, lasting joint.
 —*Duane Waskow, Marion, Iowa*

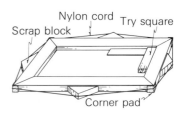

Nylon cord Try square

Scrap block

Corner pad

Scratch Beader

Simple tool makes intricate moldings

by Henry T. Kramer

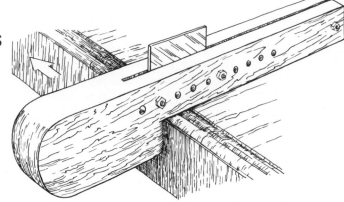

The scratch beader is a tool of many virtues. It is quickly and easily made. With practice, it is a substitute for a router (table or hand) and for molding planes. It can do things those tools cannot, depending on the particular job. It can cut any molding (or groove or rabbet) you are willing to make a cutter for, including intricate shapes.

The beader consists of hardwood stock with a projecting arm, which has a vertical saw kerf along its length. The tools are held in the saw kerf by bolts. The shoulder between the stock and the arm guides the tool as it is drawn along the edge of the work.

Making a cutter for the beader is easy. File or grind a piece of any scrap steel—old saw blades or cabinet scrapers are ideal, but in a pinch one can use almost anything. The steel should be wide enough to accommodate the desired shape plus another ¼ in. or ⅜ in. to recess behind the shoulder. Recessing the tool stiffens it during each stroke. It should be long enough to accommodate the design and stick out the top, and no thicker than the kerf in which it will be placed.

The cutter is formed by cutting and filing the desired shape, as a negative cross section, in one end of the blank. The cutting edge is filed straight across the edge of the tool. With steel no thicker than an old saw blade, a mere awareness that the trailing edge should not extend below the cutting face will allow sufficient clearance. With heavier steel, a more deliberate relief will be required, as on the sides of a tool that is to follow a curve. But do not leave any more relief than necessary. The tool cuts like a scraper, not a chisel, and it should not want to cut the wood under vertical or horizontal pressure.

If you wish to harden and temper the tool, fine. It is not ordinarily worth the effort for one-of-a-kind applications. If the shape is complex and not easily sharpened without destroying the design, hardening may be desirable. Usually one is not obliged to harden unless the molding to be cut involves a lot of wood. This is not a production tool. It is for small or non-repetitive jobs, and it permits a flexibility of shapes that production tools cannot match.

It is used by placing the beader at right angles, vertically and horizontally, to the shape or groove to be cut. With cuts of any depth, say ⅛ in. or 3/16 in. or more, the tool is first placed part way below the arm and secured tightly on both sides by two or more small machine bolts of any convenient size. The beader is then drawn along the surface to be cut, holding its shoulder against the nearest edge or surface, and at a right angle to the surface to be cut. The beader should be held upright at all times, but at the very start some slight tilt in the direction of the stroke may be useful. One or two trials will show that the leading edge of the cutter will then have the effect of providing a quite shallow cut. But as soon as the cutter has got into the wood, the beader should be used upright. As the work progresses, the cutter may have to be reset

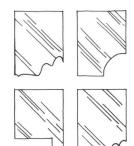

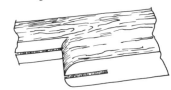

Scratch beader is easily made from hardwood and steel scraps; cutter can be bolted in saw kerf at various positions along projecting arm. Left, cutter profiles are negative cross sections of desired shapes. Drawing below shows tool's rounded shoulder, which allows the beader to follow curved edges.

deeper until the final design has been cut.

A beader will be used most often to shape an edge, but may also be used to cut a groove (for inlay, for example) or molding in the surface of a plank following a straight or curved edge. In this case the shoulder of the tool, which locates and maintains the distance between the groove (or inner edge of the molding) and the outer edge, may be rounded to about the smallest arc of the curved edge being followed. This makes it easier to hold the tool steady as you follow a curve, it keeps the distance of the cut more constant, and it permits you to keep the long axis of the tool normal, or perpendicular, to the curved edge as you follow it.

The beader is best used on hardwood and with care it will cut across the grain—even in situations where a plane or router would tear. It will not cut cleanly to the very end of a blind groove, nor, in the case of sharp angles, can it be worked right to the intersection. Work up to about a half-inch away and finish with a knife or chisel. Take care always to keep the shoulder bearing on the work as you scrape. And put a bolt through the hole nearest the end of the arm, so the saw kerf won't pinch your hand as you work.

Beaders may be made in a variety of sizes, although they are difficult to use for large moldings. Some beaders, for delicate work, are quite small. Start with simple designs; later, all sorts of applications will invite your interest. Whatever size you try, keep to the general proportions shown in the drawing. Too long a beader encourages twisting as you scrape, which is not good. Beaders don't last forever, because the cutter tends to enlarge the kerf in which it is held during use. When this happens, you'll have to make a new beader. Make one and practice on some scrap and you'll soon appreciate the versatility of this inexpensive device. ☐

Henry Kramer, 60, of Somerville, N.J. is in the reinsurance business. He'd rather make and fix tools and furniture.

Two Tools

Small saw, marking gauge

by Jim Richey

If there is a class of tools missing from modern workshops it is those simple hand tools designed around a specific function. As a result, many of us find ourselves making a delicate little cut on a small piece of wood with a giant power saw, or designing our work around our equipment.

The planemaker's saw and a small marking gauge are members of the missing class—simple hand tools whose function has dictated their design. They are related in another way: The saw is used to make the gauge.

The planemaker's saw was originally used to cut the wedge dadoes in wooden planes. It is also quite effective for sawing through mortises or wedge slots, trimming protruding tenons or pegs without scratching the wood, and sawing curves in pierced work. In tight places it has no equal.

This planemaker's saw was made by cutting teeth into the back of an old kitchen knife. If you choose to go this route, pick a long, slim carbon-steel knife of the type readily available for a couple of dollars. Avoid the harder stainless-steel knives. Knives that taper in thickness from handle to tip are unsuitable. If you want to go through the annealing and heat-treating steps (*Fine Woodworking*, Fall '76), any scrap of tool steel about 1/16 in. thick will do.

Let your plans for the saw and the thickness of the blade dictate its length, width and taper. I needed a blade that could start its cut in a 1/4-in. hole, hence the slim design.

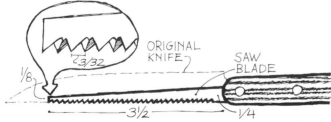

Slowly and carefully, grind the blade to shape, dipping frequently to avoid overheating. File the sides of the blade so that the front is a shade thicker than the back. Not much taper is needed, just enough to prevent binding.

Now file the business edge of the blade perfectly straight and lay out the teeth. I spaced the gullets 3/32 in. apart. To cut in the teeth, hold the triangular file level at an angle (50° to 60°) toward the handle of the saw. File every other tooth four or five strokes and turn the blade around. Holding the file at the same angle to the handle, file the remaining teeth four or five strokes. Repeat until the teeth take shape.

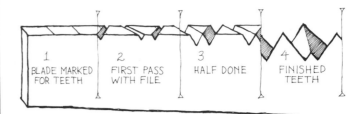

By tilting the file slightly you can give the teeth more or less rake. Old-timers claim that more rake is better for soft woods, less for hard woods. Exact angles are less important than consistency. The filing process sounds difficult but it takes only about 10 minutes.

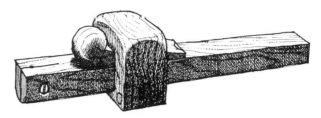

Although I have a beautiful old (but clumsy) marking gauge, I needed a small gauge designed specifically for mortise and dovetail work on thin wood. Designing the gauge around these functions resulted in the following dimensions.

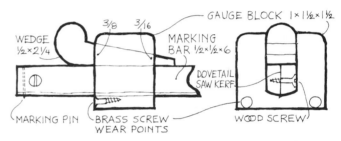

As to variations, most would prefer a wider block with more lip for general use. The wedge could be moved to the back or side. The marking pin could be installed at an angle. Design your gauge around its intended uses.

The bar was made first so that its profile could be transferred to the gauge block. The bottom rounding of the bar is quite helpful in using the gauge and should be included. I drilled two 1/4-in. holes through the block and used the planemaker's saw to cut the tapered mortise, as shown. When

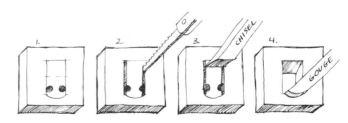

the mortise was trimmed so that the bar would fit smoothly, the wedge was rough-cut and trimmed to fit. I used a taper of 3/16 in. through 1 in. This is rather steep, but seems to hold well. Less taper would hold tighter.

The marking pin is a small brad held in a dovetail saw kerf with a screw. If the gauge is to be worked only one direction, the pin should have a knife-like point slightly angled so that the lip is pulled into the work. Those who mark both directions would prefer a pointed pin.

Wear points or a wear strip should be installed if the gauge is expected to have lots of use. I used two brass screws partially countersunk and filed flush.

Sawing by Hand

Bowsaw is best; keep it sharp

by Tage Frid

A handsaw can replace a machine-powered saw for every cutting operation. The correct use and maintenance of handsaws should be practiced until they are second nature. To saw properly, coordination of the joints in the hand, elbow and shoulder must be achieved. The biggest mistake most people make when using a handsaw is to hang onto it as if their lives depended on it, bearing down much too hard. This makes it hard to start the saw, and once the cut is started, it is difficult to follow the line. A handsaw should lie loosely in your hands. No pressure should be applied, particularly when starting the cut. Once experience is gained, a slight amount of pressure can be applied after the cut is started. Use your thumb as a guide when starting the saw.

There are many different handsaws on the market, and each one is designed for a special purpose. Handsaws are sold by length and by the number of points—a six-point saw has six teeth per inch.

The bowsaw, scroll bowsaw, offset dovetail saw and rip panel saw are the saws I have found most useful in my many years as a cabinetmaker. I don't like and would never buy a backsaw; they are clumsy and heavy. Maybe they are all right in miter boxes, but a bowsaw will do the job faster.

For general sawing, I would recommend buying a 26-in., six-point and an 18-in., eight-point bowsaw. (Lengths might vary, because most bowsaws are made in Europe and so are measured metrically.) I would also buy a 26-in. scroll bowsaw, preferably with interchangeable blades, and a 10-in., or longer, 15-point offset dovetail saw. A 24-in. rip panel saw (the standard American carpenter's saw), six to seven points, is useful for cutting big pieces such as plywood, where the bridge of the bowsaw would be in the way.

Japanese saws are good for special work. I have some but hardly ever use them, except in cramped space where I can't get in with a regular saw. The Japanese ripsaw cuts on the pull stroke. This makes the line fuzzy and hard to see when cutting joints. On the crosscut, the teeth are long and might bend when hitting a knot. Also, the saw is hard to resharpen.

For scroll work, I would of course use a band saw if I could. Or I might use a saber saw. But a scroll bowsaw will cut as fast or faster than a saber saw, and no electricity is needed. The blade on the scroll bowsaw is considerably longer than that of any other scroll saw or coping saw.

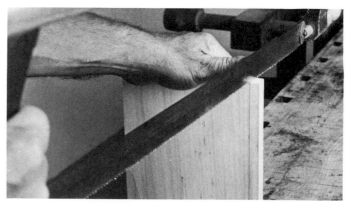

Starting the cut: Frid holds saw loosely, left thumb guiding blade, with eye, blade and cutting line all aligned vertically. Blade is angled so frame will clear wood as cut proceeds.

Dovetail saws: straight (top), offset and Japanese.

Sharpening Vise

You can make a sharpening jig out of two pieces of 3/4-in. plywood. The dimensions can be changed to suit your individual needs. Glue two pieces of maple or another hardwood on the ends of the plywood, as shown at right. These will be the jaws of the jig. When the glue has set, put the two halves together and attach butt hinges at the bottom. Screw or glue on the two side pieces, which keep the jig from falling through the vise. Then cut the jaws parallel, and saw the outside bevel. If you use a table saw, slide a piece of wood in between the two pieces of plywood, below left, to prevent the jaws from binding on the saw blade at the end of the cut. Or handplane the jaws parallel and plane off the bevel, below right. Planing a little off the bottom of the two jaw pieces ensures a tight grip at the top.

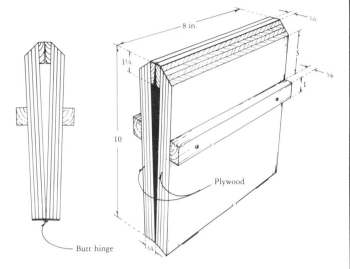

Whatever saw you use has to be kept sharp and set right. There are many vises you can buy that hold the blade during sharpening. But I make my own—it is simple to do and considerably less expensive.

For some strange reason, most new handsaws are filed for crosscutting. The first time I sharpen a crosscut saw I change it to a ripsaw (by changing the teeth from a point to a chisel edge). This makes ripping faster and easier, of course, and I find the saw works better even for crosscutting.

Before sharpening, check to see if all the teeth are the same height. If not, level them off with a mill file. Then file each tooth to a sharp point, and the saw is ready to be set. After setting, file two strokes on each tooth the length of the saw.

All handsaws have an alternating tooth setting; that is, the upper part of each tooth is bent out to one side or the other, to create a kerf that is wider than the saw blade. If the saw is not set enough it will bind. If set too much, the cut will be wide and rough, and the saw will cut more slowly. If the teeth are set more to one side, the saw will favor that side. To correct this, both sides must be reset. A properly set saw that is started correctly, with little pressure, will easily follow the cutting line. There are many good saw sets on the market. I prefer the Sandvik because it is light, easy to adjust and simple to use. It allows you to see what you are doing. Each tooth should be set approximately 1/64 in.

If the teeth are too small for a saw set, use a small screwdriver instead. Press it down between every second tooth and twist it the same amount each time.

Now the teeth are ready to be filed, with a new triangular file. Use only one edge for each saw filing; by using the same number of strokes and the same length of the file on each stroke, all the teeth will be sharpened uniformly. The file gradually gets dull, but so gradually that all the teeth will remain the same length. Turning the file to a new edge in the middle of a sharpening is a mistake, because the new side will cut deeper than the worn side. I never use an old, worn-out file. Use a new file—you get three sharpenings from each one. This way the teeth stay the same length and you won't have to level them off for many years.

When filing, press down straight on the file, just enough so the file works and doesn't skip over the metal. File both the

To level the teeth, a mill file is run the length of the blade.

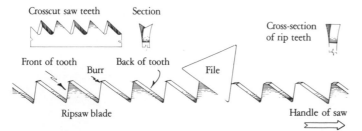

Crosscut saw teeth   Section   Cross-section of rip teeth

Front of tooth   Back of tooth   File
Burr

Ripsaw blade   Handle of saw

As teeth take shape, tiny burr points in direction of cut.

Pliers-like saw set alternately bends teeth away from plane of blade, about 1/64 in. to each side. Set must be even.

Screwdriver twisted in every second gullet will set small saws.

With fingers as stops, whole length of file is used on each stroke.

Tensioning string is wrapped four times lengthwise, woven to finish.

front and back of the teeth at the same time, working from the front toward the handle of the saw. Thus the final stroke on each tooth will be on the back, and the burr that appears when the tooth just comes to a point will be aimed in the cutting direction. Be sure to keep the file strokes at 90° to the blade. Never file or stone the face of the blade, because this would change the set of the teeth. Don't file the teeth of a ripsaw alternately, as is usually recommended in textbooks.

The saw can be refiled four or five times before it needs resetting. Of course this depends on how dull you let the saw get before you refile it. I always file my saws as soon as the tips of the teeth get shiny white. This means the saw has started to get dull. If it isn't too dull, two file strokes on each tooth should be enough to sharpen the saw.

If the wood tears up in the back when crosscutting or ripping, one or more of the teeth are too long. In this case I file across the top to even the teeth, and then refile all the teeth before setting. If the teeth still tear, as is likely to happen in softwood and especially in plywood, scribe a line where the cut will be and make a vee-cut with a chisel on the underside of the piece. This will prevent tearing.

The bowsaw is my all-purpose saw. It takes longer to learn to use than other handsaws, but once you get the hang of it, you will use it for most cutting. All my advanced students use a bowsaw, and I don't brainwash my students. Its advantage is that because the blade is narrower, there is less friction in the kerf. The blade does not whip because it is kept in tension. Because the steel is thinner than in a panel saw, the bowsaw advances more quickly, and it is easier to cut a line.

When you buy a bowsaw that uses string as a tensioning system, you usually get the saw in pieces. Even if it comes assembled, you must know how to string it in case the string breaks. Clamp the saw in the bench so that there is tension in the blade when the string is applied. Wrap the string four times lengthwise, then finish the stringing by weaving the end in and out of the strings about 10 times. Then place the piece of wood that controls blade tension between the strings. Release the tension when the saw is not in use.

When I rip with a bowsaw I clamp the board down on the bench. I can cut faster this way because I am sawing up and down and can put force into the down stroke. I use both hands so I don't tire as easily. Also, by positioning the board with the portion to be ripped extended over the bench, I have to clamp the board only once. If I stand it up in the vise, I have to keep clamping and unclamping to move it into position. If I were cutting a long board, say 8 ft., I would need a ladder if I stood the board up in the vise. The board would vibrate so that it would be just about impossible to cut.

When I rip a board with a bowsaw, I hold it so the blade is perpendicular to the board. All the force is from the right hand, with the left hand acting as a guide. I saw away from myself so that I can see the line, and so that I can move along with the cut with my arms in a comfortable position. On a 3/4-in. thick piece of basswood clamped horizontally, 10 strokes with a 26-in. bowsaw cut 9 in. With the wood vertically in the vise, the same number of strokes cut about 5 in.

For crosscutting, I use the rip-sharpened bowsaw. I lay the board flat on the bench, with the piece I am cutting off to my right, and hold the wood down with my left hand. Then when the cut is almost through I plant my left elbow on the board to hold it, and reach between the blade and the bridge of the saw to catch the off-cut.

Making a Bowsaw

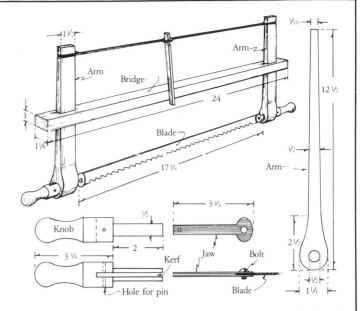

If you want to make a bowsaw, the first thing to do is to buy the blade, so you can design a saw with the right relationship between the arms, bridge and blade. A bowsaw should be as light as possible. I would use teak or mahogany for the arms, clear pine for the bridge, and maple for the knobs.

To make the arms, drill 1/2-in. holes in the arms first, then mark the wood and cut the taper using a band saw, scroll saw or scroll bowsaw. The arms should be identical. Sand the pieces and break the edges, especially where you will hold the saw. Leave the arms square where they pass through the bridge. The bridge is rectangular in section and has a through mortise near each end for the arms.

Make a 1/8-in. saw cut in the knobs for the two pieces of steel that will hold the blade. Then turn the knobs.

The steel jaw pieces are the most difficult parts of the saw to make. Two pieces go in each knob and sandwich the blade between them. One, 19 gauge, has a hole so the screw can slip in easily; the other, 17 gauge, should have a threaded hole to fit a 3/16-in. roundhead bolt, 1/4 in. long. Remember to put the knobs through the arms before fastening the steel to the knobs with a pin.

For a 17-3/4-in. blade I would make the arms 12-1/2 in. long; for a 25-3/4-in. blade I would make the arms 14-1/3 in. long. Personally I would not go through all the trouble of making a bowsaw. The wood parts are easy, but the metal parts take time, and I can buy a good bowsaw ready-made for less than $20.

When I have to resaw by hand, I start the same way as sawing a tenon (*Fine Woodworking*, Summer '76), and if it is started correctly it will naturally follow the line. I mark a line on both ends and along one edge of the board and saw down on one corner so I cut the whole end and part of the top. Then I turn the board around in the vise and saw from the other corner. This way I don't have to worry about following two lines at once—the saw drops into the first kerf and this guides it along. For cutting up plywood, I place the panel flat on sawhorses and climb right up on top of it.

For very small work I use an offset dovetail saw. With the offset, I can see the line more easily and I can use the saw for cutting flush anything that protrudes above a flat surface. I also change it from crosscut to rip the first time it needs filing. I don't like the reversible offset. It is very bulky, and because I change it to a ripsaw I can only use it one way anyway.

[Editor's note: Bowsaws are sold by Frog Tool Co., 548 N. Wells St., Chicago, Ill. 60610; Garrett Wade, 302 Fifth Ave., New York, N. Y. 10001; Silvo Hardware, 107 Walnut St., Philadelphia, Pa. 19106; Three Crowns, 3850 Monroe Ave., Pittsford, N. Y. 14534; and Woodcraft Supply, 313 Montvale Ave., Woburn, Mass. 01801. Olson Saw Co., Route 6, Bethel, Conn. 06801, makes blades for most types of frame saws.]

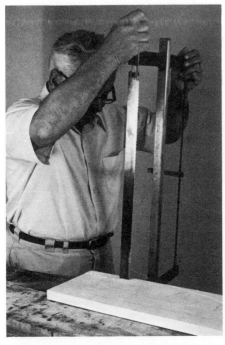
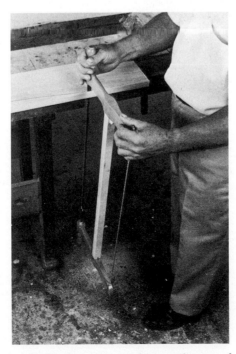

When ripping (left), left hand guides cut and right hand powers whole length of blade downward. Scroll bowsaw (center) also cuts on down stroke, away from sawyer. As saw nears end of crosscut (right), sawyer reaches between blade and bridge to catch wood.

55

Circular Saws

How to keep them sharp and running true

by Eugene Roth

Circular saws must be kept sharp. When a saw does not cut easily, it is usually dull or has lost its swage or set. Forcing the feed in these conditions will heat the rim of the saw, and the metal may expand and crack. The saw may also lose its tension and bend or break over the collar. A saw that wobbles and does not cut straight is dangerous to use and should be sent out for professional repair.

With practice and careful attention to detail, however, a woodworker can learn to sharpen and maintain circular saws in tip-top shape. The set and rake of the teeth can be adjusted to suit the type of work. The basic tools for sharpening are a good saw vise, which can be homemade, a setting stake and hammers, the correct files (mill bastard, round, cant, square mill and triangular tapered) and grinding wheels. The 60° triangular file is familiar to most craftsmen, but the cant saw file is not. It is also triangular in cross section, but with a 120° angle and two angles of 30°. It is used for sharpening saws with a very steep gullet angle, and for filing the face bevel of dado and combination blades. The square saw file is also used on dado and combination blades.

The saw-filing bench. Equipment shown here includes flat, triangular, cant and square files, swage (among files), setting hammer and anvil-and-stake (right). Conical stake accepts blades for various sizes of arbor, adjusts up and down, and moves along slot to position teeth over anvil.

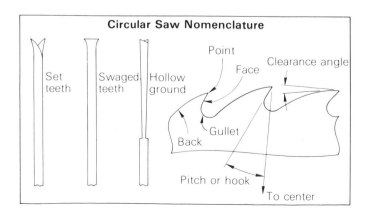

Circular Saw Nomenclature

Set teeth — Swaged teeth — Hollow ground — Point — Face — Clearance angle — Gullet — Back — Pitch or hook — To center

Circular saws are usually described by the type of cut they are designed to make, as crosscut, cutoff, rip, miter, dado, combination or planer. But to prevent binding in the wood, all circular saws are widest at the very rim. This clearance is obtained in one of three ways: setting, swaging or hollow grinding. Most common rip and crosscut saws are set, which means the tips of the teeth are alternately and uniformly bent to the right and left. Cutoff and ripsaws designed for use in green lumber are usually swaged, which means the point of each tooth is spread by hammering with a small anvil. Combination and planer saws are usually hollow-ground, which means the tips of the teeth are as thick as the hub of the saw, and the metal in between is ground thinner to provide clearance. When a new blade is purchased, it is wise to trace around it, or make a carbon-paper rubbing, to serve as a pattern later on.

There are four operations in sharpening all flat circular saws: jointing, gumming, setting or swaging, and filing sharp. To know when the saw is getting dull, watch the corners of the swage or set. They may seem sharp to the touch, but close examination will reveal a slight roundness, which will make the saw feed hard and not cut properly. Although the set seems full, the saw will bind just back of its points. The saw must be jointed below the rounded corners, and each tooth brought back to a nice, keen point.

A common error is allowing a saw blade to accumulate gum and pitch on the sides, which may cause it to run hot and snake. The best way to remove the gum is to soak the saw for a while in a strong warm solution of Oakite in water, and then rub it clean in a small box of sawdust. The gum will come right off, and the Oakite solution can be kept in a covered jar and used over and over. Never scrape off gum with a sharp tool because this will mar the finish and make the blade more susceptible to buildup.

Jointing

The first operation in sharpening by hand is jointing, to make all the cutting teeth the same height. If every tooth does not do the same amount of cutting, the unequal strain on the high teeth may cause cracks. If several teeth are unusually high, they may break off upon encountering a hard knot.

Professional saw-jointing equipment includes a powered grindstone mounted with a fixed center on which the blade can pivot. Lacking such a machine, the craftsman can joint

Eugene Roth is a foreman at Huther Bros. in Rochester, N.Y., once a leading manufacturer of circular saws and carbide-tipped blades. Huther still makes and repairs special-order saws, but most of the plant is now devoted to grinding flat and circular knives for the paper, plastic and cardboard industries. The hands in the photos belong to Eric Michaud, the only craftsman left in Huther's once-bustling filing room.

right on the table saw by using a flat vitrified medium jointer stone or a piece of broken emery wheel. The blade is reversed on the arbor and revolved at full speed, and the stone is lightly but firmly pressed against the points of the teeth. Lower the blade below the surface of the table, press the stone over the slot in the table, and slowly raise the blade. Raise it enough to grind a small shiny flat at the top of each tooth.

Gumming

Repeated filing is bound to make the teeth shallow, and grinding the gullets deeper is known as gumming, although a saw does not need to be gummed every time it is sharpened. A blade is gummed on a bench grinder with a grade 1-6 VL emery wheel, with its edge dressed round, or use an 8-in. or 10-in. round second-cut file. To keep the saw in balance, all the teeth should be gummed to the same depth. It is easy to make a simple wooden compass with a dowel center to fit the saw's arbor hole, as shown in the drawing on the next page. Use a colored pencil to mark a circle the proper distance below the points; the distance can be gauged from the tracing made when the saw was new. Then grind until the bottom of every gullet just touches the edge of the circle. Generally, gullet depth is two-fifths of the distance between the points of the teeth.

When gumming, go around the saw several times so as not to crowd the wheel by taking too deep a cut. Taking out too much metal at one time will heat the gullets and stretch the rim, and the saw will then need expert hammering on an anvil to restore its original tension. Crowding the wheel will also blue and burn the gullets, and often glaze the metal so hard that a file will not touch it. From these hard spots small cracks begin, at first invisible but gradually enlarging until they become dangerous fractures.

After gumming, the saw should be lightly jointed before continuing with the sharpening, to make sure it's still round.

Setting

A uniform, even set is most essential for an easy-running, smooth-cutting saw. An uneven set places a greater strain on some teeth and may crack them. Too much set not only puts an unneccessary strain on the rim of the saw, which can result in cracked gullets or broken teeth, but also causes it to chatter or vibrate, resulting in a rough cut. Vibration heats the rim and gullet cracks appear. If the teeth are set more to one side than to the other, the saw will lead to the side with the heavier set and may break.

There are two ways of setting teeth: with an anvil and stake, or with a saw set. The anvil and stake consists of an adjustable, conical center post that slides on iron ways to allow the edge of the blade to rest precisely over the beveled edge of a small anvil. Different anvils may be used, depending on the size of tooth and amount of set required. A special setting hammer, which has a small, flat face, is used to bend alternate teeth over the anvil. Then the blade is turned over and the process repeated.

A saw set bends the teeth by leverage rather than by pounding. It consists of a series of slots for different lengths and thicknesses of teeth, and is mounted on a handle with an adjustable gauge for regulating the amount of set. When placing the set on the tooth, permit it to drop until the point of the tooth touches the bottom of the slot, then bend the tooth over until the gauge touches the side of the saw.

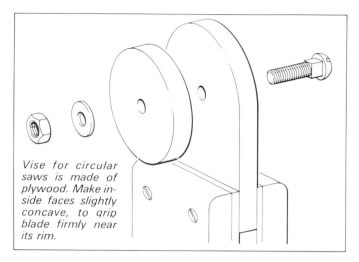

Vise for circular saws is made of plywood. Make inside faces slightly concave, to grip blade firmly near its rim.

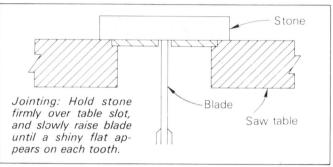

Jointing: Hold stone firmly over table slot, and slowly raise blade until a shiny flat appears on each tooth.

Thin, round-edge grinding wheel (left) is used to gum a saw blade. Balance is checked, right, by mounting blade on dummy arbor and rolling along parallel knife edges.

With anvil and stake, one sharp tap per tooth sets the saw.

57

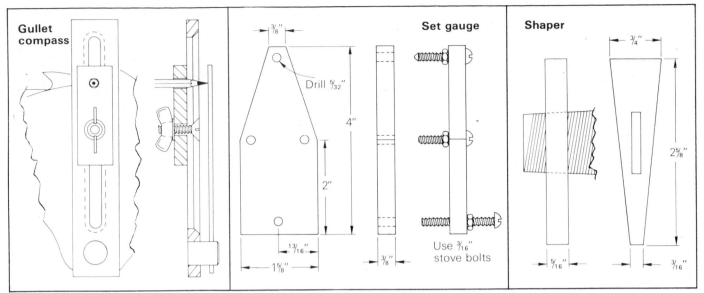

Gullet compass

Set gauge

Shaper

Drill ⁵/₃₂″

Use ³/₁₆″ stove bolts

Three saw-filing gauges. Adjustable compass, left, establishes uniform gullet depth for gumming. Set gauge, center, checks the set of each tooth. The top screw is first filed sharp, then the point is flat- *tened to about ³/₆₄-in. dia. Adjust the bottom screw to the desired set. Right, a shaper holds the file at the correct angle for regulating the set of swaged teeth. Its long side slides on the face of the blade.*

Swage, top, is placed on each tooth of ripsaw and tapped sharply to spread point. In close-up, left tooth has been spread with convex die, right tooth has then been squared with straight die.

Filing a crosscut saw: Both hands push the file in long, rhythmic strokes powered from the shoulder to ensure uniform teeth.

Since only the points of the teeth do the cutting, the set should not extend more than one-fourth of the distance down the tooth. If the set extends too far down the tooth, the blade will vibrate and cut roughly. The amount of set, as measured from the plane of the blade, varies according to the type of wood and the smoothness of cut desired. A fine set does fine work; dry hardwood requires less set than green hardwood, and softwood requires more set than hardwood. The amount of the set is always less than the thickness of the blade, and usually less than half the thickness. For dry hardwood, the set is usually .012 in. to .015 in.; for green hardwood, .015 in. to .018 in. Electric hand saws, because of the rough work they have to do, require a heavy set—around .02 in. or even more.

After determining which set works best for a particular type of cut, it is well to make a simple side gauge, as shown in the diagram, to check the set of each tooth.

Swaging

Swaging is spreading the point of every tooth. A swaged saw will cut more wood than a set saw because every tooth is cutting on both sides, and it will take a faster feed and more power. On the other hand, the cut is rough. Ripsaws for green lumber and production saws are generally swaged. Any type of saw may be swaged, although if the blade is too thin the swaged corners will be needle-pointed and fragile. If it is too thick so much pressure will be needed to spread the metal that it may crack.

Before swaging, joint, gum and file all teeth sharp, using an 8-in. or 10-in. mill bastard with two rounded edges. Swages, which are hand-held anvils with two dies set in the face, are sized according to the thickness of the saw blade. One of the dies is convex, one is flat. Use the convex die first and keep a drop of oil on it. Set the swage atop the point of the tooth and strike several light, quick blows with a small setting hammer. Keep the swage straight, so the die centers on the tooth. Then use the straight die to square up the cutting edge and give body to the swaged point.

Lightly file the sides of the teeth with a shaper, to even up the swage. A shaper can easily be made from a scrap of hard-

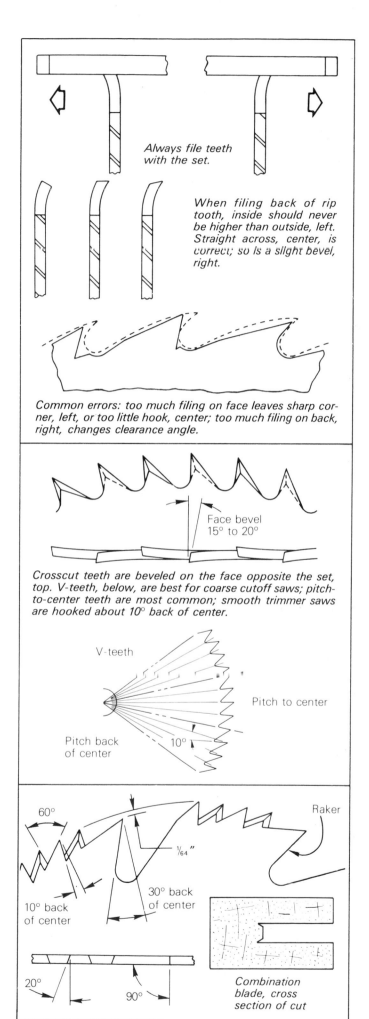

Always file teeth with the set.

When filing back of rip tooth, inside should never be higher than outside, left. Straight across, center, is correct; so is a slight bevel, right.

Common errors: too much filing on face leaves sharp corner, left, or too little hook, center; too much filing on back, right, changes clearance angle.

Face bevel 15° to 20°

Crosscut teeth are beveled on the face opposite the set, top. V-teeth, below, are best for coarse cutoff saws; pitch-to-center teeth are most common; smooth trimmer saws are hooked about 10° back of center.

V-teeth

Pitch to center

Pitch back of center   10°

60°

Raker

1/64"

10° back of center

30° back of center

20°   90°

Combination blade, cross section of cut

wood, as in the drawing. Its long side slides on the face of the blade, to guide the file at the proper angle. Use the set gauge to keep the swage uniform. Then file straight across the underside of the tooth and across the top, very lightly, with an 8-in. or 10-in. mill bastard. Be careful to maintain the original angle of the tooth and avoid dubbing off the swaged corners, as this will reduce side clearance and cause the saw to bind and burn in the cut. Finally, use a round 8-in. or 10-in. second-cut file to clean out the gullets.

Filing ripsaws

For a rip saw to cut fast and easily, the teeth should be hooked so that a line along the face passes halfway between the center of the saw and the rim (about 30° and known as ⅓ hook). When filing a ripsaw with set teeth, use an 8-in. or 10-in. mill bastard file, and maintain the original hook, shape and angle by taking the same amount off the back and front of the tooth. Usually the backs are filed straight across, though some prefer a slight bevel (about 5°). Too much bevel produces a lateral motion that causes the teeth to chatter and vibrate in the cut. When filing the backs, file every other tooth on one side all around the saw, with the set; then reverse the saw in the vise and file the other teeth, with the set. This is the only way to file the backs uniformly, either straight or with a slight bevel. The inside edges should never be higher than the outside ones.

Keep the gullets round with an 8-in. or 10-in. round second-cut file. Cracks are most often caused by sharp corners in the gullets.

Filing crosscut saws

Joint, gum and set the saw. For coarse-tooth cutoff saws use an 8-in. or 10-in. mill bastard with two rounded edges; for saws with a pitch of 5/16 in. to ⅜ in. use an 8-in. cant saw file; for pitch ¼ in. or finer use the cant saw file or a slim triangular file. The flat file used on large saws can sharpen only one face of a tooth at a time, but the cant saw file and triangular files catch the face of one tooth and the back of the next on each stroke. A face bevel in the 15° to 20° range is usually recommended for hardwoods. A somewhat longer bevel is sometimes used in softwoods, and a slightly shorter bevel in very hard woods. Most cutoff saws are made with pitch-to-center teeth and some are pitched slightly back of center, while others have V-shaped teeth. Try to keep the gullets round.

Planer saws

Planer saws are hollow-ground, and are designed for precise, smooth cuts both with and across the grain. Their teeth are in groups of three to six crosscut-type cutting spurs, followed by a deep gullet and a rip-type raker tooth. The raker is sharpened flat across the back, 1/64 in. lower than the cutting spurs. The spurs sever the wood fibers on each side of the kerf, then the raker comes along and cleans out the core of the cut. Flat-ground novelty and combination saws cut in essentially the same way, and it is particularly important with all saws of this type to make an accurate template when the saw is new, as a guide for sharpening.

To file a planer saw, you should have a special raker gauge to keep the rakers a uniform 1/64 in. lower than the spurs. Without such a gauge, joint the blade on the circular saw, then take the rakers down by filing the same number of strokes square across the back of each. Then file the spurs

All the spurs in a group on a dado blade, left, are alike. In blade blank above, right gullet is typical, left is correct.

with a 20° face bevel, maintaining the original hook (usually 10°), using the 8-in. cant saw file or the square mill file.

A block of hardwood can be used as a gauge to keep the raker teeth uniform. After jointing, leave the blade on the saw arbor and adjust the height until it can be locked by jamming a piece of plywood into a gullet and clamping the plywood to the saw table. The top raker should be very close to parallel to the table surface—adjust the height until it is parallel. Now make a block a fat sixty-fourth lower than the back of the raker, and rest the mill file on it to shape the tooth. Moving the plywood stop to the next gullet should index the next tooth, and so on around the blade.

Dado heads

First, joint the entire dado head, including all the inside cutters. File the spurs on the outside saws with a 10-in. square mill file, keeping the original bevels and stopping when the teeth just come to a sharp point. Then file the rakers and inside cutters across the top until the flat left by jointing is just gone, and finally take the same number of strokes on each raker and inside cutter. As with planer saws, the rakers and inside cutters should finish about 1/64 in. lower than the spurs, but the precise amount is not nearly so important as uniformity—use the whole length of the file on each stroke, and follow through from the shoulder. Do not touch the face of these teeth except to remove the burr left when the tops are filed.

Saw manufacturers and repair shops commonly joint all the spurs just enough to remove the dull points, then set the stop on their machine 1/64 in. deeper. They joint all the rakers and inside cutters just enough to remove those joint marks. After repeated sharpenings, it becomes necessary to gum the saw and reset the spur sections.

The spur sections of most dado heads manufactured for the home craftsman are ground straight across, with no face bevel. They will cut much better if all the spurs in a group between a pair of rakers are beveled about 20° one way, and all the spurs in the next group are beveled the same amount on the other side. Use the square file at a steep angle (about 30°) to the face of the blade, and be careful to keep all the teeth the same length. □

Sources of supply

Saw-filing tools are usually sold by large hardware stores and industrial hardware suppliers. For mail order, consult the catalogs of Woodcraft Supply Corp., 313 Montvale Ave., Woburn, Mass. 01801 and Silvo Hardware, 107-109 Walnut St., Philadelphia, Pa. 19106. Brands to look for are Nicholson (files), Disston (setting tools) and Simonds (all saw tools).

Methods of Work

Making chisels

One source of steel for making special tools is the local junkyard. High-carbon steel can be found in auto leaf springs, spring-tooth harrows, bed rails and many other things. You can determine the type of steel, or at least its relative hardness, by trial and error with a file or a hacksaw: If you can cut it or mark it with relative ease, then it is not what you want.

I needed several mortising chisels, and old bed rails lent themselves to this type of tool. Bed rails are usually 1/8 in. thick and 1½ in. across the right-angle flats. The rails can be cut with a hacksaw, but you will use a lot of blades. They are easy to cut if you first remove the temper by heating with a propane torch wherever you wish to cut.

First I laid out the design for the tang and sides of the blade, then I roughly cut out the blank with a hacksaw. I finished shaping the tool with a bastard and second-cut file, leaving the cutting edge until after the handle was driven onto the tang. The handle can be bought or turned on a lathe, or shaped by hand. To keep the wood from splitting, I used ½-in. thin-walled electrical conduit for the ferrules, and a

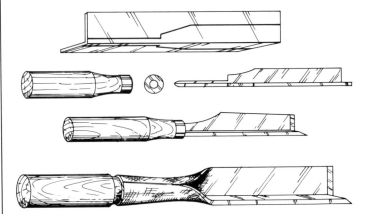

common washer on the shoulders of the tang. I predrilled the hole and drove the handle onto the tang. Then I filed the cutting edge to shape and tempered it.

My method of tempering the cutting edge is adapted from a technique I learned from an old blacksmith. First heat the metal to cherry red, place the tip in cold water for a few seconds, then file across the beveled cutting edge until a straw color appears. Then immediately and completely immerse the metal in cold water. You will have to use trial and error to get the right hardness. The propane torch is not hot enough to temper a complete cross section of bed rail.

When a furnace or an acetylene torch is available, you can make larger tools such as socket chisels and mortising chisels from bed rails and auto leaf springs. I use a tapered pin in a machinist's vise as a form for the socket. By hammering and reheating it is possible to form the socket around the pin. Then I turn handles of hickory wood to fit the socket. First drive the handle into the socket, then shape the cutting edge on a grinder and with files. Finish by tempering and polishing. —*Lester E. Rishel, Bellefonte, Pa.*

Ball-bearing collars

My wood shaper has a ½-in. dia. spindle. In using spacer thrust collars for irregular edge molding, I found that the edge of the wood gets burned from the friction of the collars.

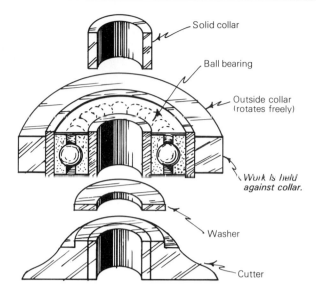

Solid collar

Ball bearing

Outside collar (rotates freely)

Work is held against collar.

Washer

Cutter

I purchased about a dozen ½-in. I.D. x 1⅛-in. O.D. sealed ball bearings, ⅜ in. thick. Next, I machined collars to half a thousandth under the outside diameter of the bearings. The O.D. of the collars were in steps of 1/16 in., starting from 1¼ in. (the collars are thinner than the bearings). Next, I pressed a bearing into each collar, using the vise to keep the surfaces parallel.

It is important to use a solid collar that matches the inner ring of the ball bearing above and below the assembly, so that when the shaper nut is tightened the tension will be only on the inner ring—the outside will float. When the wood is pressed against the outside of the assembled collar, the outside perimeter stops rotating and only the spindle with its bearing rotates. I have used a small, thin washer on each side of the bearing, which permits the same freedom of movement.
—*George P. Calderwood, Long Beach, Calif.*

Sharpening setup

I have assembled a jackshaft on two sleeve pillow bearings. The shaft diameter is ⅝ in., except for the extreme end, where it is reduced to ½ in. and rests in a ½-in. pillow block bearing. To the inside position of the bearing the shaft is threaded for a ⅝-in. thrust nut, a stop collar at the opposite end of the shaft (inside the other bearing) and between the two are spacer sleeves and thrust or side plates for as many grinder or leather wheels as one wishes.

The shaft is driven by a ⅓-HP motor rotating backwards, or

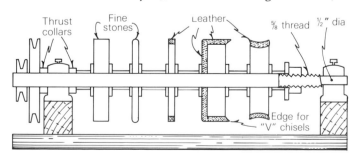

Thrust collars

Fine stones

Leather

⅝ thread   ½" dia

Edge for "V" chisels

away from you, and has two step pulleys, one for grinding speed and the smaller pulley (driving) for honing my woodcarving or regular chisels. I made the discs of hardwood and covered their sides and periphery with leather.
—*George P. Calderwood, Long Beach, Calif.*

Knife profile patterns

Because shaper knives and hand planes cut at an angle, a molding profile cannot be directly traced onto a blank and ground to shape. The method I will describe here will help you make a blade that will reproduce a desired molding pattern. First, determine the angle a of the knife as it cuts (either

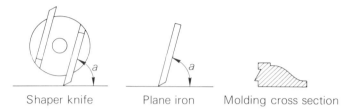

Shaper knife   Plane iron   Molding cross section

in a shaper or a hand plane). Then draw a cross section of the molding shape. To this sketch add the outline of the knife as it cuts the wood. Then draw a folding line and a side view of the knife at angle a and at its true length. Now add another folding line parallel to the knife length, and beyond it draw a knife blank. Extend

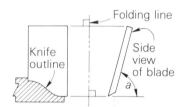

Folding line

Knife outline

Side view of blade

construction lines from several points on the molding profile, through the first folding line at 90°, to the edge of

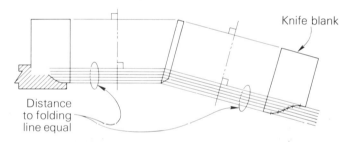

Knife blank

Distance to folding line equal

the knife length. It is possible to construct a template the actual shape and size of the knife you want to make by measuring with dividers from the first folding line back to the construction line intersection points on the molding outline, then transferring these measurements from the second folding line to the knife blank. All construction lines must pass through the folding lines at 90°.
—*Rod Davidson, Port Angeles, Wash.*

Triangle tip 1

An architect's 45° triangle is inexpensive and handy around the shop. Attach a ½-in. x ½-in. strip of walnut along the hypotenuse with No. 2 R.H. brass wood screws to make a miter square. Take care not to cut into the edge of the triangle when you scribe with a metal instrument.
—*Dwight G. Gorrell, Centerville, Kans.*

Triangle tip 2

An inexpensive but accurate plastic drafting triangle gives a perfect 45° setting on the table saw. A long wood face on the fence with sandpaper attached prevents slippage and further improves accuracy. For a perfect 90° setting on the saw gauge, turn it over, push it against the back of the saw table, and tighten.
—*Jim Richey, Houston, Tex.*

End-Boring Jig

Horizontal crossfeed makes drill press more versatile

by Steve Voorheis

The floor-model drill press is one of the most versatile machines in the small woodshop. A major limitation, however, is its lack of provision for quick and easy end-boring operations. The horizontal crossfeed end-boring jig described here is an effective means of converting a tilting-table drill press into an end-boring machine that will handle workpieces up to 38 in. long. In addition to quick conversion time, the crossfeed action facilitates boring multiple holes without removing the work from the jig and without making multiple setups. Further, the jig may be used horizontally for various housing and routing operations.

The mechanics are simple: The stationary housing mounts to the table of the drill press. Enclosed in the housing is the lead screw/traveler block assembly. Rotation of the lead screw results in the transverse motion of the traveler block, which is fastened to, and in turn moves, the crossfeed table. As the crossfeed table travels horizontally, it is guided and held in the same plane by steel keys in wooden keyways.

The fence is mounted to the crossfeed table so that fine vertical adjustments may be made with the entire jig mounted on the drill press. Finally, there is an adjustable work-stop for rapid setup and repeat operations.

After the cutting list is completed, mount the female collar of the lead screw into the traveler block. Locate the hole for the collar by measuring in from the surface of the traveler block that will mate with the crossfeed table, the same distance that the lead-screw pilot hole is in from the corresponding edge of the housing. This ensures that the axis of the lead screw will be parallel with the crossfeed table, thus preventing binding and stiffness. Mark the vertical center line on the traveler for future reference.

The end grain of the keyways and keyway blocks should be sealed with a coat of varnish before assembly, to minimize future instability. After sealing, work ⅛-in. by 5/16-in. grooves into the keyways and the keyway blocks. To ensure a proper fit, all these grooves should be located and worked relative to the edges that will face the inside of the crossfeed table.

Begin by gluing one vertical member to the back panel, carefully maintaining alignment. In the same manner, install the two horizontal keyways, making sure that the surfaces from which the keyways were worked are facing away from the back panel. Install the second vertical member, in which the lead-screw pilot hole has been drilled. Again, make sure that the correct face is towards the back panel.

Accuracy is particularly important for smooth operation. Take care to ensure squareness and parallelism. Once the glue is set, true one of the vertical edges on the jointer. Working from this edge, rip the other edge parallel. Trimming the keyed ends of the housing parallel to each other is the most critical operation. By using the table saw and a simple crosscutting "cradle," this can be reliably done. Trim one end of the housing and then rotate the work 180° in the horizontal plane to make the second trim cut parallel to the first. Clean up these ends with very light passes on the jointer.

To assemble the crossfeed table, first install steel keys in the keyways of the stationary housing. Position the keyway blocks over the keys in operating position and insert newsprint shims between the mating surfaces on either side of the keys. With keyways and shims clamped firmly to the stationary housing, mount the crossfeed table to the movable

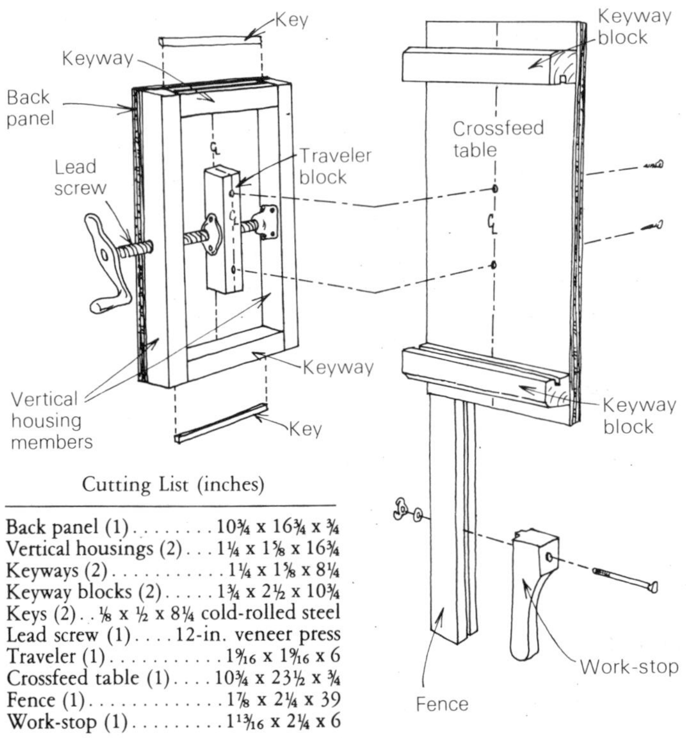

Cutting List (inches)

Back panel (1)	10¾ x 16¾ x ¾
Vertical housings (2)	1¼ x 1⅝ x 16¾
Keyways (2)	1¼ x 1⅝ x 8¼
Keyway blocks (2)	1¾ x 2½ x 10¾
Keys (2)	⅛ x ½ x 8¼ cold-rolled steel
Lead screw (1)	12-in. veneer press
Traveler (1)	1 9/16 x 1 9/16 x 6
Crossfeed table (1)	10¾ x 23½ x ¾
Fence (1)	1⅞ x 2¼ x 39
Work-stop (1)	1 13/16 x 2¼ x 6

Use any hard, dense wood, such as maple, and birch ply for the table.

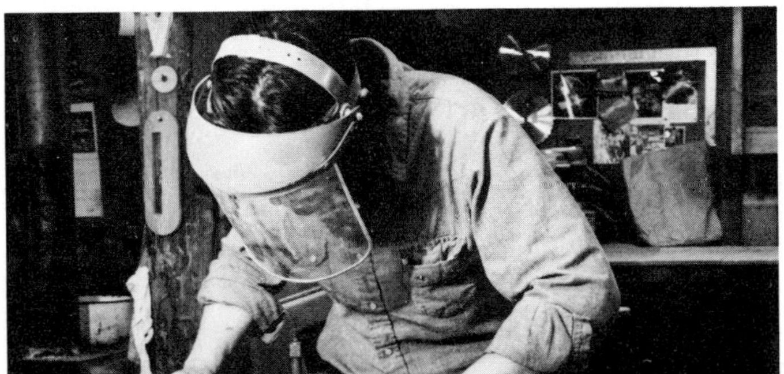

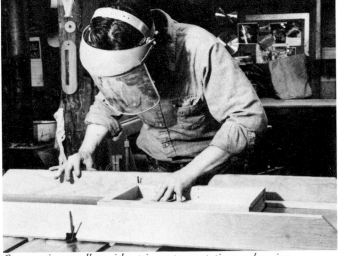

Crosscutting cradle guides trim cuts on stationary housing.

Jig facilitates end-boring (above) and routing (right). Top right, jig hooks over table edge and can be bolted through center hole of drill-press table.

keyway blocks with woodscrews and glue. Before final screwing and gluing however, it would be wise to test the crossfeed action. Alternately clamp the crossfeed table to the keyway blocks and then release the original clamps. Remove the shim material to assess the sliding action and adjust as necessary.

Insert the lead screw through the pilot hole in the housing, thread it through the female collar mounted in the traveler block and finally into the mounting base, where it is secured with a retainer screw. If the jig is built exactly as described here, it will be necessary to drill an access hole in the back panel behind the mounting base to lock the retainer screw, because there will not be enough clearance below the crossfeed table. Move the traveler block along the screw all the way in one direction and then project the vertical center-line of the traveler block down onto the back panel of the housing. Move the traveler to its other extremity and project the center-line onto the back as before. Halfway between these two points is the mid-travel position for the traveler block.

With the block at mid-travel position, transfer the traveler-block mounting screw hole locations to the outside of the crossfeed table. Re-install the crossfeed table centered on the stationary housing with the steel keys in place; attach the table to the traveler using screws only, to facilitate disassembly. Mount the fence assembly to the table with hanger bolts and wing nuts. Slightly oversized holes for the hanger bolts will permit fine vertical adjustment, for perfect alignment of the fence with the vertical axis of the drill press.

A wooden bracket attached to the back of the jig hooks over the edge of the vertical drill-press table to hold the jig in place. For extra stability during high-speed routing, add a hanger bolt, wing nut and a large wooden washer, which can be secured through the center hole of the drill table.

A stop collar may be installed on the drill-press column at the height at which the jig will most frequently be used. Then the table need only be tilted and dropped to the collar and the jig put in place. The collar also allows the jig to swing through an arc under the spindle as well as travel in and out on the screw, covering a range of positions. □

Steve Voorheis, 35, designs and builds furniture in Montana.

Scale Models
Plywood mockup illuminates design

by Bob Trotman

Because even the best drawings offer only an approximate idea of how a piece of furniture will look in three dimensions, it is often desirable to build a model. The models I make are not intended to be fine miniatures, but are built as quickly and easily as possible to see what an idea will look like. It is obviously much easier to make changes in design and proportions at this stage than when the full-scale work is underway.

Working from my sketchbook, I draw out the side view of the design in ¼ scale on graph paper, and then transfer it with carbon paper to posterboard (optional) and then to plywood. In ¼ scale, ½-in. plywood will represent 8/4 lumber, and ¼ in. is close enough to 5/4 lumber. Internal openings may be cut on the band saw (if you don't have a jigsaw) simply by cutting through at a convenient place, then gluing and doweling the cut back together. White pine is suitable for solid members such as stretchers, since it is fine-grained and easily worked. Cushions may be made of wood covered with cloth. □

Bob Trotman, 30, of Casar, N.C., is a professional woodworker.

Finished model of dining chair has fabric-covered wooden seat.

Basic Machine Maintenance
Regular cleaning and lubrication are essential

by David Troe

Many people mistakenly expect machines to work perfectly from the time they are unwrapped and think they will last forever with no attention, but the life and accuracy of machines are directly proportional to the amount of care they receive. Thoughtful attention and simple preventative maintenance will ensure accuracy, minimize the need for major repairs and increase resale value.

Woodworkers generally don't maintain their equipment as well as they should, and they often don't understand the relationship between various mechanical components of their machinery. Unlike some furniture these days, machines are designed logically—there is a reason why the components are where they are, and they are all there for some reason. Obviously not all equipment is assembled correctly by the manufacturer, but far more damage is done by unobservant protomechanics who fail to recognize the interrelationships of things. If you don't have an exploded assembly drawing of your equipment, try and get one from the manufacturer, or if your machine is an antique, see if a machinery distributor in your area has one on file that you could copy. Assembly drawings are excellent, but often not detailed enough. When you are pulling something apart, if there is any question in your mind about how it goes back together, label the parts, make sketches or take photographs. But before doing any cleaning or repairs, turn off the power or unplug the machine.

Most repairs are not outside the capability of woodworkers. Most of the tools will already be in the shop: screwdrivers, wrenches, pliers and the like. Unlike automobile repair, extremely few specialized tools are necessary. If you should encounter a situation requiring tools that you do not have, do not attempt to use a substitute that might damage the part. Pliers won't replace wrenches, nor will a cold chisel substitute for a spanner wrench. If you cannot completely disassemble a component for repair or replacement, do as much as you can and then take it to a competent mechanic. This will save the mechanic time, thereby saving you money. Ideally you should take the work to a machinery distributor with repair facilities or to the manufacturer's service center, but that is rarely practical. If the job requires more tools, skill or confidence than you possess, it can often be handled by a jack-of-all-trades machine shop, or even by a garage. If the equipment is still under warranty, it will be voided if anyone other than those authorized by the manufacturer works on it.

The regularity with which maintenance should take place depends on how much use the equipment gets. Follow manufacturer's recommendations and establish your own schedule. Unless you suspect a serious problem, such as a new noise or vibration, the only regular maintenance required is to keep your equipment clean, to keep it lubricated, to check for loose parts and wear, and to check the motor and the power transmission system. Do this at least once a week in a commercial shop, once a month in a one-person shop, and every six to twelve months in a hobbyist shop.

The first rule is to keep your equipment clean. Dust and dirt will accumulate in even the smallest and least accessible places. At the least, brush off your equipment, or better yet, use a vacuum cleaner. Compressed air is effective in blowing out dust from inaccessible areas but caution must be exercised to avoid driving the dust into other components. For this reason a maximum line pressure of 40 psi is suggested. However romantic sawdust and chips scattered around the shop may be, they are harmful both to you and to your equipment. Dust sticking to machine surfaces causes many problems: excessive wear; drying out and premature failure of bearings and ways; sticking of gears, trunnions and all sliding surfaces; *V*-belt and band-saw tire deterioration. All lead to extensive down-time if the situation gets out of hand. Also, accumulated dust is a very real fire hazard, especially in electrical switches and motors. Clean your equipment and your shop regularly and often.

Lubricate your equipment when and where necessary. Remember that excessive lubrication is at least as harmful as under-lubrication. Over-lubrication in bearings causes the lubricant to churn and heat up, which can lead to early failure. Exposed grease and oils collect dust and chips like a sponge, eventually turning into a gummy blob that restricts free rotation and easy movement. It is safer to under-lubricate frequently than to over-lubricate infrequently.

It is difficult to recommend a lubricant if there are no guidelines from the manufacturer or the distributor, but the following suggestions can be assumed to be safe. For bearings that have oil fittings, use SAE 10 to 20 nondetergent machine oil. The SAE rating refers to viscosity, not to motor oil, which should not be used. For bearings that have grease fittings, use a lithium-soda type bearing grease, NLGI (National Lubricating Grease Institute) Grade 2. Do not oil a bearing designed for grease, and do not grease a bearing designed for oil. For gearboxes, use SAE 90 to 140 gear oil. And on drill-press quill and pinion gears, try SAE 40 oil.

As a general rule, use dry lubricants on any moving part that is not subject to high speeds or where movement is for adjustment, such as on tabletops, dovetail ways, jackscrews, trunnions, fences, miter-gauge slots, tailstock spindles and the like. Wherever possible, use dry lubricants such as hard wax or graphite. Avoid silicone or Teflon-based sprays—they are extremely expensive and adversely affect wood glues and finishes. My favorite is plain old hard wax, which is inexpensive, easy to apply, and as far as anyone knows doesn't cause cancer or affect the ozone in the atmosphere. Wax provides longer service on cast-iron surfaces because it fills up the microscopic pores in the iron. You can use any paste wax or

David Troe, 25, a cabinetmaker, is director of product development at Mason & Sullivan, Osterville, Mass.

liquid wax that does not contain cleaners, because the abrasive action of cleaners would cause lapping and excessive wear. Rub in the wax well and remove any excess.

Another way to lubricate surfaces upon which wood must slide is to apply a Teflon-impregnated tape or adhesive-backed sheet. Thoroughly clean the surfaces with a grease solvent to ensure a strong bond, and extend the Teflon over any edges where it might catch on a piece of wood. The covering need not be solid—several strips of tape running parallel to the direction of feed and spanning the wood are often adequate. Planer beds, saw tables and fences are good candidates for this treatment. Look in the Yellow Pages under "Plastics" for a specialty supply house.

When lubricating with grease or oil, make sure that both the lubricants and the fittings are clean. Often oil cups and grease nipples are coated with gummy sawdust, which must be cleaned before lubricating. Oil levels are generally set by visible marks on oil cups or by the saturation of fiber wicks, but grease levels are more difficult to ascertain. Do not overlubricate. Common sense is essential in determining the correct amount of lubricant to use. Never force grease into a bearing and its housing more than half full.

Bearings

Bearings cause woodworkers the most confusion and grief. Different kinds of bearings require different treatments. Sleeve bearings, usually oil-impregnated metal but sometimes plastic, rely on a very thin lubricating film to reduce sliding friction. It is interesting to note that sleeve bearings are used both in inexpensive applications and in situations where precision is a prime requirement: at one end the lowly $9.95 drill and at the other end a metal-machining spindle costing many thousands of dollars. The difference is in the materials used, the precision with which they are made, and the complexity of the bearing lubrication system. Before modern metal-hardening technology and precision machin-

ing, which made the manufacture of ball bearings feasible, all bearings were of the sleeve type. That is why Babbitt bearings are so often found on old machines. Sleeve bearings are either full or split, and worn ones are relatively easy to replace by pushing them out of their housings. Press evenly on the rim of sleeve bearings when replacing and be careful not to roll an edge or raise any burrs. Babbitt bearings can be repoured, but this should only be attempted by someone who knows how to do it properly—it is hazardous.

Antifriction bearings are bearings in which rolling members reduce friction. These bearings fall into four categories: ball bearings, roller bearings, tapered roller bearings and needle bearings. Ball bearings are the most frequently used. Needle bearings, because of their smaller size, are used in portable power tools. Tapered roller bearings, because of their inherently high-thrust load capacity, are used in some high-quality portable drills and in lathe headstocks. Many machines have bearings that are said to be "lubricated for life" or "sealed for life," but this refers to the life of the bearing itself and not to the life of the machine or to the life of the owner. The life of a bearing can be quite short if it is improperly handled during installation, or quite long if treated with care. Sealed bearings are so named because they have a shield that seals the lubricant in and the dirt out—at least that's the theory. Care must be exercised not to damage the seals in any way. Sealed bearings can be relubricated by prying out the seal, cleaning the bearing, relubricating and replacing the seals, but this requires a bit of expertise to avoid damaging the seal so I can suggest it only to those who have patience, confidence and the skill to be gentle. For the general lot of us, when a sealed bearing needs lubrication (you'll know by stickiness, roughness or strange noises), it must be thrown out and replaced with a new one.

While most people can replace bearings, care must be exercised not to damage either the bearing or its housing. Any pressure above that which you can supply with your fingers

Rolling members reduce friction in antifriction bearings. Clockwise from above, tapered roller, needle, roller, ball bearing.

Pressing bearings

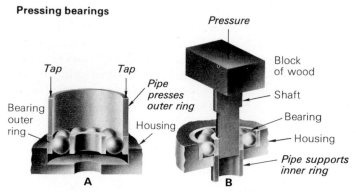

When removing or replacing a bearing, apply pressure to the ring that is fixed to the shaft or set in the housing, never to both rings at once. To replace a bearing in a housing (A), a pipe the diameter of the outer ring will distribute the force of the tapping evenly over the ring. When the shaft is then set in (B), a pipe supporting the inner ring will prevent distortion of the bearing.

V-belts

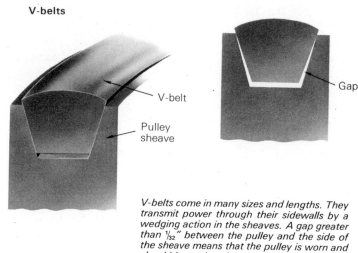

V-belts come in many sizes and lengths. They transmit power through their sidewalls by a wedging action in the sheaves. A gap greater than ¹⁄₃₂″ between the pulley and the side of the sheave means that the pulley is worn and should be replaced.

must be evenly applied to either the inner or the outer ring, never to both at the same time and never between the rings. If you don't have a section of pipe, a socket wrench or other suitable cylinder of the right size, you can turn a wooden one on a lathe, but if you are replacing the lathe bearing, you are up the proverbial creek. An uneven force on the bearing can dent the bearing races and/or ruin the trueness of the housing. Don't try to free a stuck bearing from both the shaft and the housing at the same time. If the bearing is tight, try spritzing some penetrating oil around the ring. Or heat the housing to about 250° F—the expansion will usually do the trick. If that doesn't work, the bearing can be removed with a gear puller, but that always ruins the bearing and it then must be replaced. If in doubt, take it to a good repairman.

Manufacturers use standard "in stock" bearings whenever possible to reduce costs. Because stock bearing dimensions have long been standardized, a bearing from one manufacturer can replace a bearing of the same series from any other manufacturer. All a supplier needs to know is the bearing identification number, which is etched on the side of the bearing. Tapered roller bearings have two numbers you must know—one on the cup and one on the cone. If you can't find an identification number, measure the outside and inside diameters and the width, get the speed (rpm) and phone a bearing distributor. Check in the Yellow Pages under "Bearings." You will save money by dealing with a bearing-supply firm rather than with the machine manufacturer.

When replacing a bearing, follow the reverse order from that used to remove it. Sometimes bearings are not symmetrical, so be sure to replace it in the same orientation as the original. Keep the bearing wrapped until you install it.

Neither ring on a bearing should fit so loosely as to allow it to rotate independently of its assembly. If the rings are loose, they can be temporarily fitted with an anaerobic sealant, such as Loctite. This delays the necessity of replacing the worn component. Heating to about 350° will soften the Loctite when you want to remove the bearing. Clean off all foreign material from the spindle and the housing before replacing a bearing to prevent scoring them.

Open or unshielded bearings should be cleaned once a year or as your specific situation requires. Some bearings can be cleaned while in place, but usually a more complete job will be had if the bearings are removed from their components. Never use water to clean a bearing: Wash out all the old lu-

bricant in clean kerosene, degreasing fluid or other commercial solvent, and rinse with fresh, clean solvent. An old soft toothbrush is excellent for scrubbing the parts. After cleaning, allow the bearing to dry dust-free by wrapping it in a clean lint-free cloth. As soon as the bearing is dry, rinse it in a bath of clean, light mineral oil. Until you are ready to replace it, protect it from contamination by putting it in a plastic bag. Never spin a dry bearing, and never use compressed air to dry or spin a bearing. Check the cleaned bearing for any sign of wear or damage, and replace if necessary. When you are ready to replace a grease bearing in the machine, grease the rolling elements by squeezing the correct grade of grease into the bearing with your clean fingers. The housing and the bearing should be packed no more than half full with grease. Check all bearings for adequate lubrication before running.

Unless otherwise stated by the manufacturer, lubricate the components at rest. This is especially true with electric motors, where stray oil can splash into the windings and harm the insulation. More detailed guidelines can be found in the references cited at the end of this article.

Belts, pulleys and chains

If you are experiencing vibration or a loss of power at the cutter, the problem is most likely in the power transmission system. V-belts are the most common means of transmitting power from a motor to a cutter. V-belts transmit power through their sidewalls by a wedging action in a pulley sheave. They are manufactured in standard cross-sectional sizes. It is imperative to replace belts with ones of the same series, because the different series are not interchangeable. V-belts are marked as to their series and length, but sometimes the marking wears off. Some parts lists state what series and length belt to use, though more typically they give only a replacement-part number. If the belt is old and you have no idea what to replace it with, a power-transmission supply house will be able to figure it out. Since there is some latitude in the length tolerances allowed in the construction of belts, it is essential, when replacing a belt in a multiple-belt drive, to replace all the belts, and to replace them only with a matched set of belts guaranteed to be of the same length.

If you have a machine with no belts on it, or if you are replacing a leather-belt drive system with V-belts (which there isn't really any reason to do), you can approximate the proper belt length by adding twice the distance between the centers of the shafts to half the sum of the circumferences of the two pulleys. Or wrap a steel tape around the pulley rims and give the supplier this measurement. Fractional-hp drives use the outside distance around the pulleys for belt length. Multiple-belt or heavy-duty drives use the pitch diameter. When this yields a nonstandard length, go to the next longest belt and adjust the components for proper tension.

Proper tensioning is important for both maximum power transmission and maximum life of the components. Excessive tension stretches the belts, causes heat buildup that accelerates deterioration and places unnecessary strain on the bearings, leading to premature bearing failure. Insufficient tension results in belt slippage, loss of power, vibration, whip, excessive noise and accelerated wear of the belt and pulley sheaves. Belt tensioning is a matter of feel. One method is to strike the belt with your fist—if it feels dead, it is slack. A properly tensioned belt will feel alive and vibrate. On multiple-belt drives, if you can push down on one belt so that its top face is flush with the bottom face of an adjacent belt using moderate pressure (10 lb.), then the belts are properly tensioned. Ideally belts should flex about ½2 in. for every inch of span between the centers of the driving and driven pulleys.

Old belts wear pulleys more severely than belts in good condition, so it is advisable to replace belts that are worn, frayed, cracked or split. Time and money are not saved by trying to get additional service from a worn belt. Dirty belts can be washed with soap and water. Rinse thoroughly and dry completely before replacing.

Flat-belt drive systems are found on old equipment—the trusty old leather belt—or on equipment that is run at very high speeds such as industrial overarm routers and portable power planes, both of which use a belt of synthetic rubber. Only leather belts should be treated with a belt dressing at three to six-month intervals. This dressing keeps the leather reasonably supple and improves the transmission of power. Replacement belts are available from belting suppliers and, if possible, should be purchased already spliced into an endless loop. Splicing a leather belt on a machine is difficult for the inexperienced. If you insist on doing it yourself, go to the library and read all you can about the various techniques.

The greatest problem of belt drives is misalignment of the driving and driven pulleys. Proper alignment is essential to realize maximum power, and the longest possible pulley, belt and bearing life. Angular and axial misalignment and loose pulleys all place unnecessary strain on the drive system. Use a straightedge to line up your pulleys and make sure they are secure on their shafts. If the pulley appears to wobble on its shaft, either the shaft is bent and must be straightened or replaced or the bore of the pulley is worn oversize and the pulley must be replaced. Do not try to shim an oversize pulley bore as it is almost impossible to control the concentricity of the pulley. Pulleys should also be replaced when the sides of the sheave have worn to the point where there is a gap of ½2 in. or greater on either side. The belt must not touch the bottom of the pulley sheave.

Pulleys are almost always "keyed" to their shafts, most

Misalignment

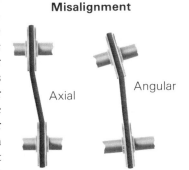

Axial

Angular

commonly with a short piece of square keystock but sometimes with what is called a Woodruff key. Replace missing keys with the same size keystock (available at all hardware stores) and don't rig a temporary replacement out of nails. When so provided, tighten the pulley setscrew(s) but be careful not to overtighten—it is easy to strip the threads in pulleys, rendering them useless. Unless you are an engineer or a mechanic, replace worn pulleys with ones of the same size. Any variation in size from the original will affect the speed at which the equipment runs.

The same general suggestions regarding alignment, tension and cleanliness apply to variable-speed belt drives. Since these are relatively new, it should be possible to contact the drive manufacturer to get lubrication recommendations. Remember that in drives of this type it is important to change speeds only when the equipment is running, so as not to damage either the belt or the pulleys.

Roller chains transmit large amounts of torque at low speeds and that is why they are often found in the feed-drive mechanisms of thicknessers. The same general suggestions concerning belts apply to chain drives, except that chains must be lubricated to operate freely. Keep the chain taut but not tight if you can adjust it. Make sure the links are free and not sticking to each other, and that the chains are reasonably clean. Since grease attracts dust, I prefer to use a dry lubricant on chains, but this also means that the chains must be lubricated more often. Roller chains, just like their bicycle-chain cousins, usually have a removable master link that allows the chain to be taken off for thorough cleaning or replacement. Chains can be cleaned with kerosene or other degreasing solvent, in much the same manner as bearings. Replace chains that show signs of rust. When the chain is off, check the sprocket teeth for wear. If they are worn, or if one side of the chain is riding on one side of the teeth, most likely the sprockets are not properly aligned. In any case, replace worn sprockets and chains.

Unless you are familiar with electric motors, do not attempt to do anything to them other than to keep them clean and, if fittings are provided, to keep them lubricated. Dust should be frequently cleaned out of motors, electrical junction boxes and electrical switches to minimize the hazard of fire. Repair or replace electric cords that are cut, cracked or abraded. Always make sure that the power is cut off when you are working around electrical equipment.

Regular maintenance need not take a great deal of time, but should be thorough and comprehensive. A little time invested on a regular basis will minimize major repairs and lost time by catching problems before they become serious.   □

Further reading

Some useful shop maintenance references:

Power Tool Maintenance by Daniel Irvin (McGraw-Hill, Inc., 1221 Ave. of the Americas, New York, N.Y. 10036, 1971).

Machinery's Handbook by Erik Oberg and Franklin D. Jones (Industrial Press, Inc., 200 Madison Ave., New York, N.Y. 10016; 20th Edition 1976).

Millwrights and Mechanics Guide (Theodore Audel & Co., distributed by Bobbs-Merrill, 4300 W. 62nd St., Indianapolis, Ind. 46206, 1975).

Selecting and Using Electric Motors by L. H. Soderholm and H.B. Puckett (U.S. Government Printing Office, Farmer's Bulletin No. 2257, 1974).

Woodshop Tool Maintenance by Beryl M. Cunningham and William F. Holtrup (Chas. A. Bennett Co., Inc., 809 W. Detweiller Dr., Peoria, Ill. 61614, 1974).

CABINETMAKING

Preparation of Stock

The essential first step is obtaining a true face side

by Ian Kirby

A face side and a face edge are true reference surfaces from which accurate measurements may be taken. Proper preparation of a face side and from it a face edge are essential preparatory steps in woodworking. If this part of the job is not done correctly, one is bound to get into serious difficulties in all subsequent operations.

Preparing a face side that is flat in width, flat in length and out of winding is analogous to pegging out the site on which a house is to be built. If this first step is taken lightly and not accurately carried out, the errors compound at every building stage. No amount of connivance will prevent difficulties from arising at every turn. Yet of all the processes in woodworking, preparation of stock is often woefully done and frequently receives only perfunctory attention. Basic woodworking books do cover the process, and it seems strange to me that in teaching, the case for it must be constantly restated. I find that even quite experienced woodworkers need to be reminded of the procedures to follow. Preparation is so elementary that people seem to treat it with contempt, saving their energies for more interesting operations.

General approach

I shall discuss the general principles and requirements of preparation before going on to the specifics of obtaining true reference faces. It's always unwise to approach woodworking procedures in an ad-hoc manner because in the main there is a sequential logic to them. Preparation is no exception.

For any one job it is best to convert and prepare all of the stock at the same time, whenever it is possible to do so. This usually saves material, time and effort, and reduces the risk of making mistakes. It also ensures that all pieces to be finished to the same dimension are machined (if you are using machines) at the same setting.

Preparation includes or at least begins with the selection of timber for the job, if only because knowing what one has to achieve from a piece of wood has a lot to do with which piece one chooses. However, selection could be considered a topic in its own right and I won't try to deal with it here. Nonetheless, the two procedures overlap when deciding whether to cut all the pieces directly to the sizes specified in the cutting list, or whether to make it a multi-stage operation by preparing larger pieces from which the correct number of smaller pieces will later be taken. This depends very much upon the available stock, and it is worth spending some time deciding how best to proceed. For machining it's usually best to work with larger rather than smaller pieces of wood. Not only is time saved, but best use is made of the length of the machine bed. Thus one maximizes the possibility of achieving flatness, since flatness is, in part, a function of the length of the machine bed. On the other hand, the wood may be so long that it is difficult to handle, or the plank may be badly sprung, cupped or twisted. Machining out these defects will require

many passes and waste a lot of material, and in such cases it pays to cut the plank into more manageable lengths first.

In preparing a piece of wood, whether it is a long plank which will be cut apart later or a single piece to be finished to a specific size, you have to assume that none of its six faces is an accurate reference surface. The first thing to do is to prepare a side which is flat in length, flat in width and out of winding.

The tools for testing these three characteristics are a long

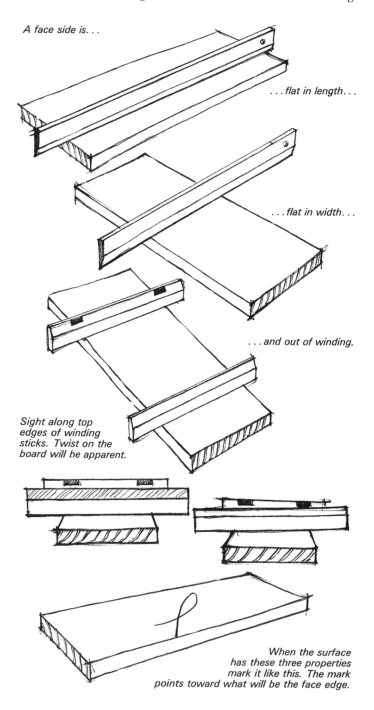

A face side is...

...flat in length...

...flat in width...

...and out of winding.

Sight along top edges of winding sticks. Twist on the board will be apparent.

When the surface has these three properties mark it like this. The mark points toward what will be the face edge.

straightedge and a pair of winding sticks. When a side of the board is flat and out of winding, it is marked and henceforth referred to as the *face side*. It is a reference surface from which further measurements are made. If it is not accurate, measurement can not be accurate.

Whether you choose to prepare one side in preference to the other on the basis of whether it will be exposed and visually important or for reasons connected to its role in constrution is inconsequential to the primary fact that there has to be a face side. However, in many situations one does have to consider whether to put the face side on the inside or outside. The decision need not be too confusing. For instance, drawer parts should have their face sides inside, and the members of a carcase generally also have their face sides inside. This way, you retain an accurate reference surface no matter what you later do to the outside. Decide which side will be the face side by thinking ahead to the consequences of having this reference on the inside or on the outside. Since the outside surfaces of any job will be cleaned up by hand-planing or sanding, or perhaps by carving, the face side will be lost if it is the outside.

Do not, however, confuse the face side with the best-looking side. Frequently the two will be on opposite sides of the board. Also, the mark that is used to designate a face side is a clear statement that the side has been prepared and is flat in length, flat in width and out of winding. Never put a face mark on a board as a statement of intent. It is an after-the-fact mark.

The face side provides the reference surface from which a face edge can now be produced. The face edge bears the same three characteristics as the face side, plus a fourth: It is at 90° to the face side. All further measuring and marking can spring from these two reference surfaces, and most of the woodworker's marking-out tools are designed to rely on them. The marking gauge, for example, is used to mark lines on the wood parallel to either face side or face edge to indicate width and thickness. Because it gauges directly from these established reference surfaces, it is only as accurate as they are.

It is usual to mark and cut to width first, because less energy is involved in removing the material than if it were thicknessed first. Whether the board is planed to width or sawn first and then planed depends on the work involved. A good rule of thumb is that if there is enough wood to take a saw kerf and leave a small amount of falling board besides, then it is worth sawing first. If not, plane directly to the line. The same is true when cutting the board to thickness. Having now four of the six faces flat, out of winding and at 90° to each other, it remains only to cut to length.

Machining the face side

The machine used to produce the face side is the jointer or surface planer. It consists of two horizontal flat tables which are adjustable in height, separated by a revolving cutter block. The lead table (infeed) is in front of the cutter block, and the take-off table (outfeed) is behind it. The take-off table is accurately set so that its surface is perfectly tangential to the arc made by the rotating cutter. Thus when the wood passes over the cutter, it meets the take-off surface with no further deflection up or down. The table is set at this height when the blades are set in the cutter block, and it remains undisturbed thereafter. The lead table, on the other hand, de-

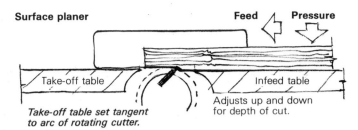

Surface planer   **Feed**   **Pressure**

Take-off table   Infeed table

Take-off table set tangent to arc of rotating cutter.

Adjusts up and down for depth of cut.

Pressure transferred from infeed table to take-off table, which now acts as a register for the remainder of the pass.

If take-off table is too high, wood will slide on the table's leading edge, causing a taper cut. If the wood is pressed onto the take-off table, the trailing end of the wood will lift off the infeed table.

If the take-off table is too low, the trailing end of the wood will be snipped off as the wood drops onto the take-off table.

Depth of cut exaggerated for clarity.

termines the depth of cut and is constantly being adjusted for this purpose.

Mechanical feeds do exist but in the main the wood is offered to the machine by hand. It is held down firmly on the lead table and moved toward the cutter. At this point the wood has no reference surface, so the lead table is acting only as a carriage. Since the take-off table is set exactly tangential to the arc of the cutter, the cut surface will coincide with its surface. It is vitally important that this contact be established and maintained throughout the cut. Thus as soon as the leading edge of the wood passes the cutter, the operator shifts his hand to the take-off table and presses downward to maintain the contact, while no further downward pressure need be applied to the wood still on the lead table. Otherwise, the wood is liable to pivot or rock about the cutter and lift from the take-off table.

So long as the take-off table is set properly and the contact maintained between it and the newly cut surface, this surface will have all three properties of a face side, although it usually requires more than one pass to achieve. But provided the wood is not too badly sprung or twisted, two fairly light cuts will usually do. Two or three light cuts usually give a better result than one heavy cut, though the feed speed is of course also important in surface quality.

If the take-off table is set too low, the wood drops as it leaves the lead table and the cutters snip off the trailing edge of the board. If the take-off table is set too high, the wood tilts as it feeds and the cut is deeper at the leading edge, producing a taper.

Many shops lack a large jointer and attempt to achieve true reference surfaces with the thickness planer alone. But a thickness planer operates by pressing an already flat surface against its lower bed, to cut the top surface parallel to it. Its feed rollers apply enough pressure to straighten cup and warp out of a board. The board straightens as soon as it leaves the machine. Thus while it will produce a smooth surface, it cannot produce a flat surface unless the board is already flat on one side. It is better to hand-plane the face side and then thickness than to attempt to produce a face side with the thickness planer alone.

If I were faced with the financial problem of having to choose between buying a wider jointer or a thickness planer, I would probably prefer the jointer because you simply must be able to produce a true reference surface from a rough board. One solution, however, would be to use a European combination machine. These have one cutter block and two tables, a jointer on top and a thickness planer below. Wadkin makes several such machines, as do the Swiss Inca and Italian Combinato lines.

Hand-planing the face side

The long jointer plane is also known as a trying plane or sometimes as a fore plane, which probably comes from the word "before"—it is the tool used before anything else. There is a similarity between the jointer machine and the jointer plane in that both have a long, true surface. In both cases this long surface is the reason they are able to produce a flat surface on the wood. The trying plane is usually 22 in. long, enough for most work.

Also, while there is no difference in level between the toe and heel of the plane's sole, as there is between the lead and take-off tables of the machine, the toe and heel part do play a similar role to the machine tables. The toe and the surface in front of the plane iron act as the initial register, but the part behind the blade is most important in imparting flatness be-

cause it is guided by the improved surface of the wood. So it is vital to maintain pressure on the rear end of the plane to ensure contact and provide progressive flatness at each stroke. Since there is no difference between the two surfaces, the inherent tendency to lift from the surface of the wood is much less apparent than with the machine.

The piece of wood to be planed should, if it is of manageable proportions in terms of width and thickness and not too badly warped, be placed on the surface of the bench against a bench stop. A less good way to plane wood is to hold it in the vise. If there is a degree of spring or twist, the pressure of the vise will probably rectify it, thereby giving a false indication of the real state of the wood when being planed. On release the wood of course returns to its misaligned state. Apart from this, the time involved in mounting the work in the vise, releasing it and changing body position to do so each time the work is checked is much greater than the time it takes to lift the wood from the bench, check it and put it down again. Further, working against the bench stop obliges one to operate the plane properly and provides tactile feedback information that one would not get if the work were in the vise. For instance, if the thrust of the plane is not directly along the axis of the wood or is not being applied horizontally, the wood will react by either toppling over or skewing round on itself. Learners will avoid forming bad habits if they plane woods on the bench in this way. The assumption here, of course, is that the bench is accurate. The surface on which one planes must be horizontal. It must be a "face side" in itself and have all the properties of a face side. A piece of wood with much of one's weight being pressed on it through the plane will easily deflect a few thousandths of an inch. If the surface it is on is hollow, it will be planed hollow. A fine shaving is only about .0015 in. thick, and there is little room for error. When a lot of wood has to be removed, sharpen the plane and move its frog back to open the mouth and take deeper cuts with each pass.

A straightedge is used to check flatness in length and width. It is necessary to hold the wood and the straightedge up to the light to ensure that no light can be seen between the straightedge and the surface being tested. Don't despise checking the board by eye at any time without instruments. It would be foolish to claim that the eye can be developed to the point where measuring tools become redundant, but one should develop as keen an eye as possible—for one's own awareness if nothing else.

To check for winding, two accurately planed, equally dimensioned pieces of wood, known as winding sticks, are placed transversely at points along the length of the surface and sighted to read for parallelism throughout. The sticks need to be long enough to accentuate the degree of winding so it can easily be seen. The amount of twist can be gauged by the deflection of the sticks, and the remedy is to plane diagonally from the high corner at one end to the opposite high corner at the other end.

If the surface has interlocked or similarly awkward grain, set the plane mouth fine, the back iron close to the blade edge and keep the blade sharp, and it will be easy to plane diagonally or at right angles to the grain. Generally, the more dense the wood, the easier it is to plane across the grain. When the board is flat and out of winding, one should be able to take a clean, fine shaving from end to end all across the surface. When the surface is flat in length and width and

Plane against a bench stop whenever possible. If plane is not held horizontal, workpiece will keel over.

If plane is not pushed in line with workpiece, it will skew off the bench.

For wide, thin stock, make a support stop. This is held in a vise or against the bench stop.

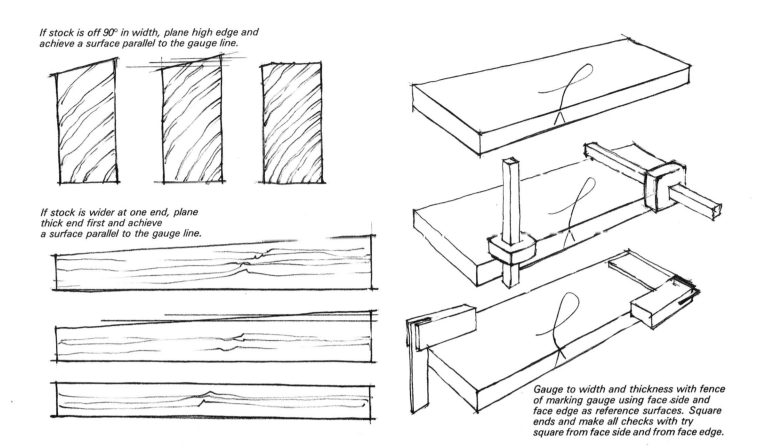

If stock is off 90° in width, plane high edge and achieve a surface parallel to the gauge line.

If stock is wider at one end, plane thick end first and achieve a surface parallel to the gauge line.

Gauge to width and thickness with fence of marking gauge using face side and face edge as reference surfaces. Square ends and make all checks with try square from face side and from face edge.

out of winding, the face-side mark is applied to it in a position to indicate which edge will become the face edge.

The face edge

Machining the face edge on the jointer is like preparing the face sides. Pressure must be applied to the take-off table in the same way, but now the face side also has to be kept firmly in contact with the fence. The fence must make a 90° angle with the jointer bed, and it's worth checking with a square every time the machine is used. Both downward and sideways pressure need to be maintained throughout the cut, and the procedure is that much more difficult to control.

When preparing the face edge on the bench with the jointer plane, the wood should be stood on its edge against the stop, for all the same reasons as before. This will not be possible when the board is somewhat wider than it is thick, and there will be no alternative but to put it in the vise. But be aware of the problems of distortion that this might cause, although the difficulty is less than with a face side. If the wood is far from being parallel it might be best to thickness the piece before preparing the face edge.

If the wood is severely angled from 90° on its edge, one must learn to hold the plane with its sole horizontal and to take material from the high edge. Some find it a help to shift the plane sideways so the high edge of the wood is cut by the center of the plane iron, but on no account tilt the plane away from horizontal in an effort to compensate. If the piece is wedge-shaped in length, the usual procedure is to get the high end parallel to the face edge and progressively to achieve parallelism down the length of the board as the width—or thickness for that matter—is reached.

The checks for flatness are the same as before, but it is also necessary to check for right-angularity between the face side and the prepared edge all the way along its length. This is

done with a try square. When the four characteristics have all been achieved, the face edge is marked as the side was marked, this time in such a way as to indicate the face side from which it springs.

Width and thickness

The next thing is to use the face side and edge as reference surfaces from which to mark and cut to width and thickness, usually to width first. The first operation may be to saw, either with circular saw or handsaw, to within planing distance of the final dimension. One should aim to saw as near to the line as possible without touching it.

The subsequent planing by machine would be done with a thickness planer and is usually a one or two-pass operation requiring only that the thicknesser be set to the given dimension, the wood fed in and collected at the other end. It is important, however, to do all pieces that are to finish at that dimension at the one setting.

Just as it is not possible to produce a face side with a thickness planer, it is also impossible to plane to width or thickness on a jointer. The necessary accuracy comes from an already established reference surface, and the jointer is not designed to work from a reference surface. There is no guarantee that parallelism will result. There are commercial attachments for jointers to convert them to a form of thicknesser, but they have limited capacity and my inclination is away from them.

Getting to width and thickness by bench methods involves gauging all around with the marking gauge and planing to the line with the jointer plane. As before, work with the wood on the bench and not in the vise.

Length

Getting the material to length is a two-part process. One end is squared off first, either with a radial-arm saw, a traveling-

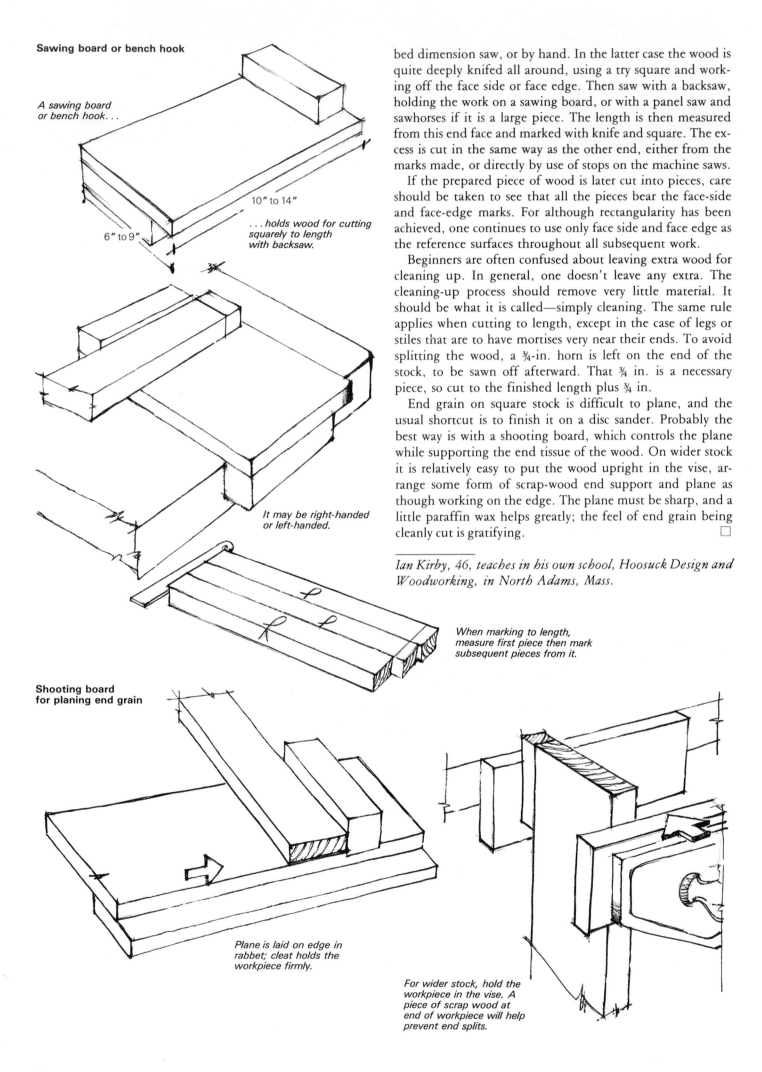

Sawing board or bench hook

A sawing board or bench hook...

10" to 14"

6" to 9"

...holds wood for cutting squarely to length with backsaw.

It may be right-handed or left-handed.

Shooting board for planing end grain

Plane is laid on edge in rabbet; cleat holds the workpiece firmly.

When marking to length, measure first piece then mark subsequent pieces from it.

For wider stock, hold the workpiece in the vise. A piece of scrap wood at end of workpiece will help prevent end splits.

bed dimension saw, or by hand. In the latter case the wood is quite deeply knifed all around, using a try square and working off the face side or face edge. Then saw with a backsaw, holding the work on a sawing board, or with a panel saw and sawhorses if it is a large piece. The length is then measured from this end face and marked with knife and square. The excess is cut in the same way as the other end, either from the marks made, or directly by use of stops on the machine saws.

If the prepared piece of wood is later cut into pieces, care should be taken to see that all the pieces bear the face-side and face-edge marks. For although rectangularity has been achieved, one continues to use only face side and face edge as the reference surfaces throughout all subsequent work.

Beginners are often confused about leaving extra wood for cleaning up. In general, one doesn't leave any extra. The cleaning-up process should remove very little material. It should be what it is called—simply cleaning. The same rule applies when cutting to length, except in the case of legs or stiles that are to have mortises very near their ends. To avoid splitting the wood, a ¾-in. horn is left on the end of the stock, to be sawn off afterward. That ¾ in. is a necessary piece, so cut to the finished length plus ¾ in.

End grain on square stock is difficult to plane, and the usual shortcut is to finish it on a disc sander. Probably the best way is with a shooting board, which controls the plane while supporting the end tissue of the wood. On wider stock it is relatively easy to put the wood upright in the vise, arrange some form of scrap-wood end support and plane as though working on the edge. The plane must be sharp, and a little paraffin wax helps greatly; the feel of end grain being cleanly cut is gratifying. □

Ian Kirby, 46, teaches in his own school, Hoosuck Design and Woodworking, in North Adams, Mass.

Pencil Gauges

A bag of tricks for marking wood

by Percy W. Blandford

The marking gauge goes back a long way in history. When the old-time cabinetmaker did not want a scratch because it might show in the finished work, he then reverted to pencil and had several ways of using it. These methods have applications today, and their simplicity makes them attractive.

The simplest way of using a pencil to gauge a line up to an inch or so from an edge is by holding the pencil between the first finger and thumb, then letting the tips of one or more other fingers rub along the edge of the wood. With confidence and a steady hand one can pull along the edge to draw a line with surprising accuracy.

For more accuracy a notched thumb gauge can be made. The wood should be long enough not to wobble as it is

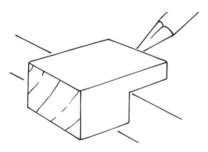

pulled along. If several lines are needed, the gauge can be made and used for the farthest one in. Then the end can be cut off.

This sort of gauge is intended to be discarded after use. However, most of us find ourselves repeatedly gauging the same width. A graduated pencil gauge allows several fixed distances to be drawn with the same gauge. The hollow provides a finger grip, and the small chamfer makes the tool slide more smoothly. Another way of getting

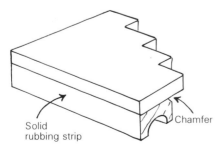

Solid rubbing strip   Chamfer

more increments in the same tools is to use the opposite side of the block or even a square block with distances in four directions (shown below), but individual gauges are less clumsy.

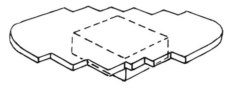

A thumb gauge used by boatbuilders could have applications in other work. A plywood deck is laid to overlap slightly, but the row of fixing nails or screws needs to be parallel with the final edge if it is to look neat. A thumb gauge is cut to fit over the plywood

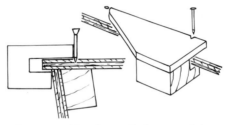

edge to guide the nails into position. For even spacing there could be an extension at the side to check the distance from the previous nail.

When the glued plywood has been nailed it is helpful to have a pencil line on top to mark where the edge is to be cut. A gauge with both legs the same length (below, left) will do this. However, there is a complication in boats—the angle of the side is not con-

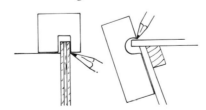

stant and may flare considerably towards the bow. A gauge with a curved cutout (above, right) conforms to varying slopes and gets the line right.

A combination square can replace thumb gauges, but it has to be set each time. Also, stock sizes carefully cut in a wooden gauge will always be the same,

while there might be variations in an adjustable setting.

Even with a stock of fixed gauges there may be occasions when a special measurement is needed, particularly in the deck-fixing type of work. A combination gauge will not mark a line of nail positions over a rough edge. An adjustable gauge for this sort of work can be made by cutting a central block

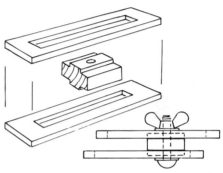

to slide in two grooved pieces. The whole thing is locked with a bolt, washers and a butterfly nut.

Notched pencil gauges have much in common with miter and dovetail gauges, so it is possible to make combination tools. A two-sided notched gauge can have one end of both sides cut at 45° for marking miters.

The tool body could be notched to mark dovetails at an angle of about 1 in 7. One side could be a slightly steeper angle for hardwoods and the other side slightly wider angled for softwoods.

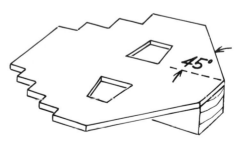

The cutouts should be wide enough to allow easy use of a pencil. They are not intended to indicate actual dovetail widths, but will be moved to suit the spacing marked on the wood. □

Percy Blandford writes on woodworking and traditional crafts in England.

Triangle Marking

A simple and reliable system

by Adrian C. van Draanen

Suppose you are making half a dozen drawers. You have cut all the pieces for them, and they are neatly stacked up. Your next steps are dovetails and grooves for the bottom. As you pick up a piece, you can probably tell whether you are holding a front, side or back. But can you tell which way is up, or which is the outside? Can you tell the left sides from the right? If the drawers are of different sizes, can you find matching pieces without remeasuring?

If you can answer "yes" to all these questions, you must have an adequate system for marking your work. If not, I'd like to suggest the triangle method.

Textbooks ignore marking. One is often advised to "mark the face," or "mark the top." But a particular method is never mentioned, and it is left to the worker to adopt or develop a system. Hence the use of lines, letters, numbers and other devices.

European carpenters and cabinet-makers use a system that employs a triangle, and nothing else. This system is widely used, and it is taught in trade schools. But it doesn't seem to be known outside Europe.

The rules of the system are:
—the triangle is an isosceles triangle and it must point up, or away, from you;
—each piece of wood must have two lines of the triangle on it.

Here is a glued-up panel, marked according to these rules:

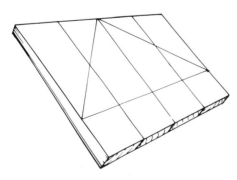

It is possible to take away each piece and put it back in the same place later. And each piece can immediately be identified. If, for instance, you were holding this piece,

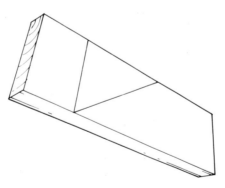

you would know right away that it is an inside piece, located to the left of the center of the panel.

If you had picked up this piece, you

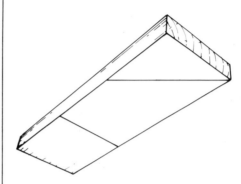

would know that you were holding it upside down. You would also know that it is the rightmost piece of the panel.

A glued-up tabletop is similar to a panel that has been rotated 90°.

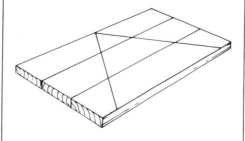

You may draw the base of the triangle on the tabletop, but it is not required and in practice it is never done. Look at each board and you'll find two lines, the two sides of a triangle that points away from you.

Now we have marked a panel and a tabletop. You can mix all the pieces any way you like and you can always put them back together. Each piece can be identified as either part of a panel (a vertical construction, because the base of the triangle is drawn at right angles to the sides of the individual pieces), or a tabletop (a horizontal construction, because the base of the triangle is parallel to the sides of the individual pieces). Just two lines give you all this information.

You may say at this stage that your own method is just as simple and fool-proof, and you are probably right. Very few constructions are as simple as a panel or a tabletop, though. When the work becomes complicated, as with drawers, the triangle method remains as simple as for the tabletop. Let's consider something that has both vertical and horizontal components, such as a door.

Here are the stiles,

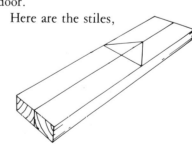

and here are the rails.

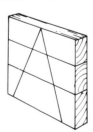

The completed door looks like this:

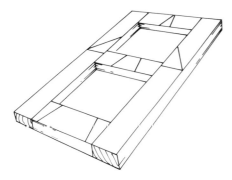

For simplicity the panels have been omitted, but you already know how to mark them. If this door had two panels of equal height, and both were marked the same way, it would be possible to get the pieces mixed up. To avoid this confusion, a double line on the second panel distinguishes it from the first.

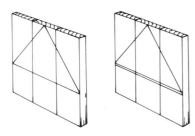

The base line on the second panel is the one to double, because it is the only line that is common to all the pieces.

Two identical tabletops would be marked thus:

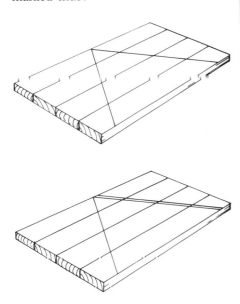

Again, a mix-up is impossible, because of the double line.

So far we have worked only with flat, two-dimensional assemblies. A set of four legs introduces a third dimension. There are front and back legs, left and right, and mortises are worked in the two inside surfaces of each leg.

A triangle drawn across the face of the front legs is clearly not enough.

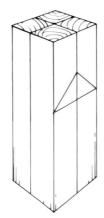

We must mark all four faces of the bundle. Going around clockwise, we draw the second triangle (A), doubling

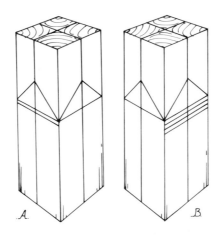

the base line, as this line is common to the two legs, then the third (three lines) and the fourth triangle (B).

It makes no difference whether the piece has four legs, or more than four

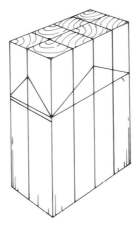

legs; they are all marked in the same manner.

Until now we have marked the sides of the stock, because that was the way the pieces had to be assembled. But in a box or a drawer, the edges, not the sides, are in the same plane; therefore marks are put on the edges.

Here is a drawer:

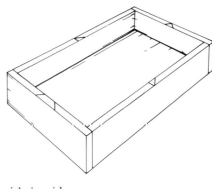

with its sides,

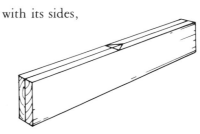

and its front and back.

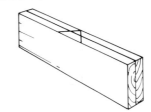

And now you can without hesitation identify this piece.

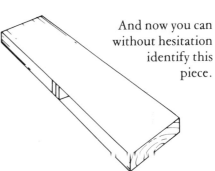

It belongs to a drawer. It is the right-hand side of it. You also know which side is the inside, which way is up, and that it belongs to the third drawer.

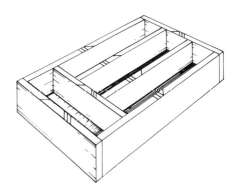

Adrian C. van Draanen, 49, has worked as a cabinetmaker in his native Holland and in Ottawa, Canada, where he is now a government computer expert.

Drawers
Logical assembly ensures proper fit

by Adrian C. van Draanen

With the exception of those who make only chairs, the makers of furniture are regularly called upon to produce pieces with one or more drawers. Often the design of the drawers must meet specific requirements. For example, a china cabinet usually has at least one felt-lined drawer, with dividers; one drawer in a desk should have provision for pens, pencils and other small supplies. Drawer exteriors may also demand special attention. A chest of drawers is a good example of a piece of furniture whose appearance depends on the proportions, shape and material of the drawer fronts.

In this article I will look at what goes into making and fitting a drawer. The methods and recommendations given here apply to traditional, first-class work, and they involve handwork. For the large production jobs a shaper or router with dovetail attachments significantly reduces the time.

A drawer has a front, two sides, a back and a bottom. The front must match or complement the piece of furniture of which it will become a part, and therefore the wood is chosen mainly for appearance. The thickness of a solid front should not be less than 2 cm (¾ in.) in order to have enough material for dovetails, and for a mortised lock if the customer wants one. As a rule the grain of the front runs horizontally. To do otherwise would result in a drawer which would have no strength without unusual measures to reinforce the joints. Moreover, the drawer front would undergo considerable dimensional changes caused by fluctuations in humidity.

These problems do not exist with plywood fronts, because the direction of the grain in the face veneers is of little consequence. Plywood fronts are often used in simple, modern furniture and in kitchen cabinets. To preserve the pattern of the face veneers, particularly when the grain is vertical, no rails show between the drawers. Because of this, and because plywood drawer fronts need a veneered top edge, their construction and fitting are quite different from solid-front drawers and fall outside the scope of this article.

The wood for the sides and back does not need to match the front. Ability to resist warping, to be hard-wearing and to finish nicely are the most important considerations. Depending on availablity, ash, beech, birch, maple, oak or sycamore can be used. Cedar, fir, pine, poplar and spruce are less satisfactory because they do not stand up to hard wear. Sides are 8 mm to 12 mm (5/16 in. to ½ in.) thick, and the back has either the same thickness as the sides or a little bit more. The direction of the grain in a drawer side must permit you to plane it from front to back along the top edge and on the outside. If the grain runs the wrong way and the drawer sides cannot be planed from front to back, you risk damaging the drawer front when fitting the top edge or when the outsides

Adrian C. van Draanen, 50, has worked as a cabinetmaker in his native Holland and in Ottawa, Canada, where he is now a government computer expert.

of the drawer are being cleaned up after assembly. The second thing is that when a drawer side has any tendency to bow, it must be placed with the hollow side out. When the bottom is put into the drawer, the side will straighten automatically. If the drawer side curves out, binding will be a constant problem. Naturally, if the side has anything more than just a slight bow, it should be rejected.

The bottom is usually made of plywood, 3 mm to 6 mm (1/8 in. to ¼ in.) thick. Heavier plywood may be used for extra-large drawers or when the weight of the contents is going to be excessive, although thinner plywood with a reinforcing center strip glued underneath it is preferred for better work. Birch and beech are good choices for plywood bottoms and they are readily available in several thicknesses. For first-class work, Douglas fir or poplar plywood should not be considered unless the bottom is lined. Convention dictates that the grain on the bottom run in the same direction as that of the drawer front. This means you have no choice but plywood when the drawer has a vertical front, since there is only one way a solid bottom can go in: with the grain running from side to side. The grooves for the bottom must be neither too tight nor too loose—in the first case, the bottom may force the sides apart or cause them to split; in the second, the drawer may rattle. It is also important that the width of the bottom be accurate, to ensure that the drawer remain square and that the sides stay straight. The bottom should be long enough to extend 2 mm to 3 mm (1/8 in.) beyond the back of the drawer, but not so long as to be even with the ends of the sides. If you should have to shorten the sides during the final fitting, you do not want to have to trim the bottom too.

Before plywood became available, and even after that but before it was accepted for high-grade furniture, drawer bottoms were always made solid. I see no advantages in using solid bottoms for contemporary work. But they are a must for certain reproductions if they are to appear authentic, and in the repair and restoration of old furniture when the original condition must be preserved or restored. A solid bottom requires a fair amount of work and it is not something that is highly visible or immediately apparent to an uninformed observer, and for that reason not appreciated.

Suitable timbers for solid bottoms are clear pine, spruce, fir and basswood. If woolens are to be stored in the drawer, aromatic cedar might be considered. Preference should be given to quartersawn boards, and the wood must be thoroughly dry. You should aim for a bottom with maximum stability and maximum freedom from warping and cupping. The boards are edge-glued to obtain a width equal to the depth of the cabinet. The grain of a solid bottom must run from side to side, so that the shrinkage and expansion of the bottom can then be allowed for at the back of the drawer, the bottom can be glued to the front, and the sides will be kept square with the front because there is no movement of the

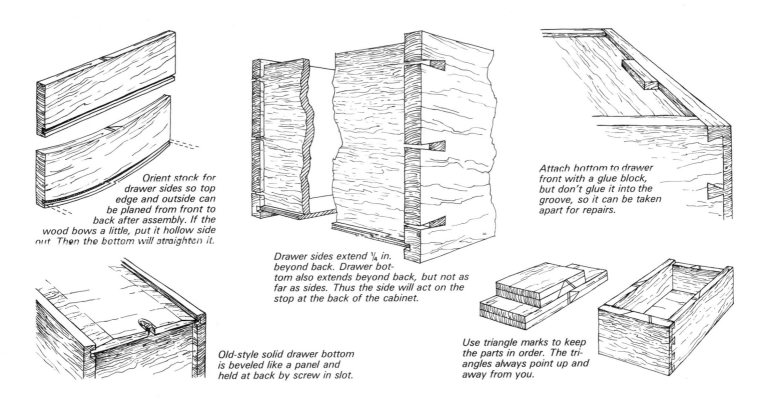

Orient stock for drawer sides so top edge and outside can be planed from front to back after assembly. If the wood bows a little, put it hollow side out. Then the bottom will straighten it.

Drawer sides extend ¼ in. beyond back. Drawer bottom also extends beyond back, but not as far as sides. Thus the side will act on the stop at the back of the cabinet.

Attach bottom to drawer front with a glue block, but don't glue it into the groove, so it can be taken apart for repairs.

Old-style solid drawer bottom is beveled like a panel and held at back by screw in slot.

Use triangle marks to keep the parts in order. The triangles always point up and away from you.

bottom in that direction. A thickness of 5 mm to 6 mm (¼ in.) is good for most drawers if they are not too wide, but in repair work or in reproductions the thickness may have to be much more. When the original was made, thicknessing was done by hand, and the sawmill did not provide boards much thinner than 1 in. The bottom was made like a panel, with the center part left the full thickness and a border about 1½ in. wide all around it planed down to ¼ in. or ⅜ in. The flat side of the panel was placed on the inside of the drawer. The width of a solid bottom must be a perfect fit in the drawer. The grain runs in this direction, and this dimension therefore doesn't change. The front to back length of the bottom (across the grain) must be such that at its driest the bottom is at least even with the backside of the drawer back, and that at the other extreme the bottom does not extend beyond the drawer sides. The bottom is screwed to the back with flathead screws. The screw holes in the bottom are elongated across the grain of the bottom, so that the bottom can move and still be held. This eliminates the danger of splitting (winter) and buckling (summer). The bottom must be glued to the drawer front with good-sized glue blocks. Do not glue the bottom into the groove at the front, because this would make future repairs very difficult. It is imperative that the bottom and the front be securely kept together, else the bottom will pull out of the groove when the wood dries.

Assembly

Assuming that all material has been chosen and cut slightly oversize, and all the components have been paired and marked (see "Triangle Marking," pages 76-77), fitting and assembly can begin. Note the order—fitting comes before assembly.

Take the drawer front and plane the bottom edge. It must be made true and parallel to the top edge, and the height of the drawer front must be a perfect fit in the drawer opening. Square one end of the drawer front and place it in the opening to scribe the other end. It does not matter whether this mark is made on the face or on the inside of the drawer front,

but cutting must be done on the face because cutting from the inside may leave the face rough. When the second end has been cut you have a front that fits the opening exactly. No force should be necessary to place the front in the opening, but there should be no clearance either at this stage.

The back is next. Its top and bottom edges must be parallel to each other. The distance between them, that is, the height of the back, is less than the height of the front. It is not possible to give exact measurements, but it is from 2 cm to 2.5 cm (¾ in. to 1 in.) less. The bottom of the back must clear the drawer bottom when the bottom is slid into place, and the top edge is lower than the sides by about .5 cm (¼ in.). This clearance at the top of the back allows air to escape when the drawer is being closed. Without it a well-fitting drawer acts like a piston. The length of the drawer back must be the same as that of the front.

The drawer sides must have a true bottom edge, and the ends of the sides must be square to this bottom edge. The height of the sides is of no consequence yet, provided that it is more than is ultimately required: The sides should be just a little too high to fit into the drawer opening. The length of the sides is equal to the full inside depth of the cabinet (from the face of the front rail to the inside of the back) minus the .5 cm (¼ in.) or so you leave in the drawer front for half-blind dovetails. In a cabinet without a back, or whose back is not sturdy enough to act as a drawer stop, measure to a rail or stop, securely fastened as close as possible to the back of the cabinet. Thus the drawer stops are always present, and fixed, and the drawer sides are fitted to these stops. It is a good practice to make the drawer sides as long as possible, even when the drawer itself is short. This is some insurance against a drawer being pulled out too far and falling on the floor, and the wear from the sides on the front rail is more even.

So now we have a perfectly fitting drawer front, a back exactly as long as the front but lower than the front, and two sides with straight bottom edges and square ends. Before putting these pieces aside, restore the pairing marks on the top edges where necessary. If the piece of furniture has more than

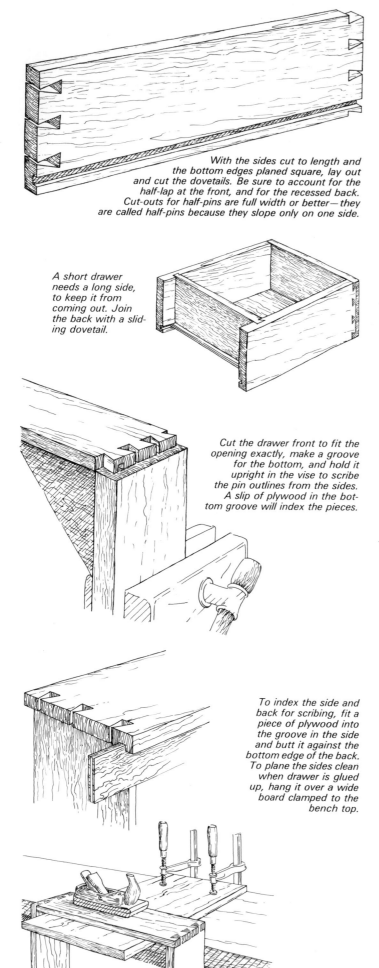

With the sides cut to length and the bottom edges planed square, lay out and cut the dovetails. Be sure to account for the half-lap at the front, and for the recessed back. Cut-outs for half-pins are full width or better—they are called half-pins because they slope only on one side.

A short drawer needs a long side, to keep it from coming out. Join the back with a sliding dovetail.

Cut the drawer front to fit the opening exactly, make a groove for the bottom, and hold it upright in the vise to scribe the pin outlines from the sides. A slip of plywood in the bottom groove will index the pieces.

To index the side and back for scribing, fit a piece of plywood into the groove in the side and butt it against the bottom edge of the back. To plane the sides clean when drawer is glued up, hang it over a wide board clamped to the bench top.

one drawer, repeat the whole procedure for each drawer.

One more thing remains to be done before the drawers can be assembled. A groove must be made in the drawer fronts and sides to receive the bottom. The reference line for this groove is the bottom edge of the drawer fronts and sides, that is, take measurements from this edge. The depth of the groove must not exceed half the thickness of the sides, and enough wood must be left between the groove and the bottom edge of the drawer to allow clearance and to support the bottom without danger of splitting the sides.

The next step is making dovetails at both ends of each side. The half-blind dovetails joining the drawer sides to the front should not present any difficulties ("Hand Dovetails," Spring '76, pp. 28-32). On the other hand, the joint I use at the back might appear unconventional to some. The sides extend approximately .5 cm. (¼ in.) beyond the back for a drawer as deep as the cabinet.

Because the dovetails extend beyond the back of the drawer, they look best when the tails are wide—almost touching each other—and the pins on the drawer back are small. The illustrations should make this clear. Dovetails are not practical at the back of shallow drawers with long sides. It is better to join the sides and the back with a sliding dovetail, in which the back is slipped into place from below, or let the back into a dado in the sides.

When all the dovetails have been cut, the location of the pins is marked on the drawer fronts and on the back. The bottom edges must be used again for reference, but because the grooves for the drawer bottom have already been made with the bottom edge as reference, the grooves can now be used to align the drawer sides, fronts and backs. Take a small piece of the plywood you intend to use for the bottom, insert it in the grooves of both the drawer front and its mating side, and the two pieces will be correctly aligned and will stay that way while you scribe the pin locations. The drawer back has no groove but it can be held against the piece of plywood to align it with the sides.

I do not dry-fit dovetail joints. They are too easily damaged in fitting, with a subsequent loss in accuracy in the final joint. By holding one piece on top of the other it is not difficult to judge the fit, and it is entirely possible to obtain perfect results without actually assembling the joint first.

One more observation before we return to making drawers. Many workers divide a space in equal parts when laying out dovetails. This results in half-pins that are often too small. Dovetails depend for their strength on a wedging action. If the two outside dovetails are too close to the edge, not enough wood is left to keep the joint tight and closed under all conditions. Severe strains on the joint may even cause a split to start at the half-pins. The answer is wider half-pins. They can be achieved either by making the two outside dovetails a little narrower than those in the center, or by setting out the half-pins first and then dividing the remaining space evenly.

With all the dovetails made and ready to be glued up, now is the time to clean up the insides of all the pieces, and varnish or paint them if you are so inclined. Finally the drawers can be put together. Care must be taken to keep them square while the glue is drying.

If you take a board or a piece of plywood, 2 cm (¾ in.) or more thick and a little bit longer than the width of your bench, and put this across your bench, you have a good support for the drawer when you are planing the outsides clean. The board must be secured to the bench, and if the inside of the drawer is already finished, the overhanging end of the board must be covered with cardboard or cloth. Clean up the outside of the drawer, and you are ready for the bottom. Some workers like to have the bottom in the drawer when they work on the sides, but leaving the bottom out is more satisfactory because it allows much better support. The drawer looks best when the bottom is just long enough to extend to the outside of the drawer back, or maybe 2 mm or 3 mm (about ⅛ in.) beyond that. It should not be quite as long as the drawer sides. When the bottom has been sanded and finished, it should be inserted and screwed to the back of the drawer. This is a first-class drawer and nails simply won't do. If the bottom is plywood, use two or three flathead screws, countersunk. If it is solid, use screws in slots to allow for movement.

Some workers like to put glue blocks on the underside of the bottom along the drawer front and sides. Glue blocks are made out of square material about 8 mm (⅜ in.) on a side and are approximately 5 cm (2 in.) long. Two of the long surfaces are coated with glue, and the block is rubbed back and forth a few times in the desired location. The rubbing will distribute the glue evenly, and if you do it right, there will be so much suction that it quickly becomes impossible to move the block. Clamping is not necessary. I believe that glue blocks are not necessary when the stock is dry and free from defects. But if there is any doubt that the drawer front or sides will stay flat and straight, glue blocks provide peace of mind.

The sides of the drawer are still too high. The height of the drawer front should be scribed onto the sides, and the top edges should be planed down to make them even with the drawer front. If you did everything right, you now have a drawer that fits tightly in the opening, more so in height than in width. This is because the height has not been changed since fitting the drawer front, but the width has been slightly reduced by cleaning off the outside dovetail joints. The reduction is hardly noticeable, but it provides just the clearance the drawer needs across its width. Clearance in height is obtained by taking one shaving off the top edges of the front and the sides. This is probably all you need to produce a drawer that fits well and moves freely. If you think the drawer is still too snug, take off one more, very light, shaving, but only after you have rubbed a candle along all the edges and tried the drawer once more. Paraffin is also good to make the drawer slide better, but beeswax or other sticky substances should not be used because they attract dust.

The length of the sides can now be checked. Where the drawer front is going to be in relation to the front of the cabinet is determined by the length of the drawer sides, because the drawer stops are already in place. The front of the drawer can be flush with the cabinet, in which case you should not have to do anything to the drawer sides. A front recessed not more than 1 mm (a fat 1/32 in.) often looks better than a perfectly flush front.

If a recessed front is desired, the sides must be shortened by 1 mm, or less. For those who have not yet been exposed to the impending metric system, your thumbnail is about 1 mm thick. As a finishing touch, slightly break the sharp edges of the drawer, give the last 2 cm or 2.5 cm (1 in.) of the top edge of the drawer sides a slope to correspond to the slope of

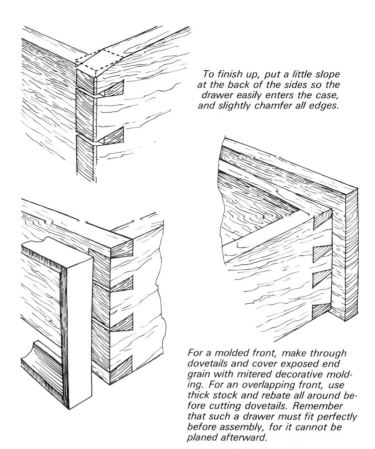

To finish up, put a little slope at the back of the sides so the drawer easily enters the case, and slightly chamfer all edges.

For a molded front, make through dovetails and cover exposed end grain with mitered decorative molding. For an overlapping front, use thick stock and rebate all around before cutting dovetails. Remember that such a drawer must fit perfectly before assembly, for it cannot be planed afterward.

the dovetails, and chamfer the protruding dovetails at the end of the drawer sides.

A drawer with a molded front is made as described above, with one difference: The dovetails joining the sides to the front are through dovetails, and the length of the sides is equal to the depth of the cabinet minus the thickness of the molding. The molding is not applied until the drawer has been fitted and all adjustments have been made. The molding covers the exposed dovetails in the drawer front. This type of drawer is reserved for more traditional work.

A drawer with an overlapping front must fit perfectly when assembled, because the oversized front makes subsequent planing impossible. The rabbeted part of the drawer front must fit in the cabinet with just the right degree of clearance, and the drawer sides must also be the right height before the drawer may be assembled. They can be planed and checked in the opening before assembly. It is somewhat more difficult to give this drawer a perfect fit because of its construction. On the other hand, the very feature that makes fitting difficult, that is, the overlap, also conceals a less-than-perfect fit. The stock for this drawer front should be thick enough to permit dovetails 12 mm to 15 mm (½ in. or more) long, with enough left for an overhang that is not going to break the first time the drawer is closed. Although this type of drawer does not seem to need stops, it is highly recommended that the ends of the sides, not the overlapping edges of the front, take the impact on closing.

A completely different way of making an overlapping drawer is to make a flush-front drawer first. The overlapping front is a separate piece attached after the drawer has been fitted. When this method is used it is imperative to have stops behind the ends of the drawer sides. If this is not done, chances are that the separate front will sooner or later become a separate front in a very literal way. □

Methods of Work

Drawer "push"

I have seen several small boxes whose beautiful forms are interrupted by a knob. Indentations for the fingers to pull the drawer out may also work against the design of the box. My father taught me an alternative to these "pulls" and that is

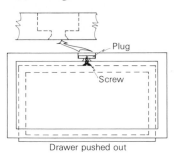

simply to push the drawer out. First drill a hole about two-thirds the depth of the thickness of the back of the box. If the rear wall is ¾ in. thick, I drill down ½ in. Now drill a small hole the remaining distance through the wall of the box, then countersink the small hole on the inside of the box. Make a plug ¼ in. thick and fasten it from the inside with a screw that will move freely through the small hole. Pushing the plug in causes the screw-head to push the drawer out far enough so that one can easily get hold of the drawer in front to pull it out the rest of the way.

—*John Roccanova, Bronx, N.Y.*

Curved edge joint

A simple system exists for making close-fitting edge joints along a curving line. This quick and reliable method works equally well for major design pieces and for rough work.

The idea is to cut both of the pieces to be joined simultaneously, as in marquetry, one above the other. The desired design is laid out on the upper one, and the boards overlapped a distance appropriate to the line. They need to be firmly but temporarily fixed in this position, by means of nails, glue, clamps, double-stick tape, etc. The assembly is then cut on the band saw with a bold and sure stroke, since any stopping and wiggling will result in a hole along the glue line. Frequently the two pieces can be held during cutting just with one's hands, doing away with the fastening.

When the waste parts are removed, the major pieces should fit together very well. Even if the sawing went off the line, at least they match. There may be a small gap evident along the glue line where the curve is sharp. This results from the radius

Edge joints can be cut by overlapping contrasting boards and bandsawing along the line of the design. Joint is then glued and clamped. Result, right, is a resawn and bookmatched pattern.

differential between the two sides of the saw kerf. In practice this is not a problem, however, because it usually can be pulled up in gluing without undue stress. A little judicious shaving at the ends would also solve this problem.

When wide boards are cut by this technique, the upper one sometimes droops out of parallel with the band-saw table. This is prevented by tacking a filler piece along its outer edge to hold it up. Joining thick wood brings out new possibilities—the lamination can then be resawn and bookmatched.

This method is good for relatively unimportant edge-joining such as in jigs, mockups and secondary pieces. Here a strong joint can be accomplished in a few seconds.

—*Sam Bush, Pottstown, Pa.*

Ogee molding

Ogee molding is easy to make using a table saw with a jointer or hand plane. By setting up a diagonal fence on the saw, the boards, usually 3 in. to 5 in. wide, are hollowed, leaving a flat section along each edge, one narrow and one wider. For

4-in. molding of the type usually used for bracket feet on case pieces, I usually leave a ¾-in. flat along one edge, which will remain flat. Along the other edge is a wider plane, which I joint or hand-plane into the graceful curve that makes this molding so useful. For safety, use a push-stick and make several passes over the saw blade, raising it perhaps ⅛ in. at each pass. The fence is simply a board with a straight edge, clamped to the table at about 30° to the line of the blade. Other moldings, chair seats and even raised panels with beautiful curves forming the rise may be made using variations of this method. —*James B. Small, Jr., Newville, Pa.*

Dip for screws

When you purchase a box of wood screws (brass or steel), dip them in a solution made of two tablespoons of bowling-alley wax dissolved in a pint of mineral spirits. Spread the screws out on a piece of kraft paper to dry before returning them to the box for storage. It will keep the brass bright, the steel from rusting and will make them go into the wood with half the effort, thus reducing breakage.

—*Charles F. Riordan, Dansville, N.Y.*

Drawer Bottoms

Six variations on a theme

by Alan Marks

Drawers have long been considered one of the most difficult elements in cabinetry, probably with justification. Done in traditional fashion, they are time-consuming and require exacting work if they are to operate properly. This accounts on the one hand for industry's preference for stapled particle board, hot-melt glues, and ball-bearing steel suspension glides; and on the other hand for the tendency of to-day's craftsmen to avoid traditional drawers in favor of compartments, shelves or pigeon holes. Dovetailed construction, however, remains the strongest way of making a drawer, and also the most attractive.

The many types of construction possible using dovetails allow for innovation and flexibility, as witnessed by these six examples from Malmstens Verkstadsskola in Stockholm. Although the Swedes agree that the dovetailed drawer is the sturdiest, they often consider the decorative aspect incidental. All of the front dovetail joints shown here are half-blind. The conservative Swedes generally eschew through dovetails in drawer fronts because they interfere with the design requirements and overall style of traditional pieces. Drawer fronts on such cabinets often are delicately inlaid with veneers or carved or profiled around their edges,

all unsuitable situations for through dovetails. Also, problems of uneven swelling and shrinkage can occur with through dovetails, when the wood of the solid drawer front shrinks while the end grain of the tails does not. Through dovetails are, however, used in the backs of drawers, where the unevenness ordinarily remains unnoticed.

French bottom

The traditional drawer bottom is made of solid wood, as opposed to Masonite or plywood. Thought to have originated in France, the so-called "French" drawer bottom floats with its grain running parallel to the drawer

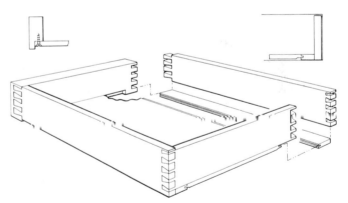

Exploded view from rear, with side and glide removed, shows how French-bottom drawer is put together. Section at left shows bottom screwed to front rabbet; right, section shows side, glide and bottom.

The little chest shown here is used to teach drawer construction at Malmstens Verkstadsskola (workshop and school) in Stockholm, Sweden. It was made in 1960 by master cabinetmaker Artur JonERöt, from drawings by guitarmaker Georg Bolin, then rector of the school. Of mahogany, it stands 65 cm (25 in.) high, 25 cm (10 in.) wide and 31 cm (12 in.) deep. From the top, the drawers are kitchen, NK, false French, French, NK with ply bottom, and side-hung. The work of Carl Malmsten, who died in 1972 at age 83, was an inspirational source for the commercial furniture style now known as Scandinavian or Danish modern. Many of his designs are still in production; his school, which he founded in 1930, is now state-owned. In preparing drawings for manufacturers, he usually offered alternative constructions and indicated the one he thought superior. The second would be accompanied by a comment such as, 'This construction probably won't even last a hundred years.'

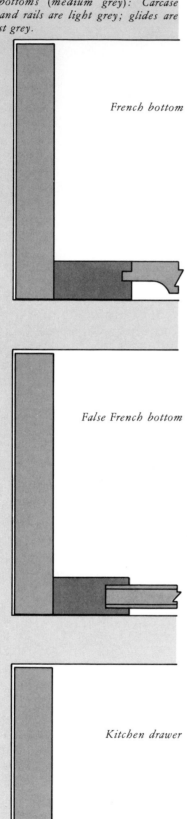

French bottom

False French bottom

Kitchen drawer

front, grooved into a two-piece frame formed by the glides. The drawer front is rabbeted to receive the bottom, which is slid home after glides have been glued to the drawer sides. Then the bottom is secured at the front with screws or a few brads, thus allowing later removal for cleaning, refinishing or repair, or else it is simply glued at the front edge. Either way, the wood bottom is free to expand and contract in its grooves. On a drawer this small, the bottom need be only 8 mm (5/16 in.) thick; it is raised 1-1/2 or 2 mm (1/16 in.) above the bottom of the glides to get around problems of sagging and scraping. The tongues should be made about 2 mm (3/32 in.) thick and 3 mm (1/8 in.) long.

The back of this drawer—and all the drawers discussed here—is made 5 mm (5/16 in.) lower than the sides; this keeps the back from scraping as the drawer is pulled out.

The bottom edge of the drawer front protrudes about 4 mm (5/32 in.) below the drawer side to act as a stop. This overhang slides into a corresponding rabbet in the carcase rail; the drawer may be made to close flush or to recess by varying the depth of the rabbet.

False French bottom

Because the French bottom is somewhat complicated to make and not compatible with large series production, the obvious shortcut is to take advantage of such dimensionally stable materials as plywood and Masonite. The resulting false French bottom simplifies construction and saves time. It looks the same at the front, but from the back the scalloped profile of the genuine French bottom is missing and three plies, two of veneer and one of Masonite or plywood, show up. This procedure creates a problem: The bottom might warp upward or become uneven if it is not restrained in some way; a tongue cut in Masonite or plywood would be much too weak. The solution is a glide with a groove wide enough to accommodate the whole thickness of the bottom, glued to the sides and butted against the front, as before. This creates a ledge inside the drawer, like the edge of the frame in conventional panel construction, which can be rounded. The final fitting of the glides is left until sides, front and back have been assembled. Then the glides are held in place at the front, marked at

French bottom, back view.

the back, and rabbeted with a chisel the small amount needed to make the bottom of the glide flush with the bottom of the side, enabling the bottom to be slid home. The drawer bottom projects into a rabbet in the drawer front and is fastened there with brads or screws and a bit of glue.

Kitchen drawer

The kitchen drawer bottom carries the cheapening of quality construction to its extreme. It is nothing more than a veneered plywood or Masonite bottom held by grooves in the sides and front and glued in place. There are disadvantages: rubbing on sides, little torsional strength, a small gluing surface, sides weakened by the groove, and a tiny gliding surface that eventually wears grooves in the rails.

NK drawer

The traditional French bottom and its counterfeit version share a weakness with most drawers made ever since

NK glide; pins are pared flush with side.

chests of drawers replaced lidded chests: the sides present a large scraping surface. This is noisy and can make the drawer difficult to extract. A solution is found in the so-called NK (pronounced enco) drawer.

NK is the abbreviation for a large store with several branches, Nordiska Kompaniet. Founded in Stockholm in 1902, a time of revolution against cluttered overdecoration in Swedish interiors, NK set up its own furniture factory. It was able to design, build and market tasteful contemporary pieces more in keeping with the timeless advice of William Morris: "If you want a golden rule that will fit everybody, here it is: Have nothing in your homes that you do not know to be useful, or believe to be beautiful."

The glides, usually 10 to 12 mm (1/2 in.) thick, are glued to the bottom of the sides and protrude about 3 mm (1/8 in.) beyond them. This is done by cutting the pins on the drawer front about 3 mm deeper than the thickness of the sides. Thus the drawer is steered by the narrow side surfaces of the glides alone. After assembly, the protruding full pins are pared flush with the sides, while the half-pins at the top and bottom of the front are trimmed to horizontal. A solid bottom is screwed or glued into a groove in the drawer front.

This construction gives ultimate ease in sliding, especially when used for high drawers, and is quite strong because of the bracing the glides provide by being glued across the corner.

NK ply bottom

The one drawer that provides all possible strengths is the NK style with a veneered Masonite or plywood bottom, although it may offend those who insist upon solid wood. The version shown here has a half-open front, intended for use inside large cabinets with doors or within secretaries with drop leaves. Since it needs no pull, the cabinet door can close quite close to the drawer front, an optimal use of space. The bottom of the front entirely overlaps its supporting rail.

In construction, the veneered bottom is cut to width such that its edges on either side lap the drawer sides by half their thickness. It is then glued into a rabbet in the glides. The glides butt against the front, where the bottom enters a rabbet. This assembly, if squared properly, automatically ensures

NK glide with low front, recessed side.

that the drawer front closes parallel to the cabinet. Excellent fits are easily made possible if the bottom and glide assembly is first fitted to the drawer opening before it is glued to the front, sides and back.

Side-hung

The side-hung drawer slides on runners inset into the cabinet sides and screwed in place. These runners also butt the end of the groove in which they ride and act as stops for the drawer. Thus the drawer front need have no overhang. The grooves may be made with a router, shaper or dado head, and squared up with a chisel. The veneered Masonite or plywood bottom acts as a cross brace for the front, back and sides. The sides are rabbeted, leaving a lip of about 3 mm (1/8 in.), and the bottom is glued, or glued and screwed, to them. At the same time it is glued to the back and let into a rabbet in the drawer front.

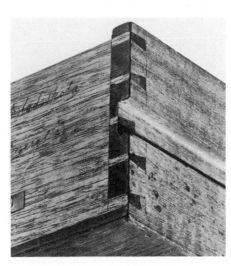

Side-hung drawer, back view.

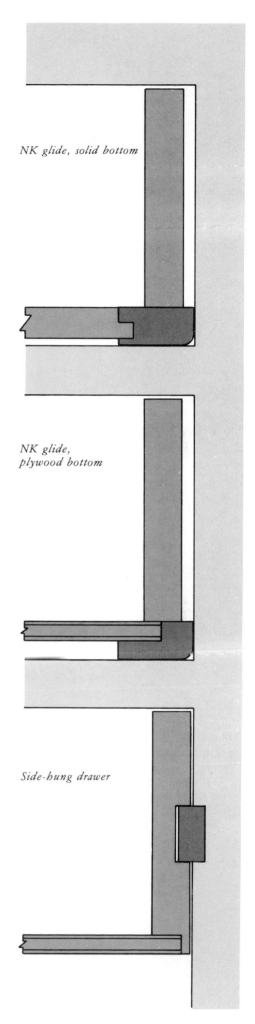

NK glide, solid bottom

NK glide, plywood bottom

Side-hung drawer

Routed Edge Joint

Fence guides router for seamless fit

by John Harra

Joint is invisible.

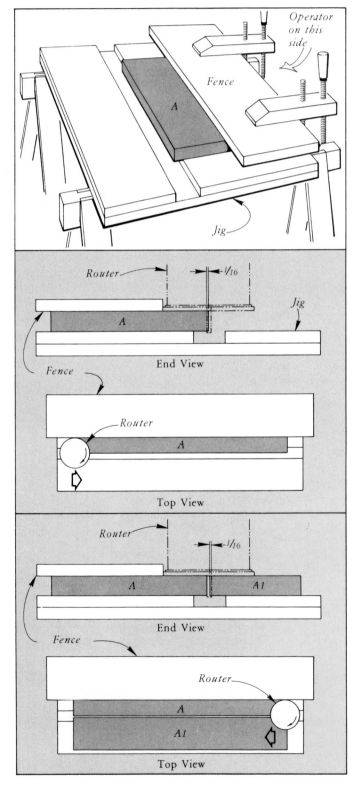

A basic task of woodworking is joining two or more pieces of wood to make a wide piece, with no apparent seam, for things like tabletops. It can be a difficult, time-consuming job and one that does not always turn out well. I have developed a system for edge-joining pieces of wood using a router, several clamps, a jig, a ruler and a fence. The results are consistently near-perfect and, with a little practice, can be achieved in a few minutes.

Ideally, two pieces of wood would mate perfectly if they were held edge-to-edge and both edges were cut smooth with a single pass of the router. Any variation from a straight line would be mirrored on both pieces. The router is a most versatile tool, but even at 22,000 rpm it isn't powerful enough to cut that way. My system uses a fence to guide the router along the edge of the first piece to be joined; then the second piece is clamped facing the first and routed against the same fence. Thus any bumps or hollows in the fence are imparted to the first piece and transferred in reverse to the second piece. A hill in one piece will have a corresponding valley in the adjoining piece. The two pieces of wood are perfect mirror images and when joined, look like a single piece of wood.

This router system of edge-to-edge lumber joining can be used to match two pieces with ''S'' curves or irregular compound curves, as well as straight pieces, as long as the curves are gentle. Thus beautiful grain patterns don't have to be disrupted by straight-line cuts. By joining along the natural flow of the grain, rather than through the grain pattern, you can build a large table apparently constructed from a single piece of wood.

The species and thickness of wood are really not critical. I've routed everything from pine to ebony. Anything from 1/4 in. to 2 in. thick can be routed easily. I have routed 3-in. thick maple using a special bit. With soft woods it is more difficult to get a clean edge because the grain doesn't shear and cut as easily and often rips away. Harder woods have more resistance and break away cleanly.

For this kind of routing, a straight bit is used because the two edges to be joined must be perpendicular to the surface of the wood and parallel to each other. Convoluted or fluted bits won't work. Nor will a bit with a narrow cutting area. The cutting surface of the bit has to be at least 1/2 in. in diameter—3/4 in. is best because the peripheral speed makes the smoothest cut with minimum friction. Also, the chips are the right size for the router motor to blow away. With larger bits, the chips are larger and tend to pile up. The bit should be long enough to cut at least 1/4 in. deeper, and preferably 1/2 in. deeper, than the thickness of the wood. The shank size of the bit is important, too. A 1/2-in. shank is preferable. If you have a small router with only a 1/4-in. collet capacity, you'll have to rout very slowly because of the tremendous strain on the bit. If the bit bends—and it can—it becomes eccentric and can whip itself out of the machine.

Now on to the process of achieving a flawless edge joint. You'll need to construct a routing jig to hold the edge of the wood off the bench so the router can cut the entire surface to be joined. Cut a piece of 3/4-in. thick flakeboard, 18 in. wide and longer than the longest boards you plan to join. Glue or nail two more pieces of flakeboard or plywood on top of this piece, one about 6 in. wide and the other about 10 in. wide, leaving a 2-in. space between them. This gap not only allows the router to cut below the surface of the wood, but also provides a path of escape for the sawdust. This is important because unexpelled sawdust can work around the bit, fill up its normal clearance space and cause it to whip dangerously back and forth.

Rest the jig on sawhorses, rather than your workbench. Four large clamps—I prefer wooden jaw clamps—will be needed to hold the lumber on the jig. The routing fence can be made from any piece of 3/4-in. material such as flakeboard or plywood. It should be at least 6 in. wide and at least 4 in. longer than the lumber you'll be routing.

Mark the pieces of wood to be joined (A-A1, B-B1, etc.) so it will be easy to identify matching pieces. It's best to match all the lumber you'll need for the whole tabletop first, and then join it together. Take either piece from a pair to be joined and place it—let's say it's A—on top of the jig so that the edge to be routed is over the slot in the jig. Then place the fence on top of A. The key to the operation is the distance between the leading edge of A and the front edge of the fence. It must be a little more than the distance from the cutting flute of the router bit to the outer edge of the router base. To determine this distance, first insert and tighten the router bit. (Be sure the router is unplugged and the off-on switch is off.) With a ruler flush against the bottom of the router, rotate the bit by hand so that it just ticks the end of the ruler, and read the distance to the edge of the router base. The distance varies from router to router, but let's say it's 2-1/2 in. The fence is then clamped down at both ends so that it is exactly this distance from the edge to be routed plus 1/16 in. This means the router will be cutting away 1/16 in. from the leading edge of the lumber.

To begin routing, stand between the clamps with the fence in front of you. Hold the router with the left hand and turn it on with the right hand. Place the router flat on piece A with the bit just off the wood to the right. You will rout from right to left so that the blade, which is rotating clockwise when seen from above, is cutting into the wood. Holding the router firmly, bring it toward you against the fence, and move it slowly into and along the wood from right to left.

After routing A, turn the router off and leave A clamped in place. Place the adjoining piece of wood, A1, on the jig so that the edges to be joined are facing each other and separated by the diameter of the bit (in this case 3/4 in.). Now, move piece A1 1/16 in. closer to piece A—the amount of wood you will remove from A1. Clamp A1 down and check both ends to be sure that the distance from A is exactly the

Operator guides router along fence from his left to right to cut 1/16 in. from second piece of wood.

diameter of the bit less 1/16 in. If the gap is too narrow, the router may stall. And if you have to interrupt the cut, you are almost certain to ruin it.

Now turn on the router and, standing in the same position, place it at the left end of the jig, with the bit just off the edge of the wood. You'll be routing from left to right this time. The router rests on both A and A1, and is held against the fence. In this position it will cut off 1/16 in. from A1, but nothing from A.

After you've finished routing A1, turn the router off. Unclamp A1 and bring it forward to A (which is still clamped in place) to check for errors. If the pieces don't quite match, you can rout another 1/16 in. If there are gaps, you haven't routed deeply enough. If the pieces have been routed correctly, there is only one position in which the boards will join. When the right alignment is found, the seam will virtually disappear. Pencil a fine line across the joint to help match the pieces again when you're ready to glue them.

The same procedures can be used to join wood along curves. Visually match the grain of the pieces to be joined. Mark the faces of the pieces P and P1. Draw the desired cutting line on P and using a band saw, sabre saw or hand saw, cut along this line. Place P over the mating piece P1. Trace along the line you've cut and cut piece P1. You'll now have two roughly-mated pieces. Again using P, trace along a new piece of wood to be used as a fence and saw along this line. Follow the same procedures for setting up the wood and routing as for a straight-line joint. Curved edges routed in this manner will not be perfect mirror images, especially when the curve is severe. But a slow curve or a gentle ''S'' curve will fit together nicely to form a clean joint.

Flaws in this system are caused by flaws in the wood. Avoid severely twisted wood, narrow boards and wood with knots. Cupped or bowed wood can be clamped flat for routing and planed level after glue-up. Rout the flatter board first, tacking a piece of plywood on top of it to obtain a stable surface. Finally, a word about grain. What you have to do is stop and think, which way is the grain going? Then if the router is tearing it up flip the wood over to reverse the grain.

John Harra, 33, owns the John Harra Woodworking Studio, a cabinetmaking shop and school in New York City.

Tambours
Precise measuring and machining make slats run smoothly

by Alphonse Mattia

Tambours are flexible doors, made up of a series of thin wooden slats. They are either glued to a fabric backing or threaded together with wires. The slats have tongues at each end, which run in tracking grooves cut into the carcase. Tambour doors can open vertically, as in a roll-top desk, or horizontally, as in a buffet.

Most people refer to tambours as "roll-tops" because of the familiarity of the American oak roll-top desk. Tambours, however, originated in France during the 17th century. Tambours were very popular in Louis XV (1715-1774) and Louis XVI (1774-1792) work, and again in England during the Sheraton period in the early 19th century. They did not reach the general public in America until the oak roll-top desk came into fashion early in the 20th century. Tambours are also used in Scandinavian contemporary furniture.

Tambours are efficient and offer several advantages over other door systems. Space is saved because doors do not swing out from the carcase. They give greater access to the carcase opening than sliding systems where the doors must overlap. Tambours can also follow or accentuate graceful curves in the piece. Wired tambours offer the advantage of allowing the back of the tambour to be exposed, since it is not covered with fabric. The fabric-backed method stabilizes the tambour and controls warpage better. I prefer the fabric method and will concentrate on it in this article.

Design

Tambours are a sophisticated door system, which must be an integrated element of a total design, not attempted as an afterthought. Every aspect of the piece should be planned out, from shape or form right through to details, because tolerances and clearances are very important considerations.

The initial concept should be developed through sketches and made final in accurate full-scale drawings. Mock-ups should be made where full-scale drawings do not supply enough information.

Precision is essential. The tongues must be of a shape and size that will slide smoothly in the grooves. The carcase must be glued up square with duplicate tracking grooves directly opposite each other. Design a form that you will be able to control accurately through the building stages. This is not to say that your piece must be a rectangle, but keep your first attempt fairly simple and small.

With vertical tambours, weight becomes important. A large tambour that opens from the bottom may be too heavy, and one that opens from the top may fall open under its own weight. If you plan to have a reverse curve in the track, you will have to cut a clearance angle on the sides of each slat.

One common problem with tamboured pieces is that warpage in the carcase will affect dimensions between the tracking grooves, usually at unsupported corners or over long expanses. Be sure your carcase is structurally sound. Internal parts can be designed to add rigidity to the carcase. Tamboured pieces often have a false back and sides, which conceal the fabric side of the tambour when it is opened and also prevent the contents of the cases from interfering with the travel of the doors. They may also support compartments, partitions, shelves or drawers. These parts have to be located to allow enough clearance for movement of the doors. I try to

Designer/craftsman Alphonse Mattia is assistant professor at the Boston University Program in Artisanry.

Left, author's writing cabinet, bubinga and figured maple. Above, detail of Richard Tannen's tall maple cabinet; fixed slats are filler strip.

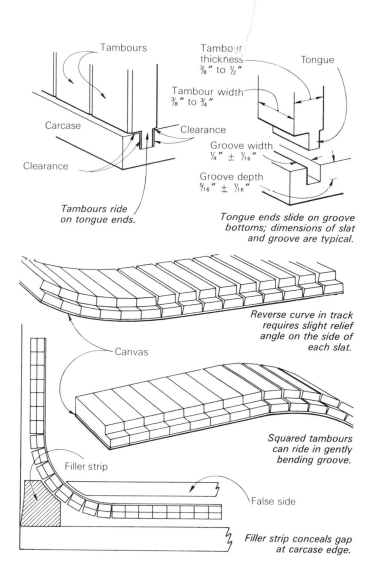

Tambours

Tambour thickness 3/8" to 1/2"

Tongue

Carcase

Clearance

Clearance

Tambour width 3/8" to 3/4"

Clearance

Groove width 1/4" ± 1/16"

Groove depth 5/16" ± 1/16"

Tambours ride on tongue ends.

Tongue ends slide on groove bottoms; dimensions of slat and groove are typical.

Reverse curve in track requires slight relief angle on the side of each slat.

Canvas

Squared tambours can ride in gently bending groove.

Filler strip

False side

Filler strip conceals gap at carcase edge.

provide as much clearance as possible to prevent later problems, such as rub marks on the tambour surface. The space where the tambour enters the carcase can be made to appear narrower by use of a filler strip or a thickened carcase edge.

Tambours are usually shouldered on the exposed side to conceal the carcase groove. The tambour can then be fitted to the groove at the tongue without distorting the shape of the tambour. Tracking grooves vary in width, depth and radius of curve. Generally speaking, tracking grooves range in width from 3/16 in. to 5/16 in. They may be smaller in delicate, silk-backed work, or larger in heavy applications. Grooves should be a little deeper than they are wide. A 3/16-in. groove should be about 1/4 in. deep; a 1/4-in. groove should be 5/16 in. deep.

Tambours for a 1/4-in. groove might range from 3/8 in. to 3/4 in. wide, and from 3/8 in. to 1/2 in. thick. The tambour width is the dimension parallel to the direction of the groove; the tambour thickness corresponds to the width of the groove. A rectangular tongue (wider than it is thick) will ensure steadier travel in the groove. For a narrow tambour, say 5/16 in., I would probably switch to a 3/16-in. groove for this reason.

The radius of the tracking grooves should be checked carefully to make sure that the tambour can travel the bend comfortably. This can be checked on paper. Draw the groove by using a compass to construct two parallel lines at the proper radius. Be sure that a paper rectangle the size of the tambour tongue will fit in the groove. This will tell you a lot, but is no substitute for routing a sample groove to the desired radius in a piece of scrap plywood and testing a glued-up sample of

your tambour. A 6-in. square of tambours can easily be made by cutting the appropriate tongues on one end of several short strips and gluing them to the fabric with Titebond. This should not take long and will be well worth the effort.

One last word about design—you should decide how you will attach the handle to your tambour, because the attaching strip may interfere with internal parts of the cabinet.

Making templates and routing grooves

A template, or pattern, for routing the tracking groove is needed to transfer the groove accurately from the drawing to both sides of the carcase. The easiest way to make grooves is to run a router against the template. It is best if a single template can be reversed for alternate sides of the carcase, so that slight inaccuracies in the curve will be duplicated.

Before you make the template, decide how it will guide the router. I usually use rub collars, which are available for most routers in a variety of sizes. Choose a size that has a convenient distance from rub surface to cutting edge. You will have to account for this distance when you construct your template. A 1/4-in. bit with a 1/2-in. O.D. rub collar will give you a difference

Router and rub collars.

of 1/8 in. This means the template has to be 1/8 in. smaller than the inside line of the groove.

You could run the router directly off the edge of the router base, but this can be inconvenient. The router will be more difficult to handle and discrepancies in the template will be magnified because of the large distance from the base-plate edge to the groove.

Get the bit and collar before making the template. It is very annoying to construct a template for a 1/2-in. rub collar and then find out that the local hardware dealer has every size except 1/2 in. A new carbide bit will help make a clean, clear track.

Once you know the size of the rub collar, you can construct accurate template lines on the full-scale drawing. To parallel a curved line, set a compass to the distance that you want between the two lines. With the point on the original line, lay out a series of arcs from the line. Then construct a new line through the top points of the arcs by using a French curve, flexible drawing spline or bending sticks. Circular arcs can be drawn with a compass.

When you draw the template, consider reference points that you can use to orient the template on both sides of the carcase. The template can be laid out to conform to some fixed line or shape on the carcase, such as a bottom edge or corner where the groove does not pass. Templates can be clamped in place, or better yet, screwed down in two or more inconspicuous spots that can be filled later. Screwing the template down will save you the aggravation of having to move clamps during routing. These screw positions can also provide an ideal reference for locating the template on the sides. A template attached in this manner can be removed, cut down and relocated to pattern other grooves in the cabinet (unless you plan to make a duplicate cabinet, in which case you'll want to keep all the templates intact). For example, the same template could be used to flush-trim the outside shape of the

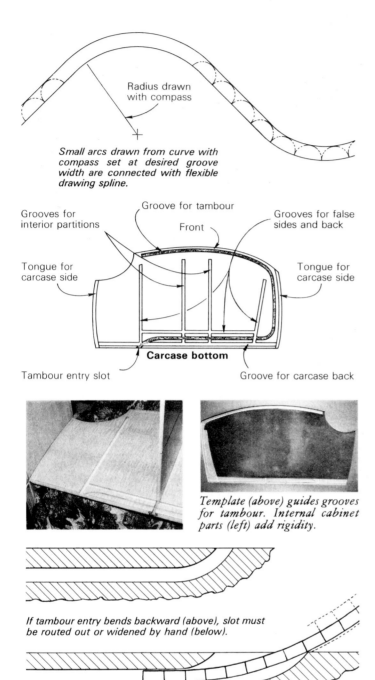

Radius drawn
with compass

*Small arcs drawn from curve with
compass set at desired groove
width are connected with flexible
drawing spline.*

Grooves for
interior partitions

Groove for tambour

Front

Grooves for false
sides and back

Tongue for
carcase side

Tongue for
carcase side

Carcase bottom

Tambour entry slot

Groove for carcase back

*Template (above) guides grooves
for tambour. Internal cabinet
parts (left) add rigidity.*

*If tambour entry bends backward (above), slot must
be routed out or widened by hand (below).*

carcase, then be removed, cut down and relocated to rout the tambour grooves, removed, recut and relocated to cut grooves for the false sides, back, shelves and other internal parts.

Template lines should be transferred from the full-scale drawing to the template with tracing paper. I glue the tracing to a piece of Masonite or Baltic birch plywood using spray adhesive or rubber cement. Fir plywood has too many voids that will cause problems when routing. Cut the template as accurately as you can, cutting on the waste side of the line. Lumps can be filed, but be sure you check the accuracy of the template against the full-scale drawing. If inaccurate, it's best to get a new piece of Masonite and start over.

Note that tambour entry slots can be part of the template, or hand-cut later if that is easier in your particular design. Remember that if the entry slot bends backwards, you have to cut a clearance angle on the tambour, or else widen the slot.

To familiarize yourself with the feel of running the router against the template, fasten the template to a piece of scrap

plywood and make a trial cut. The router cuts best when run against the direction of rotation. This may mean that on one side you will have to lower the router down into the wood to start the cut. This is awkward, but is better than trying to run with the rotation. I usually rout at full depth with a carbide bit. Most routers are slightly inaccurate, and two settings may make a tiny ledge in the groove that will cause later problems. Make sure the bit is fastened securely in the router. Some ½-in. routers do not hold ¼-in. shank bits snugly. It is common for a ¼-in. bit to slip in the collet. If this happens you will have to fill the grooves, reset the bit and rerout. Other routing mistakes can sometimes be repaired the same way. It may be necessary to widen the groove slightly at a tight radius, to aid tambour travel. This can be done by removing the template, filing the radius a tad, relocating and rerouting. Or the radius can be eased during sanding.

After the first groove is routed, orient the template on the other side. Double-check positioning and rout again. I sand grooves with little fitted sanding blocks. They should be sanded as smooth as possible without deforming them. Finish with a coat of thin shellac and polish with paste wax.

With the grooves complete, continue building the rest of the carcase. Prefinish the inside before assembly. Take precautions to ensure that no glue will run into the grooves or into areas with limited access, such as between a false side and the carcase side. Make sure that your cabinet is glued up square.

Machining the tambours

Tambour slats will be ripped longer than their finished size. Then they will be shaped, presanded and glued to a fabric backing. After gluing up, the tambour will be cut to its final length, and shoulders and tongues will be cut on the ends. Plan on making about one-third more tambours than you need. If you need 60, make 80 or 90. This will not require that much more time or material, and it is convenient to be able to discard chipped or warped tambours. Tambour stock should be sawn down to 3-in. to 5-in. widths, 1 in. or so longer than the finished length. Anything much wider will be difficult to resaw. Then resaw the sections about ³⁄₁₆ in. thicker than the finished thickness. (This depends on the length of the tambour—shorter tambours require less excess than longer ones.) These slats should be allowed to warp, at least overnight and preferably for several days. Then the slats should be dressed down to the finished thickness.

Now slats should be ripped to width. Rip a few to see if they are coming off the saw fairly straight. A little bit of warp can be tolerated in this dimension. A light jointer pass between each sawcut will help keep the tambours straight. If they are warping too much you will have to rip them oversized, allow them to warp again, dress them on the jointer and either thickness-plane or rip them to exact width. It is best to avoid running them over the jointer—this is dangerous with such small strips. If you must, make sure the jointer knives are sharp and use a push-stick. Now cut the strips to length, leaving ¼-in. to ½-in. excess at each end. Remember to account for the tongues.

When the tambours are cut to size, they should be stacked with stickers between them so they are exposed to air on all sides. Stickers should be of equal thickness and should be placed directly over each other just as when stacking lumber. I find it is better not to restrict movement and warpage. Later, before assembly, you can discard the worst tambours.

Tambours can be machine-shaped in many ways, but if you plan to do this there are a few things to remember. If they are completely rounded over on the top surfaces, you may have to cut the tongues ahead of time, because a rolled-over tambour might not sit flat on the glue-up board. Rounded tambours and most other shapes require presanding. Tambours that have a relief angle to travel in a back curve can also require presanding. On a first attempt keep shaping fairly simple, such as a simple chamfer or cove cut on the edges of the tambours to accentuate the individual strips.

To shape the tambours you will need a shaper or a router mounted in a table. Set the chamfer or cove bit to the proper height. Clamp a fence at the right distance. Clamp finger boards in place to hold the tambours tightly against the fence and table. Push each tambour through with the next one. Try not to pause when picking up the next one, as this can cause burn marks. Repeat on the second edge of each tambour.

If you have to cut a relief angle, make a jig that will hold the tambour securely as it is slid past the angled blade of the table saw. You need hardly any angle at all. Slide the tambours through once for the first side and again for the second.

If you are going to presand, make another jig to hold the tambour. A few minutes of work here will save a lot of time later. Rabbet a piece of wood to receive the tambour and hold the tambour in place with two small stop blocks. Tambours should be stacked again with stickers while you prepare a glue-up board.

Gluing up

You will need to make a board that will hold your tambours tightly together and flat and square while you glue the fabric onto the back. I use a piece of ¾-in. chipboard. It should be about 2 in. wider on each side and about 8 in. longer (2 in. at the back, and 6 in. at the front of the board) than the size of the tambour you are gluing up. Make sure you figure on enough tambours to recede into the carcase, so that you will not see the last slat when the door is closed.

Dress two pieces of wood about 1¼ in. to 1½ in. wide and as long as your glue-up board. Cut a rabbet in each piece that will receive the thickness of the tambour. The rabbet should be tight, so that when the strips are screwed down they will clamp the tambours firmly to the board. For the ends of the jig, make three thinner strips to fit under the rabbet. These should be the same length and thickness as the tambours, and about 1¼ in. to 1½ in. wide. Also make two or three pairs of opposing wedges the same thickness as the thinner strips. These will be used to clamp the tambours tightly together.

Screw the first rabbeted strip down to the particle board. Then screw down one of the thinner strips, checking with a framing square to be sure that it is 90° to the rabbeted strip. Put the tambours in place, face down, and screw down the other rabbeted strip. Once the strips are aligned, loosen the screws and remove the tambours.

Lay out the tambours on a flat surface, face up. Sort out the worst and arrange the remaining ones for color and grain pattern. You can tolerate a reasonable warpage between tambours, because it will be forced out by the clamping action of the glue-up board. Discard any tambours that arch severely away from the flat surface.

Slide tambours face down into the jig in the order you want. Keep in mind where the handle will be attached. Slide

Stickered tambours dry unrestrained; warped ones will be discarded.

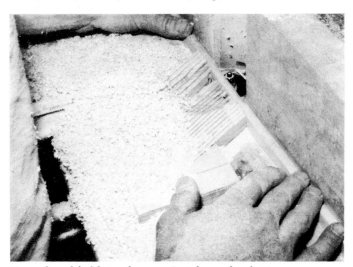

Finger board holds tambour against fence, for shaping.

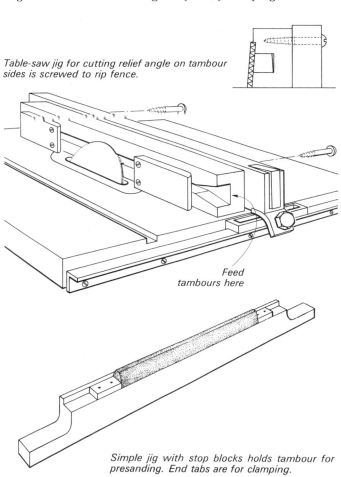

Table-saw jig for cutting relief angle on tambour sides is screwed to rip fence.

Feed
tambours here

Simple jig with stop blocks holds tambour for presanding. End tabs are for clamping.

Glue-up board

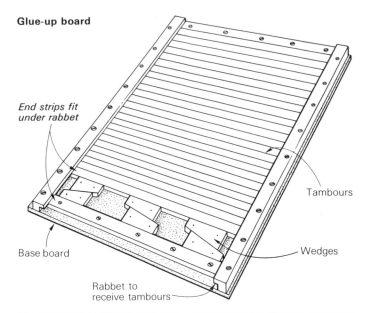

End strips fit
under rabbet

Tambours

Base board

Wedges

Rabbet to
receive tambours

Glue is brushed on a tambour section. Then a veneer hammer, working from center to edges, smoothes out the canvas.

After tambour is glued up, tongue shoulders are sawn (left), then waste is routed from front and back (above). Canvas flap is for attaching handles.

in one of the remaining thinner strips. Screw down the last strip about 2 in. behind the second strip, depending on the size of the wedges. Then tap the wedges into place to squeeze the tambours together tightly. You don't need any more pressure than is necessary to take out warps and close gaps, to prevent the glue from oozing down between the tambours. Screws in the rabbeted strips should be snug but not all the way home. While tightening the wedges to close gaps, you may need to tap the tambours down flat to the board with a scrap piece. Continue to tighten the screws in the rabbeted pieces and the wedges until the tambour is tight and flat. Then lock the wedges with a few brads.

An alternative method eliminates the third thinner strip and the wedges. Draw the whole tambour up tight with two or three bar clamps. Then screw down the second thin strip and remove the clamps. This works, but you must be careful not to deform the glue-up board with clamp pressure.

While silk, linen and leather can be used as a tambour backing, I prefer unprimed canvas. A good art-supply store will have a selection of canvas types and weights. Generally, 10-oz. canvas is best.

Now calculate the distance between the shoulders of the tambours. The tambours are still longer than final dimension and you want to be sure the canvas will clear the tongues. Remember, canvas stretches. Subtract about an additional ⅜ in. on each side. The canvas should be about 2 in. or 3 in. longer at one end than the tambour, for attaching the handle.

Now you are ready to start gluing. You can use Titebond or liquid hide glue, but I recommend hot animal glue for two reasons. Hot glue can be reheated with an iron, allowing you to correct minor problems. And, if used at the right consistency, it will not penetrate between the tambours. It should just begin to bead up as it runs off the mixing stick—like a thick syrup. You will need a veneer hammer (page 172) or a suitable wooden alternative.

It is important to get a good bond on the first tambour. Be careful not to get glue on the adjacent thin strip of the glue-up board—wax or masking tape can be used as a glue resist. Spread the glue with a 1-in. or 2-in. brush over about a 4-in. section of the tambour. Start at the handle end. Move quickly—you do not want the glue to cool. Lay the canvas over the tambour, and remember to allow for the overhang for the handle. Be sure the canvas is straight and centered. Now, using the veneer hammer, work from the center toward the ends to even out the glue and smooth the canvas. You don't need a lot of pressure. Draw the hammer parallel to the tambours. If you draw the hammer perpendicular to the tambours you will stretch the canvas, causing the tambour to roll backwards when taken out of the glue board. Then the tambour will not lie flat. You are trying only to even out the glue, smooth the canvas and ensure a good spread of glue. Try not to overwork, or you will saturate the canvas with glue, causing it to become brittle when dry.

Working quickly, flip the canvas back over the area you have just done and pull the canvas back from the glue about ½ in. in a straight line. This will ensure a good overlap of glue. Spread another 4-in. section, lay the canvas back over the tambour and smooth out with the hammer. Repeat over the entire tambour. Don't wait for the glue to dry each time. You may be surprised at how easily the canvas pulls back from the glue. Don't worry—the bond will not be strong until the glue has completely dried and matured. Don't tug on

Making tongues

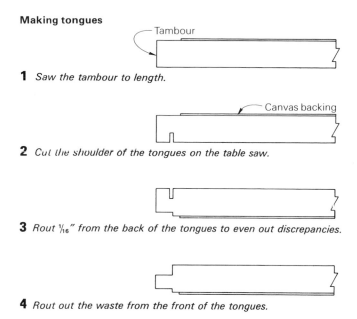

1 *Saw the tambour to length.*

2 *Cut the shoulder of the tongues on the table saw.*

3 *Rout ¹⁄₁₆″ from the back of the tongues to even out discrepancies.*

4 *Rout out the waste from the front of the tongues.*

Making handles

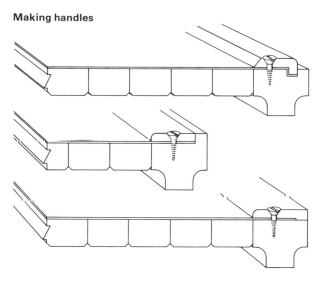

Handles, whatever the design, are usually attached with a backing strip that is screwed to the back, sandwiching the canvas. A lip conceals the canvas from view.

the canvas. Let the tambour dry overnight before you remove it from the glue-up board. Leave the tambour straight after you remove it—don't flex the joints yet.

Fitting tambours

All tambour measurements should be tested with an extra tambour strip and checked at intervals along the grooves in the carcase. It is common to have some variation in the distance between the grooves, so measure for a tight fit at the narrowest point. The tambours should run on the ends of the tongues, not on the shoulders, to avoid causing rub marks on the carcase. It is better to start with a tight tambour and to plane or sand it to a perfect fit.

First cut the tambour to exact length. Trim excess canvas from the back end and tape the handle flap out of the way before running the tambour through the table saw. To figure the length, measure the distance from the bottom of one groove to the bottom of the other groove at the narrowest part of the carcase. The tambour should be just shy of this dimension (about ¹⁄₃₂ in. shorter). Since you will want to center the canvas over the tambour, you will need to make two settings on the table saw, running the best edge against the fence in the first pass.

The tongues are formed by first sawing the shoulders, then routing out the excess wood above the tongues. This way, the router will not chip the exposed edges of the tambours. To make the shoulder cut, set the saw fence to the length of the tongue—much safer than running the whole tambour between the blade and the fence. Make sure the shoulder cut allows clearance between the tambour and the carcase. Finally, you'll need to remove ¹⁄₁₆ in. from the back of the tongue after the shoulder is cut, to even out discrepancies. Therefore set the height of the blade ¹⁄₁₆ in. lower than the thickness of the finished tongue.

After cutting the shoulders, I remove the excess wood with a shaper or router table setup. Set the fence a little short of the length of the tongue (the saw kerf from the shoulder cut is a safety zone) and use a straight cutter bigger than the length of the tongue. Set it just high enough to kiss off the back of the tambour—¹⁄₁₆ in. is plenty—and run both edges. Then raise the bit, flip the tambour over, and rout the front

side. Whole chips will fly off, so safety glasses are essential.

Now try the tambour. It probably won't fit. Try to figure out which dimension is off before going wild with the rabbet plane. Problems can be caused by too long a tambour, too thick a tongue, too little clearance at the radii, or shoulders that rub. A sharp rabbet plane, a crisp 90° sanding block and patience are necessary to fit the tambour. As you get close to the final fit, use finer sandpaper. When the tambour is running smoothly, polish with paste wax. You can also lubricate sparingly with paraffin, but too much will gum up the track.

Handles, finishing and stops

The tambour handle should be an integrated part of the total design, relating to other details on the piece. You want a handle you can grasp easily. One that is too narrow or extends out too far will be prone to binding. If you wish to install a lock or latch, you will have to design the handle with enough material to accommodate it.

Cut stock for the handle with tongues on the ends. This can be done by hand, with a dovetail saw. Try the handle in the groove to check the tongues. Then do all necessary shaping and sanding. The canvas should be trimmed slightly smaller than the width of the handle. I like to size the canvas end with a little Titebond to prevent unraveling.

Handles are usually attached with a strip of wood that is screwed to the back, sandwiching the canvas. I like to cut a slight lip on the edge of the attaching strip to conceal the canvas when the door is open. This lip is easier to cut before the strip is ripped off a larger piece of wood. Attach the handle to the tambour on a flat surface and make sure it is tight against the first tambour before you try to install it in the carcase. Once the holes are drilled you can remove the handle, install the tambour in the carcase and screw on the handle.

Apply finish before you install the tambour. Spread the tambours open, and use a dry brush or rag between them. Don't get finish on the fabric or you will shorten its life.

Plan on making a stop. The handle won't do because repeated use will weaken the canvas where the handle meets the tambour. A ripped canvas will mean a big repair job. Stops can be strips screwed or glued to the inside of the back of the carcase or small pieces screwed into the grooves. □

Shaped Tambours

by Bob March

Traditional tambours run on horizontal or vertical tracks and they can follow various curves. But they always have a flat back, which make it difficult to do a lot of shaping on the front. While it would be possible to make the tambour thicker, it could become so heavy that it couldn't be opened easily. This can be overcome with a system of concealed counterweights, which I considered for the desk shown here.

A counterweight didn't seem in keeping with the open nature of the desk I was making, so I decided to eliminate the flat backing. The tambour top is 48 in. wide, so I reduced the canvas to two 10-in. strips down the edges. Then, with conventional shaper jigs, I shaped the tambour slats in the center so they would curve back behind the plane of the canvas.

The first problem that arises when you shape a tambour this way is that it will not be able to go around a corner unless you also taper the portion that is behind the plane of the canvas. The amount of taper can be figured by drawing an end view. In this desk I decided to exaggerate the taper, so there would be open slits in the center portion of the tambour. I felt this would go well with the rest of the desk, which has many open slits in the end and across the back. The slats were tapered with the thicknesser. Then the tambour was hot-glued to the canvas with a veneer hammer.

The handle was attached with hot glue after the tambour was installed in the desk. It was designed with two gripping points, one at each end, which transmit the stress of opening and closing directly to the canvas strips. Its form also seemed to go well with the concave shape of the front.

The additional work this approach requires is well worth the increased shaping possibilities. On this desk the shaping was quite subtle, but the soft curve of the tambour, the top and the back slats made a significant difference. One could also exaggerate the shaping, possibly even making the individual slats from laminations. □

Bob March, 28, a graduate of the School for American Craftsmen in Rochester, N.Y., teaches at the Worcester (Mass.) Craft Center.

Desk, of vermilion, is 58 in. by 26 in. by 46 in.

Chinese keyed splice shown in photo and drawings joins leg to desk.

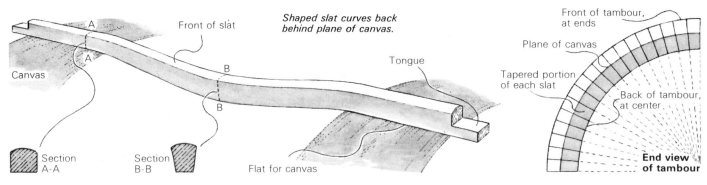

Of the Cylinder Desk and Book-Case

by Thomas Sheraton

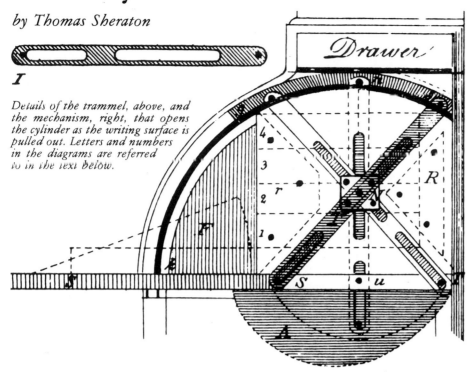

Details of the trammel, above, and the mechanism, right, that opens the cylinder as the writing surface is pulled out. Letters and numbers in the diagrams are referred to in the text below.

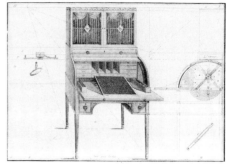

Sheraton's cylinder desk, reprinted from The Cabinet-Maker and Upholsterer's Drawing Book.

EDITOR'S NOTE: Thomas Sheraton (1751-1806) was a cabinetmaker and a cabinetmaker's son, although there is little evidence that he actually built any of the pieces so carefully described in his *Cabinet Maker and Upholsterer's Drawing Book*. He seems to have acted like a freelance designer, noting down what was being made in London, then peddling his drawings and notes to the trade. He died a pauper, little knowing that he would emerge as the namesake and principal chronicler of the furniture of the late 18th century. His drawing book is available as a handsome $5.95 paperback published by Dover, 180 Varick St., New York, N.Y. 10014, from which the following excerpt is taken. We've modernized the spelling and deleted material extraneous to the cylinder-fall itself.

First, observe the slider is communicated with the cylinder by an iron trammel, as *I*, so that when the former comes forward, the latter rises up and shows the nest of the small drawers and letter holes, as appears in the design. When, therefore, the slider is pushed home even with the front, the cylinder is brought close to it at the same time. In this state the lock of the long drawer under the slider secures both the drawer itself and also the slider at the same time... The trammel *I* is a piece of iron near a quarter thick, an inch and quarter broad, with grooves cut through, as shown at *I*. *S*, in the profile, is the slider; and *g*, *12*, *h*, the

cylinder. The trammel *T* is fixed to the cylinder at *h* by a screw, not drove tight up, but so as the trammel will pass round easy. Again, at the slider *S* a screw is put through the groove in the trammel, which works on the neck of the screw, and its head keeps the trammel in its place; so that it must be observed, that the grooves or slits in the iron trammel are not much above a quarter of an inch in width. When the slider is pushed in about half way, the trammel will be at *u* and its end will be below the slider; as the plate shows; but when the slider is home to its place, the trammel will be at *T* and *g*. The center piece with four holes is a square plate of iron, having a center-pin which works in the upper slit of the trammel. It is let into the end of the cylinder and fixed with four screws. To find the place of this center, lay the trammel upon the end, as *T-h*, in the position that it will be in when the slider is out, and with a pencil, mark the inside of the slits in the trammel. Again, place the trammel on the end as it will be when the slider is in, as at *T-g*, and do as before; and where these pencil marks intersect each other will be the place of the center-plate. The figures *1, 2, 3, 4*, show the place of the small drawers. The triangular dotted lines with three holes, is a piece of thin wood screwed

on to the end, to which is fixed the nest of small drawers, forming a vacuity for the trammel to work in. *F* is a three-eighth piece veneered and cross-banded, and cut behind to give room for the trammel. This piece both keeps the slider to its place, and hides the trammel. The next thing to be observed is, that the lower frame, containing two heights of drawers, is put together separate from the upper part, which takes the cylinder. The ends of the cylinder part are tenoned with the slip tenons into the lower frame and glued. The shaded part at *A* shows the rail cut out to let the trammel work... The cylinder is jointed to its sweep in narrow slips of straight-baited hard mahogany, and afterwards veneered. If the veneer be of a pliable kind it may be laid with a hammer, by first shrinking and tempering the veneer well, which must not be by water, but thin glue. If the veneer be very cross and unpliable, as many curls of mahogany are, it is in vain to attempt the hammer. A caul in this case is the surest and best method, though it be attended with considerably more trouble than the hammer. To prepare for laying it with a caul, proceed as follows. Take five or six pieces of three-inch deal, and sweep them to fit the inside of the cylinder. Fix these upon a board answerable to the length of the cylinder. Then have as many cauls for the outside of the cylinder, which may be made out of the same pieces as those for the inside. Take then quarter mahogany for a caul to cover the whole veneer, and heat it well. Put the caul screws across the bench, and slip in the board with the round cauls screwed to it; and then proceed, in every other particular, as the nature of the thing will dictate. □

Methods of Work

Mortising plane

Here is an old design for a plane to cut mortises when inlaying hardware. It works like a router plane, but can reach places the router can't go, such as when inlaying hinges in door jambs. Because the two side pieces are raised from the sole, the corners of the blade can cut right up to shoulders and moldings. I have found a 14-in. plane most useful, as it gives a sure surface for hardware up to 7 in. long. Of course the plane can be made longer or shorter.

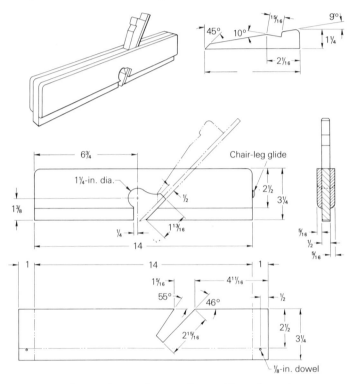

You need one piece ⅝ in. x 3¼ in. x 16 in. of maple or some other dense wood; two pieces ⅜ in. x 3 in. x 16 in. that may be a contrasting wood if you like; one piece ⅝ in. x 1½ in. x 6½ in. for the wedge; and one piece of steel ¼ in. x ½ in. x 9 in. Oil-hardening steel, which comes in 18-in. lengths, is well-suited; that is why the iron is 9 in. long. After the steel is cut and ground, send it out to be hardened or do it yourself.

First make the centerpiece, which is notched and finished to ½ in. thick. Drill two ⅛-in. holes as shown and insert two dowels, to locate the side pieces during glue-up. Plane the side pieces to 5⁄16 in. thick and clamp the assembly together, using cauls for straightness because the sides are so thin. Clean out the glue where the wedge and iron will fit, and clean it off the bottoms of the side pieces. When the glue has set, cut the plane to length, locate and drill the 1¼-in. hole and complete the cut-out shape. Round the edges of the upper part of the cutout, so the shavings will slide off easily.

Now make the wedge and fit the iron. Move the iron back ¼ in. from the bottom and tap the wedge home, then correct the sole for straightness. If you true the plane without the iron and wedge in place, it may change when they are pressing against the wood. To lower the iron, tap it at the top. To move it up, tap on the back of the plane. To protect the wood, you can hammer in a chair glide or inset a hardwood striking button. To remove the iron completely, tap against the notch in the wedge. —*Tage Frid, Foster, R.I.*

Louvered Doors
Router jig cuts slots

by William F. Reynolds

Woodworkers at the U. S. Capitol are often called on to match the decor of an earlier age. When the Architect of the Capitol decides that a room must be renovated or redecorated, woodworkers like Ned Spangler, a cabinetmaker for the U. S. Congress, must rise to the occasion and improvise techniques to carry out the project. An example of the challenge, and the solution, is the production of louvered doors. Before air conditioning, Washington offices were extremely humid, and louvers allowed air circulation into cabinets, which kept the contents from mildewing and prevented doors from sticking. Although louvers can be difficult and time-consuming to make, they are elegant and dignified.

Spangler has a shortcut for making the louvered doors he is so often required to build. As Spangler says, "The job has to be done right, and right the first time." His router jig turns out slotted stiles quickly and precisely. It could be adapted to make a series of mortises, such as for crib slats.

The jig consists of two long hardwood posts mounted on plywood, a square piece of Masonite screwed to the baseplate of the router, and two router carriages that slide along the posts and guide the router as it cuts the equally spaced, mirror-image slots on opposite stiles. The jig shown here is designed for a ¼-in. router bit, and for ⅞-in. thick stiles for a

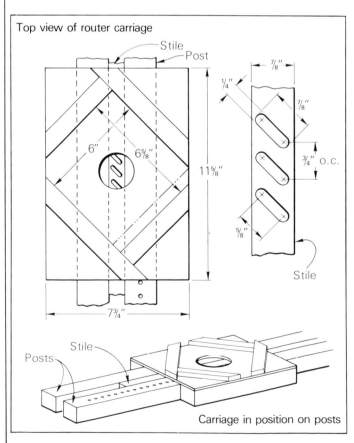

Top view of router carriage

Carriage in position on posts

Test slots are checked for accuracy of angle, fit.

Spangler routs a slot; screwdriver indexes carriage.

The completed door—elegant and dignified.

30-in. door, with 1-in. wide slats angled 45° and spaced ¾ in. on center along the stiles.

The posts, cut from birch or similar hardwood, should be long enough to hold the stiles firmly, with perhaps an extra foot on each end. For this jig, the posts are 5 ft. long and 1¾ in. square. They are mounted parallel to each other and ⅞ in. apart, on a plywood base, so that a stile fits snugly between them.

To mount the router, cut a 6-in. square from ¼-in. Masonite. In it drill three holes to match those for screws in the router base, and one of ¾-in. dia. in the center, for router bit clearance. Then screw the square to the base of the router.

Next, drill holes in the posts for stops for the router carriages. These equally spaced holes determine the spacing of the slots, and therefore of the louvers. Drill 1-in. deep holes, ¼ in. in diameter, down the top of either post, starting and ending 8 in. from each end. Space the holes for minimum clearance between louvers, in this case ¾ in. on center.

The two router carriages slide along the posts. At each stop, they allow the router to travel the exact length of the 45° slot it must make for the louver. To make these carriages, cut two pieces 7¾ in. by 11⅛ in. from ¼-in. plywood and lay out a 2-in. diameter hole at the center of each. These holes will help align the louver slots and allow clearance for the router bit. Cut four pieces, 2 in. by 1¾ in. by 11⅛ in. Nail two to the underside of each plywood plate, to form the carriage sides and keep it centered as it moves along the posts.

Four pieces, each 1 in. wide by ½ in. thick, position the router base plate atop the carriage and allow it to travel only far enough to cut a slot. Starting from the center of the uncut hole, measure to each side and lay out a rectangle 6⅜ in. by

6 in. at 45° to the sides of the plywood. The router base will travel within this rectangle. For the second carriage, the long sides of the rectangle should slope 45° to the other side; thus the two will produce mirror-image slots. Make sure that this is so before nailing the pieces in place to frame the rectangles. Then cut the 2-in. center holes. With this setup, the router travels ⅝ in. to make a slot ¼ in. by ⅞ in. long. If you use a bit larger than ¼ in., adjust the router travel distance to the length of the slot minus the diameter of the router bit.

To cut the first slot, set one stile between the posts and place the carriage on top. Mark the stile where you want the cut to end, perhaps an inch from the end of the stile, with the router travel from lower right to upper left. Stand a sample slat, cut short, on the stile inside the hole in the jig and align the sample so it marks the area for the first slot. Put a ¼ in. screwdriver in the post hole nearest the point where it will hold the jig in place while the slot is being cut. It may be necessary to move the stile slightly, leaving the screwdriver in the selected hole, to achieve perfect alignment.

Set the router bit to make a test cut, on this or on a test stile. Cut to the required depth, usually ⅜ in. to ½ in. Successive cuts are located by advancing the screwdriver to the next post hole and moving the carriage along.

To cut the slots in the opposite stile, use the second carriage. Always make a trial cut to check for alignment. If the first slot matches the one on the mating stile, then the others will too. If you have measured exactly, the job should go quickly and the louvers should fit the first time. □

William F. Reynolds is a Washington-based free-lance journalist and an amateur woodworker.

Entry Doors

Frame-and-panel construction is sturdy, handsome

by Ben Davies

Exterior doors are the problem child of architectural design. They are required to perform three functions: seal off an opening from the exterior air, open to allow passage and then reseal, and be attractive. All this from wood, a material that can change in size as much as an inch over the width of a typical opening. While each of these functions might be separately accomplished with ease, their combination into one design creates problems.

Single-panel board-and-batten constructions of edge-glued lumber are generally too unstable for exterior doors. They cast or wind unless great care is taken in the selection and seasoning of the lumber. They also expand and contract so much with the seasons that sealing against the weather is impossible. These shortcomings can be overcome by using frame-and-panel construction and, in fact, most doors are made this way. The style is relatively stable and offers great flexibility of design. Even the familiar commercial veneered doors are a variation of the frame and panel—the panel is reduced in

thickness to veneer and glued over the frame rather than inserted into grooves, and cardboard honeycomb or wood cores support the veneer. These doors succeed admirably in the first two functions a door must perform, but fail miserably at being attractive.

The frame-and-panel door has been in use for so long that its construction is well understood, and variations on its designs have been thoroughly explored. When any construction method remains dominant for hundreds of years it can mean only that it works quite well.

The standard size for entrance doors of new construction in the United States is 3 ft. wide by 6 ft. 8 in. high. A walnut door of this size can weigh 80 lb. to 100 lb. or more, depending on the thickness of the panels and the amount of glass. This is considerably heavier than a softwood or hollow-core door of the same size, and great care must be taken to ensure that the joints are well designed and well constructed.

I have seen a number of doors fail that were constructed

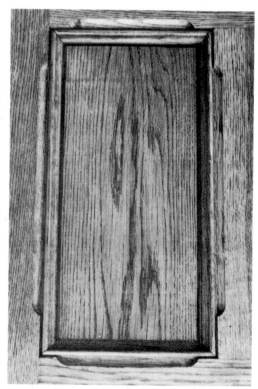

Routed sticking stops short of corners in raised-panel door, left, but continues around corners of flat-panel door, center. Both are Honduras mahogany. Detail from oak door, above, shows routed sticking combined with molding.

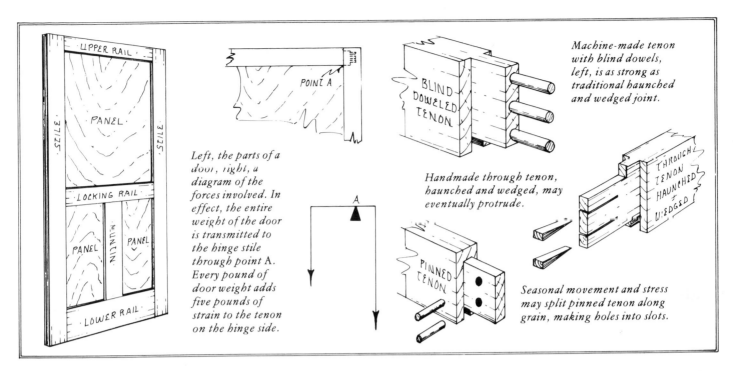

Left, the parts of a door, right, a diagram of the forces involved. In effect, the entire weight of the door is transmitted to the hinge stile through point A. Every pound of door weight adds five pounds of strain to the tenon on the hinge side.

Machine-made tenon with blind dowels, left, is as strong as traditional haunched and wedged joint.

Handmade through tenon, haunched and wedged, may eventually protrude.

Seasonal movement and stress may split pinned tenon along grain, making holes into slots.

with a mortise-and-tenon joint pinned through the cheek with dowels. A stronger joint is one with blind dowels inserted into the end of the tenon and bottom of the mortise. I use a 3-in. deep mortise and tenon with three or more 1/2-in. diameter blind dowels to join the stiles with the rails. Interior parts of the frame, such as muntins, are joined to the rails with smaller tenons, usually made to fit the groove cut for the panels, and are also blind-doweled. For flat panels I ordinarily use a 1/2-in. deep groove in the rails and a 3/4-in. deep groove in the stiles. This difference is to compensate for the greater shrinkage that occurs across the grain of the panels.

Several factors make blind dowel pins preferable to through-the-cheek pins. The first is visual. Dowels through the cheek are often chosen because they give the same sense of rigidity to frames as dovetails give to casework. While they do make a door look sturdy, the time will surely come when that particular effect is not wanted.

More importantly, I believe the blind-doweled tenon to be stronger than one pinned through the cheek. A tenon with blind dowels need not be haunched because the dowel pins not only make the tenon effectively longer, but also transform a stub tenon into a haunched tenon. Thus the glue area of the tenon becomes about one-third greater. And a stub tenon can be made more quickly than a haunched tenon.

Dowels perform two main functions. One is to prevent the tenon from sliding out of the mortise and the other is to counteract the bending moment of the weight of the door about the point where the tenon enters the stile. The lever arm through which the through-the-cheek dowel must act is necessarily about 3/4 in. shorter than that of the blind dowels. In a 3-in. tenon this difference translates into 25% greater strain on the pins. It is very important to understand that on a 36-in. door with stiles 6 in. wide, every pound of door weight adds about 5 lb. of strain to the dowels on the hinge side of the door. The wider the door and the narrower the stiles, the more intense the leverage. The maximum length of a through-the-cheek dowel is the thickness of the

Ben Davies makes doors and furniture at Muntin Woodworks in Chattanooga, Tenn. He has taught philosophy.

door, while the blind dowel can be twice as long as the width of the stile minus the tenon length. The extra dowel length is significant because part of the glue line between the dowels and their holes is end grain joined to long grain.

I have not discussed the through wedged tenon because this joint must be made by hand, a relatively time-consuming operation. However, the joint is strong, although in the long run the tenon will protrude slightly from the stile.

The total strength of a blind doweled mortise-and-tenon depends on two factors: the shear strength of the glue line that joins the cheek of the tenon to the wall of the mortise, and the lesser of the tensile strength of the wood in the dowels and the shear strength of the glue line around the dowels. The dowel joint is strongest when the outside dowels are as far apart as possible without getting so close to the end that the tenon is split by hydraulic pressure from the glue.

A mortise and tenon can be strengthened by increasing the size of the tenon, thereby increasing the glue area. The thinness of the glue line is also quite important—the thinner the better. The smoother the walls of the mortise and the sides of the tenons, the better the adhesion of glue to wood. I use a chain mortiser to make the mortise, and for the tenons, either a tenoning jig on the table saw or a single-end tenoner, which cuts with a cylindrical head like a jointer. But the tools used are not as important as getting a close fit.

While the decline and fall of Western civilization is widely anticipated, these things do take time, and until the event actually occurs there are few circumstances in which a door will be exposed to moisture other than that which is in the air. Therefore I generally use aliphatic resin (yellow) glue on doors that will be protected by a porch. This glue has worked out well in practice. In order to be classified ''waterproof,'' a glue joint must withstand boiling water for some hours without losing strength. If you plan to boil your doors, phenol resorcinol glue is what you want. No matter what glue is used, be sure to seal both ends of the door with polyurethane varnish, even if the door is to be delivered unfinished. This is often neglected by the painter.

Wooden panels for a door can be flat or raised. Raised panels are somewhat easier to fit, because with flat panels the fit

Federal law requires manufacturers to use tempered glass, but permits leaded glass panels as long as no single piece of glass is larger than 30 sq. in. and no opening is large enough to pass a baseball. Beveled octagonal glass, left, is a framed panel within a panel.

must be precise—very nearly tight enough to split the stile or rail but not so tight as to actually do it. Something can be gained by slightly tapering the edge of a panel by a hand plane or belt sander but this requires a very light touch. Any irregularity or dip left by the plane will show up distinctly where the panel enters the frame. When using panels of glued-up stock, it is a good idea to design the door so that no panel is wider than about 12 in. This is particularly true where there is a cutout in the center for glass. If the panel and glass fit tightly, the wood of the panel may split at its narrow point when contracting, rather than moving in its grooves. Of course, don't fragment a design just to obtain narrow panels.

If a wide panel is necessary, flat-cut veneer over plywood will give great stability. Or large panels themselves can be made up as another frame within the frame of the rails and stiles, if the changing grain directions do not do violence to the design. A number of coats of polyurethane varnish on the door will inhibit the transfer of moisture from wood to air and reduce the shrinkage-expansion oscillations.

Often an integral part of the doors I design is a piece of stained glass that is curved or in some other way not rectangular. Installing the glass in the irregular opening can be a problem. The easiest solution is to let the glass into a groove when gluing up the door, in the same manner as for a wooden panel. This is quick and convenient, but impossible to repair. It is best to avoid this method unless the door is going to lead a quiet life in the interior of a mausoleum. Gentle curves can be glazed with moldings of steamed wood. First, a rabbet is cut with the router, then the glass is bedded in glazing compound, and finally the molding is steamed and put into place. I sometimes make a virtue of the necessity for fasteners to hold the molding and work brass screws into the de-

sign. Silicone caulk is excellent and long lasting, but it is also a glue and the window will have to be cut loose with a razor blade if it has to be removed. If curves are too acute for steam-bent wood, an extremely flexible brown plastic panel retainer can be used. It is available from Minnesota Woodworkers Supply, Rogers, Minn. 55374.

If neither steam bending nor plastics is appealing, you can use the band saw or sabre saw to cut a molding out of solid stock to fit the line exactly where glass and wood meet. This works well, but is time-consuming. Leave the stock 1/2 in. or more thick, make the cutout, then fashion some detail on the edge complementary to the sticking (the shape cut into the inside edge of the frame) on the door.

The sticking on all commercial doors is done so that the detail runs the full length of the stile. Its mirror image, called the cope cut, is then made on the shoulder of the tenon. The corner resulting when the door is assembled is a crisp line, much like that made by mitered molding.

The most economical way for a small shop to make these cuts is with matched coping and sticking cutters for the shaper. Knives can be purchased with standard copes and stickings already ground and many companies will grind a set to your specifications. I use a single-end tenoner with cope heads, which is somewhat more cumbersome to set up than the shaper but has the advantage of easily cutting a tenon as long as 3 in. and making the cope at the same time. Also, matching beading and coping bits are available for the router, and one could fashion a set of wooden hand planes to do the job. Skill and patience with hand tools can make a joint as well as a ton of machinery can, and also will lead one in the direction of simpler, less cluttered designs.

Relying on sticking to provide the detail on the inside edge of the frame works well if the panel design is rectangular and raised panels are used. However, when the design includes curved or flat panels, it is often better to eliminate crisp corners by cutting the sticking with a router after the frame is clamped up without the panels. The effect is to soften the corner, draw the eye away from the frame and emphasize the shape of the panels. Although subtle, the difference is important to the overall feeling of the door. Attention is diverted from the outline to the interior, for the most part unconsciously. Generally, soft corners are best suited to less formal designs, although this is not a hard-and-fast rule. Making use of this detail can be a powerful tool for the designer in trying to achieve a desired effect.

Moldings around the panels give a similar effect to conventionally cut sticking, but far more depth and detail are possible. The door can be made up with everything square and the moldings then glued into place. There is a problem here of wood movement, best solved by fastening the molding to the frame, leaving the panels free to expand and contract. Silicone-type glues will stretch a great deal while still holding their bond. Better yet, put the molding around the panel like a picture frame, with a channel or a tongue on its outer edge to fit to the door frame. No glue is needed to hold the panel or the molding in place.

Lately I have been experimenting with a molding that is H-shaped in cross section, with excellent results. The open ends of the H are cut to fit the stiles and rails on one side, and to fit the thickness of the panel on the other.

It is difficult for me to say anything really useful about design because only its superficial aspects can be discussed meaningfully. Much nonsense is spoken and written in an attempt to intellectualize style and lump it together with technique. More often than not, good design is a matter of trial and error combined with the designer's ability to recognize those combinations of color and form that succeed and, just as important, those that do not.

A number of design techniques, although they will not generate successful designs all by themselves, are nonetheless helpful from time to time. One of these techniques is to use a geometric form where possible rather than a free form.

Beveled glass takes on a multifaceted gemlike appearance when used in openings that are regular or irregular polygons. These same polygons around a free-flowing piece of stained glass give a visual reference that controls the curves on its interior. I suspect this explains why Art Nouveau was less successful in architecture than it was on a smaller scale. Its paintings were bounded by rectangular frames and its small objects and furniture by rectangular walls. Its architecture had no regular boundary and consequently appeared grotesque. Descriptions of space will go where they will but the human mind is Euclidean. And why should these geometric devices not succeed? Much of the diversity and beauty found in nature has as its foundation the geometric, crystalline structure of inorganic materials. A designer can do a lot worse than to mimic nature. At least it helps avoid appearing contrived.

Another interesting tool comes from the arithmetic series 0, 1, 1, 2, 3, 5, 8, 13, 21, 34, and so on. These are called Fibonacci numbers and each number in the series is the sum of the two preceding numbers. After the series has progressed for a while, the ratio between any two adjacent numbers stabilizes at 1.618. All this would be only of academic interest if someone had not noticed that the Parthenon fits neatly into a

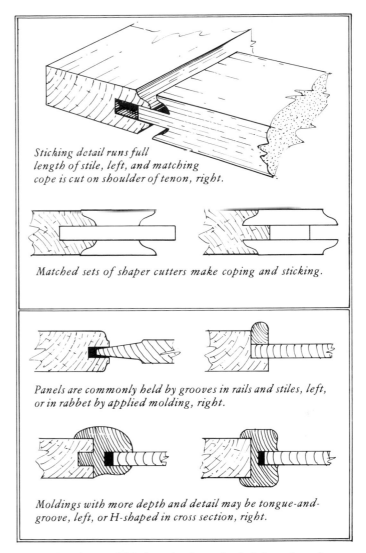

Sticking detail runs full length of stile, left, and matching cope is cut on shoulder of tenon, right.

Matched sets of shaper cutters make coping and sticking.

Panels are commonly held by grooves in rails and stiles, left, or in rabbet by applied molding, right.

Moldings with more depth and detail may be tongue-and-groove, left, or H-shaped in cross section, right.

rectangle whose width is 1.62 times its height; that the exquisite, logarithmically spiralled shell of the chambered nautilus can be generated with this ratio; that the proportions of some of Leonardo da Vinci's paintings, as well as those of Mondrian, seem to be determined by this ratio. A rectangle of this proportion, known as the golden rectangle, is frequently used in art and architecture. It has obvious applications to both doors and casework. Of course we do not want every rectangle to have these proportions, but it can be helpful to know the relationship.

These examples do not begin to scratch the surface. They are from one category of one mode of our awareness. That is, they are visual and oriented toward form. Within the visual mode there are also techniques for generating color and texture. And most often neglected are the other senses: smell, touch and hearing. The interplay and blending of techniques with a material as diverse in its nature as wood allows limitless possibilities for design.

And yet, when a door or piece of furniture succeeds, it is due to the designer's sensitivity rather than to manipulation and awareness of techniques. In much of the work where the golden rectangle has been found, the designer was unaware of the mathematics involved; the proportion just *looked* right. No doubt it is very easy to do a perfectly hideous piece based on the golden rectangle, or on any geometric figure for that matter. Techniques are just toys with which to play—they do not guarantee good design. Good design is simply done, not generated by formula.

The Right Way to Hang a Door

by Tage Frid

When I make a door I first make the doorcase (frame). I make the inside of the doorcase 3/16 in. larger in height and width than the door itself. If the door is to be painted, I allow a little more for the paint. I bevel the edges of the door a little toward the closing side, so that if dirt or paint should fill up the corners of the frame, the door will still close tightly.

If I am using two hinges, I place them approximately one-sixth of the height of the door in to the center of the hinge. With three hinges, I center one and move the other two out closer to the top and bottom. The hinges should be mortised half into the door and half into the frame. Here is where the mortising plane (as described on page 96) comes in handy, as it will fit into the lip of the frame.

When fitting the hinges to the jamb, inlay the top hinge so that the door will fit tightly against the jamb when it is closed. But inlay the bottom hinge a little less, so there will be a gap of 1/8 in. or so in the back. Setting the hinges this way will leave the whole door cocked at a slight angle, which is much exaggerated in the drawing. The space will not be the same the whole way around. I do this because as a hinge starts wearing the door

will begin to droop down. Hinges set as described will allow for this droop and the door will fit much better throughout the life of the hinge. It is especially necessary to do this with modern stamped and rolled hinges. You can see in old doors that haven't been hung this way the extent to which drooping occurs.

When I install the door frame I have all the hardware—hinges, locks, latches—already installed in the frame. I use wood shingles as shims to level the frame and fasten the hinge side first. Then I hang the door into the frame, close it and shim it until I get the spacing I want all the way around the door. Then I fasten the rest of the frame to the studs on the wall.

If I really want to do it right, I use a door-frame dovetail on all four corners, with the pins in the horizontal pieces. The joint is designed so that when you fit the door you can make the frame narrower or wider without a gap showing. Also, if the door should shrink or expand, I can take the outside molding off and wedge in or shim out the door frame to fit the door without getting a gap and without having to plane the door and refit the hardware. And this joint is much stronger than the usual method of nailing the corners together.

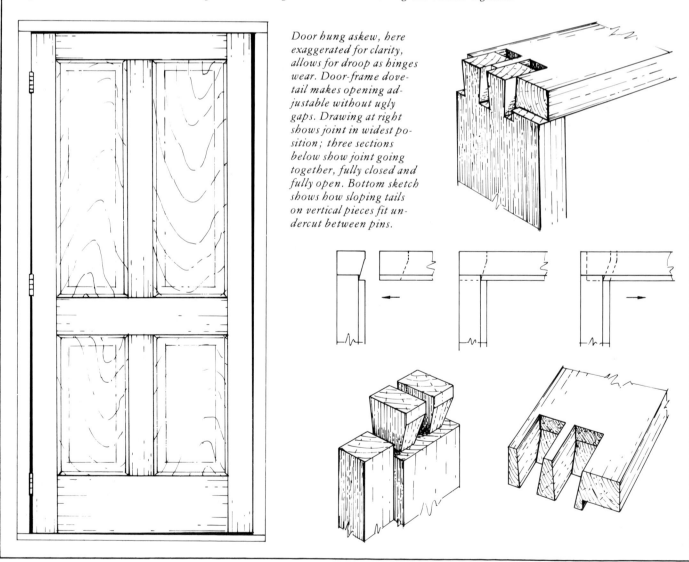

Door hung askew, here exaggerated for clarity, allows for droop as hinges wear. Door-frame dovetail makes opening adjustable without ugly gaps. Drawing at right shows joint in widest position; three sections below show joint going together, fully closed and fully open. Bottom sketch shows how sloping tails on vertical pieces fit undercut between pins.

Hanging a Door

Another way to get it right

by Willis N. Ryan III

EDITOR'S NOTE: *When we published Ben Davies' article "Entry Doors" (page 98), we asked Tage Frid to fill a page telling how he hangs a door. Frid obliged with details of the intricate dovetail jamb joint he learned as a carpenter's apprentice, and we added a headline that read, "The Right Way to Hang a Door" (page 102). Several readers objected, and rightly so, for there is no single "right way" in woodworking. There are many ways, and the "rightness" of each can be judged only by the results. Here, Willis N. Ryan of Fayetteville, N.Y., describes the method "taught to me by a cantankerous and exacting builder before he retired." Ryan adds that he has been hanging doors for 15 years, "and seriously for the past five."*

When a door jamb has been cased out it should have and retain a clean, unbroken, molded-in-place appearance. With a painted door especially this requires the jamb to be set securely, its head fixed, and the casing miters glued. The paint fractures we usually see shouldn't be there.

In new construction, figure back from the door size to determine the rough opening. In remodeling, the rough opening and jamb stock can usually be made to accommodate a standard door. Extensive trimming of the door is always a last resort. If the rough opening is greatly out of plumb you will need extra clearance for the jamb. Normally ½-in. clearance in width is plenty.

When I make a jamb the sides are rabbeted to accept the header, the header is glued and toe-nailed to the sides, and then the sides are nailed to the header. Then I nail temporary spreaders to the jamb about 8 in. from top and bottom, extending past each side by about 6 in. The spreaders hold the jamb in plane with the wall and keep the sides of the jamb parallel during installation.

This jamb assembly's inside dimensions are larger than the finished door by ½ in. in height and ³⁄₁₆ in. in width. It is tacked in place through the spreaders, with the sides plumb and the header level. Both sides are then scribed to the floor. The clearance allowed for the door depends on the hand of door and the run of the floor; if the floor is level ³⁄₁₆ in. is fine. The jamb is pulled out of the opening and cut to the scribed lines. When put back in the opening the jamb will meet the floor correctly, and its header will be level.

When setting the jamb, keep the sides plumb and true. If the hinge side of the rough opening is plumb, nail the jamb directly to it. If not, do the minimum necessary shimming on the hinge side and keep the shims near where the hinges will be placed. Shim and nail the latch side at top, bottom and middle. When the jamb is secure and true, remove the spreaders. This method is very trustworthy and, once you're used to it, very fast.

Always use three hinges, unless you're hanging a door under 5 ft. or a hollow-core. Each butt hinge is designed for a specific door thickness, size, weight and for the usage it will receive. Solve your hardware problems by taking your business to a firm that specializes in hardware, not a hardware

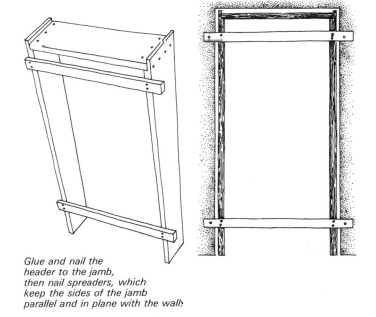

Glue and nail the header to the jamb, then nail spreaders, which keep the sides of the jamb parallel and in plane with the wall.

store. For doors that are heavy, much used or equipped with a mechanical closer, ball-bearing hinges are available in most sizes.

To hang the door, drive two nails into each side of the jamb to act as temporary stops. Set them back from the edge of the jamb slightly more than the thickness of the door. Set the door in the opening and wedge it against the hinge side of the jamb. Check the top of the door for even clearance. If it runs one way or the other, plane the top of the door.

I use a router template to inset the hinges. If you're going to lay out the mortises by hand and chisel them, careful figuring here will save much trouble later. If your hinges are insufficient or the door is extraordinarily heavy, you can increase the depth of the inset with each higher hinge to produce an even clearance between the door and hinge side of the jamb.

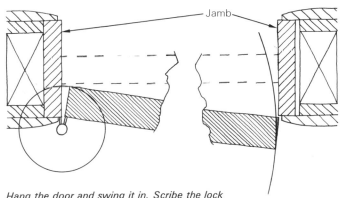

Hang the door and swing it in. Scribe the lock edge ³⁄₃₂ in. from where it meets the jamb, and plane a bevel. Sectional view shows why: Center of swing is hinge pin.

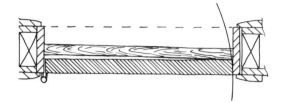

Door (hatching) closes with satisfying thunk when stops are correctly placed. Hinge side stop is held away from door for its entire length and head stop (section above) curves from there to meet the door at the latch side. Latch stop touches the door at top and bottom but bows away in between (right, exaggerated for clarity.)

If you're using the right hinges, a common door, and your jamb is set solidly, this won't be necessary.

Split the hinges and screw half to the door and half to the jamb. Knife-thread screws are a worthwhile investment. Hang the door, and swing it in. Unless the door is very wide it won't close completely, because the inside swinging edge of the door will hit the edge of the jamb. Set your scriber for $3/32$ in. minimum and scribe the inside of the door where it meets the jamb. Pull the door off, plane a bevel on the edge to the scribe line, and rehang the door. Any further planing can usually be done without removing the door. When the lockset is installed correctly, a little outward pressure against the door will bring it into plane with the jamb.

To install the casing trim, first cut all the miters, leaving the sides overlong. Then nail up the header casings. To find the proper length of a side piece, simply set it upside down against the wall and mark where it meets the header piece. Glue the mitered joints.

The door's performance is fine-tuned by the installation of the stops. When closed, the door should be held under slight tension between the lockset bolt and the upper and lower-most points of the stop on the lockset side of the jamb. The stop should be slightly bowed away from the door between those two points. The stop on the hinge side is held away from the door its entire length, and the stop on the header curves from there to meet the door on the latch side. If this tension is too great the lockset will feel sticky. If it is too little the door will feel loose. Properly stopped, the door will have a very light spring when opened, and give a solid, satisfying thunk when closed. □

More Doors

Mock-up shows deep mortise and tenon, with H-section molding that straddles frame and holds panel.

Mahogany door to Panayi's shop has arched panel and shell carving. Two square tapered pegs driven through each mortise cheek lock the tenon in place.

Michel Panayi of Houston, Tex., runs a two-man shop that specializes in solid wood frame-and-panel doors. This door, of cypress, was designed around the customer's glass. Panayi favors cypress for exterior doors because it is both weather-resistant and strong.

Oak entry way has elegant Louis XVI flavor, evidence of Panayi's French training. He uses traditional construction techniques, and his work is influenced by early French designs. Panayi has tried in-line doweled tenons (pages 98-101), but prefers the pegged joint. He buys lumber locally and mills it himself. His work backlog is six months.

A Two-Way Hinge
Careful routing makes screen fold

by Tim Mackaness

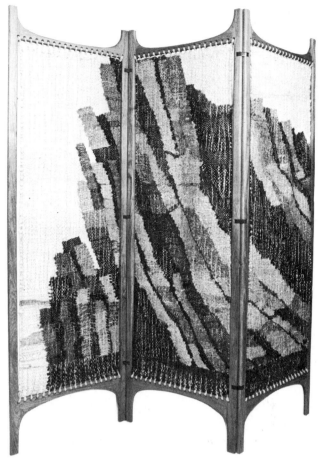

Many folding screens must be able to fold up like a concertina as well as stand alone as a triptych. Traditional hardware companies offer few acceptable hinges for the two-way folding screen. An attractive and functional concertina-type screen hinge can be made of wood by a sequence of careful but simple router cuts.

The hinge, visually symmetrical, can be de-emphasized if made of the same wood as the screen, or exaggerated to produce an interesting design detail by choosing a wood of contrasting color. Either way, a strong wood must be used. This design may be adapted to screen stiles of almost any thickness. The screen shown is made of ⅞-in. stock. I've found that wood thinner than ¾ in. is too fragile. In any case, remember that the hinge pivots about the center of the dowel pins, which are concealed by inlays.

The use of round-over bits to produce a machine fit for the inlays and to radius the hinge member is handy and yields a very precise piece, but equally fine results can be achieved by carefully rasping and sanding the radius by eye. A practice hinge made before you confront the actual screen will build your confidence, let you determine the proper tolerances and provide a handy crutch for future hinges. □

Folding screen of teak and rosewood made by author, with 'Columnar Basalt' tapestry by Judy Nylin. Dowels reinforced with mitered glue blocks join rails and stiles. Curve is bandsawn after assembly, then template-routed to make all three panels identical.

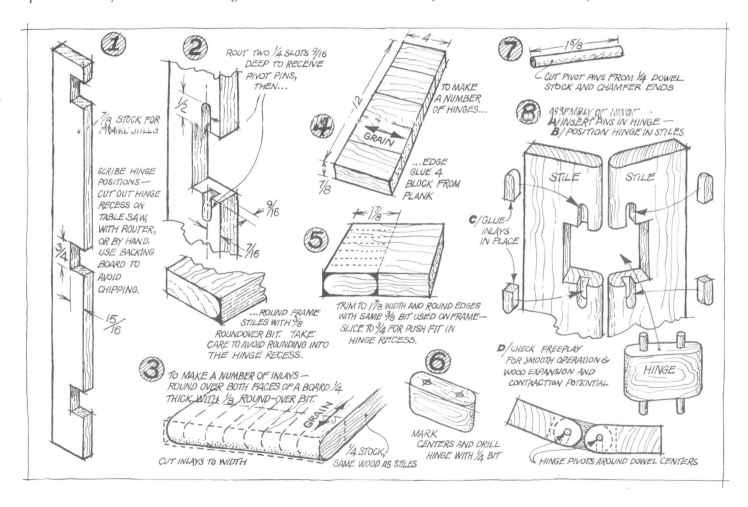

Designing for Dining

Dutch pull-out extends table for guests

by Tage Frid

There are several different systems to choose from when making an extension dining table. Some you can purchase ready-made; they are usually quite expensive. Of the ones you can make yourself, I prefer the "Dutch pull-out" dining table. It is both simple and fast to make.

The tabletop consists of two pieces of plywood, both the same size, one mounted right above the other on the base. The lower piece is cut into three sections—two of them are the leaves, and the third is a fixed center piece. The top rests on the center piece and the leaves and is held there by two vertical dowels sitting loosely in guide holes. Thus it is free to move up and down but not from side to side. The leaves are mounted on long tapered slides that allow them to be pulled out from the ends. The slides travel in grooves in the end aprons and in a supporting rail across the center of the table base. As a leaf is extended, the taper makes it rise slowly throughout its travel to the level of the top. As the leaf rises, so does the top, until the leaf is fully extended and clear of the top. Then the top drops down again, flush with the leaf. Before the leaf can be pushed back in the top has to be lifted high enough to clear, then the top settles back down onto the center piece as the leaf travels back to its original position.

I made the table illustrated here 25 years ago, and it took four or five days, including veneering and edging plywood for the top. Once you understand the system, the work is easy and should go very quickly. You'll have to make four slides and only eight mortise-and-tenon joints. Other than wood for the base and the slides, you need hardwood-veneered ply-

wood, two 3/4-in. dowels and edging for the top.

In addition to being easy to make, the leaves store right inside the table and are easy to pull out, even with the table set. If uninvited guests show up just when the food is on the table and you are ready to sit down, and they apologize for interrupting your meal but hint that they haven't eaten yet themselves, before you know it they are invited to join you. With most extension systems you would have to clear the table before you could enlarge it. But with the Dutch pull-out you can pull out the leaves without disturbing the setting at all.

There are several important dimensions you must consider when designing a dining table. Since the seat height of a dining chair is usually about 18 in., the height of the table should be between 29 in. and 31 in. I usually use 30 in.—this seems to be most comfortable for the average person. And since people differ in height more from the hip down than from the seat up, the distance from the floor to the bottom of the table apron should be at least 24 in., so that someone's long legs or fat legs aren't the legs holding up the table. In the length, I like to allow 24 in. for each person, so no one feels squeezed in. I try to place the legs so that no one ends up with a table leg between his or her own. (The easiest way to avoid that situation is to make a pedestal or trestle table.)

A place setting—dishes, glasses, and so on—is about 14 in. deep. So the minimum width of the table must be 30 in., or else you may drink the wine of the person across from you. Whenever possible, I make dining tables 42 in. wide, to leave space in the center for food, wine, flowers and condiments.

Leaves of Dutch pull-out store right inside table and can be extended from either or both ends without disturbing dishes.

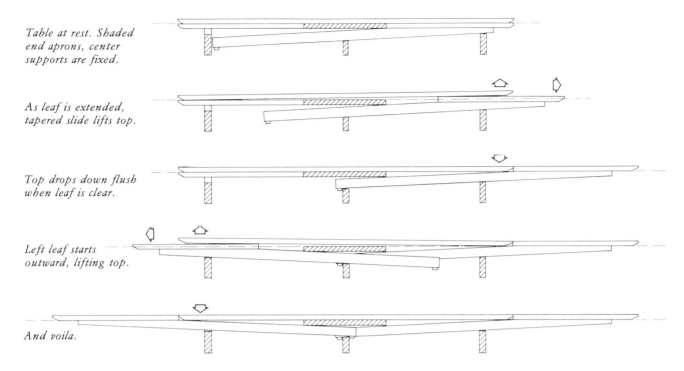

Table at rest. Shaded end aprons, center supports are fixed.

As leaf is extended, tapered slide lifts top.

Top drops down flush when leaf is clear.

Left leaf starts outward, lifting top.

And voila.

The table shown here was designed for a very small room and is only 32-1/4 in. wide, about the minimum.

For the last 12 years I have belonged to a gourmet club made up of seven men who cook for each other once a month during the winter. We have five good meals for ourselves, and at the last dinner of the season, two of us cook and the wives are invited. I feel that half the success of a meal is a result of how it is presented, and how comfortable each person is.

There is nothing worse than being seated near one end of a long, straight table and trying to talk with someone on the same side at the other end. If you want to see the person, you have to lean in so far that you might get gravy on your ear. The most logical shape for a table is round or oval, so everyone can see each other. And with a round table, each person uses less space because the chairs and elbows are out in a bigger circumference. A simple Dutch pull-out cannot be used on a round table, although complex systems using the same idea have been thought of. But a Dutch pull-out will work for a table with curved sides, though the overhang between the top and the leaf will not be the same all the way around (which I don't mind). I prefer to curve the sides slightly.

In designing a Dutch pull-out, remember that the less overhang there is between base and top, the bigger the leaves can be. This is because each leaf must travel its full length outward before it can clear the top. The tail end of the slide to which the leaf is attached of course travels the exact same distance. But the slide can't go any further than the inside length between the apron and the center support, less about an inch for the stop. Therefore, when you have chosen the length of the closed table, you can decide how much the top will overhang the base and calculate the length of the leaves. Or you can decide the length of the leaves and figure the overhang. One determines the other.

The measurements given in the drawings were taken from the old table in the photographs, and I will use these dimensions to explain the system. But you will want to use your own dimensions and make the table to suit your own dining area.

When my table is closed it is 50-1/2 in. long. I decided the top should overhang the base by 4 in. all around. Since the apron is 7/8 in. thick, the aprons and overhangs at both ends

Partly open view from below shows system of slides, stops.

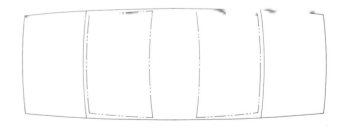

System works with curved sides, although overhang is uneven.

Table has beveled edge and careful rounding where leg joins apron.

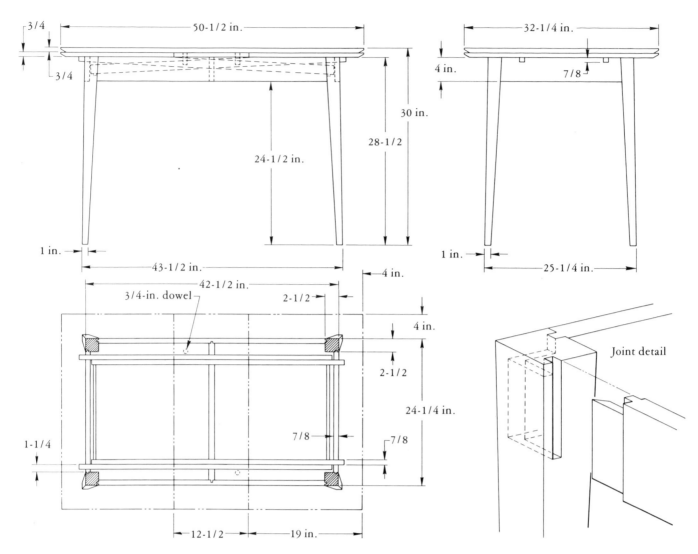

Joint detail

add up to 9-3/4 in. Deduct that from 50-1/2 in. and you get 40-3/4 in., the inside length of the base. Divide that in half (20-3/8 in.) and deduct 1-3/8 in. for the stop and half the thickness of the center support, and you get 19 in. for each leaf. Thus the table will extend 38 in., its open length will be the sum of the leaves and top, or 88-1/2 in., and the width of the center piece will be the difference between the leaves and the top, or 12-1/2 in.

If I had started with both the open and closed lengths, I would follow the same calculation in reverse to find the overhang. Since my table measures 50-1/2 in. closed and 88-1/2 in. open, simple subtraction gives 38 in. for the combined length of the leaves. Add the thickness of the two aprons (1-3/4 in.), both stops and the center support (2-3/4 in.) and you get 42-1/2 in. Deducting this from the length of the top gives 8 in. So the top would be allowed to overhang the base by 4 in. at each end.

The table base consists of four tapered legs joined to an apron that is 4 in. deep. I used haunched tenon joints in the legs. If the tenon came up through the leg in a slip joint, you would have to clamp across the cheeks when you glue the pieces together. By leaving the leg solid on top this is not necessary; you need clamps only in the direction that will pull the tenon into the mortise. To get as much strength as possible, I let the two mortises meet and cut the ends of the tenons to 45°, but left a 1/8-in. space between them for expansion. Use a tongue and groove to join the center support across the base. This piece will guide the slides and serve as a place to run the stops against to keep the leaves from falling out.

Because the tabletop is loose and the slides are glued and screwed to the leaves, the top and leaves must either be made out of plywood or be made using frame-and-panel construction. If you use plywood, you should get a top grade. You can buy it already veneered, or veneer it yourself, or you can paint it, stencil it or finish it however you like. I veneered the top and leaves together, so the grain would follow when the table is open, applied solid wood edging and beveled it. There are two reasons to bevel it. First, if the table gets used a lot, there might be a little play in the dowels and the beveled edge will help to hide discrepancies; second, when the leaves slide down, they will slide more easily.

The success of your table will depend on your accuracy in laying out and cutting the four slides. Be sure that the wood you use is straight. I usually cut the slides oversize and leave them for a few days to give them a chance to warp. Then I joint and thickness-plane them to size, in this case 7/8 in. thick and 1-1/2 in. wide. Their length is the inside measurement of the base (40-3/4 in.) plus the 7/8-in. thickness of the apron plus the 4-in. overhang, or 45-5/8 in. The slides will be trimmed shorter later, for looks, but they have to be full length now, for measuring.

The ends of the slides that hold the leaves must be cut at an angle so that they will wedge the leaves up to the level of the tabletop as they are being extended. On this table, the top and leaves are 3/4 in. thick. Thus each leaf must rise 3/4 in. when it has traveled 19 in., its full extension. From one end of one of the slides, measure down 19 in. and square the line off. Then make a point 3/4 in. over on the same end. A line connecting this point with the edge of the 19-in. mark will give the angle at which to cut the slides.

To be sure that all the slides will have the same angle and be cut exactly the same, you should construct a jig. Square a piece of plywood about 6 in. wide and a foot longer than the angled portion. Place the slide over the plywood with both marks (the ends of the line you have drawn) just touching the bottom edge of the plywood. Then trace the end and the other side of the slide and bandsaw out the shape.

With the table-saw fence still at the same setting you used to cut the plywood jig to width, insert the slide into the jig and make the cut. Use the same setup for all four slides and you can be sure they will all turn out the same.

The slides run in slots in the end aprons and the parallel center support. One pair of slides travels inside the other pair, and the two run side by side in the slots in the center support. To lay out these grooves, mark lines on top of the apron at both ends, 1-1/4 in. from the inside edge of all four legs. With a long straightedge, transfer these lines to the center support. Mark the thickness of the slide to the *outside* of the table from these lines on one apron, and to the *inside* of the table from the lines on the other. On the center support, mark the thickness of a slide to *both* sides of the center line.

The grooves on the end aprons must be the same depth as the slide at that point, so that the leaf will clear the apron as it is extended. To find this depth, measure in 4 in. from the tapered end of the slide and cut the groove to the exact depth of the slide at this point, in this case 7/8 in.

To find the depth of the grooves in the center support, first mark its location onto the slides, in this case 25-1/4 in. from the tapered end, or half of the length of the closed table. Then push the tapered side down flat and measure the depth at the marked point, in this case 1-7/8 in. This is the minimum depth that will allow the leaf to rise 3/4 in. in its travel; the grooves may be cut a little deeper if you wish.

Now that all the measurements and cuts have been made, the tapered ends of the slides can be trimmed. I wanted the closed slides to extend 1 in. beyond the apron, so I cut off 3 in.

To assemble the table, place the slides in the grooves with the angled sides up. Put the leaves in position (don't forget that you just trimmed 3 in. off the end of each slide), and glue and screw the slides to the leaves. To locate the stops, extend the leaves 19 in. and mark where the slides pass through the center support. Then screw on the stops at this point.

The central plywood piece is screwed to the base above the central support. It prevents the leaves from falling down when they are pulled out and locates the tabletop. Drill two 3/4-in. holes in the central plywood piece between the slides and the apron; these are the guide holes for the top.

Now push the leaves in and locate the top in its correct position. Clamp it down to the leaves and mark the location of the guide holes on the underside of the top. Then drill and glue two 3/4-in. dowels into these holes. The dowels should be about 2-1/4 in. long, since the top has to move up a full 3/4 in. while the leaves are being extended.

When you push the leaves back in you have to lift the tabletop. To prevent scratches that would result from the tabletop sliding on the leaves, I glued two strips of felt to the bottom of the top. Use hot hide glue or rubber cement.

Contributing Editor Tage Frid is professor of woodworking and industrial design at Rhode Island School of Design.

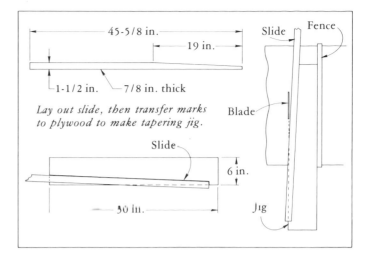

Lay out slide, then transfer marks to plywood to make tapering jig.

Ripping the taper: Jig guarantees four identical slides.

Push taper flat to measure depth of slot at center support line.

Slots for slides are cut in aprons, center support.

Wooden Clockworks

Design and construction require ingenuity, care

by John R. Lord

Clocks—old and new—are a subject of very personal interest to me, not only from the standpoint of historical value but also from one of design. It follows that the approach by which I design and construct my clocks is also personal. I hasten to mention that clock design and construction have been thoroughly documented down through history (further reading, page 117) and I make no claim as to the classical propriety of my designs or means of executing them. As an artist I formulate a careful plan at the outset. But then, within certain parameters of scale, strength and function, I may do almost anything, even violate all rules of horology, to pursue my vision. That confession out of the way, let us proceed.

I shall endeavor here to explain how clocks work, how to design a clock mechanism from scratch, and how to make it out of wood. The designing is not very difficult once the principles of escapements and gears are understood, and the manufacture is within the reach of an amateur craftsman with average facilities. A clock could be made entirely by hand, tediously. But there is no complete plan in this article, for I want most of all to encourage original design. Although a clock can be made to tell accurate time, it is a mistake to be constrained by this historically recent requirement. With the works exposed, face and hands can be absent, allowing greater appreciation of the marvelous machine called clock.

A clockwork is a transmission ma-

John R. Lord, 29, of Waterloo, N.Y., has designed and built eight wildly different clock-like mechanisms. He has a master's degree in fine arts and design from Syracuse University.

chine, a train of intermeshed gears and pinions, set in rotary motion by the kinetic energy of a falling weight. An escapement mechanism divides the weight's long fall to the floor into tiny increments. A swinging pendulum regulates the rate at which the weight is allowed to fall, eking out its energy in brief, uniform and countable bits.

My romance with clockworks and timepieces (the term clock, strictly, denotes an hour-striking device as well) overtook me in London when I visited the National Science Museum. Some of the oldest running tower clocks are there, iron machines of great complexity and beauty, dating from the 14th century. I spent hours studying them as they beat the inexorable seconds.

Clockwork is not the product of a linear evolution, nor did it spring whole from any single source. It represents the convergence since the Middle Ages of several diverse technologies. Toothed wheels as a means of transmitting power were described by Archimedes, and ancient Greek artisans used them in complicated devices for computing the relative positions of the sun, moon and planets. This technology was preserved by Arab civilization and transmitted to Europe in the 12th century. The escapement was invented in China in the 9th century and reached Europe 500 years later, when monks developed weight-driven clockworks regulated by an inertial escapement called "verge and foliot." These clocks had no dials—they were used to automatically strike the prayer bells. In the 16th century, when faces were added to tower clocks, most had only an hour hand. A minute hand, while technically possible, would have been pointless. The mechanisms were too inaccurate to give

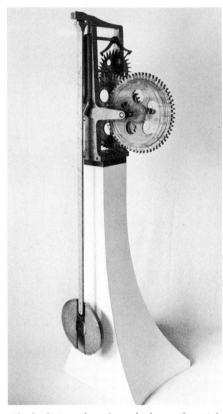

Clock designed and made by author ticks off the seconds but has no hands. Frame and pendulum are bird's-eye maple; large wheels are laminated from strips of various hardwoods with wooden teeth set into slots sawn in rims. Original wooden escapement has been replaced by experimental version of acrylic plastic (top center); base is Formica-covered plywood on hardwood framework. Pendulum has effective length of one meter and beats once a second; escape wheel has 30 teeth; center wheel (extreme right) rotates once in 144 minutes.

meaning to the minutes, and anyway, few cared.

Clocks did not become accurate until the pendulum regulator replaced the verge and foliot. For a pendulum of any given length from suspension to bob, the period of oscillation is constant, regardless of the amount of swing or weight of bob. This was noticed in the middle of the 17th century by several observers, among them Galileo and Christian Huygens. Although Galileo made the first drawings of a pendulum clock, the Dutch astronomer Huygens first built one.

Most early clocks were hand-forged of iron, by blacksmiths. Not far into the 15th century, brass became more widely available and was quickly

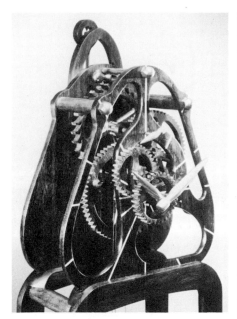

Starting from the Thomas plans and using a Shopsmith with hand tools, Richard Heine of Santa Monica, Calif., built four clocks like this. Now he has formed a company, The Finest Hour, and is tooling up to produce about 20 a month to retail at $2,000. The clock stands 65 in. high. Case and works are Brazilian rosewood; hands and pendulum bob are cocobolo. The wheels for the prototypes were made by pasting paper patterns on the wood and bandsawing. Now Heine uses a metalworker's gear-cutting machine. These clocks use a watch-type escapement, a close cousin of the recoil anchor. The lever spans only three teeth, minimizing expansion problems, but the price is a complex escape wheel with fragile short grain across many of its teeth.

Crutch — Suspension

Back plate

Escape lever

Escape wheel - 30
Escape pinion - 8
Spacer

Thomas with clock

Front plate

Latch

Bob

Shaft cover

Seconds

Weight arbor

Timing nut

Ratchet

Minute wheel - 30

Second wheel - 60

Minute pinion - 8

Second pinion - 8

Hours

Center wheel - 64

Minutes

Figures represent number of teeth

Pawl

Crown wheel

Cannon pinion - 10

Hour wheel - 32

This exploded view of an all-wooden clock is taken from an 8-sheet set of plans developed and sold by Ralph D. Thomas, shown at right with his prototype. Thomas, a Western Electric executive, got interested in clocks 15 years ago, after helping his son make a gear-driven gizmo for science class. He found that although many old clocks use wooden wheel trains, none was made entirely of wood, so he made one. It takes 40 hours to build and comes apart.

Thomas sells his plans for $4.50 from his home at 1412 Drumcliffe Rd., Winston-Salem, N.C. 27103; the plans are also available from Constantine, 2065 Eastchester Rd., Bronx, N.Y. 10461.

adopted because it is much easier than iron to shape. A simultaneous interest in watches and smaller clocks demanded increased use of brass, although supply continued to be scarce until the Industrial Revolution because of the tortuous process by which it was made. A melt of copper and tin was poured from a crucible into a flat puddle and hammered by hand to workharden it. The brass was reheated red, cooled and hammered some more, then cut to shape and filed smooth.

Wooden patterns were probably necessary for making these early clocks, and some enormous mechanisms were made entirely of wood, in the tradition of grist mills. Smaller wooden clockworks were made in backwaters such as the Black Forest of Germany, and in Colonial America. The American tradition of wooden wheel trains, using scarce metal only for arbors and escape wheels, continued during the development of mass production after 1800, but by the middle of the century the

same Industrial Revolution had made brass readily available and wood was replaced. Many factory-made wooden clocks of 130 years ago are keeping good time today.

How clocks work

People usually don't understand just what it is that drives and regulates a pendulum clock. The most common questions are, ''Where's the motor?'' and ''How does the pendulum make it go?'' Although the swinging pendulum is the eye-catching part of most clocks, it is simply a regulator. All the energy comes from the gravity-induced fall of the suspended weight (which can be replaced by a coiled spring or an electric motor). The wheel train transmits this kinetic energy to the time-computing motion works for display by the hands, and also to the escape mechanism. The escapement's release-relock sequence passes tiny impulses on to the pendulum, making up for frictional losses and keeping it swinging. In turn,

each beat of the pendulum allows the escapement to unwind, thereby emitting a tick or a tock.

All this time-computing and power-transmitting wheelwork could be removed, reducing the clock to its bare minimum: A weight hung from a cord wrapped directly around the arbor of an escape wheel with escape lever, crutch and pendulum (diagram on next page). This clock would run, but that's all. If it had a 30-tooth escape wheel and a one-meter pendulum, it would count the seconds. The weight acts through a lever arm whose length is the radius of the arbor, thus exerting force to turn the escape wheel. Unlike a spring or even an electric motor, this force never fluctuates and it needs no care other than periodic rewinding.

Instead of an escape wheel with 30 teeth, which would rotate once a minute, the minimum clock might be made with a single wheel of 1,800 teeth. Connected to the same one-meter pendulum, the wheel would ro-

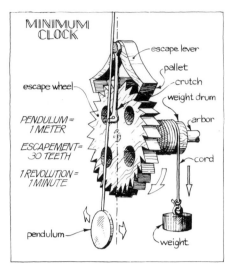

MINIMUM CLOCK

- escape lever
- pallet
- crutch
- weight drum
- arbor
- cord

escape wheel

PENDULUM = 1 METER

ESCAPEMENT = 30 TEETH

1 REVOLUTION = 1 MINUTE

pendulum

weight

Minimum clock would tick off the seconds, but that's all.

'Clock IV', by Lawrence B. Hunter of San Diego; 86 in. high, 36 in. wide, 19 in. deep; made of walnut with ⅛-in. birch dowel in an edition of six, $3,500 each. Hunter, a sculptor, writes that he is 'trying to eliminate the nonessential and distill down to the very essence of the clock and its skeletal structure, then organize the parts into a visual whole.' The great wheel has 160 pin-type teeth, the escape wheel has 72 teeth, the lantern pinion has eight leaves. The pendulum beats once in 1¼ seconds, and the single hand turns once an hour.

tate once an hour, still counting every second. But an 1,800-tooth wheel is hardly practical. This is why clockmakers use a train of wheels and pinions. The essential tick-tock mechanism remains the same.

Tick, tock

The diagram at left on the next page breaks the release-relock sequence of the escape mechanism into the stages that produce a tick and a tock—two seconds in the life of the clock. This is a recoil-anchor escapement, so called because the lever is shaped like an anchor, and because there is a small backward motion at the end of each beat.

Aside from the precise shape of the wheel and lever, which I will discuss shortly, the physical requirement here is that their arbors be mounted below the suspension point of the pendulum. The crutch, which transmits the impulse to the pendulum, is an extension of the arbor that carries the escape lever and embraces the pendulum rod without being attached to it. This ensures that the pendulum will beat freely without hindrance of friction. Note that the escape lever may be below the wheel or alongside it, as long as it is balanced to rock freely.

Without the governing influence of the pendulum, the escape mechanism would oscillate rapidly and irregularly, expending the energy of the system in a whirring clickety-clack. Thus the pendulum is the soul of the system, forcing it to eke out its store of power, second by second. It accomplishes this by virtue of the physical laws innate to it: A pendulum of given length, unhindered by frictional drag, will swing from side to side in a given time and that time will be constant no matter how wide the arc of swing. (This is not strictly true when the arc is very wide, but it is true when the arc is only a couple of degrees.) Further, a pendulum one meter long will always take one second to swing. Since each swing of the pendulum releases one-half tooth of the escape wheel, a 30-tooth wheel will rotate once a minute, and tick each second.

The time of the swing depends upon the length of the pendulum and the acceleration of gravity, which varies minutely according to latitude and elevation above sea level. The time of swing has nothing to do with the weight of the bob, as long as the bob is heavy compared to the weight of the arm

from which it hangs. The formula is:

$$t = \pi \sqrt{\frac{l}{g}} \quad \text{or} \quad l = \frac{t^2 g}{\pi^2}$$

where t is the time of one swing from left to right in seconds, the familiar π equals 3.1416, l is the length of the pendulum and g is the acceleration of gravity, 32.17 ft/sec² or 9.81 meters/sec².

If the beat is to be 2 seconds, the pendulum will be 13 ft. ½ in. (or 4 meters) long; if the time is 1½ sec., the pendulum is 7 ft. 4 in. (or 2.25 meters) long; if it is one second, the pendulum is 39.14 in. (or 1 meter) long; if the time is a half-second, the pendulum is 9.8 in. (or 25 centimeters) long. A clock is adjusted by minutely changing the length of the pendulum, usually by means of a thread and nut at the suspension point or under the bob.

The escapement

Whether the aim is a timepiece or a kinetic sculpture, the design process should begin with the pendulum and escapement. There are many types of escapement; the traditional workhorse is the recoil anchor shown here. It is a simple yet eminently workable design. The escape wheel and the escape lever (the anchor) are laid out together, as in the diagrams at right. The one shown is right-handed and turns clockwise. A left-handed wheel will also work. The most difficult procedure is spacing the 30 points around the circumference of the wheel. No matter how careful you are with an adjustable drafting triangle, there's always something left over at the end. I treasure an old 60-tooth ratchet wheel I found at a scrap yard. I can draw the wheel the size I want, plunk the master down on it, and extend lines from its points to the wheel's circumference.

The configuration shown, where the back of each tooth drops directly to the base of the next at the root circle, is sturdy enough for wooden construction. Wear will be least when the wheel is lightest, however, and narrower teeth are best for fabrication in brass or plastic. To draw them, construct a second circle tangent to a 20° angle from a radius, its vertex at one of the points on the rim. Draw the backs of all the teeth tangent to this circle, just as the fronts are tangent to a 10° circle. I have made escapements of solid and laminated wood, iron, and acrylic plastic, and

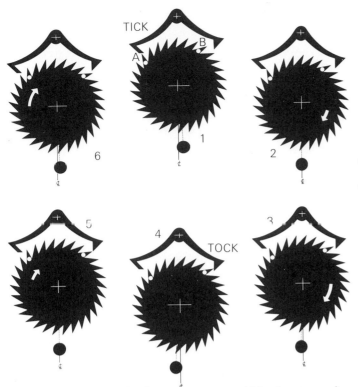

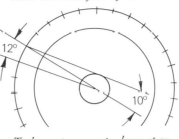

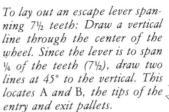

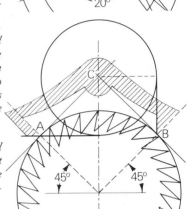

To lay out an escape wheel of 30 teeth: Draw circles of outside and root diameter, i.e. 6 in. and 4½ in. Divide circumference into 30 equal parts (12°). From one of these points, draw a radius and a line making an angle of 10° with it. Draw a circle tangent to the 10° line. Draw lines from each point tangent to the 10° circle. These lines define the front faces of the teeth. Connect each point to the root of the previous point. This defines the back face of each tooth. For a wheel of brass or plastic, draw a second circle at 20° to a radius and make the back face of each tooth tangent to it.

To lay out an escape lever spanning 7½ teeth: Draw a vertical line through the center of the wheel. Since the lever is to span ¼ of the teeth (7½), draw two lines at 45° to the vertical. This locates A and B, the tips of the entry and exit pallets.

Draw tangents to the wheel through A and B. They intersect at C, the center of the escape lever axle. A tangent is perpendicular to a radius.

Draw a circle at C whose radius is one-half the distance between centers. Draw tangents to this circle through A and B. These tangents define the faces of the entry and exit pallets. The remainder of the escape lever may be any shape.

Two seconds in the life of an escapement, told in six steps reading clockwise. Sequence begins with a tick (1) as the tooth A smacks the entry pallet and the pendulum swings toward its rightmost point. The turning escape wheel pushes the entry pallet (2), rocking the lever and sending an impulse via the crutch to the pendulum as it begins to swing leftward. Tooth A escapes (3) and the wheel turns, but immediately tooth B is caught by the exit pallet, tock, stopping the motion (4). Tooth B pushes the exit pallet (5), rocking the lever and prodding the pendulum toward the right. Tooth B escapes (6) and the cycle repeats.

have settled on plastic.

The escape lever shown embraces one-quarter of the wheel's circumference, or 7½ teeth. This is the most common configuration, and (if you have no taste for geometric construction) the distance between arbors is 1.41 times the diameter of the wheel. The number of teeth embraced can be up to one fewer than half the total, and as few as two or three. The layout procedure is the same. The difference is the distance between arbors—the more teeth, the farther they are apart; the fewer, the closer together.

This construction locates the active faces of the entry and exit pallets, and the distance between arbors. These are the only absolutes—the form of the rest of the lever is left to the designer. But absolute precision is essential in locating and fabricating the active surfaces, else the clock won't run. The tips of the teeth and the pallets must be as smooth and hard as possible, allowing no irregularity in their motion. Some makers saw out the bearing surfaces and replace them with a denser material, a watchmaking practice whereby tiny,

flat jewels are cemented to the pallets. They do not wear and they are absolutely smooth.

The importance of the pendulum in all this contrasts with the relative simplicity with which it can be made—the Thomas clock uses a croquet ball on the end of a dowel. It must be suspended above the escapement, on a vertical line with the wheel arbor. The suspension may be as simple as a strap of leather or a steel shim stock, a point set in a dimple (Thomas), a knife edge in a groove—anything that allows the pendulum to swing freely in a flat, smooth arc.

The exact location of the crutch is a function of the arc or swing and of the amount of rock designed into the escape lever, and is best found by experiment and observation. The exact shape of the crutch may range from a flat stick with two protruding dowels that embrace the arm, to wherever your imagination takes you. One caution: Not more than ⅟₃₂ in. of space should exist between the crutch forks and the arm, or the impulse won't be of sufficient duration ever to catch up.

'Clock III' by Lawrence Hunter uses a verge-and-foliot escapement. The horns atop the clock swivel majestically back and forth, taking two seconds each way, releasing a tooth of escape wheel each time. Wheel has 15 contrate teeth—that is, teeth are parallel to arbor rather than perpendicular to it.

'Inventor Released,' escapement-mechanism sculpture by David and Marji Roy of South Woodstock, Conn. Powered by the hanging weight, the L-shaped arm rises to kick escape lever, releasing a tooth and allowing large wheel to rotate a full turn clockwise or counterclockwise. The Roys produce a variety of escapement sculptures in limited editions that retail in the $100 to $250-range.

The time train

In the diagram below, the time train of a typical clock is spread out on a line. It proceeds in two directions from the center wheel: To the right, it energizes the pendulum and is regulated by it; to the left, it computes and displays the hour. The weight's energy is transmitted via the center wheel, which drives the pinion of the second wheel (so called because of its position in the train, not because it counts the sec-

onds); the second wheel drives the pinion of the escape wheel. Proceeding the other way, the pinion of the center wheel (the cannon pinion) drives the minute wheel, whose pinion drives the hour wheel. The figures are the tooth counts of each wheel and pinion.

If you should somehow have access to a computer and plotter, it can be used to lay out very accurate wheels. It can also lay out elliptical wheels, square wheels and star-shaped wheels. They must run in identical pairs, and always turn end-to-side. They do not turn at a constant speed, but rather at double speed half-way around, and half-speed the rest of the way, averaging out where they ought. They seem to gallop.

The wheels are generally arranged—but needn't be—to run the minute and hour hands from a common center, which requires a hollow arbor called a cannon tube concentric with the arbor of the center wheel.

For convenience, the weight drum may also be on a hollow arbor concentric with the center wheel. Note that the weight drum may be connected to another whole train of wheels. These have nothing to do with computing the time, but rather with how often one must rewind the clock. Thirty-day movements are common in brass clocks, but in wood old friend gravity takes his vengeance in the form of friction and inertia at each connection. When the time is told, most of the weight's energy is lost. The longer the movement, the more slowly the weight must fall, and the more freely the mechanism must turn. Eight days is about the limit in wooden clockworks.

The ratios in the diagram are used in many grandfather clocks, but they aren't sacred. The point is to make the minute hand rotate once for 60 turns of the second hand, and the hour hand once for 12 turns of the minute hand. Many different wheel ratios, a few specified in the chart opposite, will do the same thing. These combinations will be most useful to the maker of wooden works, but others can be figured from the logic below. For practical purposes, begin with a one-meter pendulum and a 30-tooth escape wheel.

This pendulum beats once a second, and each beat releases half a tooth on the escape wheel (each tooth acts twice, once on each pallet of the escape lever). Thus the 30-tooth escape wheel rotates once a minute, or 60 times an hour. Its arbor is therefore a good place to mount the second hand. Since the escape wheel and its pinion are fastened to the same arbor, the pinion must also rotate 60 times an hour. In one hour the pinion's eight leaves will engage 60 × 8 or 480 teeth on the second wheel, thus turning it eight times. The second wheel pinion also turns eight times, engaging 8 × 8 = 64 teeth on the center wheel. The center wheel has exactly 64 teeth, so it will rotate once an hour. Put the minute hand here.

Turn now to the motion work to the left of the center wheel. The cannon pinion, 10 teeth, is fastened to the center wheel arbor and therefore rotates once an hour or 12 times in 12 hours, thereby engaging 120 teeth on the minute wheel. Since it has 30 teeth, it will have to rotate four times in 12 hours. The minute pinion also rotates four times, so in 12 hours its eight teeth will engage 32 teeth on the hour wheel, which happens to have exactly 32 teeth. It will rotate once in 12 hours. The hour hand goes here.

Notice that in 12 hours, while the hour wheel rotates only once, the pendulum beats once a second—an astonishing 43,200 times. In any gear train, the number of rotations of the last pinion to one rotation of the first wheel will be equal to the product of all teeth in the wheels divided by the product of all the leaves in the pinions. In a clock, the teeth in the escape wheel are multiplied by two because each acts twice. The pendulum itself is the last pinion, one beat being one ''rotation.'' Thus,

$$\frac{32 \times 30 \times 64 \times 60 \times 30 \times 2}{8 \times 10 \times 8 \times 8} = 43{,}200$$

A typical time train, spread out for clarity. Numbers are teeth in wheels, pinions.

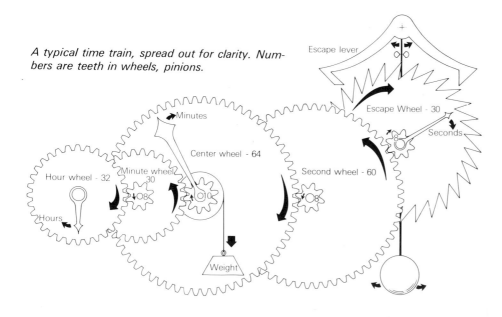

Clock Trains						
Center Wheel	Second Wheel	Second Pinion	Escape Wheel	Escape Pinion	Pendulum beats/min.	Pendulum Length
48	40	8	30	8	30	156.5"
64	40	8	30	8	40	88"
96	90	12	30	12	60	39.14"
64	60	8	30	8	60	39.14"
68	64	8	30	8	68	30.5"
80	80	8	30	8	100	14.1"
96	80	8	30	8	120	9.8"

	Motion Works			
Chart above relates number of teeth in each wheel and pinion to pendulum beats and lengths, to rotate center wheel once an hour. Chart at right specifies teeth in 12-hour motion trains.	Cannon Pinion	Minute Wheel	Minute Pinion	Hour Wheel
	10	30	10	40
	12	36	12	48
	16	40	10	48

Chiming clock train made by M.C. Hall of Austin, Tex., right, is alongside a 19th-century Eli Terry movement. Hall, 74, a retired aircraft tool engineer, adds an extra wheel, a deadbeat anchor and brass bushings to get a 30-day movement. Front and back plates are quartersawn white oak, wheels are quartersawn black cherry, one-piece arbors and pinions are maple. Terry's pinions are holly.

Wheels and pinions

A complete discussion of the geometry of wheels and pinions would fill a book. For clockwork purposes, consider two rollers pressed tightly together, one driving the other. The smaller, the pinion, is the driven; the larger, the wheel, is the driver. The relative speed of each would depend on their diameters, and if slippage could be prevented, rollers would drive a clock. In practice, teeth are necessary and teeth must mesh just as smoothly as if the wheels were plain rollers. The effective size of intermeshed gears is the size of the imaginary rollers, and is called the pitch circle. The teeth must be shaped so that the transmitted motion is absolutely uniform, or the clock will stop.

In engineering practice, for a wheel with N teeth, the relationship between the pitch diameter PD and the outside diameter OD has been standardized:

$$PD = OD \frac{N}{N+2}$$

For gears to mesh at all, the number of teeth in the wheel and the leaves in the pinion must be directly proportional to the diameters of their pitch circles. Engineers call this the pitch of the gear, and specify it by the number of teeth per inch of diameter of the pitch circle. Thus a 7½ in. wheel with 60 teeth is 8-pitch. So is a 1-in. pinion with eight leaves. The wheels in the Thomas clock are 8-pitch.

The Thomas clock uses the type of gears engineers use to transmit power. The teeth of the wheels and pinions have the shape of involute curves. Historically, clockmakers settled upon cycloidal teeth, a shape that is easier to make and equally efficient, since a clock doesn't transmit great amounts of torque. Cycloids generated by circles come in pairs, and one pair matches a straight line with an epicycloid that is so close to circular that the difference doesn't matter. The mating teeth are shaped as in the diagram below. When they are made of brass, the faces of the pinion leaves are radial; when made of wood, they are made parallel. The small circle that defines the profile of the wheel teeth is half the diameter of the pinion's pitch circle, and the arc is struck from midway between two teeth, on the pitch circle of the wheel.

While it would be convenient to design pinions with very few leaves, the practical lower limit is eight. This is because friction is markedly higher when gears begin to interact before the meshing teeth pass an imaginary line connecting the center of the wheel and pinion, compared to when they mesh after this line. With a pinion of fewer than eight teeth, the interaction begins before the line of centers; with eight, at the line; with more than eight, after the line. The situation is improved with the lantern pinion—even with as few as six pins, the action begins well after the line of centers. A lantern pinion will mesh well enough with both cycloidal and involute wheels, and also with tinker-toy style teeth made of dowel.

Wheel construction

Most woodworking shops aren't equipped for the specifics of gear cutting, so it becomes necessary to invent. An index wheel is the handiest tool, in

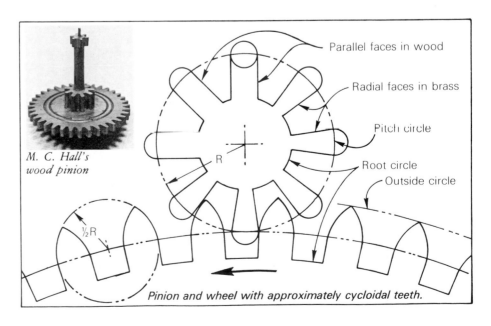

M. C. Hall's wood pinion

Parallel faces in wood

Radial faces in brass

Pitch circle

Root circle

Outside circle

R

½R

Pinion and wheel with approximately cycloidal teeth.

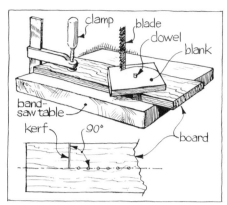

A piece of plywood can quickly become a circle-cutting jig for the band saw. Space holes for a dummy arbor along a line perpendicular to the blade. Carefully adjust guides, rotate blank into the blade.

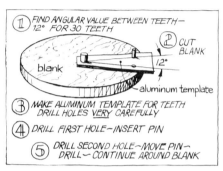

① FIND ANGULAR VALUE BETWEEN TEETH— 12° FOR 30 TEETH
② CUT BLANK
blank
12°
aluminum template
③ MAKE ALUMINUM TEMPLATE FOR TEETH DRILL HOLES *VERY* CAREFULLY
④ DRILL FIRST HOLE~ INSERT PIN
⑤ DRILL SECOND HOLE~ MOVE PIN~ DRILL~ CONTINUE AROUND BLANK

An aluminum or brass template, carefully made, will space holes around a blank.

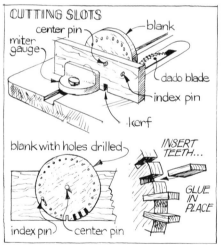

CUTTING SLOTS
center pin
miter gauge
blank
dado blade
index pin
kerf
blank with holes drilled
INSERT TEETH...
GLUE IN PLACE
index pin
center pin

Use the table saw to turn the holes into slots. The trick is aligning the first hole with the dado blade, so the slot will be perfectly radial. Then drill through a hole for the index pin, and all the slots will be radial.

Lantern pinion from Lawrence Hunter's 'Clock IV' engages pin wheel laminated of seven veneer layers, five of them running around the rim and two running crosswise.

terms of accuracy gained and time saved, but it is rarely available. Fortunately there are ready substitutes. I urge constant surveillance of junkyards and scrap machinery for any gears of reasonable size and some number of teeth which will divide into usable numbers and provide a pattern for tracing. Two of the best to own have 60 teeth and 96 teeth. Between them they yield 2, 3, 4, 5, 6, 8, 10, 12, 15, 20, 24, 30, 32, and 48 teeth. The next best alternative is a protractor and an adjustable triangle.

Another home remedy is a jig for cutting round wheel blanks, as in the diagram at left. Much cut and try goes into clockwork and the ability to generate wheels easily and quickly is a big help. With well-adjusted saw guides, a sharp blade and care in alignment, this jig will deliver a very accurate blank.

There are several alternatives regarding the actual fabrication of clock wheels. At its most basic, a wheel is no more than a single, solid disc of wood with teeth cut into its circumference. The easiest way to make one is to draw a full-size paper pattern, glue it onto the wood, and cut around the profile with a jigsaw, band saw or coping saw. The problem with this type of wheel is seasonal movement of the wood, short-grain fragility and difficulty of replacing a broken tooth in case of disaster.

As a hedge against the wood's tendency to warp with the weather, I laminate wheels of several narrow strips, or of pie-shaped wedges. I usually mismatch each strip with respect to the next according to the annual rings; veneers can be inserted between pieces for further visual interest. I've seen wheels cut of birch plywood, very stable.

I use inserted teeth because if one becomes damaged, it can be replaced singly. This necessitates sawing a series of radial slots in the rim of the wheel. I do this by first drilling a ring of properly spaced holes, using the template shown in the diagram. If the template layout and initial drilling are not absolutely accurate, the last hole will have a very strange relationship to the first. But the job can be done with care.

Thus far we have a set of holes evenly spaced around the wheel. We could press dowels into them and use them as pin wheels, which also allows interesting variations such as right-angle drives. To cut the holes into slots to accept inserted teeth, I use the table-saw

Close-up of author's clock shows laminated wheel construction with inset teeth and lantern pinions. Crutch is bandsawn from laminated veneers, pendulum rod is bird's-eye maple, suspension is a piece of leather caught in a saw kerf.

jig shown in the diagram. The difficult part comes only once, in aligning the blade with the first hole to be cut. Once this position is ascertained the locating pin is fixed and the rest of the slots follow like clockwork.

Such a simple jig is bound to chip the wood as the blade exits, but I find chipping minimal and anyway it is later negated by turning each wheel on a lathe. I do this both for esthetic reasons and to reduce the weight of the train. The result is a flat-bottomed radial slot ready for the inset tooth. I thickness a straight board and rip it to width, then slice the teeth to length and glue them in place. Once mounted, I file the faces of each tooth by hand to a close fit.

Pinions can be made just like small wheels, of solid or laminated wood. But they are tricky and I prefer the lantern pinion. It consists of two circular plates of wood, plastic or metal, with the necessary number of holes spaced around the pitch diameter. Leaves are simply short lengths of dowel or acrylic rod pressed into the holes. One of the circular plates can be eliminated and its holes drilled directly into the wheel.

The distance between centers of two mating gears ought to be the sum of the radii of their pitch circles. In practice, this is a good place to start. But it is best to put each pair of wheel and pinion on dummy arbors and adjust the distance until they turn most freely.

Most clock problems come from improperly depthed wheels. There must always be some clearance between the outside diameter and root diameter of mating wheels, and enough clearance between tooth faces to allow a little backlash. The remedies usually involve careful sanding. A stick the shape of the space between two teeth, with sandpaper glued to it, is a useful file. Sometimes the sanding goes too far and a tooth must be built up with a slip of veneer, or be replaced.

I've used dowel for the arbors on which the wheels ride, and I've turned my own dowel to try and avoid warping and swelling. But dowel vacillates between squeaky tight in the bushings to such looseness that the clock becomes a locked-up woodpile. I therefore switched to aluminum—I like the juxtaposition of color and texture, and it just plain works. However, many makers find dowel entirely satisfactory.

The arbors turn in bushings in the frame that keeps the clock together. The Thomas clock doesn't use bushings, merely countersunk holes lubricated with graphite to keep friction down. Others drill oversize holes and press bearings into them. In my effort to maintain high tolerances, I machined bushings of a very dense and stable monomer-impregnated maple. It is made by putting the wood in a vacuum to remove the air from the cells, then flooding it with plastic resin, which fills the voids in the wood and hardens. I machined the bushings several thousandths of an inch oversize and pressed them into the frames. They

probably aren't necessary.

Once I've settled the layout of the holes, I tape the front and back frame pieces together and clamp them to the drill-press table. I drill one hole most of the way through, then turn the whole thing over and come back the other way, to avoid a bad chip-out. Then I press in a bushing or a dummy arbor and proceed to the next hole.

Because I want to emphasize the personal nature of design, I won't dwell on the details of the frame. It can be full front and back plates, or very skeletal supports just where they are needed for the wheel arbors, as long as they are absolutely rigid and parallel.

A ratchet-and-pawl system is the most direct way to wind up the weight and couple it to the wheelwork, as in the diagram below. The pawls may be attached directly to the center wheel, as in the Thomas clock, and the weight suspended by a pulley system to increase the time between windings. Or the pulleys may be eliminated by fixing the pawls to a separate great wheel, coupled by a pinion to the center wheel.

As the weight drum is wound up (by hand in my clock, but most use a couple more wheels and a key), the pawls back over the ratchet. When the weight is fully wound, the pawls move forward and engage the ratchet. I chose not to display the weight and so hung it from a fine cable inside the base of the clock. You may want it to be an integral part of the design. I've used a 7-Up can full of lead—since it is hidden, its lack of charm is not noticed. After the clock is running, tinkering and wear will eliminate some friction, and the beast will of its own accord run more easily and require less weight. I suggest avoiding cast lead weights and using a container full of sand, lead shot or ball bearings—some easily divisible material. □

Further Reading

[Editor's note: Of the books listed, Britten's and Grimthorpe's are in print. For the others, check libraries and used-book stores.]
Britten, Frederick James, *Old Clocks and Watches and Their Makers*. 8th edition. Edited by Cecil Clutton et al. New York: E.P. Dutton, 1973, $40. The 7th edition, published in 1956, is more complete.
Gordon, G.F.C., *Clockmaking, Past and Present*. 2nd edition. London: Technical Press, 1949.
Grimthorpe, E.B., *Rudimentary Treatise on Clocks, Watches and Bells*. Luling, Tex: Caldwell Industries.
Milham, Willis I. *Time and Timekeepers*. New York: Macmillan, 1923.

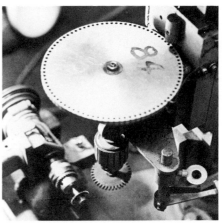

Wheel-cutting machine designed and built by M.C. Hall is indexed by interchangeable aluminum wheels mounted on the same shaft as chuck that holds the work. Assembly is lowered into saw-type cutter which is shaped to remove the space between two teeth at a single pass.

'Clock II' by Lawrence Hunter is regulated by dowel-pin escapement, above, with tinker-toy motion works, below.

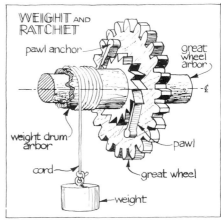

Weights hang from pulleys on cord wrapped around arbor, and ratchet engages pawls on great wheel, which couples to time train via pinion on center wheel arbor. Or, pawls may be attached to center wheel itself.

A clockmaker's depthing tool, this one designed by M.C. Hall. Upright arms pivot at baseplate, allowing large wheel (foreground) to mesh with pinion (concealed by smaller wheel). When teeth mesh perfectly, points (left) may be used to strike arcs, on which arbor centers must lie.

TURNING AND CARVING

Spindle Turning

How to sharpen and use roughing-down and coving gouges

by Peter Child

For turning between centers, standard roughing-down gouges and coving gouges are best. These spindle gouges have only two shapes of blade. The roughing-down tool has a deep, U-shaped flute ground straight across with no pointed nose, and the coving gouge has a shallower flute with a pointed "lady's fingernail" nose.

Roughing-down gouges have an even thickness of metal all around the cutting edge and a very short single bevel of 45°. Unlike bowl gouges, they have no keel. Three sizes are commonly available: ¾ in., 1 in. and 1¼ in. The first and last sizes should both be the choice of the turner if possible; the 1-in. size is the economy combination tool.

Coving (spindle) gouges have a longer bevel than roughing-down gouges. Four sizes will handle all the turner's requirements: ¼ in., ⅜ in., ½ in. and ¾ in. Any work requiring larger coves, hollows or long curves can be done better with roughing-down gouges, so gouges larger than ¾ in. aren't necessary. Both roughing-down and coving gouges should have long, heavy-duty handles to facilitate control—mine are at least 10 in. long.

Gouges are cutting tools. They fashion a cove or hollow by cutting down from each side alternately until the desired shape is reached. A gouge is rarely the exact size of a desired cut. A customer of mine complained that a ¾-in. gouge supplied was in fact ¹³⁄₁₆ in. and consequently of no use to him. He was obviously misusing the gouge as a forming tool, pushing it straight into the revolving wood and scraping out a hollow which he required to be exactly ¾ in. across. Using a

gouge as a scraper is wrong. An important woodturning principle is that cutting tools always work from large diameter to small: Revolving wood cannot be properly cut "uphill." This means that the tool must have room to work, especially at the bottom of the cove, so it is impossible to cut a ¾-in. cove with a ¾-in. gouge. It would be better to use a ½-in. gouge.

Most woodworking tools are properly shaped by the factory grinder and finisher, and sharpening is all that is needed before using them. Woodturning tools are an exception and have remained so, despite the efforts of professional turners to educate manufacturers. So be very critical regarding the shape and bevel length of brand-new gouge blades. You may find that a roughing-down gouge is not ground straight across, a condition which must be remedied on the grindstone. The bevel length will almost certainly be too long, not the correct angle of 45°. Sometimes a lot of metal (and money) has to be ground away before the correct angle is reached. As a temporary measure, a very short 45° angle can be ground on the longer bevel. This is against another basic woodturning principle, which is that no tool has more than one bevel on the cutting edge. Successive grindings, however, will eventually get down to one bevel of 45°. Do not try this dodge on new coving gouges.

The grindstone is an important tool in the turner's shop and should be used not only as a "grind" stone but as a "sharpening" stone. The grit grade must not be so coarse that a sharp edge cannot be ground, or so fine that an edge can easily be burned at the tip. A good medium grit is a Carborundum (silicon carbide) dry wheel A54-N5-V30W or an equivalent grade. The diameter should not exceed 7 in. and the width should be at least 1 in. The stone should revolve towards the user at the fastest speed possible, although not

English master turner Peter Child, author of The Craftsman Woodturner, *wrote about turning bowls in the Winter '76 and Summer '77 issues of* Fine Woodworking.

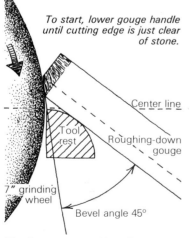

To start, lower gouge handle until cutting edge is just clear of stone.

Center line

Tool rest

Roughing-down gouge

7" grinding wheel

Bevel angle 45°

To sharpen a roughing-down gouge, hold the blade on the rest and lower the handle until the cutting edge is just clear of the stone. Roll the bevel slowly from side to side, keeping the point of contact at right angles to the stone. As the bevel comes up (photo sequence), *the bright mark shows the operator for the first time where he is removing metal. Lift or lower the handle until the center of the bevel is reached, then continue to roll the blade with no variation in height until the bevel starts to hollow out and fit the stone.*

faster than the safety rpm marked on its side. Safety glasses are a must, but provided the stone is maintained and used as described, I don't find other guards essential.

The stone must be kept to its original shape and completely free from dirt, swarf and glazing. As an example, after, say, three new tools have been shaped and sharpened, the stone will need cleaning. This is achieved with either a diamond or star-wheel dressing tool. The latter is much cheaper and just as effective.

Hollow grinding is when the whole of the bevel of the tool, from heel to sharp edge, is in full contact with the stone's circular surface, and thus takes on the negative contour of the stone. Grinding has to stop at the exact moment the cutting edge of the tool comes in contact with the stone. This sounds simple but when I watch my pupils trying to do it I realize how frustrating doing this properly is to learn.

Beginners at grinding usually make several common mistakes. First, they hold the tool far too firmly and stiffly when approaching the stone. The more relaxed hold is with one hand over the tool, holding it down on the rest, with just the fingers of the other hand around the handle. There should be just enough firmness to hold the tool in place. An efficient stone of the right grit will do its work all by itself and need not be pushed. Pressure leads quickly to burning, whereas with no pressure the tool can be rested on the running stone for considerable time before it even gets hot.

Inclining the head to one side to see if the tool is being presented at the proper angle is another common fault. There is little control when watching from the side. The head and eyes should always be directly behind the blade and handle.

Another fault—lifting the blade off two or three times to inspect it—results in the bevel surface looking like a badly plowed field. It is almost impossible to replace the blade at the exact grindstone height from which it is taken.

Roughing-down gouges

With a roughing-down gouge we are grinding a straight-across edge, and it is important to roll the blade so that at all times it is at right angles to the stone. With a right-handed operator, his right hand on the handle keeps the tool at this angle, and his eyes on the edge tell his hand what handle adjustments to make. The diagram and photos show how to proceed. A stream of sparks traveling on top of the flute indicates that the edge has been reached, and I advise beginners to stop right before or just at this point. What happens is that the edge is broken into thousands of little cutting burrs or sawteeth, like a tiny breadknife or steak knife. Such an edge works well in woodturning and when blunt is quickly and easily resharpened. Over-grinding the edge produces only comparatively few thick burrs, easily broken and blunted by the revolving wood. To avoid over-grinding, stop as soon as the sparks travel on top of the edge. Then the operator should point the gouge straight at his face and look directly at the edge. The places that reflect light have not yet been reached by the sparks. After two or three more careful passes on the stone, these areas of light should have disappeared and the edge will be sharp. Another test is to feel around the inside of the flute with a fingertip. There should be a minute roughness all around. I now go directly to the lathe, without any attention from the oilstone, where the tool cuts efficiently for a short time before it needs to be resharpened. When this is required, the heel of the bevel is put into contact with the stone

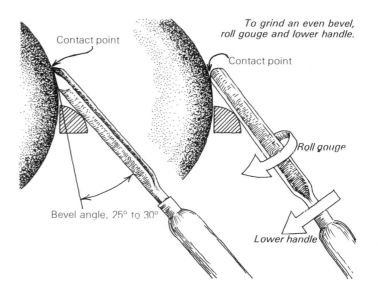

To grind an even bevel, roll gouge and lower handle.

Contact point

Contact point

Roll gouge

Bevel angle, 25° to 30°

Lower handle

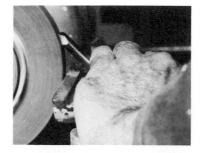

Start sharpening a coving gouge at the center, then roll the blade over to the left while lowering the handle, as in the drawing. The blade rides up so that its left edge contacts the stone at the same height the center did. Then roll to the right the same way (photo, top and above left). To hone by hand (photo, right), brace the gouge against the lathe and move the stone around the bevel. Keep the stone in firm contact with the point and heel.

and the handle is gradually lifted until the sparks appear at the edge—it takes just a few seconds.

The beginner, who should stop grinding just before the hollowing-out bevel meets the cutting edge, should hand-hone to a finish with a flat medium to fine oilstone, keeping it firmly in contact with the heel of the bevel and the edge of the tool, in a dead straight plane without any rocking motion. The partly hollow-ground bevel will save time in sharpening, because there is less metal to remove than if the bevel were totally flat. The tool can be used for a considerable period, hand-honing at frequent intervals until the hollow in the bevel almost disappears. Then it must be formed again. A completely hollow-ground tool is perfect, a dead straight bevel is good, but the slightest trend towards a "belly" or roundness of the bevel means the tool is useless.

Coving gouges

I have a "black-iron" coving gouge, entirely handmade before I was born, which is a beautiful tool to use. The underside is slightly more than a half of a circle in shape and a finger moves around it smoothly without hindrance. Imagine a pencil cut lengthwise down just above the diameter; the bigger portion would be the same shape as my gouge. A gouge works with a rolling or scooping action, depending on the task, so it should be obvious that the fully rounded pencil shape is ideal for both purposes, the underside offering no resistance to the edge of the tool rest.

Nowadays, for cheapness or lack of skilled labor, most coving gouges are brutally stamped out by machine, which, at best, can produce only a half circle. At worst the underside of the tool has two almost straight sides, two corners and a semicircular bottom. Imagine this doing a smooth full roll on a rest! It is well worth the time to remedy these defects by grinding—it would be exceedingly difficult to make them worse. Again, the blade of the gouge is not likely to be the ideal shape. Common faults are a second bevel at the tip, a flattened cutting edge, the top not nearly rounded over, leav-

To rough from square to round: lift the handle until the edge contacts the blur, traverse from left to right and roll the gouge.

End of first cut; small chips are 'corners' wood. Now go back again, slowly rolling the gouge, handle always lower than cutting edge.

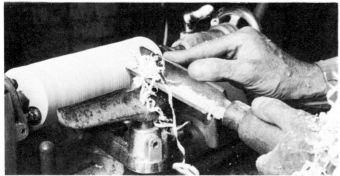

When wood is cylindrical, gouge produces long, even shavings.

ing corners, (the term "lady's fingernail" is very descriptive of the proper shape), and often the bevel is not long enough.

Unlike the roughing-down gouge, which always has a 45° bevel, the bevels of coving gouges can be varied to suit the user, although they must not be too short. As a guideline, measure the breadth of the bevel of the roughing-down gouge, and at least double this for the coving gouges. The bevel of the ¼-in. gouge will perform better if it is longer than that of the ¾-in. gouge.

Begin grinding with the blade on the rest, flute up, with the point of the gouge in the middle and just clear of the stone. Unlike grinding the roughing-down gouge, it is not good enough just to roll the blade from side to side because this operation would soon remove the point. The handle must be lowered as the blade is rolled to the left, so the extreme left-hand corner rides up to the same height that the point was when the operation started. The movement is then reversed, raising the handle as the point rolls onto the stone and lowering it as the right-hand edge comes around. A beginner should try some dry runs on a motionless stone, experimenting by look and feel with the movement needed to grind the bevel evenly. I keep the handle straight up and down during the whole operation. A beginner might find it easier to move the handle slightly from side to side, although I don't think the bevel can ever be ground as evenly this way. Again, the grinding need not be continued right to the edge. The safer but more laborious method of hand-honing can finnish it off.

Roughing down a cylinder

Any piece of wood about 10 in. long and from 2 in. to 3 in. square with lengthwise grain will do for practice in roughing down a cylinder. Unseasoned wood of medium hardness will cut more easily and show the beginner if he is using the tools correctly. Mount the wood between centers and adjust the tool rest at a height just below center line and about ⅛ in. clear of the corners, testing this by rotating the wood by hand. Lathe speed should be anywhere between 1,000 and 2,000 rpm. Place a lamp at the back of the lathe so that it shines on the work but not in your eyes.

Start the lathe and stand back. You will see a distinct round shape, surrounded by a blurred border. The blur is the corners of the wood, which progressively have to be removed. Place the 1¼-in. gouge on the center of the rest, handle lower than the blade, flute directly uppermost, edge above and just away from the work. The left hand (assuming a right-handed turner) should be over the flute, holding the blade quite firmly down on the rest. Lift the handle until the edge contacts the blur. There should be only a slight jolt. Working from either direction, take the gouge along the rest to the end and back again, removing small chips of wood on the way. The chips will increase in size as the work progresses, until a cylinder shape results. Do not concentrate the gaze on the tool edge all the time—when you feel it is cutting properly, look at the top of the revolving wood, where you should actually see the cutting action. You can stop the lathe at intervals to see what is happening, or without stopping, trail the finger tips lightly over and around the back of the turning wood. Any slight irregularity means it is not circular at that point.

Stop the lathe when the wood is a cylinder. Don't worry now about exactness of size all along the length. At this stage you can demonstrate to yourself in safe, slow motion the correct cutting, not scraping, action of the gouge. Place the gouge on the rest, flute facing upwards with the heel of the bevel touching the wood. This means that the handle will be held well down from the horizontal and the actual cutting edge will be just clear of the wood. Have the lathe turned slowly by hand. The blade will be in contact with the wood, just rubbing it lightly. Move the gouge slowly along, and at the same time gradually lift up the handle. When the angle of cut is correct, the edge will start to remove a thin shaving and the bevel will be in full contact with the wood surface. If the handle is lifted too high, the bevel will leave the wood, the cutting action will stop, and the resultant scrape of the edge will not only remove wood in a most unsatisfactory manner but will also immediately blunt the sharpest of edges.

Working with the flute facing fully upwards all the time is not a good idea, because only the center of the edge is cutting. The whole edge has been sharpened and so it all can be used—roll the gouge as it travels along the rest. The 1¼-in. gouge is a powerful tool that can remove large quantities of wood in a hurry. Unlike the bowl gouge, it has no ugly tendencies. If the butt of the handle is braced on the hip and the legs splayed, the blade can be swung from end to end by sideways movement of the hips. The body powers the cut, the hands control it.

Long slow curves are easy with the 1¼-in. gouge. Cut with light pressure, starting from the extreme left end of the wood, then roll gradually towards the middle, increasing pressure and thereby removing more wood at the center. Stop, and repeat the cut from the right side towards the center. Watch the top of the wood while cutting, because this helps keep the curves smooth.

For surface smoothing hold the gouge down on the rest with the flute over on either side. Bring the handle up until the blade starts cutting. Don't roll the blade, but watch the top of the wood and take smoothing cuts by pulling or pushing the blade along the rest.

Some economists think they can take a large-size heavy-duty pointed-nose coving gouge with a shallow flute, grind the nose square, and use it in place of a deep-throated roughing-down gouge. This does not work nearly as well.

Cutting coves, hollows and balls

Imagine a large capital "S" standing upright as in normal print. Lean it over to the right at an angle of 45°. Gouges can make the "ball shape" (top of the "S") and the hollow (middle and tail). It is impossible to cut the cove at the tail of the "S" in one operation, because after cutting halfway the gouge would be forced uphill. Coves can be scraped uphill, but no amount of abrasive paper will eliminate the damage caused to the wood fibers.

To form coves, make a cylinder between centers, about 2 in. in diameter and of any length. Use a pencil on the rest, and with the wood revolving, mark a line, then another one not more than ¾ in. away from the first, and not less than ⅝ in. Pick a ½-in. spindle gouge, and with the flute on the left side of the rest, try to enter the point into the line on the right. Unless you are lucky, the gouge will skid along the rest to your right. Until the point of the gouge has penetrated the wood there is no back-up support from any part of the bevel. The turning wood rejects the gouge and makes it skid.

Position the tool rest below center height so that with the gouge held completely horizontally, on its side, flute facing

To start a cove, hold the gouge firmly and push its point in slowly.

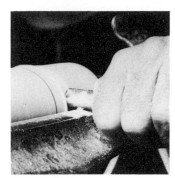

Remove half the waste in one cut by pushing firmly in and rolling the gouge onto its back. Right, the finished cove.

left, the point of the gouge is pointing directly at the right-hand line and in a position to make contact at center height of the wood. Push the point forward so that it is just in contact with the wood and hold it there, rubbing the surface. Holding very firmly, push the point in slowly. Only very little penetration is needed—1/16 in. is too much. Once some penetration has been achieved without skid, the danger is all over. If you still cannot manage it, remove the skid marks and make small notch marks with a parting tool instead of pencil lines, then proceed. Now, holding firmly down on the rest, push straight into the wood while twisting the gouge so that it is turning over on its back (flute ends up facing upwards), removing, quite brutally, half the waste wood towards the left. Try to remove this half in one attempt. Otherwise you will leave a "collar" of waste in the center of the cove.

Repeat from the left-hand line and remove the other half of the wood. If you find you do leave a collar, you are not taking out enough waste with the two cuts, or else you are trying to do too large a cove with too small a gouge. The result of these two scooping cuts does not look pretty, but the cutting actions that follow clean it all up nicely.

Using the right-hand side of the cove again, present the blade, flute facing left, with the point at the position at which the cut has to start. Keep just inside the rough-cut beginning—otherwise you will skid away again. Keeping the bevel just slightly away from the wood will enable you to put the point in and start the cut. The handle will be just down from the horizontal and a little over to the left. The full cut is completed by swinging the handle over to the right (thereby bringing the bevel into contact) and proceeding down the right-hand slope, gradually rolling the gouge over on its back

To start a ball shape, rub the bevel on the line, roll the gouge and lift the handle. Start each successive cut a little closer to the center line, but don't move the tool along the rest during any one cut.

(flute up) to finish at the bottom of the cove. Do not go past center of bottom. Sometimes I will allow just a little way past so that this area cleans up nicely without ridging.

Reverse the directions and cut down from the left-hand line. If you do not attempt heavy cuts you can do these alternate ones nice and slowly, watching and feeling the cut working properly. Alternate cuts from side to side will deepen and shape the cove to your satisfaction.

The coving gouge, which many beginners think is just for hollows, can also form quite attractive ball shapes. Right at the full diameter it cannot finish as cleanly as the skew chisel or the beading and parting tool, but it can get quite near.

Make the usual practice cylinder, 2 in. in diameter between centers. Somewhere along cut down a groove to about ½-in. in diameter. To give room for the gouge to work, widen it to 1 in. in length. Repeat the process 2 in. away so that you are left with a 2-in. block with room to work at either side. Pencil a line around the center of the block. Then pencil two more so that the wood has three equidistant lines running around it. We will start work from left to right.

With the lathe stopped place the gouge on the wood with the point upwards at the right-hand line, the bevel straddling the line, and the flute up. Turn the lathe slowly by hand. Keeping the blade on the rest and at a right angle to the wood, slide the blade down the wood, keeping the bevel rubbing, until the point takes hold and starts a small cut. Keep this going by gradually twisting the blade over to the right while progressively raising the handle. This action continues until the corner of the block has become slightly rounded and the gouge comes off the cut. You will find that the gouge has to be rolled and the handle lifted a surprising distance to accomplish such a short area of cut.

Start the lathe and do a similar cut, increasing the rounded area. Do another with the lathe stopped, slowly so that you can feel how much more freedom and lift you have to give the tool to keep it going over each full cut. Then you can gradually progress back to the block's center line, increasing the rounded area down to the ½-in. short spindle. You are cutting from large diameter to small with the bevel rubbing all the time. Down at the ½-in. spindle, the gouge will have been rolled over so much in order to keep it cutting that the flute finally ends up facing completely right.

Ensure that whatever hand is on the rest does not move along at all during any one cut. Keep your tool bevels at the correct length, hollow ground or dead flat, and sharpen often. And above all, do not try to cut wood uphill. □

Methods of Work

Tapered turning head

When lathe-turning candlesticks or other items with a center hole, the hole can be perfectly centered by drilling it before turning, and then using a tapered turning head, such as the one shown. If the candlesticks are to be for standard ⅞-in. diameter candles, taper from a large diameter of about 1⅛ in. to a minor diameter of about ¹³⁄₁₆ in. or slightly less. The important dimensions are ⅞-in. diameter at ½ in. to ¾ in. from the small end, along with a smooth, straight taper.

The predrilled wood blank is slipped over the tapered head. Take care not to overtighten, as the taper will split the blank if too much force is applied. Making the overall length of the taper about 2¼ in. and using the diameters given provide good tightness and tool clearance for standard candlesticks.

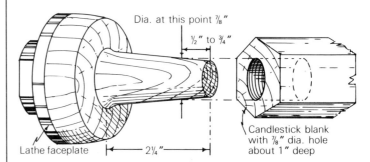

Cutting away stock from the top of the turning adjacent to the tapered head shortens the workpiece and consequently loosens the grip of the head, so if you must cut at that point, be sure to remove only a small amount before stopping the lathe and retightening the tailstock. When finished, the work can be removed easily by backing off the tailstock and moving the work slightly from side to side until loosened. The result is a perfectly centered hole. This method has one other advantage: You proceed with turning *after* you know you've drilled a good clean hole. The same concept can be applied for other center-hole pieces as well by turning other tapers with different diameters. If you have several tapers, it's best to mount each one permanently on its own faceplate to ensure concentricity.   —*L. L. Chapman, Newark, Ohio*

Steel-wool holder

Cut a hollow rubber ball into two pieces, one smaller than the other (for two different sizes). Into each piece place steel wool and use, instead of final sandpaper, for finishing your projects. The ball will keep the steel wool together and also keep it from sticking your fingers. I find that steel wool makes a better finish than sandpaper on the clocks I build. For sanding round pieces on the wood lathe I use a homemade tool. Take a piece of pipe in a length to suit your needs and split it in half lengthwise, then weld a handle on it. Lay sandpaper or steel wool in the cup and hold with your thumbs back from the work.   —*George Eckhart, Kenosha, Wis.*

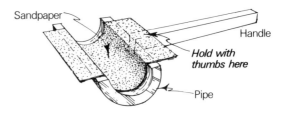

Small Turned Boxes

Grain direction determines technique

by Wendell Smith

Walnut box, 6-in. diameter.

Small wooden boxes offer the woodturner an excellent opportunity to try his hand at design. I would like to describe some techniques I use to make boxes for storing small items such as jewelry. One approach to the design of such turnings that I particularly like is to inlay circular veneers into box lids. The availability of many figured veneers allows an almost unlimited number of attractive wood combinations. Some wood/inlay combinations I enjoy are: walnut/thuya burl, padauk/ebony, maple/ebony, cherry/tulipwood, mahogany/madrone burl, mahogany/amboyna burl, walnut/*Dalbergia sp.* (rosewood, cocobolo, kingwood, etc.).

Depending upon whether the grain is to run horizontally or vertically in the completed box, the sequence of operations in box turning is somewhat different. I've divided the discussion according to this difference.

Grain is horizontal

Turning boxes of horizontal grain involves primarily faceplate techniques. Useful lumber thicknesses are 2 in. and 3 in. With 2-in. stock, I generally use the full thickness for the base, and resaw another piece from an adjacent section of the same board for the lid. This point is quite important, because differences in color and texture between boards can be very apparent if one is used for a base and another for a lid. A

Wendell Smith, 46, is a research associate in color photography at Eastman Kodak in Rochester, N. Y. His turnings, which he sells through art galleries, have been exhibited in several juried craft shows. Smith uses a Rockwell-Delta lathe and Sorby gouges.

3-in. blank may be resawn into 2-in. and 1-in. pieces for the base and lid, thus permitting the figure to carry through from top to bottom. Resawn lid blanks should be given ample time to return to equilibrium with the ambient humidity prior to turning. Then glue round waste blocks of 3/4-in. plywood with paper interleaving to the bottom of the base and the top of the lid. Polyvinyl acetate (white) glue and brown wrapping paper serve the purpose satisfactorily. The faceplate, of course, is screwed to the waste block.

I turn and finish-sand the inside of the lid first. The lid is then removed from the lathe and the glue block split off. The base of the box is placed on the lathe, and a shallow recess turned to accept the lid with a snug fit. The base is now capped with the lid, and the two held together with a flat center in the ball-bearing tailstock. The support of the tailstock eliminates the necessity for a tight jam fit. Unless a jam fit is very tight, slippage may occur when turning the base and the lid together, which invariably burnishes the wood. And a very tight fit may require prying to remove the lid, which can easily damage the box. Before capping the base with the lid, the top edge of the base is sanded. Thus, those surfaces on the base and lid that contact each other are now complete, and so is the inside of the lid. With this arrangement, the side of the box and lid may be worked together, and then finish-sanded. Before removing the tailstock, the lid is "clamped" to the base by wrapping the joint with masking tape. I use 1-1/2-in. tape, which is amply strong.

The top of the lid is now finished as desired. One precaution: If a knob is desired, it is usually better to add a separately turned one rather than to turn the lid and knob from the

Grain is horizontal in 3-1/2-in. diameter cherry box, left, with koa veneer inlaid into its lid, center. Box at right is goncalo alves,

4-1/4 in. in diameter. Although both boxes are plain cylinders, subtle changes in shape make each distinct.

same piece. Because a large amount of wood must be removed from the top of the lid to leave a knob, re-equilibration of the lid with the ambient humidity may lead to cupping.

Upon completion of the top of the lid, the masking tape and lid may be removed and the interior of the box finished. Boxes in which the grain runs horizontally rather than vertically are more prone to develop sticking lids with humidity changes. Consequently, the interior of the box should be sanded until the lid fits loosely. For this type of box, a loosely fitting lid is a properly fitting lid.

There is a trick to removing waste plywood blocks that prevents damage to the bottom of the finished turning. The splitting wedge (an old plane blade) should be inserted between the two layers of the waste block closest to the paper interleaving—not between the waste block and the paper. This removes about 80% of the plywood. The remainder, still glued to the paper, has no strength and is easily pried off with a chisel. Scraping and sanding complete the job.

To inlay a veneer into a box lid, the first step is to soak, press and dry the veneer. Once dry, the veneer should be kept under moderate pressure to keep it flat until ready for use. It is then clamped with a circular wooden block against a wooden faceplate previously flattened in the lathe. The wooden block is held in place with a ring center in the ball-bearing tailstock. The ring center indexes the block for later re-centering at the gluing stage. The block should be about 1/8 in. smaller in diameter than the desired circle of veneer.

A tool rest is now brought as close as possible to the veneer and block. With the lathe running at a slow speed, the veneer is cut using a skew or diamond-point chisel. Using this method I have cut circles with undamaged edges even from recalcitrant veneers such as burls.

To prepare the box lid for the veneer, I first turn a slightly undersize recess. A ''straight-across'' scraper is used to flatten the bottom of the recess. The diameter of the recess is carefully enlarged by using a parting tool to pare off a small amount at a time. This means frequently stopping the lathe to test the fit, a tedious but necessary process. The fit should be snug—anything less results in an unsightly glue line. I remove the tightly fitting veneer for final gluing with the shop vacuum cleaner, using the last gentle gasp of suction after the vacuum has been turned off.

To attach the veneer, I use a polyvinyl acetate (white) or an aliphatic resin (yellow) glue, both of which are water-based. Put the glue on the box lid—not on the veneer. A water-based glue applied to the veneer will cause the veneer to expand rapidly and it will be difficult to fit it into the recess. Finally, the inlay is clamped in place in the lathe using the same circular wooden block (previously indexed with the ring center for re-centering) as was used in cutting the veneer, with waxed paper inserted between the veneer and block. After overnight drying in the lathe, the lid may be finished.

Grain is vertical

I generally turn vertical-grain boxes (such as a ring box) from 2x2 spindle-turning stock. Because the lid is separated from the base on the lathe, allowance must be made for some waste.

The blank is first placed in the lathe between centers and turned to a cylinder. A shoulder is then turned at one end to fit tightly into a homemade chuck, as shown in the diagram,

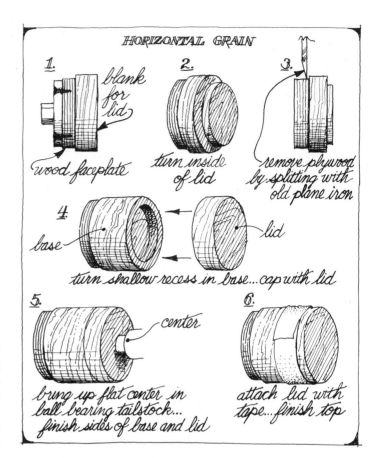

Horizontal-grain box in cherry, 10 in. diameter, 2-1/4 in. high, shows design possibilities permitted by the method diagrammed above. Lid is mostly finished with tailstock for support, then taped in place for final shaping of knob.

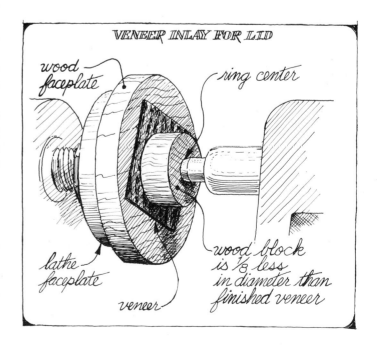

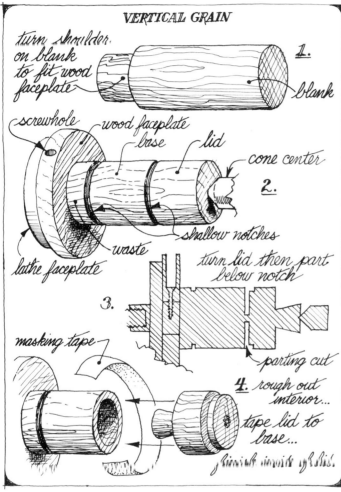

VERTICAL GRAIN

1.
turn shoulder on blank to fit wood faceplate

blank

2.
screwhole
wood faceplate
base
lid
cone center
shallow notches
waste
lathe faceplate

3.
turn lid then part below notch

masking tape
parting cut

4. rough out interior...
tape lid to base...

and securely fastened with two countersunk screws.

The lid can be prepared in two ways. If the wood is figured, it is desirable to have the figure carry through from base to top in the completed box, as shown in the photograph. Consequently, when the lid is parted from the base, it must go back on the same way it came off. If the wood has little or no figure, it is somewhat easier to prepare the lid in the reverse sense; that is, after parting from the base, the lid is turned around and refitted. Since the method for figured wood is more involved, I'll describe it in detail.

The cylindrical blank, fastened to the chuck, is mounted in the lathe with a cone tailstock center supporting the free end. After truing so that the cylinder runs smoothly, a shallow notch is cut with the parting tool where the lid will meet the top of the base. A second shallow notch is cut at the bottom of the base, no closer than about 1/2 in. from the chuck. These notches assist in visualizing the relative proportions of the base and lid and other aspects of the design of the box. In estimating the height of the lid, about 3/16 in. extra should be allowed at the tailstock end for later removal of the cone center mark. Shrinkage and expansion are not much of a problem with vertical-grain boxes, so a knob may be turned as an integral part of the top.

The knob and top of the lid are first roughly turned to the desired shape. Then the lid is parted from the base, the parting tool entering the cylinder about 1/8 in. below the notch previously cut between base and lid. The interior of the base is next partially roughed out to accept the inverted lid, which is fastened to the base by wrapping the two with masking tape. This automatically centers the lid, and its inside, including the shoulder, is now easily finished. A slicing cut with the skew is ideal for finishing the bottom of the lid, as this exerts little force and leaves a surface that requires a minimum of sanding. After sanding the bottom of the lid and shoulder, the masking tape and lid are removed.

The turning of the remainder of the box is similar to the method for horizontal-grain boxes. The interior of the base is first enlarged so the lid will fit snugly. The tailstock is brought up, and the side of the box and lid are worked together. The joint is then taped, the tailstock removed, and the handle and top of the lid completed. One must take very thin slicing cuts at the end of the handle to avoid breaking it. Finally, the lid is removed and the interior of the box is completed.

I remove the box with a parting cut that goes nearly to the center of the cylinder. To prevent fibers from being torn from the center of the base, I terminate the parting cut when about 1/4 in. of wood remains. Parting is completed with a coping saw, leaving the 1/4-in. nubbin of wood on the box. The box is then turned around and snugly fitted to the approximately 1/2 in. of waste wood still protruding from the chuck, by turning the waste wood to size. The box is supported with the tailstock cone center touching the nubbin, and all but the very center of the base can be cleaned up with a slicing cut of the skew, followed by light sanding. The nubbin is then removed with a jeweler's saw and any remaining waste sliced off with a chisel. Hand sanding completes the base.

Homemade chuck holds cylinder with vertical grain, photo at top, for turning sequence shown in the drawing. At left is soft maple box, 1-7/8 in. in diameter and 5 in. high, with separately turned knob of walnut. Myrtlewood box, right, is 2 in. in diameter and 3-3/4 in. high.

Turning Spalted Wood
Sanders and grinders tame ghastly pecking

by Mark Lindquist

*Spalted maple bowl
(5 in. high, 11 in. dia.).*

Just as spalted wood is not like ordinary wood, so turning spalted wood is not like turning ordinary wood. New methods must be found. Spalting refers to the often spectacular patterns of line and color that occur when water and fungus invade downed wood and begin to rot it (*"Spalted Wood,"* Summer '77, pp. 50-53). These processes of decay change the wood's chemical and cellular structure, and its physical properties. In particular, the density of spalted wood varies enormously and unpredictably. Highly spalted zones are much softer than surrounding, more ordinary wood. The differences in density cause hideous pecking in turning, and spalted wood requires extremely tedious sanding before a smooth surface can be achieved.

My father and I, over the past decade, have developed an abrasive method of turning spalted wood. We rough out the blank with conventional turning tools, then, with the wood still whirling on the lathe, we shape and finish it with an assortment of abrasive body grinders and disc sanders. Our method also works on conventional woods and can be considered an alternative to traditional turning. But it transforms the working of spalted wood from an impossibility to a fascinating challenge.

I like to use pieces that have dried for at least three years after harvesting. Occasionally, if the wood was already dry when harvested and feels okay after a year, I attempt to work with it. But in turning the wood this soon, there is always a risk that it will crack or warp.

First, I use a Rockwell #653 power plane to expose the patterns and figures in the aged block of wood. It planes a swath 4 in. wide, has an optional carbide-tipped helical cutter (which I strongly recommend), and can handle just about any hard surface. I cut the ends off the block cross-grain to expose the end grain, which often is the key to the picture or figure of the spalting within. If the piece has been properly prepared and aged, cutting an inch or so off each end will usually take out end-grain surface checks and cracks. It is best to saw the blank so that the bowl lip faces the outside of the tree, and the pith side is toward the bottom of the bowl. This may seem extravagant, but it makes sense to have a bowl whose lip is less liable to crack later. I have also made reasonably successful bowls by turning end grain up towards the lip. The best way is to turn side grain, so that the bottom of the bowl has side grain and the sides or walls have end grain. Usually, the best figure or picture is in the end grain, so this is also an esthetic advantage.

Once you have visualized the bowl within the chunk of

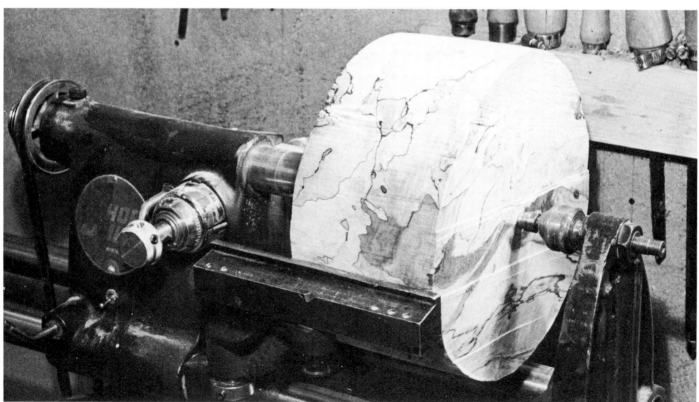

Before turning, Lindquist exposes the pattern with a power plane, cuts out surface checks and cracks, and decides on the orientation of the bowl. Then the blank is bandsawn cylindrical and mounted di-rectly on the faceplate with self-tapping screws. The bowl is turned between centers as much a possible and at low speed to avoid problems caused by the varying density of spalted wood.

wood, examine the piece all over for checks and cracks. Determine which side is the bottom and which is the top by deciding whether the cracks may be turned out or eliminated. With a compass, scribe a circle larger than the top of the bowl will be, and another that is the minimum size of the bowl. Somewhere in between, scribe the line on which you will cut the blank. Cut out the blank on a band saw—a ¼-in. skiptooth blade works well—and center and mount the faceplate on the bottom side of the blank.

Normally, I use ¼-in. self-tapping sheet metal screws, ¾ in. long, to mount the faceplate directly onto the wood. This method has both advantages and disadvantages. There are usually harder and softer zones within a piece of spalted wood. While the wood is spinning rapidly on the lathe, it is easy for the tool to grab and catch in a soft spot that meets a hard spot. This wrench may be violent enough to rip the bowl loose from the faceplate. I've found that the more usual method, gluing the wood to a waste block with paper in between and screwing the waste to the faceplate, simply is not strong enough to withstand the wrench. In addition, the blank may be unbalanced because of its varying density, and screwing the faceplate directly to the wood is safer. Afterward, I plug the screw holes with turned pegs that over the years work themselves slightly out, but as they do so they also lift the bottom of the bowl just off the table, protecting the underside finish. Although gluing to paper isn't strong enough, a bowl can be glued directly to a waste block, which can be cut off after turning. And often the stock is large enough to turn a bowl with an extra-thick base, containing the screw holes, for cutting off later.

Once the faceplate is mounted on the bowl, and the bowl on the lathe, I chuck the headstock with the bowl up to the tailstock. Free faceplate turning is dangerous with spalted wood, again because of its varying density. Whenever possible, it is best to keep the bowl between two centers. Now with the lathe running at low speed, I rough the outside of the blank. I use carbide-tipped scraping tools, which I make myself; you can use conventional or carbide scraping tools or cutting tools. I prefer carbide because the black zone lines in spalted wood are very abrasive and quickly dull steels. Whatever tools you use, the first time you try spalted wood you will be shocked, disappointed and amazed, all at once. Spalted wood cuts like butter. It seems to be mush. But it pecks. Great chunks just tear out of the surface, leaving ugly pits and pockets behind. It will seem impossible to repair and you will want to throw the blank away. But don't, not yet.

Cone separation

First, rough out a fat version of the bowl you want to make. The inside may be removed by any traditional turning method, but with a large chunk of spalted wood the cone separation technique is a sensible choice. This trick removes an intact cone from the block of wood, which may be remounted and turned into another, smaller bowl. This is a good technique but requires confidence and care: If the tool catches deep inside a large blank, the lathe shaft will bend.

To separate the cone, I use a long, thick and strong file with its teeth ground smooth. I make the cutting edge on what was once the edge of the file, not the face, so the tool is rather thicker than it is wide. Grind the end to a short, sharp bevel, on the order of 60° or 70° and keep the corners sharp. Then add a long, sturdy handle for leverage.

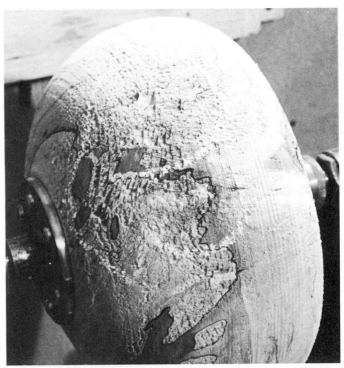

Spalted wood is a turner's nightmare. Rough turning yields pitted surface, with pockets nearly ¼ in. deep. Dark patches are hard wood; soft areas appear light. Black zone lines define patterns.

The lip and the face of the bowl are trued up with a long, straight borer, to prepare the blank for cone separation.

Start the cut at the inside rim of the bowl, and aim for the bottom center of the bowl. Make the cut at least twice as wide as the tool, for clearance. Once you have penetrated deeply enough to make a cone of the piece that normally would have been chips, use the same tool to begin cleaning out the sides of the bowl. The idea is to save the center section for another bowl or possibly two, and to keep the bowl between centers until it is almost completely roughed out. When the blank at last begins to look like a bowl inside (you can peer behind the cone, which is still attached at the center), take the whole thing off the lathe and place it on the floor, preferably on concrete. Using a spoon gouge and mallet, strike the center of the cone—with the cutting edge of the chisel facing end grain, not side grain—a good sharp whack. If you have done it right, a few subsequent blows will pop the cone right out. If you try to go at the side grain, there's a good chance you will split the bowl in half. Play with the method and find the best way for you—the point is to get the cone out without damaging the bottom of the bowl.

Once the bowl is remounted on the lathe, the inside must be cleaned up and the piece finish-scraped (not that it will do much good, for the more scraping that is done, the worse the

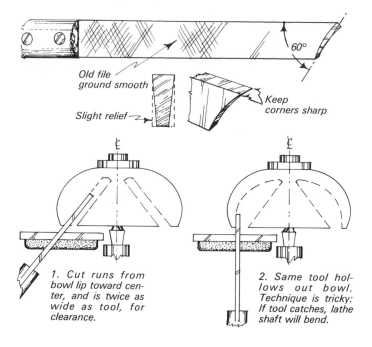

Old file
ground smooth

Slight relief

Keep
corners sharp

60°

1. Cut runs from bowl lip toward center, and is twice as wide as tool, for clearance.

2. Same tool hollows out bowl. Technique is tricky: If tool catches, lathe shaft will bend.

Cone separation: Above, a cut twice the thickness of the file divides the center cone from the bowl. After subsequent cuts have roughed out the interior of the bowl, the cone can be freed with a spoon gouge and mallet, below. A few sharp whacks of the mallet, with the cutting edge of the chisel facing end grain, will do the trick. The cone can later be made into another, smaller bowl.

chips keep coming out all over in what appears to be a turner's nightmare). At any rate, disregard the appearance of disaster, and let the bowl stand as it is, with all its blemishes.

Microwave drying

If occasionally I find that the bowl I've turned is still too wet to sand and finish, I leave it about an inch thicker than I want it to be all around. With white glue I paint the places that look as if they might crack—especially the end grain. If the wood is wet, the glue usually takes a while to dry and sometimes only becomes pasty. Then I pop the rough-turned bowl into a microwave oven. As I understand it, the microwave oven speeds up the molecules in the mass of the object, causing friction that results in heat. Not just heat, but a very even heat throughout the mass. Whole green pieces crack, but drier, merely wet pieces, especially in the rough shape of a bowl, dry out quite well without any cracking.

This approach is experimental, but here's the drying sequence I've found best: After I've turned the bowl over-thick and have it painted and placed in the oven, I try "shooting" it for 20 minutes on defrost. Defrost must be used, otherwise the bowl heats up too fast and is sure to crack. When the microwave is set on defrost, it cycles for a minute, then stops for a minute, then resumes, and continues this cycle until the timer stops. I've found that for bowls about 5 in. deep or 12 in. in diameter, 20 minutes is a good first cycle. After the first cycle, the bowl will heat quite rapidly and must be cooled. I usually leave it right in the oven for another 10 or 20 minutes, then check it for cracks, repaint it if necessary, then zap it again. Depending upon how wet or green the bowl is, it may be dry enough to finish after three or four cycles. Each bowl reacts differently, so times vary. If the piece is very special, I start out slowly (10 minutes on defrost), cool for another 10, then recycle all day. Usually the bowl will move considerably, which is to be expected, but cracks won't start.

I am still experimenting with microwave drying, and would like to hear from others who've tried it. Although the trick works in a pinch, I don't think there is any substitute for air and time. Thorough air-drying is the only way to allow all the richness and mellow color to come out.

Equilibrial abrasion

Torn end grain is always a problem in woodturning. In traditional turning, using as sharp a chisel as possible, gouging and shearing produce relatively smooth, "planed" surfaces. This requires much skill and a delicate balance between a sharp edge and perfect technique. My alternative uses industrial abrasive tools and products.

Turning hard, brittle spalted wood creates and leaves deep cavities and pecks in the surface. No amount of scraping with the sharpest of tools will improve the situation. When we first worked with spalted wood, my father and I would spend hour after knuckle-bending hour sanding through the pecks and chips to achieve a uniform surface. One spalted bowl would consume several sheets of coarse-grit paper and a lot of grueling work. Eventually, all the pecks and chips would disappear and the bowl could be finished. By the time we arrived at that point, all of the creative energy of making a beautiful bowl was gone, and it had become just a chore to endure.

After several years of searching and talking to other turners who were experimenting in the area, we arrived at a theory that we now call equilibrial abrasion. The shaft of a lathe

About bowls

I turn my bowls for appearance and artistic expression more than for utilitarian function. This may be a controversial approach among woodworkers, although it is in accord with artists and sculptors who accept a work for itself and not for its utility. As I see it, the bowl's function is to command the space of a room, to light its environment. Its function is to display the beauty of nature and to reflect the harmony of man. It is wrong to ask the spalted bowl to function as a workhorse as well, to hold potato chips or salad or to store trivialities. The bowl is already full. It contains itself and the space between its walls. The bowl is simply a vehicle in which the grain and patterns of the wood may be displayed. The patterns and colors are natural paintings, the bowl a three-dimensional canvas.

Complete and utter simplicity is required in the making of the spalted bowl. The simpler the form, the more uncluttered the surface for the wood to display itself. If we make bowls with lots of curves and decorative lines, the forms within the form fight with each other and with the wood. Wood that is spalted has become graphically oriented. To understand the art of making a spalted bowl, first understand the art of the ancient vessel. Study ancient Chinese and Japanese pottery vases, bowls, and tea-ceremony cups. Look at the work of Rosanjen. Investigate Tamba pottery. Study the masters and see simplicity at its very best.

—M.L.

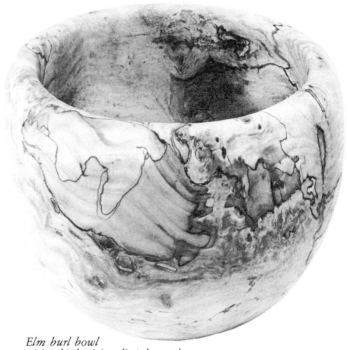

Elm burl bowl
(6 in. high, 6 in. dia.) by author.

---

turns clockwise. Most common rotating shop tools also turn clockwise. But if the shafts of two clockwise rotating tools are put together face to face, they oppose and rotate in opposite directions. We've found that two counter-rotating forces, with proper control and balance, can reach a state of equilibrium. We use abrasive discs on auto body grinders, rubber disc sanders and foam-pad disc sanders while the lathe is turning. Rather than holding the sandpaper still while the bowl turns, the spinning sandpaper works in the opposite direction against the spinning wood. The physics of the interaction aren't clear, but in practice there is a point—and it's not difficult to find—where the two rotational forces balance each other. The tool seems to hover over the work, and the sanding dust pours away in a steady stream. The counter-rotational system easily overcomes the problem of end-grain tearing. It does not eliminate the problem, it merely deals efficiently with it. And while this method won't replace the turning gouge and scraper, it incorporates the past and offers a new alternative for difficult woods.

Our method began in experiments with "flap-wheel" abrasives, at a time when it was difficult even to get flap wheels because the manufacturer, Merit Abrasive Products, Inc., was offering them only as an industrial product. Today they are also marketed for the hobbyist. We began by grinding the interior surface of a bowl—the biggest and most time-consuming problem—with a coarse-grit, 6-in. flap wheel driven by an electric drill. The outside surface wasn't so bad because it was accessible and conformed naturally to sanding. So, with counter-rotational abrasion using the flap-wheel accessory, the inner surface of the bowl was sanded much more easily than by hand. Soon I tried my auto body grinder with a coarse disc on the outer surface of the spinning bowl. At first, this was scary and dangerous, but after practice and with faith in myself and my tools, I found out how to achieve a perfect abraded surface. The tool and the application of it to wood were not new—but using the body grinder with the bowl spinning in the opposite direction and actually shaping the bowl with the grinder were new to us. With practice, the body grinder, a heavy and unwieldy machine, can become a sensitive instrument that improves with constant playing.

With such rapid sanding, the whole room immediately becomes full of dust, thick enough to cut with a knife. So an essential accessory is an efficient blower system located above and to the left of the bowl, facing it from the front of the lathe bed. Positioning is a matter of preference, but the best position is the one that sucks the most dust and is out of the way. The dust must be sucked up before it can enter the room, or it is impossible to work, breathe or see.

A simple squirrel-cage blower obtained from a local scrap yard will work fine for moving the dust. The best kind is a blower with a cast-iron housing, ball bearings, and at least a 6-in. diameter intake opening. Six-inch galvanized stove pipe works well and is cheap. The motor for the blower should be at least ½ hp and turning at 3,500 rpm. The on-off switch should be located near the lathe, since the blower is frequently turned off and on. An alternative to the blower is a large fan in the wall in front of the lathe to suck the dust out of the room. But I prefer the blower because I can direct the intake pipe to the area releasing the most dust.

After success with the body grinder, I got a smaller hand-held grinder that is easier to control, to use with finer grits. I use it with 120-grit floor-sanding discs to prepare the outside of bowls. I also use a small, flexible, rubber-backed disc on the interior of the bowl. Both Merit and Standard Abrasives make a system called quick-lock or soc-at that connects the sanding disc to the pad with a screw or snap fastener, making grit changes quick and easy. My usual grit sequence begins with 24, then 36 or 50, then 80, then 120 followed by finish-

The bowl interior is ground smooth with a disc attached to an electric drill. A suction system located above the bowl removes the clouds of dust that lathe-sanding creates.

ing papers. If the wood is especially soft, I leave out the 24 grit. Thus equilibrial abrasion can prepare the whole bowl for final finishing with hand-held sandpaper.

Speed is the key to these techniques. If the bowl turns faster than the disc, the bowl will overpower the disc. The disc must spin almost twice as fast as the bowl (unless it is burning the wood) in order to achieve equilibrium. There must be a balance of power and an overbalance of cutting action. In interior abrading, the disc should reach a flow, a floating movement, gliding back and forth from the bottom of the bowl to the lip, and each pass grinding off excess wood. Preparation sanding calls for careful control, discipline and knowledge. Use high-speed drills (1,000-1,800 rpm), especially two-speed drills, but not variable-speed drills, since they can't take too much force. A low-cost drill can't be used—it will merely burn out. When you hit equilibrium, the tool will appear to be suspended or within a magnetic force-field, free to vacillate in any direction. This can occur only when the tool is properly cutting the wood. A good strong drill will really cut, and the bowl will quickly take shape.

I usually start by abrading the interior of the bowl, using the electric drill with a 3-in. locking disc and a 24 or 36-grit abrasive. Some pieces of wood will finish up more quickly if the initial sanding of the end-grain portions is done with the lathe turned off. With others, I start immediately on the whirling wood. As you face the front of the bowl, place the disc on the right side. This may seem wrong, but the wood comes off much more quickly than it does on the left side.

Author rests body grinder on hip and pushes it from headstock to lip to sand bowl exterior.

The point is to try different sides, different angles, different approaches until the right way is found. In abrading the exterior, I rest the grinder on my hip and use my weight to push it toward the bowl, moving from headstock to lip. Near the end of the pass, I pull up the handle, turn my hand over on the handle, and reverse the direction to complete the lip, all in one movement. The idea is to get motion and control going together, to think of the grinder or the tool as an extension of the hand, but, most importantly, as a sensitive instrument. Paying attention to the sounds will pay off. The right pitch will tell you that the speeds are right. Ticking means the disc has a tear in it and will soon explode; click, click, click means there is a crack in the bowl; bump, bump, bump means there is a soft spot that the grinder is wearing away faster than the rest of the bowl.

An important caution: Do not attempt to use the body grinder on the bowl without proper safety measures. Wear goggles and make sure there is no loose clothing about. Be careful about ripped discs—plan on ripping about a dozen or so to start—and above all, know how to operate the grinder on a stationary surface before attempting to use it on a concave spinning surface. Lack of caution can easily prove disastrous for both the operator and the equipment.

Finishing
After the surface of the bowl is prepared with the disc sanders, the diagonal scratches caused by the grinding must be removed. If you use a heavy-duty foam-rubber pad ½-in. thick behind the sandpaper, the marks come out quickly since the foam pad keeps the paper from heating up and maintains a uniform surface. Aluminum-oxide or silicon-carbide sanding sheets work best with spalted wood. To take the scratches out, I use 100 grit, then 150, 220 and finally 320 grit. Occasionally, I'll go to 400 and maybe to 600 grit, but for the most part, 320 does the job. With spalted wood, usually anything finer than 320 discolors the surface and clogs the pores, leaving a grey mousiness. I do a little hand-sanding if the marks haven't come out, but if the pad sanding has been done right, and not rushed, usually 320 polishes and no marks are left. For the inside bottom of the bowl, I use a foam pad glued to a disc attached to a drill, and I finish the scratches or circular concentric lines with 220 and 320 grit. I glue turned pegs in the screw holes and sand the bottom flat using a disc attached to a drill press. The bottom of the bowl is also finished to 320 and signed.

I make up foam pads, starting with the 3-in. rubber sanding disc mounted on an arbor that is commonly sold for home auto body work. First I glue on a ½-in. layer of industrial foam, then I use the auto body grinder to shape the disc and foam to what I need. The handiest shape seems to be a cone, its wide part outward. Then I spray the foam with disc adhesive and stick cloth-backed aluminum-oxide paper to it. Many of my sanding tools are cut-and-try, made from scrap. A useful heavy foam for all sorts of sanding tools is sold in sheets and tubes by refrigeration suppliers, as insulation.

The best finish that I've found so far is an oil, urethane, and buff finish. Mix equal parts of raw linseed oil and high-gloss polyurethane varnish. Wipe on one coat and immediately wipe off. Repeat the next day. Allow to dry at least one week and then buff with tripoli, a buffing compound. Once the bowl has been buffed with tripoli (available at hardware stores), the finish may be hand-rubbed and polished with a

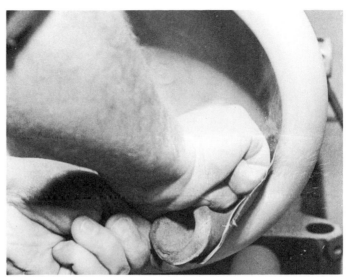

The bowl is finish-sanded in increasingly finer grits, with a ½-in. foam-rubber pad held behind the sandpaper.

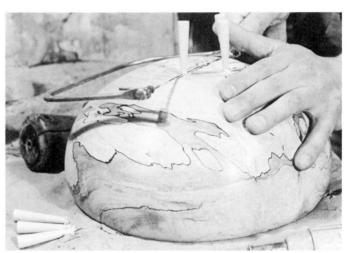

After finish sanding, the faceplate-screw holes are filled with turned wooden pegs, which are glued and pounded in. Then they are trimmed, and the bottom of the bowl is sanded flat with a disc attached to a drill press.

soft cloth. This seals the oil finish, yet is very thin, allowing all of the wood to come through. Most finishes may be used on spalted wood, and experimenting will uncover the best one for your tastes.

If the wood is extremely soft, plain polyurethane will work well. If the wood is soft and has become discolored, buff it first with a cotton bonnet. The bonnet will pull out the dirt and the finish will take better. Or blow off the dirt, if you have compressed air. If the bowl is extremely soft and a high-gloss finish is desired, apply multiple coats of clear Deft, but after approximately twenty coats, it's best to sand off about half the build-up to an even coat. Best results are without sanding between coats. Most often, the oil/urethane finish works the best, for color and character. Obviously it is not a non-spotting, non-marking finish, but it is not intended to be. A much more utilitarian finish may be applied by building up several layers of urethane, but I'm not much interested in it. □

Mark Lindquist, 29, of Henniker, N.H., is a sculptor who earns his living by turning and carving spalted wood and burls. He is writing a book about his techniques.

Laminated Turnings

Making bowls from stacked rings, bottles from tall staves

by Garth F. Graves

Awoodturner wishing to make large bowls or cylinders will be fortunate to find a suitable piece of premium stock that has been spared from being reduced to veneer, resawn into milled boards, or subjected to the sculptor's chisel. The alternatives are unseasoned blocks that are rough-turned, set aside to dry, and final-turned again (*Fine Woodworking*, Summer '76, pp. 37-39), or shells laminated from standard stock. Turning forms may be built up from an unlimited selection of choice, seasoned hardwoods. Premium stock may be laminated into a form and size that accommodates the most ambitious project, and design opportunities in size, patterns, shapes and applications are limitless. Laminated shells are as strong as pieces turned from solid blocks, and lathe time and material costs are significantly lower.

Turning blanks may be built up horizontally, by stacking rings, or vertically, with beveled staves. Shallow containers such as bowls and trays lend themselves to stacking, while tall, slender forms usually dictate the assembly of vertical staves. Added design interest can be achieved by contradicting the common logic—there is no reason that stacked rings cannot form a tall cylinder, or that shallow, wide bowls cannot be made from vertical staves. Constructing the blanks gives the craftsman great control over the final form; subtleties often transform a nice turning into something special.

The technique of stacked rings is based on overlapping concentric rings, cut at an angle from a single piece of 1-in. surfaced stock. Experimentation with the concept can produce a fairly wide range of shapes. The surface pattern of the finished piece can be controlled to some degree, and the pattern can be accentuated by inserting alternating pieces of contrasting woods at the rim, the base, or in the wall of the bowl.

The geometry of cutting all the rings from a single source board somewhat limits the shapes obtainable (diagram on opposite page). The concentric rings, cut at a 45° angle, are laminated to form a hollow conical blank for turning. The angle of cut, the width of the rings and the thickness of the wood govern the cross section of the blank. For this basic method, any increase in depth will proportionately increase the diameter. Variations of these parameters will change the assembled profile. The practical limits are quickly reached and for more scope two source boards become necessary.

Using two or more boards for alternating rings increases the possibilities. Inserting straight-walled rings between the angle-cut rings makes the form taller and reduces the slope of the wall. But I've found that the best method is to alternate diagonally-cut rings from two source boards. This reduces the slope of the wall; the thicker walls allow greater design variation. Further variations include leaving a wide ring at the top for a flare, a flange or a handle. The pieces from which the rings are cut may be segmented and laminated in many ways or built up to almost any size.

For proper bonding, the boards used for stacking should be milled and planed truly flat and evenly thick, free of ripples, valleys, pecks and checks. The circles can be cut by hand or with a jigsaw or sabre saw. But before cutting, draw a random series of concentric circles on the underside of the stock to aid alignment during assembly. The saw blade must have a starting hole, but instead of a single large hole, which would remove too much wood, drill a series of small holes in line with the arc of cut and at the angle of cut.

Keep the grain parallel from ring to ring, so seasonal movement won't break the bowl. Allow glue joints to set under pressure, attach to a faceplate, and you're off and turning.

I've seen many otherwise fine turnings marred by screw holes in the bottom, the result of attaching the faceplate directly to the wood. Glue a square of scrap to the turning blank, separated by a single sheet of newspaper. The paper will separate when a knife blade is forced between the scrap and the finished piece, and the faceplate may be securely screwed to the scrap piece.

Laminated rings are only one way of building up blanks for turning. The assembly of a number of wedge-shaped staves to form a cylinder opens more opportunities for project design. A wide variety of shapes and sizes are possible—from large cylinders to bowls, buckets, or salad sets. All can be produced from standard milled stock of premium woods, but making cylinders of vertical staves requires care. Clean, true cuts are essential and provision must be made for fitting ends to the cylinders. The same principles apply to compound-angle forms that would result in conical blanks.

Success comes from properly joining the staves; the angles are critical. The table at right contains information on various final diameters, the number of staves required, the angles of cut, and the outside width of each. It also gives the general mathematics for any size cylinder. The thickness of the stock and the number of staves will govern the wall thickness of the finished piece. The more staves, the more circular the blank will be, and therefore the greater the usable thickness.

After the staves are cut to the proper angles they are assembled dry into cylinder form and checked for fit. Some adjustment is possible by trimming angles or adding segments, to compensate for miscalculations in the cutting angle. Remember, any error is multiplied by the two surfaces and by the number of staves used.

The photo sequence (turn page) highlights the application of this technique. Note that thick stock was required by the widely varying diameters of the finished pitcher; 1-in. stock would be prepared in the same way. When the shape restricts access to the inside, as in the piece shown, I find it helpful to diagram the cross section. I use inside calipers or dividers to measure along the center line at 1-in. increments, then I dia-

(please turn page)

Garth Graves, 40, of San Diego, is a designer and prototype woodworker. He used to be an aerospace technical writer.

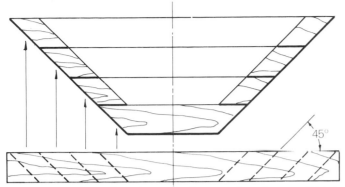

Cross section above shows how a single source board, cut at 45° into rings whose width equals the thickness of the stock, can be stacked into a conical turning blank.

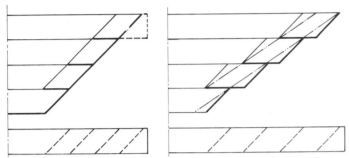

The top ring may be cut wider, left, to turn a bowl with a flaring rim. Increasing the ring width to 1½ times the stock thickness, right, permits a slightly wider bowl but possibilities are limited.

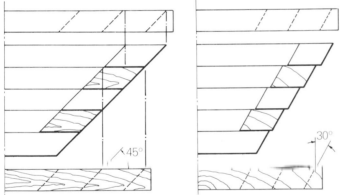

Two source boards, cut at 45° into rings twice as wide as they are thick, allow much more variation in shape. Note that the alternating rings are offset by half of their width. To make a steep bowl with thick walls, cut two boards at 30° into rings 1½ times as wide as they are thick, as at right.

Bowls are turned from stacked rings of ¾-in. teak.

Author turns woodenware in teak from staved cylinders; decanters are about 12 in. high. Chart below relates cylinder diameter, number of staves and stave width. Half-angles are the amount of saw-blade tilt from the vertical when cutting staves.

θ Angle	N Qty. Reqd.	Half-Angle Cut	STAVE WIDTH W_1 for given diameters				
			3 in.	5 in.	7 in.	9 in.	10 in.
90°	4	45°	3	5	7	9	10
60°	6	30°	1¾	2⅞	4	5¼	5¾
45°	8	22½°	1¼	2⅛	2⅞	3¾	4¼
30°	12	15°	¾	1⅜	1⅞	2½	2¾
15°	24	7½°	⅜	⅝	1	1¼	1⅜

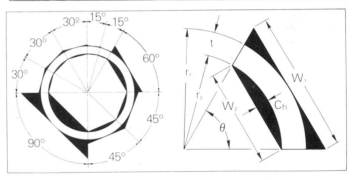

The diagram above left shows a few of the regular divisions of a circle and the relationship between the number of staves in a cylinder and the stock thickness required to produce a given wall thickness. The enlarged section through a stave, right, defines the terms for the following equations. Once you decide what you want to make, the math gives minimum dimensions. Keep angles precise but keep outside width and thickness fat, to have wood for working.

Here, N is the number of staves and θ is the included angle of each; thus, $\theta = 360° \div N$; r_1 is the outside radius of the finished cylinder and r_2 its inside radius; t is the wall thickness and thus $t = r_1 - r_2$; W_1 is the outside width of a stave, W_2 is the inside width; C_h is the chord height and thus stock thickness $T = t + C_h$.

If you have decided on the number of staves and the radius of the cylinder, solve for the width (W_1) of each stave:

$$W_1 = 2r_1 \tan \frac{\theta}{2}$$

For example, if you want a cylinder that has an outside diameter of 8 in., and it will be made of twelve staves ($\theta = 30°$), then, $W_1 = 2 \times 4 (\tan 15°) = 8 \times 0.2679 = 2.14$ in. Set the table saw at 75° (90° minus the half-angle, or 180° ÷ N), and cut each stave so it is at least 2.14 in. on its outside face.

To find the minimum thickness of the stock (T) for a given wall thickness (t), first solve for the chord height:

$$C_h = r_2(1 - \cos \frac{\theta}{2})$$

In the previous example, if the wall is to be ½ in. thick, then $C_h = 3.5 (1 - \cos 15°) = 3.5 (1 - 0.9659) = 0.119$ in. Since $T = t + C_h$, $T = ½ + 0.119 = 0.619$ in.

To find the width of the inside face of a stave, solve:

$$W_2 = 2r_2 \sin \frac{\theta}{2}$$

In the previous example, $W_2 = 2 \times 3.5 \times 0.2588 = 1.812$ in.

gram the measured diameters onto a cross-sectional view. This way I can determine the wall thickness anywhere. A design change in the final stages need not conform to the inside profile, as long as the wall doesn't get too thin.

A cylinder formed of staves doesn't expand and contract the same way as one turned from a solid block. Shrinkage will occur evenly around the circumference and across the wall thickness but the form won't become ovoid. If shrinkage is expected, any lids should be fitted loosely.

Segmenting permits variations that would not be considered if the cylinder were turned from a solid piece. I don't hesitate to embellish a segmented piece with handles, pouring spouts or whatever the design requires. One container shown earlier includes a spout. Prior to assembly, I scored the stave where the spout would go about one-half the way through, and did not glue the portion to be replaced. After the final turning, this piece was easily cut away. A rough-shaped spout, cut to the same half-angle, was glued in place for final shaping. The handle, although attached separately, could have been added in the same way. □

1. *Shopsmith saw table is tilted to half-angle; hollow-ground blade produces good gluing surface.*

2. *Check fit dry, then clean surfaces and glue. Author supplements cord wrap with vise-grip chain clamps or band clamp. Keep the assembly vertical.*

3. *With the top turned true to the sides, the cylinder is screwed to a faceplate. Screw holes will be turned away later.*

4. *First the outside diameter is roughed, then the bottom and lower inside diameter are finished to receive the base.*

5. *Cylinder is removed from lathe and replaced by stock for base. Author usually turns a rabbet so base will plug in snugly.*

6. *Tailstock feed applies pressure for gluing cylinder to its base.*

7. *Now the inside top and the whole outside of the cylinder may be turned to their final shape.*

8. *Use the lathe bed as a holding fixture for adding handles, spouts—whatever the design requires.*

Compound-Angled Staves

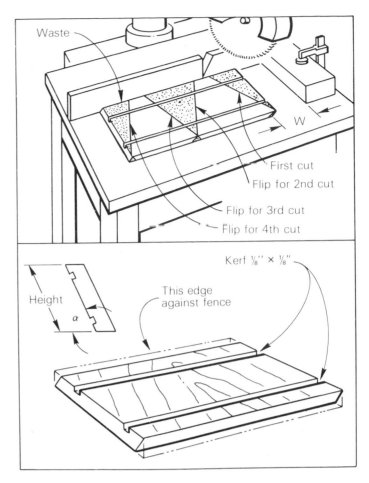

The previous discussion covers building up conical turning blanks from stacked rings, and cylindrical blanks from beveled staves. The next logical step is to make a bowl-shaped blank from staves that are both tapered and beveled.

Robert M. Hewitt, 47, a structural engineer from Mechanicsburg, Pa., has developed a simple method for cutting the staves with his radial arm saw, and for clamping them together with a nylon cord.*

Hewitt's method assumes you have already determined the number of staves (N) in the bowl, and the angle α between the side of the bowl and the table. To cut the segments on a radial arm saw, you'll need to know angle a, the bevel setting of the saw blade and arbor, and angle b, the miter setting of the saw arm. The formulas are:

$$\text{angle } a = \frac{180°}{N} \sin \alpha$$

$$\text{angle } b = \frac{180°}{N} \cos \alpha$$

For example, a bowl with 12 staves sloping at 60°:

$$a = \frac{180°}{12} \sin 60° = 15° \times 0.866 = 13°$$

$$b = \frac{180°}{12} \cos 60° = 15° \times 0.5 = 7.5°$$

If he wants the grain to be vertical in the finished bowl, Hewitt selects a wide board at least an inch thick and crosscuts it into strips whose length equals the height (h) of the finished bowl plus an allowance for cutoffs and for truing up the bottom before gluing it to the base. He bevels the edges to the same slope α as the staves will make with the base, and saws two shallow kerfs near the edges, as shown in the drawing. The kerfs will hold the nylon cord during glue-up.

Next, with the saw blade tilted to angle a and the arm at angle b, he makes the first cut at one end of a strip of stock. Use an adjustable drafting triangle to set the saw accurately. Next he locates and fixes a stop to the table so that the dimension W is the width of a stave at the base of the bowl. This can be guessed, or calculated with the equations given on page 139. He flips the stock over, indexes it against the stop and makes the second cut, producing one of the 12 staves required. Flipping stock again, he makes the next cut, and so on until he has all 12. Hewitt leaves the saw set up so he can adjust one stave to compensate for error and close the bowl.

Assembling tapered staves is tricky, and Hewitt has a tricky solution. He writes "Lay the tapered staves together on a sheet of paper, face down. They will form a segment of a circle, like a pie with a large piece removed. Outline the assembled pieces, and number them so they can be replaced in the same order. Apply contact cement to the paper and the out-

side face of the staves between the cord kerfs, trim the paper to the outline and cement the staves to it. This will allow you to pick up all the staves at once, close the bowl and see how they fit." One stave may have to be adjusted to make all the joints close tightly and it is usually easiest to cut a new one at a slightly different bevel angle.

Hewitt continues, "When the staves fit, lay the bowl out flat again on the bench, cut two lengths of nylon cord and knot them into loops a bit larger than the circumference of the closed bowl. Apply glue to all the mating surfaces, close the staves to form the sides of the bowl, slip the nylon cord into the kerfs and use a dowel to twist the cord for clamping pressure." When the glue is set, Hewitt glues the top of the bowl to a disc of plywood and centers it on the lathe. Then he turns the bottom of the blank true, and glues on what will be the bottom of the bowl. He now can turn and finish the bottom and outside, mark the center, reverse and remount, and part off the plywood. The bowl is completed in the conventional manner. Sometimes he puts a contrasting veneer between staves, for visual interest. He recommends finishing with four coats of satin urethane varnish, rubbed with pumice and oil. This seals the wood completely and prevents expansion and contraction of the wood segments. —J.K.

Blank is glued to waste disc so foot may be trued and bottom attached. Right, cherry bowl with horizontal grain and walnut base.

---

*Hewitt's method was presented last March at the annual Woodturning Symposium in Newtown, Pa. This year organizers Al LeCoff and Palmer Sharpless plan two symposia, the first on March 17, 18, and 19, and the second on June 16, 17, and 18. For more information, contact LeCoff at 520 Elkins Avenue, Elkins Park, Pa. 19117.

Rings from Wedges

by Asaph G. Waterman

(Now imagine that a cylinder is made from very short vertical staves—no taller than the thickness of a board. The staves become wedges, and the cylinder is squashed into a ring. Several such rings can be stacked up to form the blank for a bowl. Asaph G. Waterman of Camillus, N.Y., has devised a tablesaw jig for cutting wedges, and a plywood-and-angle-iron jig for gluing them together.)

There are several advantages in using this technique: The wood need not all be the same thickness, so scraps left over from other projects can be used up; wood with nail holes and other imperfections can be used with minimum loss; no end grain has to be turned, especially important in soft woods like butternut or sumac; and striking effects can be obtained by gluing contrasting pieces of veneer between the wedges.

Accuracy in assembly is very important. The jigs I will describe are for making eight-sided (octagonal) rings, but the same principles apply to jigs for any number of wedges.

The two sliders for the table-saw jig may be made of steel, aluminum or hard wood. They should fit your table-saw grooves accurately, but must slide smoothly. Make the body of the jig, as shown in the drawing, of any stable wood ⁵⁄₄ thick. The angle, 67½° for an octagonal ring, must be accurate because any error will be multiplied by 16 in the finished blank. The triangular wedges for the first layer come to a point, to fill the bottom of the bowl, but succeeding rings must be wider to allow the bowl to flare, and cut off (truncated) at the point to save turning work and avoid waste. The pointer on the jig is used to gauge the width of the truncation. Face the working surface of the jig with coarse carborundum cloth to keep the wood from sliding.

The assembly jig consists of an octagonal plywood base to which are screwed eight 2½-in. lengths of angle iron, drilled and tapped for tightening bolts. I have jigs in two sizes—one an octagon 11 in. from face to face, with sides about 4½ in. wide; the other 14½ in. from face to face with 5¾-in. sides. I use 1-in. by 1-in. by ⅛-in. angle iron. Don't use aluminum angle because the threaded holes won't stand continued use. One side of each piece of angle iron is drilled in its center and tapped for a ⁵⁄₁₆-in., 16-pitch machine screw or cap screw. The other side is drilled ⅜ in. from each end and countersunk for ¾-in. flathead wood screws.

Because the layers have varying diameters, I use spacer blocks in sets of eight between the tightening screws and the wedges themselves. My jigs will make a bowl 11 in. in diameter; a larger bowl of course requires a larger jig.

To make a bowl, I first saw eight pieces that come to a point, turning the board for each cut. Make sure the pieces fit, lightly sand each edge, and, since the main problem in this work is getting the points to meet exactly, avoid it by

sanding the points off flat. Later I drill out the center of the octagon with a tapered bit and turn a tapered plug to fill the hole. I usually run grain of the plug parallel to the grain of the layer itself. Use the small assembly jig with appropriate spacer blocks to glue all the wedges together at once. Protect the jig surface with waxed paper, wipe off the excess glue and let set overnight. If the pressure of the screws forces a wedge to rise, use a C-clamp to force it back down. When the glue has set, fasten a faceplate to the layer and take a thin cut on the lathe to smooth and true the surface.

I make the wedges for the second layer the same way, except I move the pointer on the sawing jig about an inch out from the blade. When the glue has set, fasten this layer to a faceplate, placing the screws near the center so the holes will disappear during turning. Smooth one side and use C-clamps to glue both layers together, staggering the glue lines. Now true both surfaces on the lathe.

At this point a two-layer bowl can be turned or a third layer may be added. To make the larger third layer, move the arrow about 1½ in. out from the blade. You can add as many layers as you like, to get as deep a bowl as you want. □

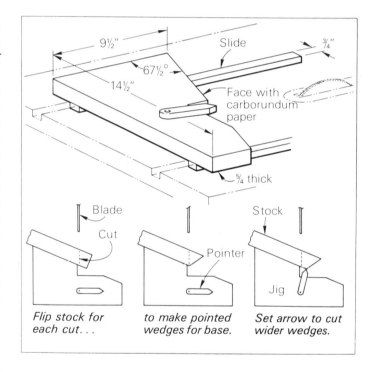

Flip stock for each cut...   *to make pointed wedges for base.*   *Set arrow to cut wider wedges.*

Assembly jig consists of angle iron bolted to plywood plate, drilled and tapped for cap screws. Use spacer blocks between screw and work.

Staved Cones
The general mathematics

by Thomas Webb

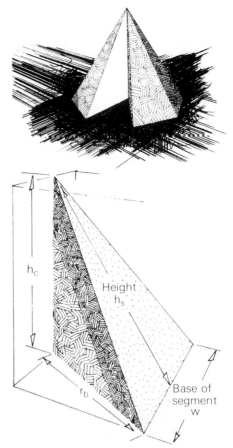

An equal miter joint for a rectangular, box-like construction will result from cutting adjoining edges of the stock at 45°. But what if we need to miter a shape that isn't rectangular? What if, for instance, the shape has seven similar sides that must lean in (or out) rather than standing parallel to one another?

Such non-rectangular forms can be thought of as sections of faceted cone-like shapes. By thinking of forms you wish to make as sections of cones, you can determine the geometry of the flat pieces needed to make those forms. You need only specify the height and base dimensions of the imagined cone, along with the number of sides you want it to have. The formulas will then tell you what shapes to cut to produce the faceted cone shape. Further alterations of the size of these pieces can produce any section of the specified cone. Combining sections of different cones can produce an infinite variety of three-dimensional shapes.

Some of the formulas look complicated, but with a table of trigonometric functions it is fairly simple to do the computations; they can be done in minutes on a calculator with trig functions.

A right cone has a circular base and is symmetrical around an axis running through the center of the base to the tip. The axis is perpendicular to the plane of the base; the length of the axis from base to tip is the cone's height (h_c). A right cone can be described in terms of its height and the radius of its base (r_b); α designates the angle between the surface of the cone and its base.

A right cone can be constructed from a flat sheet of flexible material such as paper or thin metal. The shape to be cut from the flat stock is a circular disc with a wedge removed, and the straight edges of the wedge

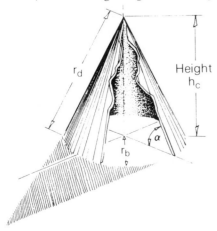

Height
h_c

are radii of the disc (r_d). When the cut radii are pulled together, a right cone is formed; the center of the disc becomes the tip of the cone, the perimeter of the disc becomes the base and r_d becomes the length of the side of the cone.

If you know the height and radius of the base of a right cone you want to construct, the following formulas specify the size of the disc you'll need and of the wedge to be cut from it.

$$r_d = \sqrt{r_b{}^2 + h_c{}^2}$$

$$\theta = 360° \frac{r_b}{r_d} = 360° \cos \alpha$$

Since θ equals the number of degrees remaining in the disc after the wedge is removed, $(360° - \theta)$ equals the angle of the wedge itself.

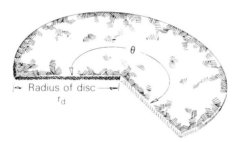

θ

|← Radius of disc →|
r_d

In some circumstances it is useful to specify the base angle α rather than the height of the cone. In this case first solve for h_c using the following formula:

$$h_c = r_b \tan \alpha$$

then apply the previous formulas.

A right cone can be approximated with thicker, less than flexible materials such as wood by cutting compound-angled staves and assembling them around a central axis. The result is a faceted "cone;" the more staves used, the closer the approximation to a true cone.

It helps to imagine that the faceted cone just fits inside an actual cone of similar dimensions. In this way we can see the important dimensions h_c and r_b as they relate to the staves to be made. Follow these steps to determine the size and shape of the staves.

First, decide on the height (h_c) of your cone, the radius of its base (r_b) and the number of staves (N) you want to use to make it.

Compute r_d, which is equivalent to the length of the edge of a stave, by:

$$r_d = \sqrt{r_b{}^2 + h_c{}^2}$$

Compute the width at the base (w) and the height (h_s) of each stave by:

$$w = 2r_b \sin \frac{180°}{N} \qquad h_s = \sqrt{r_d{}^2 - \left(\frac{w}{2}\right)^2}$$

Knowing the height of the stave (h_s) along with its width (w) at the base, you can lay out on your stock what will be the exterior surface of each stave. Remember that the height of a stave is measured along a line that bisects its base at a right angle.

To determine the saw setting for cutting

Height
h_s

Base of
segment
w

h_c

r_b

the miter angles on the sides of the segments, first calculate angle α for the shape you are making:

$$\tan \alpha = \frac{h_c}{r_b}$$

Then use this formula to find angle Ω, the table-saw setting for the side cuts:

$$\tan \Omega = \sin \alpha \tan \frac{180°}{N}$$

If you are making a complete faceted cone shape, you may want to have a flat bottom on it. First calculate the base angle β relative to the exterior surface of the segment, from the formula:

$$\tan \beta = \frac{h_c}{r_b \cos \frac{180°}{N}} = \frac{\tan \alpha}{\cos \frac{180°}{N}}$$

Then find the saw setting for the base cut by subtracting angle β from 90°.

Remember that the sides and bottom of a

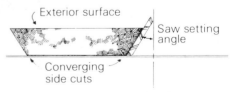

Exterior surface

Saw setting
angle

Converging
side cuts

stave converge; the interior surface consequently is a scaled-down version of the exterior surface. □

Tom Webb, 32, is a sculptor and assistant professor of art at the University of Akron, in Ohio.

Laminated Bowls
Simple cuts produce complex curves

by Harry Irwin

Bowls can be turned from seasoned wood, green wood or laminated wood. The results from seasoned or unseasoned stock are similar, but the bowls produced from laminated wood are quite different. I wanted to turn some bowls but since I don't have a chain saw or a drying room, using green wood seemed beyond my capability. And I couldn't afford to purchase a large slab of seasoned hardwood either. Therefore, I turned to making bowls from glued-up wood. When I began, I did not know what form my laminations would take; the laminated bowls I had seen didn't seem especially attractive. So I decided not to look at any how-to literature and just try it on my own. The four bowls shown here are the results of my experiments.

If I could have turned bowls from solid stock I don't know if I ever would have tried this type of lamination. But now I am hooked on the idea. The field of complex laminations is new and unexplored. Haphazard gluing can be unattractive, but with some creative thinking the laminations can enhance the beauty of the wood. Glue lines may not be pretty but they are no uglier than the mortar that holds bricks together. If a bricklayer makes an elegant archway he must taper his bricks; to do so he increases the mortar-to-brick ratio. The same is true for the woodworker. If he wants to achieve a bend or design through lamination, the glue-to-wood ratio will increase. Both cases are legitimate uses of materials, and neither should be criticized for its use of adhesives.\The work should be judged by the finished product.

Harry Irwin, 26, a former carpenter, is a woodworking teacher living in Cambridge, Mass.

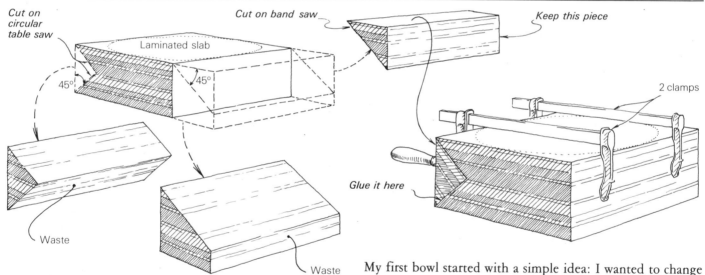

Bowl of cherry, oak, mahogany and teak, 6½-in. dia.

My first bowl started with a simple idea: I wanted to change the usual horizontal glue lines of a laminated bowl. I accomplished this with some risky end-grain gluing. I glued together pieces of cherry, oak, mahogany and teak. This block was clamped to the miter gauge of the table saw, for safety and accuracy. Then two careful 45° crosscuts caused a 90° chunk (a right triangular prism) to be released from the end grain, as shown in the drawing. This cut had to be carefully done because any unevenness would result in a poor and potentially weak glue line. The 90° must be precise too—it is easy to check with an accurate try square. From the other end of the block I cut the same shape, only here the grain is at a 45° angle to the hypotenuse instead of perpendicular. This cut, because of its length, must be done on the band saw. It will not be gluing surface so its flatness is of no special importance. This same end is then cut square for clamping. Because of the end grain, I sized the surfaces with a liberal coat of plastic resin glue. After it soaked and dried a little I applied some more and clamped it. The clamping procedure is very easy—two clamps will do the trick—then it's on to the lathe.

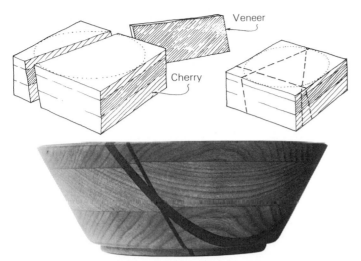

Cherry and mahogany bowl, 7⅞-in. dia.

Next, I decided to pass thin sheets of mahogany through a laminated block of cherry wood. On the table saw I set the miter gauge and the sawblade for a compound angle cut. In between the two halves I sandwiched mahogany veneer. After it dried I repeated the process two more times. In the end each piece of mahogany intersected the other two, as shown in the sketch. When the blank was turned on the lathe, the mahogany became hyperbolas. The most interesting parts proved to be the intersections of these hyperbolas.

Gluing this bowl turned out to be harder than I had expected. The angle cuts, under pressure of clamping, caused the two halves to slip apart. I solved this problem with some awkward clamping from all six sides. The unorthodox cross-grain gluing might lead to the eventual destruction of the bowl. But the thin veneers of mahogany might not have the strength to break the glue joint, just as thin layers of plywood survive their cross-grain gluing. Time will tell.

The gluing problem I encountered in the previous bowl gave me an idea for the next one. It also sent me from the table saw to the band saw. So far I was making straight cuts and the lathe was changing them into curves. This time I decided to cut a curve. I started with a block made of cherry, oak, mahogany and walnut. Through this I cut (vertically) a gentle arc. In between this arc I placed thin strips of walnut and cherry. The work was first clamped together dry, to find the gaps. Then I removed high points on the spindle sander. The final gluing was easy to do. The problem of slipping I had experienced with the previous bowl was gone, because the two arcs aligned themselves naturally. Bending wood can be difficult and time-consuming: The bending jig must be made to duplicate the curve, and steam is needed to achieve the bend. But here the bending jig is no extra work since it is also the finished bowl, while the thin laminations form easily to the arc without steam.

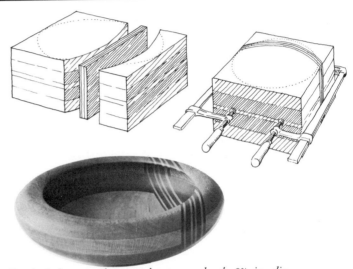

Bowl of cherry, walnut, mahogany and oak, 9¾-in. dia.

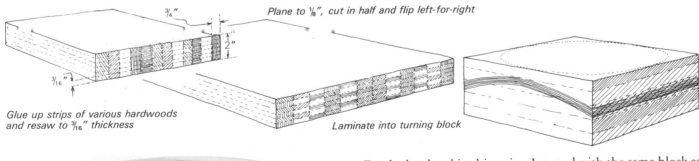

Glue up strips of various hardwoods and resaw to ³⁄₁₆″ thickness

Plane to ⅛″, cut in half and flip left-for-right

Laminate into turning block

Bowl, 9¼-in. dia., of cherry, walnut, mahogany, oak, poplar, teak.

For the last bowl in this series, I started with the same block as before. But this time the arc cut through the block went along the horizontal plane. The veneer to be laminated in this space also had to be glued up. I glued strips of teak, poplar, oak, cherry and walnut, all ¾ in. by 2 in., together edge to edge. They were resawn on the band saw with the fence set at ³⁄₁₆ in. A sharp blade is needed for this cut or else the blade will wander. The sheets were passed through the planer to bring their thickness down to ⅛ in. and to remove the saw marks, thus ensuring a good glue joint. They were turned left over right and at the end grain an inlay pattern appeared. Again this block was clamped dry to find the gaps that had to be sanded away. Once glued and turned, the curved laminations in the center of the bowl became a continuous wave around the bowl. □

The Flageolet

Basic woodwind is turning, drilling exercise

by Kent Forrester

Over the last couple of centuries, most woodwind instruments (flutes, clarinets, oboes, and others) have accumulated a bewildering variety of keys, levers, springs, bushings and extra note holes. Because of this, making a woodwind instrument seems beyond the skill of the average woodturner. However, stripped of modern embellishments, woodwinds make interesting and relatively easy woodturning projects.

The modest little woodwind known as the flageolet is not as versatile as a clarinet and not as pretentious as an oboe (you'll never get a job playing it in the Philharmonic). But it has nevertheless been a favorite of musicians for centuries—the 17th-century diarist, Samuel Pepys, loved his flageolet almost as much as he loved barmaids. With a pleasant, high-pitched piping sound and a range of more than two octaves, the flageolet can be used both for accompaniment (it goes particularly well with guitars and voice in folk music) and for solos.

To make a flageolet, first cut a 1-in. turning square 14 in. long out of the best hardwood you have. Cherry, walnut and maple are fine for flageolets; rosewood, cocobolo and ebony are even more handsome.

The boring operation will require support for the tailstock end of the wood. Buy a brass or steel plumbing tee with an inside diameter of at least 1/2 in. and an outside diameter of no more than 7/8 in. Also pick up a 4-1/2-in. long piece of pipe, threaded on one end, that can be screwed into the bottom of the tee. This pipe will be mounted in the lathe's tool post.

Now drill a hole about 3/8 in. deep in the center of the end of the stock, of the same diameter as the outside diameter of the tee. Drill a 1/2-in. starter hole for your bit in the center of the previous hole. Because the stock will be turning on the tee, rub soap inside the larger hole to reduce friction.

Now mount the stock between a headstock spur and the tee jig. With the tee loose in the tool post, pull it up so that the end of the tee enters the hole in the stock. Mount a 1/2-in. twist drill bit in a chuck in the tailstock and push this bit into the starter hole in the stock. This 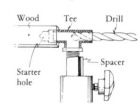 will center the tee on the lathe. Cinch up the tee tightly, lock it to the tool post and lock the tool post to the lathe bed.

A 1/2-in. shell auger mounted in the tailstock will bore a straight, smooth hole. A bell hanger's bit (of the type electricians use) or a 1/2-in. twist drill mounted on a bit extender

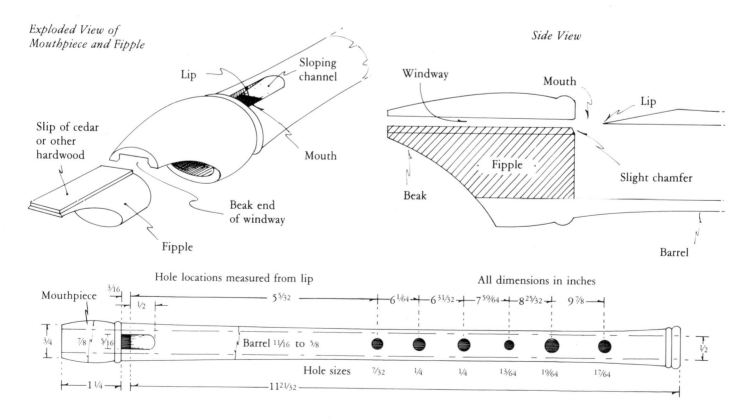

Exploded View of Mouthpiece and Fipple

Lip · Sloping channel · Slip of cedar or other hardwood · Mouth · Beak end of windway · Fipple

Side View

Windway · Mouth · Lip · Fipple · Slight chamfer · Beak · Barrel

Hole locations measured from lip · All dimensions in inches

Mouthpiece · 3/16 · 1/2 · 5 5/32 · 6 1/64 · 6 31/32 · 7 5/64 · 8 25/32 · 9 7/8

3/4 · 7/8 · 5/16 · Barrel 11/16 to 5/8 · 1/2

1 1/4 · 11 21/32

Hole sizes · 7/32 · 1/4 · 1/4 · 13/64 · 19/64 · 17/64

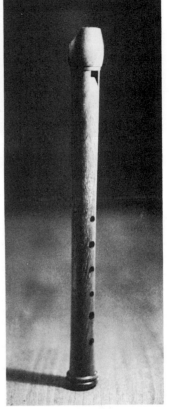

The flageolet is basically a whistle; sound is produced when wind hits sharpened edge of lip, formed by filing sloping channel in front of mouth, left. Note hole locations are carefully measured from lip, right.

Flageolet is held in V-block, left, to file channel behind mouth that forms upper surface of windway. To sand inside of bore, right, garnet paper is wrapped and glued around dowel and chucked in lathe.

will also do the job. These bits will drift a little, but the stock is cut oversize to allow for it.

Carefully measure the distance to the spur and stick a piece of masking tape on the bit where it must stop. Run the lathe at its slowest speed, drill slowly and clear the chips frequently. Now remove the stock from the lathe and saw off the end, in small increments, until the hole appears.

To facilitate turning, plane or saw off the corners from the 1-in. stock. Now place a cone-shaped abrasive wheel with a 1/4-in. or 1/2-in. shank in a chuck in the headstock and a cone center in the tailstock. Mount the wood between these two cones and cinch up tightly so that the abrasive cone grabs the stock and turns it. Turn the flageolet to shape and sand.

Begin shaping the mouth by drilling two or three 5/32-in. diameter holes. Then file to the dimensions of the rectangular shape, as shown in the drawing. Now measure from the lip and drill the six note holes. To sand the inside of the bore, wrap and glue sandpaper around a 3/8-in. dowel and chuck the dowel in the lathe. Then turn on the lathe and run the bore over the sandpaper until it is smooth. Smoothness is important, so go down to 120 or 220 grit.

To make the windway, use a flat file that is 5/16 in. wide or less. File a channel at the center of the top of the bore until the underside edge of the area that will form the lip is flat. Cut and file the sloping channel that forms the sharp edge of the lip. Now finish filing the channel back of the mouth, to form the upper surface of the windway. A piece of soft wood or leather in the mouth will prevent the file from damaging the lip. Continue filing until the lip, as you sight down the windway, is about 1/64 in. below the top of the windway.

To make the fipple, cut a 1/2-in hardwood dowel to length and sand a flat that is 5/16 in. wide. On this flat, glue (with waterproof glue) a slip about 1/16 in. thick of maple, cherry or cedar. If you use maple or cherry, coat the surface with var-

nish to prevent the grain from rising. Moisture has so little effect on cedar that all it needs is a coat of penetrating oil. Sand this slip until it is 1/64 in. below the lip when, fipple in place, you sight down the windway. The height of the windway at the mouth end will now be 1/32 in. and the lip will appear in the center of the windway. The height of the windway at the beak end is not critical, but 1/16 in. or a

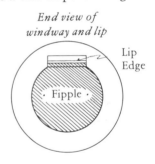

End view of windway and lip

Lip Edge

Fipple

little more is about right. Now cut the beak to shape.

To hold the flageolet, let the instrument rest on your thumbs and use the first three fingers of each hand to cover the six note holes. Rest the mouthpiece between your lips and blow with sufficient strength to produce a soft, steady tone.

The primary scale is produced by uncovering each hole in order. The lowest note, "C," is produced when all holes are covered. The semi-tones (half-notes) are produced by withdrawing the tip of your fingers so that they cover only half the holes. The second octave is achieved by blowing harder.

Test your flageolet by running through at least two octaves. If the low notes are very weak (almost inaudible), remove the fipple and increase the chamfer or sand the fipple lower. If the high notes will not blow, you have sanded the fipple too low.

To eliminate air leaks between the fipple and the bore, coat the fipple with hot wax before you insert it. Finish the bore and the exterior with a few coats of penetrating oil or varnish.

Kent Forrester, 39, is associate professor of English at Murray State University, Murray, Ky. He researches and builds medieval, Renaissance and 18th-century woodwind instruments.

Methods of Work

Better V-block

I made a flageolet (see page 142) and ran into difficulties in laying out and drilling the holes and in holding the flageolet down while working on it. Although I used a *V*-block, the slightest jiggle caused misalignments that became painfully evident after all the holes were bored. By adding two clamps atop the block and using a fence for the drill-press table, I was able to drill the holes in successive flageolets precisely and predictably. Mounted in a workbench vise, my modified *V*-block held the flageolets securely while I worked the windways, channels and slots.

To make this *V*-block, you need less than 2 ft. of construc-

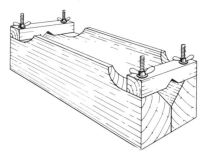

tion-grade 2x4, 6 in. of 1x1 and four hanger bolts with wing nuts and washers. The two 45° bevels that make up the 90° *V* are planed on the jointer and then carefully aligned before gluing. The clamps and the coves at the end of the body are bandsawn; a spindle or drum sander does a nice job of cleaning up the curves. Most of the dimensions are not critical.

—*Bernard Maas, Edinboro, Pa.*

Mounting flute blanks

Those of us with limited equipment and money sometimes need merely to think a little harder than those with the equipment we lack. In "The Flageolet," Kent Forrester advises mounting the drilled blank on the lathe with chuck-mounted abrasive cone centers to turn the flute to shape. Those without a chuck and abrasive cones can use this trick:

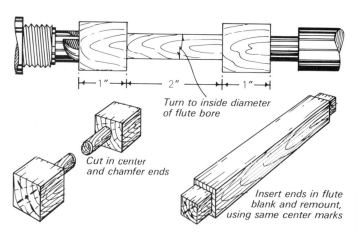

1" — 2" — 1"

Turn to inside diameter of flute bore

Cut in center and chamfer ends

Insert ends in flute blank and remount, using same center marks

Turn a 1-in. blank to the diameter of the bore, leaving about 1 in. at each end square. Cut this piece in half, chamfer the round ends and insert them into the bore of the instrument. This assembly can be remounted on the lathe, using the same live/dead orientation and the same spur indentations. If the live end slips, masking tape might solve the problem, but I didn't need it.   —*Bob Raiselis, New Haven, Conn.*

Aztec Drum

Resonating tongues produce sound

by Ray Nitta

The drum is probably the earliest and most universal musical instrument. Used in initiation rites, magic, dance, religious ceremony, war, rock concert or symphonic orchestra, the hypnotic effect of rhythmic drumming is known to all cultures and peoples.

The instrument described here is patterned after the teponaztli, an ancient Aztec drum. Unlike the conventional skin-covered membranophone, the teponaztli was a unique idiophonic instrument with tongue-like protrusions to produce the sound. Perhaps best described as a two-keyed xylophone, the teponaztli resembled a narrow wooden barrel laid sideways. An H-shaped incision cut laterally into the top formed two tongues that vibrated when struck. The teponaztli was tuned by altering the thicknesses of these tongues to create different pitches, the most desirable being those with intervals a minor or major third apart. The hollow interior of the drum was its resonant chamber and a rectangular opening on the bottom of the instrument increased its volume, like the acoustical port on a guitar. The teponaztli was placed on a stand and played with rubber-tipped mallets (cured latex).

I have used the sound-producing principles of the teponaztli to make the drums shown here. The design, tongue proportions and resonant chamber have been carefully worked out to produce a pleasant progression of natural tones with good volume ranging around minor and major thirds to diminished and perfect fifths, just as in the original drum. The two tongues used by the Aztecs have been increased to six: three low-pitched bass tones and three contrasting higher ones. The woods used by the Aztecs can be expanded to include other resonant hard and soft woods such as padauk, redwood, bubinga, fir and Hawaiian koa.

Multiple factors govern the sound produced by this drum, among them the size and shape of the resonant cavity, the length and width of the tongues and the environment in which the drum is played. Any wood may be used for the sides and bottom of the drum, but the type (hard or soft) and grain of the top govern the sound. A softwood top makes a low thud. I advise using an even-grained hardwood: The harder the wood, the more crisp and metallic the sound.

The dimensions and proportions used here are to give the woodworker a concrete example to follow. However, there are no limits to what can be done to modify this basic design or to create a new one.

Cut the wood to the dimensions shown. The top slab is where the sound-producing tongues are to be cut. The 1/8-in. lauan ply on the bottom acts as a pliant membrane that mellows the tones. Remember to allow enough wood for the corner joinery. Although simple butt joints work well,

Six-tongued drums of various woods. Inlaid dots mark location of purest tones. Drumsticks are 3/8-in. dowels fitted with superballs.

A dovetailed drum ready to assemble and cut. Butt joints, locking miters or rabbets may also be used to join sides.

dovetails, locking miters or rabbets enhance the strength and beauty of the corners.

Make an acoustical port with about the area of a silver dollar in one of the long side pieces. This opening supports the bass tones and amplifies the sound. Carefully glue the pieces into a well-sealed box. I find that vibration-resistant aliphatic resin glue works best.

Draw the tongues onto the top as shown in the diagram. Drill eight 3/8-in. holes at the tongue bases to serve as slit stops. Cut the tongue pattern with a saber saw. If the resultant pitches don't ring clear, enlarge the base holes to 1/2 in. or even 5/8 in. This will narrow the base of the tongues and make them more flexible.

Gluing the box together before cutting the tongues, a reversal of usual procedure, allows the maker to experiment with tones. By starting the cutting in the center (without predrilling slit stops), the maker can cut, strike the drum, cut again, and so on until the desired tone is achieved. The top is firmly supported on all edges and is unlikely to split.

Now tap along the length of each tongue with a drumstick and mark the spots where the pitch seems purest, with the

fewest overtones. These nodes are the spots to aim for when playing the drum. While they can be marked with paint, inlaid wood is prettier. I drill with a 1/2-in. spade or Forstner bit and plug with a 1/2-in. dowel, then sand smooth.

To finish the drum, round and form the edges with a drawknife and a plane. Sand with 80-grit garnet, then 120, and finish with 220. I use three coats of Watco and apply the final coat with 600 wet or dry sandpaper.

Make the drumsticks from 3/8-in. dowels 12 in. long, and 10-cent superballs from a toy store. Drill the balls with an 11/16-in. bit and press on.

Stands should be made to keep the drum from rattling when played on the floor or table and to increase its resonance. Good cushioning pads can be made from 1/2-in. foam or felt glued to matching blocks of wood.

The drum is magic. Place it on the foam stands, cradle it in your arm or set it on your lap. Start by playing softly and try to sustain a simple beat (about heartbeat tempo). Become one with the sound, let it move and merge with the natural rhythms of your body and feel the influence and power of the drum to move you physically, emotionally and spiritually.

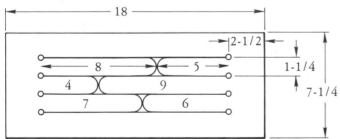

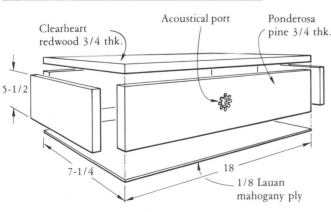

Clearheart redwood 3/4 thk.

Acoustical port

Ponderosa pine 3/4 thk.

1/8 Lauan mahogany ply

Author and drum. Nitta teaches curriculum development to teachers in Berkeley, Calif. His Aztec drum was designed as a project for beginners in school shops on restricted budgets.

Left, these tongue lengths produce pleasing bass and treble tones. Woods and dimensions can be changed to suit the maker.

Carving Lab

A basic exercise for beginners

by Robert L. Buyer

Woodcarving classes are usually unstructured meetings where a teacher advises and helps a student with a carving project. This method has the advantage of enabling a student to produce a finished carving immediately. The disadvantages are needless time spent fumbling around, often discouraging results, and at times the creation of poor work habits. This is how I learned to carve. I've often thought that some simple exercises in basic tool handling would have helped me tremendously, and would have reduced the time it took to learn.

Therefore, in preparing to teach woodcarving last year, I developed a tool lab to introduce the basic techniques. It went rather well, and I hope it will help both novice carvers and other teachers. I am not advocating hours of tedious exercises, one after another, which must be mastered and yet produce only chips. These exercises concentrate on the gouge, parting tool and veiner, and how the various cuts are affected by the grain of the wood. Just experiment with it and observe carefully at each step.

You'll need a piece of soft wood (pine or bass) at least 6 in. wide, 10 in. long and 1/2 in. thick; two clamps for holding the wood to the bench; one or more carver's mallets, preferably of different weights and styles; a carpenter's square, soft pencil and a broad felt-tip marker; and three straight (not bent) carving tools—one gouge (such as a 5-sweep, 20 mm), one veiner (about 12 mm) and one parting tool (about 6 mm).

Please don't rush out and buy a kit of tools just for this exercise. If you have access to professional tools through a school or a friend, by all means use them. If you don't have access to tools and are sure you want to take up carving, then the three

tools needed for this exercise constitute a beginning set and should be bought individually. You will be ahead of the game, both artistically and financially, if you buy full-size, professional-quality tools one at a time. As you gain skill, you will learn exactly which ones to buy next. A few fine tools are much better than a roll of small, clumsy ones. Swiss tools (my favorites because of their iron, shape and octagonal handles) currently cost between $5 and $10 each, and the three specified here can be purchased for about $20 total.

1. Draw a series of parallel lines on the wood, about an inch apart. Draw some lines parallel to an edge, some perpendicular to this edge and some at a 45° angle. With the marker, shade between the lines to make a band parallel to the edge of the board, another band perpendicular to the edge and a third band on the diagonal. Now clamp the wood securely to the top of the workbench, with the clamps as close as possible to the ends of the board.

2. Use the gouge and mallet to cut across the grain and remove the shaded band perpendicular to the edge of the board. Hold the gouge in your minor hand (left if you are right-handed) and the mallet in your major hand. Drive the gouge across the board from near to far, first cutting one edge of the shaded band, then the other.

3. Make a cut along the grain to remove the shaded band parallel to the edge of the board, again holding the gouge in your minor hand. Use the mallet to drive the gouge along the board from right to left, first cutting along one edge of the shaded band, then the other.

4. Now remove a diagonal band of wood, still holding the gouge in your minor hand. Use the mallet to drive the gouge across the board from near to far, cutting along one edge of the shaded band, then the other.

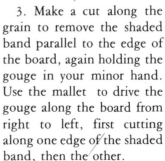

5. Observe the edges of the diagonal cut you just made, and note which edge is smooth and which feathered. Repeat the cut that made the feathered edge, but this time drive the

Carving lab equipment includes (left to right) gouge, veiner, parting tool and mallet. Clamps hold down board marked for cutting; lines parallel to grain are drawn on underside of board.

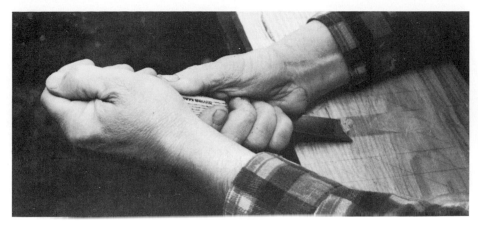
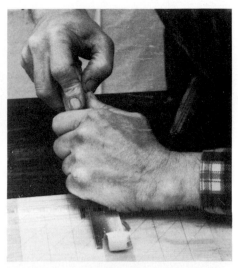

Above, gouge cut across the grain, made toward the carver. Minor hand powers cut, while major arm rests on stock for control. Right, major hand powers gouge cut across the grain, made away from the carver, with minor forearm as anchor and elbow as pivot.

gouge from far to near. Now this edge will be smooth.

6. Carve away another diagonal band, this time using the veiner to cut each edge line. Drive the veiner from far to near for one edge and from near to far for the other, so that both edges are smoothly cut. Then use the gouge and mallet to clean out the wood between the veiner cuts. Carefully compare these results with the band cut by the gouge alone. Repeat, but this time use the parting tool instead of the veiner.

7. Use the felt-tip pen to draw an arch-like design on the wood, as in the diagram. The band should be about an inch wide, and the design should begin and end at the edge of the board. Carve out the band, using the veiner or parting tool followed by the 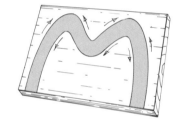 gouge, as in step 6. Change direction as necessary to get smooth edges all around the design.

Mallet powers gouge; guiding hand holds center of tool and pivots from elbow.

8. Now repeat all of the preceding steps, but change hands—carving tool in the major hand, mallet in the minor hand. Try the exercises again, this time without a mallet.

9. If you have more than one mallet, or access to other carving tools, try the same exercises with them and carefully compare the results using large and small tools of the same shape, or tools of different shapes, but the same size.

By now it should be very clear that a carving tool produces a smooth edge on the side that cuts with the grain, and a feathered edge on the side that cuts against the grain. The tools can cut toward you or away from you. You can hold them in either hand, and you should be able to select the proper tool for a task. You are well on your way to becoming a carver.

The following is advice about using carving tools. These points are presented not as gems of wisdom cast off by the sages, but as the condensate of the blood, sweat and tears of a dozen years of carving.

—Drive parting tools and veiners without rocking motion. Drive gouges with one rock per cut, to get a slicing action.

—Use the proper-size tool. Never "bury" the corners of a carving tool in the wood. If both corners are not visible you are cutting too deep or using the wrong size or shape of tool.

—Always keep two hands on tools: either one on the carving tool and one on the mallet, or both hands on the carving tool. Never use the palm of the hand as a mallet.

—For easy identification, position the carving tools on the bench (not on the work) so the cutting edges face you.

—To rough out carvings in-the-round or remove the ground of a relief carving, cut across the grain, usually with a veiner and mallet.

—Draw lines on the carving with a parting tool.

—Finish cut with gouges, using a slicing cut and no mallet.

—In lettering: First, incise the center; second, cut from each side to the center; then cut serifs.

—In relief carving: First, remove ground; second, set in edges; third, smooth ground close to final depth with no. 3 spoon and/or carver's router; fourth, model carving.

—Use a soft pencil and dividers frequently to check dimensions on the plans and redraw on the stock.

—Whenever possible establish "points" of measure on the carving and plans. Mark these points with an X. Points are usually extremities (such as the tip of the nose, center of the head, bottom of the throat) and joints (ankle, knee, hip, shoulder, elbow, wrist).

—Begin the carving at the place containing the most excess wood. Continue by carving away layers of wood—do not work on one area until it is complete, then move on to another. Instead, work on the carving as a whole, going around and around and making smaller and smaller cuts as you approach the final dimensions.

Bob Buyer, 45, is a technical writer who also teaches wood-carving and runs a sawmill/lumberyard in Norton, Mass.

Chain-Saw Carving

Furniture and sculpture from green logs

by Jon Brooks and Howard Werner

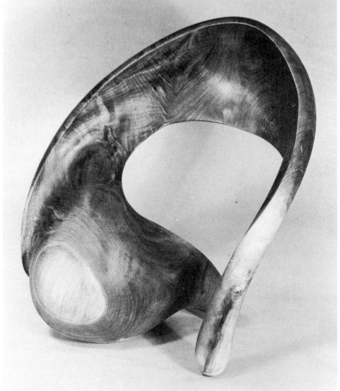

Brooks' walnut chair (38 in. high, 33 in. wide.)

We use the chain saw to carve furniture and sculpture from green logs, roots and branches. Although we live several hundred miles apart, we've worked together on techniques for the last several years. The chain saw, although not designed for this kind of work, has become our main tool for both roughing out and final shaping.

Our furniture or sculpture often begins directly in the wood, using forms suggested by the shape of the log, or forms that are revealed as wood is removed. A contorted limb may suggest a chair, an interesting crotch or hollow may predict a bowl, or a hollow log may hint at a stool. Other times, a form is developed in the mind or through sketching. The work begins with the search for a suitable log in which to execute it. Excellent free material can be found in local tree dumps, with hundreds of logs and stumps to choose from, or at the town dumps, from tree surgeons, orchards and on private land with standing snags or fallen trees.

Almost any wood is good carving material, although apple and oak are more prone to cracking and checking than most species. Spalted wood is exquisite, but it is best to avoid pieces with soft spots or excessive rot. In most species, rot takes years to progress to this point, so many downed trees, particularly disease-killed elms, are still in good shape.

Walnut checks less than most native hardwoods. Crotch sections in particular, because of their interlocked grain, hold together well against the stresses of drying. Maple and cherry, although not as stable as walnut, are still good woods for carving. Coniferous woods carve easily and oiled juniper and cedar look particularly fine. Whatever the wood, the main thing is to develop the form in the direction of the wood fibers, for strength. Experience and experimentation will show what can be done and what should be avoided.

We own both electric and gasoline-powered chain saws, but do most rough carving with the gasoline saw because it is more powerful and not tied to electrical lines. We own Stihl gasoline saws and are familiar with the range AV20 to AV45. (The AV stands for antivibration, a system that makes the saw less exhausting to handle in long carving sessions.) We've found that smaller saws aren't up to the work and larger ones are too heavy. What saw you select depends in the end on your size and the scale of work you plan to do. A Stihl AV45 weighs 15 lb., has a 16-in. bar (bars up to 30 in. long are available) and generates 4.5 hp. It can be used to carve pieces ranging in size from large bowls to 8-ft. sculptures.

A gasoline saw is very noisy—ear protection must be worn—and its exhaust fumes mean it can't be used indoors.

Left, maple bowl by Werner (24 in. high, 14 in. wide, 19 in. deep). Above, Werner's 'Double-Pocket Form' (walnut, 29 in. high, 22 in. wide, 17 in. deep).

The electric saw, quieter and without fumes, is excellent for indoor carving and is especially suited to final shaping of a piece. A Milwaukee, for example, has both a 16-in. bar and a 20-in. bar and weighs 18 lb. It is large enough and powerful enough to carve major pieces, and because it runs at a constant speed, it's easier to control than a gas saw. But it feels very heavy after a long working session. A lighter, less expensive saw is fine for small, detailed carving.

Before carving, the basic lines of the piece are marked directly on the log with chalk. It's best to strip off the bark first, since it veils the shape of the wood and often has embedded dirt, which quickly dulls the chain.

We begin, much as a whittler begins, by paring gently curved slices from the log, the way a penknife cuts shavings from a stick. These first slicing cuts are made with the center of the bar, with the tip entirely clear of the wood. For deeper cuts and tighter curves the technique is similar to chip carving—two angled cuts meet at the desired depth toward the center of the log to release a large wedge or block of wood. In this way the bulk of the excess wood can be removed, leaving an angular, faceted form.

Next, the hollows and concave areas are worked into the form. To develop a hollow, we use the tip of the saw to make a series of closely-spaced, parallel cuts. Each cut starts at the farthest side of the hollow, with the bar held at right angles to the surface and the length of the saw at an acute angle to the wood so that the bottom of the nose makes first contact. Then the saw is drawn across and the nose dropped into the wood to feel out the bottom of the hollow. A felt-tip marker line on the bar can be used to gauge depth. A deep concavity can be worked in several stages. As the cut gets deeper, the saw's speed must be increased. Working this way, the nose of the saw is never close to a 90° corner and so it won't kick back. Then another series of close, parallel cuts is made at right angles to the first set, creating a checkered pattern. The resulting squares of wood measure an inch by an inch or less and can easily be kicked or knocked away by brushing back and forth with the tip of the saw. When the squares have all been poked out, the hollow is cleaned up and and its shape is refined with the tip of the saw, scraping back and forth to make an even surface.

Extreme care must be taken in tight hollows. When the tip is near anything close to a right-angled corner, the cutters can catch on the upper wall and throw the bar back toward the operator's head and body. Always be wary, especially near a tight corner, and expect the kickback. Try to absorb and control it by holding the saw firmly in front of the body, below waist level, with the arms kept straight.

Some saws are made with an anti-kickback device, usually a lever that, when triggered, instantly stops the chain. When a kickback does occur, the operator's wrist hits the lever before the saw can rotate back far enough to do damage. However, the safety device won't trip if the operator holds the front handle on its side, rather than on top. We've also used anti-kickback chain, which has a double raker tooth, and have found that kickback occurs less frequently.

The plunge cut is another way to remove a large, mostly surrounded chunk of wood, such as that removed to form the hollow between the seat, back and arms of a chair. The wood is approached with the bar at a slight angle. As the nose begins to cut, the motor is quickly lifted and the bar is pushed straight into the log. A very sharp chain and high

From tree to finished form: Above, Werner begins with a promising walnut trunk that includes the stump of a branch. First he chalks the lines on the log and slices away the waste. Convex forms are refined and smoothed by scraping lightly back and forth with the edge of the saw bar. Deep pockets are formed with the nose of the saw by tracing a cross-hatch pattern and breaking away the waste. Top right shows the sculpture as shaped by the chain saw. Right, 'Two-Hooded Form' has been dried, finish-carved and sanded (66 in. high).

149

motor speed are necessary right from the start so the chain doesn't catch and recoil or jam. When the blade is plunged to full depth, the cut can be made into a slot before the saw is withdrawn. Successive slots are made around the waste wood, to free it as an intact chunk.

A large cutout can be started with a plunge cut. But thin walls and delicate pierced forms require scraping from both sides at the center of the area to be cut out to produce a small circular breakthrough that can be enlarged.

With the bulk of the waste removed, we mark out the precise lines and edges desired with chalk. The tip of the gasoline saw is used to trace over these lines carefully, repeating several times to reach the proper depth. Exact contours can be achieved by scraping the bar or tip back and forth across the wood, the face of the bar at right angles to the surface. Here the electric saw is best. A broad, sweeping motion with even saw pressure shapes large curves; a slight change in the approach angle of each sweep prevents the bar from falling into the grooves created by previous cuts. Consistent pressure with rhythmic motion produces smooth, controlled surfaces.

Grain direction is the crucial factor in determining the thickness of a wall. When a section of a carving is made up of head-on end grain, we rarely carve it thinner than three or four inches and expect it will crack. A long-grain section, on the other hand, can be as thin as half an inch and will usually remain intact. On an irregular form, most of the walls are somewhere between these two situations and one must learn through experience what's safe. If we make an error in judgment and part of a carving cracks right off the main form, the piece can be redesigned, even if only as firewood. If a lot of work has already been invested, a broken piece can be rejoined with dowels and glue, or with an inlaid butterfly key.

Many of these operations, raking and scraping in particular, are very hard on the saw bar and chain. It is necessary to keep the chain sharp at all times and the saw may have to be sharpened several times a day. A small electric sharpener works well for grinding out chips caused by dirt, stones and metal in the wood. A hand file with a chain-saw sharpening gauge is fine in the field. We usually file the teeth at a 35° bevel, switching to 30° for very hard or frozen wood. It's important to make the same number of file passes on each tooth, to keep them even. Irregular sharpening will cause the bar to wander as it cuts and control will be difficult.

When carving green wood, shield the piece from direct sun, which rapidly causes checking. The wood should be kept close to its original moisture content while it is being worked and can be shrouded in plastic to be left overnight. A large carving in green wood will inevitably crack and check. It doesn't take much experience to predict where cracks are likely to open and how serious they are liable to be. Cracks are virtually certain on end-grain sections and on surfaces containing the pith of the tree. We accept the cracks as an important part of the texture of the work; all we do is soften the edges to prevent splintering and integrate the cracks into the piece. Sometimes a crack pattern enhances the work so much that it is worth enlarging, or altering the design to play it up. But sometimes an end-grain section is too delicate to withstand checking, and the best solution is to coat that part of the wood with white glue to retard drying.

When we're done with the chain saw, the work has a rough texture but it is very close to its final form. The wood must be dried before it can be sanded and finished. We store pieces in

Elm lounge chair by Brooks (36 in. high, 54 in. long, 26 in. wide). Carving sequence is shown at right.

a shed or garage for at least four months, usually for a year, and sometimes for two years, depending on wall thickness and species. When a piece is about ready for finishing, we store it indoors for a couple of months first. We've experimented with shaping, sanding and oiling the green wood directly, thinking the oil might slow down the drying. But the escaping moisture destroys the finish and the wood surface changes too much during drying. We now season everything before the final sanding and oiling.

From the chain saw we go to a sander-grinder with a 7-in. disc, the type used in auto body shops. Sometimes we begin with a pad as coarse as 16 grit, but 36 grit or 50 grit is usually coarse enough to remove the chain-saw marks and refine the contours. Then we go to 80 grit and 100 grit, to smooth the surface wherever the grinder is able to reach.

We like to go directly from chain saw to grinder, but sometimes a more detailed form or the slower evolution of a design requires more refined tools. Carving gouges, a ball mill (a cutting burr about the size of a golf ball), Surforms, rasps, rifflers and files are the most useful. Standard bench planes make quick work of large convex surfaces, and violinmaker's planes also help. The Surform is especially effective in shaping difficult edge contours. When a shape cannot be achieved with one tool, we try another. Our techniques aren't rigid—they develop and change from one piece to another.

For final finishing an electric drill with a foam-backed pad is used, starting with coarse grit and working slowly up to 220 grit. These pads are small and will fit into areas the grinder can't reach. Still, there are always areas too small for the disc and they can be reached with rifflers, files and sandpaper backed with leather or Styrofoam, or wrapped around a small wooden block. On any piece, the sanding takes much more time than the carving.

Last, we sand by hand, using a leather backing pad or a Styrofoam block to remove swirls and scratches left by the disc. Then the work is ready to oil. We've used Watco oil, but we've come to prefer at least three coats of a 1-2-3 mixture of boiled linseed oil, varnish and turpentine. After the last coat has dried for at least 48 hours, we apply a good-quality paste wax and take care to avoid build-up in the cracks. ☐

Jon Brooks, 32, makes furniture in New Boston, N.H. This winter he is guest instructor in woodworking at Rochester Institute of Technology. Howard Werner, 26, an RIT graduate, is craftsman-in-residence at Peters Valley, Layton, N.J.

Shapes and Forms

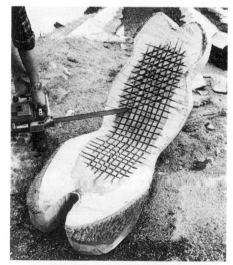

Elm lounge chair begins as a cylinder of tree trunk. First, great wedges of wood are removed to block out the chair form. Brooks pares the outline of the chair, then hollows the seat and back by cutting a crisscross network with the nose of the saw. Then he simply kicks away the waste wood.

The shapes and forms of my finished pieces can be divided into two categories. The first category has been influenced by the shape of the original found material. An example is the walnut chair, which is carved within the limits and integrity of the original crotch section of the tree. Sometimes I rough out a chair to expose the figure of the wood and leave it as a block to study. The outside shape is determined by reflecting the grain patterns—parts are emphasized or played down to get the desired effect. Root sections, curved limbs and trunks are also forms that will influence these pieces.

The second category begins with a straight, cylindrical section of wood. Then I impose a preconceived idea by working subtractively and releasing the form. Examples of this are 'Wood Falls' and the elm chair. Landscapes, horizon lines, water, cloud formations and the wood grain itself are elements which influence the form. 'Wood Falls,' conceived at Art Park in Lewiston, N.Y., is an attempt to reflect the nearby Niagara River and to capture the feeling of wood rolling down a slope toward the river. This piece asks the viewer to become visually and physically involved by providing benches for seating while viewing the landscape and the wood forms. People have made a path beside it down to the dock on the river. The exterior shape of the elm chair is an attempt to capture the human form. I tried to create the illusion of a seated person, which a person would sit upon. It was basically preconceived as a lounge chair and carved from a cylindrical tree section.

Because wood is a warm and inviting material, it is easy for one to become physically involved when it has been sanded and oiled to a very smooth surface. The rounded forms relate to the human form and to the wood grain. Too often in viewing solid objects we tend to see only the exterior form. As wood splits in drying it reveals an inner spirit and force. Rounding the splits on the surface unites the exterior form with the internal spirit and makes it easier to look at and touch. Wood splits, warps, expands, contracts; it has lived and it is living. While working with tree sections all these characteristics are heightened. To accept and move with these forces rather than to resist them is my primary objective.

—Jon Brooks

'Wood Falls' by Brooks is 15 ft. high, 15 ft. wide, and extends intermittently for 100 ft. down a hillside in the town of Lewiston, N.Y. It is carved in red oak, elm, maple and walnut, and permanently bolted to buried concrete pillars.

Methods of Work

Carving gouge

Before shelling out a lot of money for carving tools, I always think about what I want to carve and what tools I'll need. Often the tools will cost me nothing if I make them myself. To make a small carving gouge, I use a hardened steel cut

nail. The tapered shape needs little grinding. I don't bother grinding off the head; I just grind it down with the rest of the shaft, grinding one side flat and the other three sides into the curve I want. Then, holding the blank in a vise, I file the inside groove with a round (chain-saw) file. I grind a tang and mount the gouge in a hardwood handle, often with the bulge, or palm-grip, up, for easier carving at a shallow angle. Then I sharpen, putting the bevel on the inside, with file and slipstone. —*J. B. Small, Jr., Shippensburg, Pa.*

Veneer strip thicknesser

For decorative inlay and border work, it is often an advantage to have all the strips of uniform thickness, or to alter the thickness for a special design. A simple scraper thicknesser assembled from scrap hardwood will do a quick and accurate job. A trued-up 2-in. square about 14 in. long forms the body of the jig, while two identical rotating arms (say 1 in. by 2 in. by 5 in.) support the scraper and adjust the cut and thickness by means of a common pivot bolt (say ⅜ in.). The scraper is clamped to the arms with two small *C*-clamps.

To use the thicknesser, clamp one end of the body in the vise and loosely position the arms at an appropriate scraper

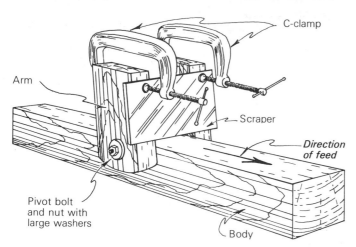

angle. Clamp the scraper to the arms as shown, using shims on the body to determine thickness and to orient the edge parallel. Tighten the pivot nut and make fine adjustments by tapping with a hammer. Feed the strips under the scraper in the direction shown and pull them through. Sometimes it helps to angle the strip to the blade. If the strips pull hard, rotate the arms and take a lighter cut. When sharpening the scraper, file straight across only about three-quarters of its length, then taper away at the end. This will permit starting the strips under the scraper near one arm, then sliding them over under the straight-cutting section for thicknessing. —*William D. Woods, Phoenix, Ariz.*

152

Relief Carving
Traditional methods work best

by Rick Butz

Relief carving has been around for a very long time. Exactly how long nobody is really certain, although archeologists agree that it predates written history. However, it was not until the 17th and 18th centuries that relief carving reached its peak of technical skill in the West. During this period, woodcarvers created works of such beauty and grace that few can equal today. And yet, despite this technical brilliance, it was only a few generations until the age of machine industry brought this period to an end. Looking back, we can see that the effect of changing priorities was a decline in certain types

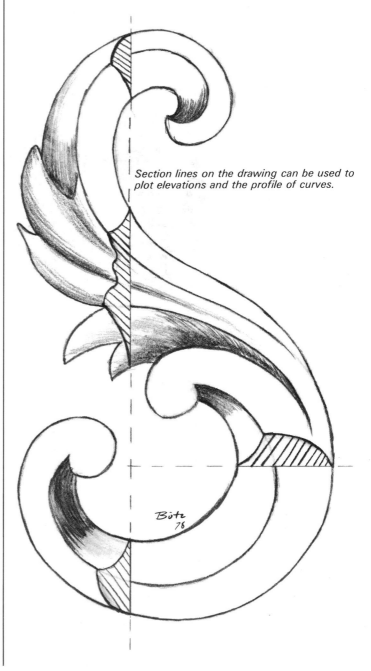

Section lines on the drawing can be used to plot elevations and the profile of curves.

of knowledge. Skills and methods that were once common knowledge have become, at best, uncommon.

The result is that today many woodworkers might wish to incorporate carving into a furniture design, but they shy away on grounds that it would involve far too much time to be practical. This should not be the case. If a relief carving is approached with a sense of purpose and organization, all the work can be done by hand with surprising speed and efficiency—and considerable pleasure too. Whether the design is contemporary or traditional, a tasteful carving can add richness and depth to any woodworking project.

Loosely defined, relief carving is a method of creating a raised design that appears to stand free of the background. The distance that separates the raised portion from the background determines whether the carving is high relief or shallow relief. In either case, the basic carving steps are always the same. First, the background is carved away and smoothed. This leaves a raised design and a level background. Second, the design is shaped and smoothed. It is important to complete all background carving before doing any work on the free-standing parts of the design. This is not an arbitrary rule, but rather a method that greatly simplifies the work.

In addition, the carving must be well planned out in advance. Not only should the design be clear on paper, but each step of the carving should be carefully thought out and systematically completed before the next is begun. While this may sound overly technical and confining, the creative worker will find instead that such planning allows greater flexibility in shaping the wood. By solving basic problems first, one may concentrate more freely upon the work at hand. Relief carving, if approached in an orderly fashion, will continue to demonstrate that in many cases, handwork is still one of the most efficient ways to shape wood.

Before any carving can begin, it is essential that tools be razor sharp, able to cut cleanly and smoothly. A properly sharpened gouge will leave the wood with smooth polished facets. Correct sharpening is probably the greatest mystery of woodcarving, but it is often an unnecessary stumbling block. In addition to the variety of European and Oriental sharpening methods, we have several generations of Yankee ingenuity to contend with. For example, I know a very good carver who uses half a dozen stones to hone his tools. Another, equally good, sharpens only with sandpaper and spray lubricants. So who is to say what is best?

The reasonable solution is to follow whatever method works best for you without abusing the tools, and the best teacher is experience. One effective method uses only a flat stone of medium grit and a revolving cloth wheel. The gouge is sharpened with a rocking motion on the stone, using plenty of oil, until an even wire burr can be felt along the edge.

Rick Butz and his wife Ellen are professional carvers who live and work in Blue Mountain Lake, N. Y.

Relief carving tools (from left): V-tool for outlining, three gouges for general shaping, long bent grounder for backgrounds, spoon gouge, and flat or firmer gouge. The blank is butternut, held to the bench by a long screw from underneath.

Next, the bevel is polished on the cloth wheel until the metal burr wears off. This will leave a razor edge. A small amount of buffing compound applied to the cloth will speed the process. A razor edge can be achieved with only a little practice, and the resulting polishing of the cutting bevel to a mirror finish noticeably reduces the friction of the tool as it cuts.

While sharpening is essential, the edge is only a small part of a woodcarving gouge, and many neglect caring for the rest of the tool. A high-quality gouge that fits your hand actually does produce a better carving. I'm not sure whether this is purely a psychological reaction, or if it is because you have better control of a tool that feels comfortable.

Even the best of woodcarving gouges should be carefully checked over for anything that does not feel quite right. It is not unusual for a new tool to have sawdust and splinters embedded in the varnish of the handle. This should be sanded smooth. Also check the metal surfaces of the tool for any rough edges. I am not surprised to find wicked burrs of metal in the brass ferrule on a new handle. These should be filed and sanded smooth, or else some particularly nasty injuries may result.

Many old-timers took the finish right off the handle to prevent blisters and calluses, much on the same principle as stripping an ax handle. The exposed wood was then soaked in oil and wiped clean. The oil not only sealed the wood, but left a porous finish. It also hardened the end grain of the handle as heat was generated by the striking mallet, which helped prevent fraying and splitting.

After the wood has been selected and the design accurately marked out, work can begin. Before cutting into the wood, it is helpful to pause for a few minutes and imagine just how the completed carving will appear. With practice this visualizing will not only help solve problems well in advance, but will also create the feeling that your hands are shaping the wood almost without conscious effort. By fixing the image in your mind, your hands will be guided by subconscious mental processes. This is not a new principle, but rather a means of helping to develop a "woodcarver's instinct." This feeling develops naturally after years of experience. However, a little practice will speed the process considerably.

The design I chose for the photo series that begins on the next page is a traditional variant taken from an old family table. It offers excellent practice in all areas of carving.

153

1 **Outlining** The first step in relief carving is to cut around the design with a *V-tool*. Such outlining serves as a starting place for isolating the raised portion of the design from the background. The cut should be made ¼ in. to ⅛ in. out from the edge of the design and must not get too close to any delicate details. These can be shaped later, when there is less chance of damage.

A mallet is often helpful in making the outline cuts, although care must be taken to avoid splinters running into the design. The best way to prevent unwanted splintering is to carve according to the flow of the wood grain. If your tools are sharp and the wood still splinters and tears, try approaching the cut from a different direction.

With a gouge of medium sweep, a series of cuts is made from the waste area toward and meeting the outline cut. This widening of the outline allows enough clearance to trim up the edges of the design. Make the walls of the design vertical by taking a small flat firmer or a gouge whose sweep is similar to the curvature of the design and cutting straight down. This procedure is referred to as "setting-in."

By continually enlarging the outline cut and smoothing down the walls of the design, the background can be sunk as deeply as wanted. A mallet of comfortable weight is helpful in these steps to tap the gouge lightly. However, take care not to drive the point too deeply, or a broken tool can result, especially if the wood is dense. Remember too that up to this point, the raised portion of the design remains untouched. The object of outlining and setting-in is to cut away all wood that will not be included in the raised part of the design.

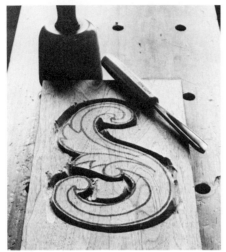
Outline the design with a V-tool.

Trim the edges vertical.

The design is outlined and set in.

2 **The background** Once the outline of the design has been clearly defined, work can begin on taking down the background waste areas. When this task is approached in an orderly manner, the grounding out can be efficiently completed strictly by hand. While this work can also be done with an electric router, a good professional woodcarver in times past could cut and clear a background in less time than most of us could even set up a power tool.

The best technique for cutting out a background, especially in softer woods, requires a firmer and a mallet, although a shallow #3 or #5 gouge can be used. With these tools a series of parallel cuts is made, one in back of the other. These are spaced in rows about ¼ in. apart and preferably across the grain. By lightly driving the gouge into the waste wood just behind the previous line of cuts, the waste will chip away. Roughing out should be done layer by layer if the background depth is to be very great. But take care not to drive the gouge deeper than necessary, or extra smoothing work will be required.

When the background has been completely roughed out, it is worked smooth using a gouge of fairly shallow sweep. Take care to arrange the smoothing cuts in an esthetically pleasing manner, as they form the finished background. Leveling and smoothing are sometimes easier with a bent gouge called a grounder. It is especially useful where lateral clearance is restricted, although in many cases a regular gouge will work quite well.

However, where working room is really cramped, such as inside a sharp curve, a

Remove background waste with closely spaced vertical cuts.

A #5 gouge levels and smooths rough cuts.

Spoon bent gouge works in tight places.

spoon bent gouge can be indispensable. These tools are available in a great assortment of sweeps and widths, yet they are probably the least used tool in many woodcarving sets. Part of the reason for this is the natural tendency of the spoon shape to be used in a scooping motion, which greatly restricts its usefulness.

Instead, the spoon bent gouge should be positioned at the angle where it just begins to cut. Then, carefully but firmly, it should be drawn across the wood without changing the angle. In effect, this produces the same cut as a long gouge. However, instead of beginning the cut at 15° to 30° to the work, the tool can be held at almost 90° to the work. This allows carving background areas inside deep recesses.

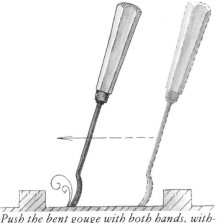

Push the bent gouge with both hands, without changing its angle of attack.

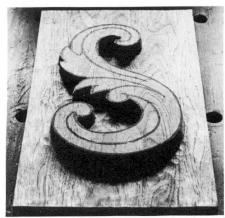

The background is now completed, and modeling can begin.

3 Modeling With the previous steps completed, the raised portion of the carving will stand free and clear from a smooth, level background. The design can now be modeled, first by roughly shaping the contours and then by smoothing the shapes with clean finishing cuts.

The roughing out is best done by carefully making cuts that round off sharp angles from the top downwards. For rough-shaping the outer portions of a curve, use a flat firmer or a gouge of slight sweep. For the inside curves, use a gouge of greater curvature or quicker sweep. This will help prevent unwanted splintering. The lines that form valleys between the leaves can be cut to depth with a *V*-tool and then rounded smooth.

These roughly shaped surfaces are then finished off with long smooth "sweep" cuts. These final cuts distinguished the professional works of old. This technique is used for finishing both the inside and the outside surfaces of the curves. Begin by steadying the blade of the tool with your left hand. The palm rests firmly upon the surface of the carving. By pushing the tool with the right hand and pivoting on the palm of the left, the edge of the gouge can be made to follow a very well-controlled curve. By experimenting with the point where the left hand pivots, a great variety of arcs can be achieved to follow the curves of most carvings. This requires a bit of prac-

tice, and like all carving techniques should be done with either hand. It is a very useful and satisfying technique.

For inside curves with concave surfaces, a bent or spoon-shaped gouge of considerable sweep is useful. On the other hand, a flat straight gouge can be used for convex, outer curves. Be careful to note changes in the direction of the grain so that the cuts will not be fuzzy, but smooth and polished. This will eliminate the need for smoothing with sandpaper, which should be avoided on any fine woodcarving. Sandpaper destroys the

The waste is gone, and finishing cuts can now be made.

tool marks that bear witness to serious handwork, and in an age of some very good plastic imitations, this is a serious consideration. If esthetic considerations require an absolutely smooth surface, then that is a different matter. But never substitute sandpaper for good technique and discipline.

As a final note, in doing any woodcarving, try not to lose your sensitivity to the nature of the wood. If you find yourself fighting the carving, if your tools produce ragged, splintered chips instead of smooth graceful shavings, then something is wrong. Make sure your tools are absolutely sharp, the wood is correct, and that you are working in the proper direction—with the flow of the grain. □

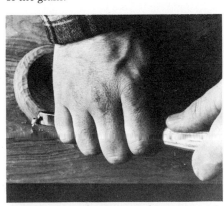

A firmer smooths the outside curves, again with long sweeping cuts.

A quick gouge rough-shapes the wood on the inside curves.

Long sweep cuts leave a smooth finish. A bent gouge or spoon gouge may be best for inside curves. The right hand powers the tool, while the edge of the left hand rests firmly on the work.

The finished carving.

Ball and Claw Feet

How to carve them

by A. W. Marlow

When combined with a cabriole leg, the ball and claw foot is a well-known furniture support dating back to ancient times. The industrial version is hardly recognizable—reason enough for every interested craftsman to develop his own.

Few amateurs are satisfied with their ball and claw carvings. To illustrate the process, I've chosen cabriole legs with ball and claw feet made for a wing chair. To many craftsmen, shaping cabriole legs is an uncertain process, but this step-by-step procedure should be simple to follow. The ball and claw foot on a tripod table requires the same basic carving cuts, but the claw placement is different—the claws come in over the ball horizontally for a more natural look.

1 The average blank size for a cabriole leg, regardless of length, is 2¾ in. by 2¾ in. To make a pattern, follow the line drawing, which is laid out in 1-in. squares. Place the pattern on a blank, as shown in the drawing and the photo at right. Keep the front knee curve toward the right-angled front corner and outline in pencil.

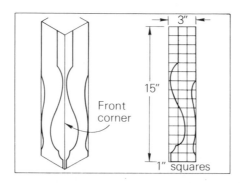

2 Shaping a cabriole leg can be quite simple when done on a band saw. Saw the first surface as shown at right, ending the cut before the waste piece is completely severed. This keeps the second or right-angled surface in place for the second cut. After the second cut has been made, turn the block back to the first surface and finish sawing the short, uncut portions of each curve.

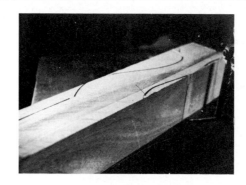
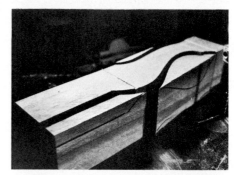

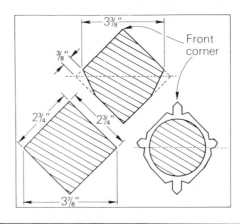

3 The next step is physically a minor one, but of major importance. Without it, the side claws look like wings sticking out. The line drawing shows three full bottom views of a leg as it is shaped. The first view shows the leg as it comes from the band saw. In the center drawing, a ⅜-in. wedge has been removed from each side claw to lessen the total width and give a more pleasing and realistic appearance to the finished foot. In the photo, a ¾-in. #3 gouge is used to chip away the wedge of wood. The third drawing adds the contour of the ball and the veiner cuts made in the next step.

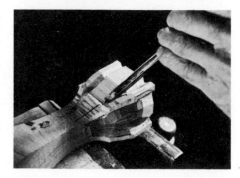

4 Now hold a pencil or ball-point pen as shown in the photo at right. Using your middle finger as a bearing against the wood, mark each side of each corner about ¼ in. in from the edge. These are the guide lines to follow when roughly positioning the claws with a ⅜-in. #41 veining tool. Continue the V-cuts into the angle area (as in the photo at far right), gradually lessening them in depth. If these feet are being cut in mahogany or walnut, you'll need a mallet to cut the rough V's.

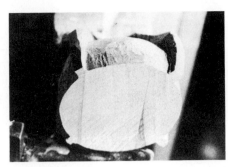

5 The next step is to shape the ball and claws. In the first photo the claws of the foot have been narrowed closer to the finished width and the ball has been cut about halfway between rough and finished condition. When cutting the ball, check frequently to see that it is reasonably round, because if any adjustment must be made, the depth of the claws must follow

the ball radius. Up to this point, the claws still retain the original band-saw outline and must be trimmed down to an average height of ¼ in. In the center photo the #3 gouge is used to trim the claws. Front and back claws will need more trimming than the sides, and the knuckles, of course, will peak above the connecting bones.

In the last photo the ball of the foot has

been smoothed down to finished size and radius. Also, the claws are another step closer to finished shape, leaving only the work of rounding bones and knuckles. The back claw follows the ball contour until it reaches the apparent knuckle immediately above the cuticle and nail.

---

6 The foot in the photo at right shows real promise of what to expect after a little more work. Take time to carefully round the claws from the ankle down to the knuckle above the cuticle. Now check the length of the nails. This dimension is not crucial, but shoot for ½ in. from the bottom up to the cuticle where they will be about ¼ in. wide by ¼ in. high. Before forming the nail, use a medium-width #7 gouge to press cross-grain over the top for a clean-cut cuticle, shown on the extreme right. Down the sides, instead of continuing to use the #7, choose a medium-width #3 gouge and press to clean-cut the full cuticle. Reduce the nail size so the cuticle appears to overlap the nail and taper the nail to about ⅛ in. by ⅛ in. at the bottom.

Study the lower side claw in the photo. Yours should now look like this except for

the slightly rounded depression between cuticle and knuckle. That slight curve must be made carefully, first from the knuckle down, then from the cuticle upward, still using the #3 gouge.

After nail cutting, pencil in the web curve. As shown in the photo, the arc starts and ends just above the lower knuckles, although the placement is not critical. Some carvers of old felt that the web should start halfway between the knuckles.

Forming the web is a repeat performance of cuticle cutting. A #4 gouge about ½ in. wide should be close to the needed radius. Because of the larger area, tap the gouge with a mallet for a clean parting cut. Make tapered shaving cuts with a #3 gouge in the area of the web line to raise the web about 1/16 in. above the ball. Look at and feel the ball for any bumps that should be removed

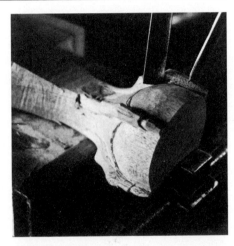

or any adjustments in contour that would improve its appearance.

---

7 So far, carving has ended at the ankle. Use a spokeshave to round the leg corners. Start at nothing where the curve swings into a wing block, to be attached later. Increase the radius as the tool descends, ending at the ankle in a near round. Round the high point of all knuckles.

Sanding may be done thoroughly, or slightly, leaving some tool marks. A smooth-looking job calls for a first sanding with 80-grit garnet paper followed by 120 grit. Wear rubber gloves to protect your finger tips and nails. If carving is planned for the knee, sand only to above the ankle. Should the knee be plain, sand to it now.

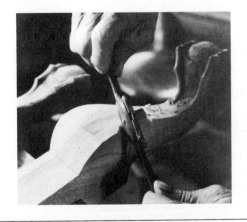

---

8 Infinitely varied foliage patterns are used on the knee for decoration. Lay flexible pattern board over the knee surface and outline the curves on the board as shown at right. Then pencil in your choice of design for carving. The photo at far right shows what to strive for. □

Andy Marlow, 74, a consulting editor for Fine Woodworking, *designs and makes traditional furniture in York, Pa.*

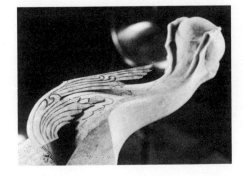

Cockleshell
Giant carving gives corner cupboard class

by Franklin H. Gottshall

The beauty of a corner cupboard can be greatly enhanced by incorporating a hand-carved cockleshell in the design. Such a shell is sure to be a show stealer, and from this standpoint alone it is worth all the effort it takes to make.

It took me two weeks to build and carve the shell shown, which measures 34 in. across on the inside at the base. Some storage space is lost on the shelf where the shell is put, but the great amount of interest it imparts more than compensates for the loss.

I designed this cupboard to be as high, wide and deep as possible, in order to have maximum storage space. This permitted me to put in such a large shell. I was fortunate to find a 2-in. plank of California sugar pine 22 in. wide and 16 ft. long at the lumberyard. Others may not be able to duplicate my good fortune and will have to glue several planks together to achieve the required widths.

The layers needed to build the shell up to height can be bandsawn out of glued-up segments. Ten semicircular layers were required to build up this shell. The table gives the sizes I

cut. Smaller shells would, of course, require less material. With proper planning there is very little waste.

When the layers have all been sawn to shape, they should be joined together on the outside of the arc with glue and wood screws. I used 2½-in. #14 flathead screws and countersunk the heads.

It is important to be careful when drilling holes for these screws so there is no danger of cutting into the screws when carving or smoothing up the inside of the shell. Arrow *A* in the diagram at the top of the next page points at the line to which waste must be trimmed. The dotted lines on layers 8 and 9 show the waste formed on the inside of the shell by stacking the layers. This waste must be removed. A cardboard template with a 17-in. radius curve may be used to help you do this smoothing properly.

Before you start to carve, glue a facing board to the front of the shell. This ensures a flat surface, while hiding the glue lines and other imperfections. Notice the direction of the grain on the facing board. A 45° angle cut on both ends of the top of the board positions the shell easily for carving.

Start smoothing the inside of the shell with wide gouges. Finish with sharp scraper blades and garnet paper. Use coarse-grit garnet paper first, and finish up with finer grit paper until the surface is completely smooth.

The broken line *B* shown in the top diagram is one of several you should draw to help you space the widths of grooves and fillets uniformly. The shell shown has 19 grooves. You can make more or fewer, but I advise making an odd number. First draw center lines where each groove is to go, making the first up the center of the shell. Then you can draw border lines for each groove and fillet. There is no great harm if a fillet at the bottom of the shell is a little wider or narrower than the others, but the grooves should all be the same width. A cardboard template helps lay out these lines.

Because it will be difficult to space grooves and fillets close together near the bottom, it is better to use another design here to fill this small area, as I did on my shell.

When all the carving and smoothing has been done on the inside, you are ready to cut the molding around the scalloped edge on the front of the shell. I cut mine with a router.

Put as many coats of finish on the outside of the shell as you put on the inside. This prevents unequal drying, which causes checking or splitting. This should be done before fastening the shell into the cupboard. I used several coats of spar varnish on the back of the shell. The inside was finished with pale green latex paint. I anchored this shell by screwing the outside of the bottom layer into the back of the shelf, and the top into the top of the cupboard. □

Franklin Gottshall, of Boyertown, Pa., is a retired industrial-arts teacher. He has written 14 books on furniture making, woodcarving, design and crafts.

Hand-carved cockleshell enhances large corner cupboard.

Dimensions of each layer

No.	Inside	Outside
1	17"	20"
2	16¾"	19¾"
3	16½"	19¼"
4	15¾"	18½"
5	14¾"	17½"
6	13½"	17"
7	11⅛"	16"
8	9½"	14"
9	5¾"	12"
10	*Do not bandsaw inside.*	10"

Table above gives inside and outside radii for laying out ten semicircular layers, numbered from bottom of shell to top. If a board wide enough for the largest layer cannot be obtained, several planks can be glued together to get the necessary width. Several layers can be bandsawn on the same segment of board to minimize waste. In the diagram below, the first, sixth and ninth layers have been nestled on a segment made by gluing three boards together edge to edge.

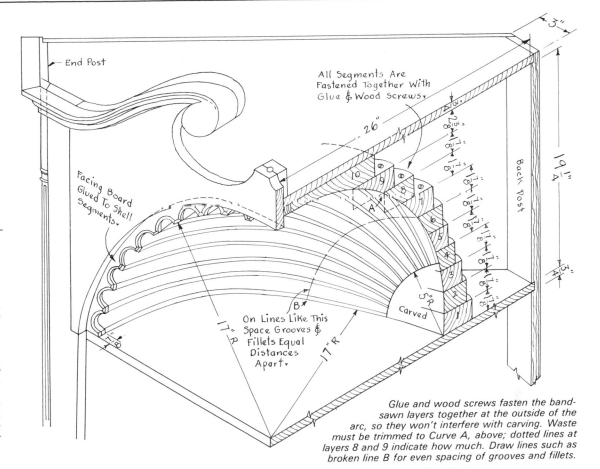

Glue and wood screws fasten the bandsawn layers together at the outside of the arc, so they won't interfere with carving. Waste must be trimmed to Curve A, above; dotted lines at layers 8 and 9 indicate how much. Draw lines such as broken line B for even spacing of grooves and fillets.

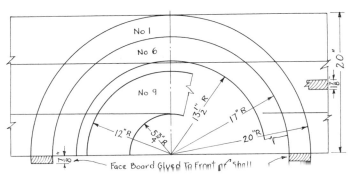

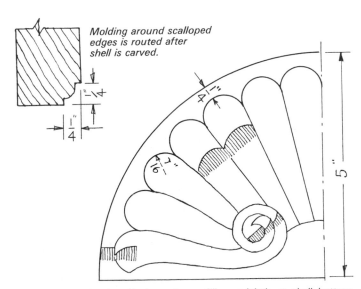

Molding around scalloped edges is routed after shell is carved.

Small shell-and-volute design, above, fills semicircle at shell bottom. Right, angle-cut faceboard steadies shell as Gottshall carves grooves.

BENDING AND VENEERING

Steam Bending

Heat and moisture plasticize wood

by William A. Keyser, Jr.

Ever wonder how old bentwood furniture parts were made or how ribs for boats are formed? Probably by steam bending. This process uses steam or boiling water to plasticize the wood so that it can be bent, usually over a form or mold. Upon cooling and drying, the bent piece retains its shape. The distinct advantage of steaming is that the grain of the wood follows the curve, thus eliminating the short-grain problems associated with bandsawn curves.

Of course a lamination, i.e., several thin pieces glued together in the curved position, will also do the job. But there is something nice about one integral piece of wood making the bend, with the grain following the curve. The time required to resaw and surface all the laminations is saved, no wood is lost to saw kerfs and ugly glue lines don't surface if the bent piece is subsequently carved or shaped. Also, a lot fewer clamps are required.

Steam bending has shortcomings. The most troublesome is accurately predicting springback. A laminated member will conform very closely to a mold; the greater the number of laminations, the less it will spring back. In steam bending the results depend upon the grain structure of each piece of wood. Local eccentricities—knots, checks and cross grain— will affect the final curve much more than in lamination,

where the process itself tends to homogenize the structure of the member. This disadvantage becomes critical when exact duplicates must be made. Also, some breakage or rejects can be expected in steam bending. If ten pieces are required, bend twelve or thirteen.

When deciding whether to steam-bend or laminate, reason it out this way: If the member must start precisely at some point *A*, negotiate a specific curve and end up exactly at point *B*, and do so repeatedly, the odds are better if you laminate. If the relative positions of *A* and *B* are not critical, or if their relationship is maintained by the rest of the structure and if there is some tolerance in the path taken from *A* to *B*, then the integrity of a single piece would justify steam bending. Where either process is appropriate, the material and time saved in steam bending by not resawing settle the question.

The piece of wood to be bent is placed in a closed container or steam box and bathed in steam generated by boiling water. The steam gradually softens the structure of the wood and makes it flexible. The wood is then forced around a mold and clamped in position. The outside circumference of the wood must usually be reinforced with a metal strap. The shape of the mold is determined by the curve desired, with due allowance for springback. The bent piece is either left clamped on this mold to cool and dry, or it is immediately placed on a separate jig to hold it in position during drying.

When the piece has cured and is removed from the mold or drying jig, it usually springs back slightly. With luck, it now

Bill Keyser, 41, is professor of woodworking and furniture design at Rochester Institute of Technology. He's currently writing a woodworking textbook.

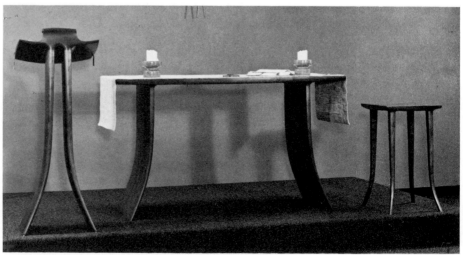

Ark at Interfaith Chapel, University of Rochester, is 8 ft. high and made of steam-bent teak angled and then joined edge-to-edge to create the shell's compound curve. Pieces bent off-the-corner become legs of small table in chapel at Geneseo, N. Y.; plain bends joined edge-to-edge support altar and lectern.

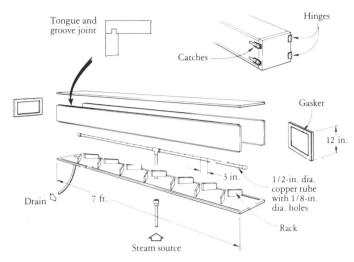

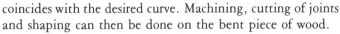

Keyser's steam box is made from one sheet of ordinary 3/4-in. plywood and is supported on sawhorses.

Wet steam for bending can be generated in a variety of ways. Keyser uses a kerosene-fired wallpaper steamer.

coincides with the desired curve. Machining, cutting of joints and shaping can then be done on the bent piece of wood.

When wood is steamed, the heat and moisture soften its fibers and allow them to distort with respect to one another, thus permitting the piece to bend. Steam at 212° F warms the wood and whatever moisture is already in the fibers; the moisture in the steam supplements the initial moisture content of the wood, especially in those fibers near the surface. Apparently, pressurized steam doesn't help much; in fact, there is some evidence that it makes the wood brittle and is detrimental to successful bending.

It's important to make sure the steam is saturated with moisture. Bubbling the steam through a trough of water or leaving some free water lying in the bottom of the steam box will ensure this. Generally, the wood should remain in the steam for about one hour per inch of thickness. Steaming for longer periods of time doesn't increase the bendability much.

Generating steam

Steam can be generated in a variety of ways; I use a kerosene-fired wallpaper steamer. Electrically heated versions are available from Warner Manufacturing Co., 13435 Industrial Park Blvd., Minneapolis, Minn. 55541. Local paint and wallpaper stores often rent them. The steam-generating units from home sauna baths can also be used. One unit, the Hot Shot Model MB4L, is available from Automatic Steam Products Corp., 43-20 34th St., Long Island City, N.Y. 11101. A lidded 5-gal. can with a filling cap and a hose fitting brazed or soldered into the lid also works well. It can be heated on a large camp stove, plumber's furnace or open fire.

The steam box can be made from one sheet of 3/4-in. exterior fir plywood, either C-C, B-C or A-C grade, depending on how much you want to spend, with the best face toward the inside of the box. You could use marine exterior grade, but it's not necessary. Tongue and groove the corners, or butt and screw them. A manifold can be made from 1/2-in. dia. copper tubing drilled with 1/8-in. dia. holes every 3 in. Introduce the steam through a hose adapter and tee midway along the length of the manifold, to equalize distribution. A drain hole for the condensation should be provided at one end, with a hose adapter to carry the water to a floor drain or outside the shop. A rack or some other method of supporting the wood above the manifold should be provided so the wood doesn't lie in the condensate. I use blocks of wood screwed to the bottom and angled toward the drain end of the box. A coat or two of porch and deck enamel or marine paint, inside and out, will preserve the steam box for years. Assemble the bottom and two sides, install the manifold, drain and rack, and paint the interior surfaces before putting on the top. Use a good waterproof glue and brass screws at the corners. Both ends should have hinges, gaskets and catches. Thus, the box can be loaded from either end if short pieces are being steamed, or very long pieces can be run right through the open-ended box and the gaps stuffed with burlap or rags to contain the steam. When the box is supported on sawhorses or on a permanent stand, slant it slightly so the condensate runs toward the drain.

Selecting wood

Some species of wood steam-bend better than others. I've found that white and red oak, walnut, ash, hickory, pecan and beech bend well. Cherry is not quite as good, and it's just barely possible to bend teak and mahogany. Softwoods do not bend well. The tables below show the relative bendability of various species, expressed as a percentage of unbroken pieces, and the limiting radii of supported and unsupported bends in 1-in. stock. Such tables have been compiled to guide industrial users and are only approximations—the craftsman's best guide is experience.

Bendability of Domestic Hardwoods		Limiting Radii of Curvature (in inches for 1-in. stock)		
	% Unbroken Pieces		Supported By Strap	Unsupported
Ash	67	Afrormosia	14.0	29.0
Beech	75	Alder	14.0	18.0
Birch	72	Ash	4.5	13.0
Elm, soft	74	Beech	1.5	13.0
Hackberry	94	Birch, yellow	3.0	17.0
Hickory	76	Douglas fir	18.0	33.0
Magnolia	85	Ebony	10.0	15.0
Maple, hard	57	Elm, white	1.7	13.5
Oak, red	86	Hemlock	19.0	36.0
Oak, white	91	Hickory	1.8	15.0
Pecan	78	Mahogany	36.0	32.0
Sweetgum	67	Oak, white	0.5	13.0
Sycamore	29	Oak, red	1.0	11.5
Tupelo	42	Spruce, Sitka	36.0	32.0
Walnut, black	78	Teak	18.0	35.0

U.S. Forest Products Laboratory, *Wood Handbook: Wood as an Engineering Material*, 1974.

W.C. Stevens and N. Turner, *Wood Bending Handbook* (Princes Risborough, England: Forest Products Research Laboratory, 1970).

163

Industrial research has also found that air-dried wood at a moisture content of 15% to 20% is best for steaming. But I have bent some species of kiln-dried wood at 8% to 12% MC with good success. If difficulties arise and the wood seems too dry, try soaking it in water for a day before steaming. The added moisture is absorbed mainly by the fibers near the surface and will evaporate quickly when the heated wood cools.

Stock for bending should be selected for straight grain and must be free of cross grain, knots, checks and other defects. I have found that flatsawn stock bends better than quartersawn; that is, the annual rings of the board should run parallel to the mold, as closely as possible.

Preparing the stock

It is best to place the heartwood side of the board on the inside of the bend. The board should be jointed and thicknessed, but usually not to finished dimension, particularly if the stock is thick. With cross sections 1-1/2 in. x 4 in. and larger, it is best to leave a little extra stock so the final profile can be sawn or otherwise worked to final form after bending. But having the stock smooth on four sides before bending prevents cracks and splits from propagating from a surface irregularity such as sawmill or circular-saw marks. A small chamfer, perhaps 1/16 in., on all four edges of the stock also helps prevent splits from starting at points where the grain might be slightly crossed. On thin stock or where curvature is not great, I sometimes presand the parts before bending. Although steam raises and sometimes discolors the grain, at least the mill marks are gone and all that is required after bending is light scraping and final sanding.

The piece of wood to be bent should always be several inches longer than the desired finished length. During bending the ends frequently are distorted and these defects can be cut off later. An end coating (such as that used around kilns, or ordinary oil-base paint or roofing cement) spread on the end grain before presoaking or steam bending prevents excessive absorption of moisture and subsequent end-checking during drying.

It is usually better to cut joints after the piece is bent; however, I have cut mortises and tenons before bending where they occurred on the straight portion of a member.

In any bend, the distance L around the outer convex side of a curve is longer than the distance l around the inner concave side. Ordinarily, when stock of length l is bent around a curve the outer fibers stretch (or go into tension) to attain the additional required length (L-l). Wood plasticized by steam will stretch only very slightly before fracturing (failing in tension), but it can be compressed to a much greater degree. The fibers in compression slip, compress, bend and distort without failing. Therefore, the objective is to begin with the plasticized stock at length L, prevent the outer convex fibers from stretching (going into tension), and force the inner concave fibers to compress

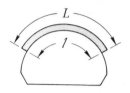

(and therefore shorten to length l). This is done by fitting the outer surface of the stock with a heavy steel strap securely welded or bolted to steel end blocks. Assuming the strap does not stretch as the wood is bent, the end blocks push against the inner fibers, compressing them to length l.

Straps and molds

I use 16-gauge cold rolled steel for straps on stock up to 1/2 in. thick, 1/16-in. hot rolled steel for stock 1/2 in. to 1 in. thick and 1/8-in. hot rolled steel for stock 1 in. to 2 in. thick. I make end blocks from angle iron or channel iron at least 1/4 in. thick, or solid steel bar stock when available. Don't underestimate the amount of force the end blocks must withstand when bending heavy stock. Frequently the force is great enough to bend the angle iron. Welding corner blocks behind the angle iron helps prevent this.

The strap must be wide enough to cover the full width of the stock being bent, and end blocks must be large enough to cover the entire end of the piece. When bending stock thicker than 1 in., I fasten each end block to the bending strap with at least three 1/2-in. dia. bolts. When I buy the strap material, I get it long enough to accommodate quite long stock. Then I can redrill the holes and rebolt the end blocks to reuse the strap for other bends. Chemical reaction with the steel strap will discolor the surface of most woods. Discoloration is usually removed in subsequent shaping and finishing, but if it is objectionable, use stainless steel straps or cover them with polyethylene sheeting.

The plasticized wood member must be bent around a mold. This mold must be very strong, must support the full width of the bent piece and must accommodate some clamping arrangement for drawing the wood around the curve. A male mold is always used, so that it will support the inner fibers of the bent wood. I make many of my molds from discarded telephone-pole crossarms (about 4 in. x 5 in.) glued into a blank and bandsawn to shape. Stacked 3/4-in. thick fir plywood or laminated 2-in. construction lumber also works well. Regardless of construction method, strength is the key word, because incredible forces can be generated in bending a piece of wood around the mold.

It is important to allow for springback when shaping the mold, so that after the bent part is released it assumes the intended shape. Only experience will teach how much to overbend in compensation for springback. Among the variables are the nature of the curve, thickness of the wood and species. Usually the more gentle the curve, the more one must compensate. It seems that the more the fibers on the concave side of the member are displaced, the less they spring back.

Wood fits tightly against strap between solid steel end blocks, which extend outward from small clamps to provide leverage. Then assembly is clamped to center of mold to prevent initial buckling and quickly pulled around. After setting for 15 minutes, wood is clamped overnight to drying jig, left.

Keyser puts the hot wood into the strap, which has been warming atop the steam box. A clamp at each end secures it to the heavy channel-iron reverse levers, tight against the end blocks. Speed is essential; do a dry run to make sure mold, clamps, tools are handy.

When making molds, I work from the full-size drawing of the piece and guess at the amount of springback. I cut the mold, bend a trial piece and then revise the mold if necessary.

If only one piece is to be bent, the strap and wood can be left clamped to the mold for a day until the piece cools and dries thoroughly. If several pieces must be bent, it saves time to construct a drying jig. This allows you to bend, remove the clamp and strap after about 15 minutes, and clamp the wood onto the drying jig. This frees the bending strap and mold for the next piece to be bent.

I usually allow one day per inch of thickness (or fraction thereof) for the bent piece to cool, dry and set before removing it from the mold or drying jig.

Bending in one plane

The simplest bend is a single curve in one plane. In bending a 1-1/2-in. x 5-in. x 56-in. piece of walnut around a 10-in. radius mold, I've used a giant cross-bow arrangement. Be careful with this method; don't take a chance on lightweight equipment failing and recoiling. I use two 1-ton heavy-duty chain hoists for the job. The wood is removed from the steamer and placed between the end blocks of the bending strap, which has been warming on top of the steam box. The strap is secured to the wood by a clamp at each end, then the strap and wood piece are aligned and clamped to the center of the mold. This is important because as bending progresses, the wood will try to pull away from the mold at the tangent point and will immediately crack if not clamped tightly there. Continue to wind the chain hoists and pull the piece around the mold as quickly and smoothly as possible, until the bend is complete. You have only a few minutes to work, for the longer the bending operation takes, the more the piece cools and dries, and the greater the risk of failure.

When the curve is this severe, the compressive forces against the end blocks become great enough to overturn the

Cross-bow mold is made from telephone-pole crossarms and fitted with one-ton chain hoists. Center clamp at base of mold and two more clamps hold wood firmly in place as hoists pull it around.

165

Bend is complete. Enormous compressive forces are apparent in slight curve away from mold's ends, despite heavy reverse levers.

After two days on mold, wood still springs back, left. Bar clamps, right, shackle bent pieces to minimize further springback.

Catastrophes: Tension failure, top, indicates loose or overturned end blocks and too-narrow strap (discoloration); compression failure, bottom, occurs when bend is too tight or wood is too plastic.

steel blocks and allow the strap and wood to recurve away from the mold. To counteract this tendency, a reverse lever made from heavy channel iron is bolted through the strap to the end block. This lever, pushing against the back of the strap, prevents the end block from overturning.

In good weather and when a helper is available, the mold may be staked to the ground and a car or truck used to pull the bent piece around the mold. The steamed piece with the strap in place is clamped to the mold on one end of the curve, and the other end of the strap is fastened to a tow chain. The advantage is that the piece can be pulled around very quickly; the danger is that lightweight chains can snap and recoil.

A few cautions are in order; live steam is dangerous stuff. The steam box and steam generator should not seal tightly, to avoid building up pressure inside. You must be sure the generator doesn't run dry and burn up. Wear heavy gloves when handling the steamed wood, and when opening the box, beware of scalding your face in the blast of steam. If you wear glasses, the steam will fog them.

Failures

Much can be learned from pieces which have failed during bending. In tension failure, the fibers on the outside surface of the bend simply pull apart. It is the result of reduced end pressure caused by the end blocks not fitting tightly against the ends of the wood or distorting during bending. The outer fibers go into tension instead of the inner fibers being compressed. If the bending strap is not wide enough to cover the entire piece of wood, a crack is liable to start at the unsupported edge. Wrinkling, or compression failure, occurs on the inner surface because of over-plasticization, too tight a bend or a bad choice of species for the particular bend.

Bends without a strap

Bending without a strap and end blocks is possible only when the curve is slight or the stock is very thin. I have found that the difference between the lengths of the outer and inner faces of the bent piece should be less than 3%, although this varies from species to species. For 1-in. stock, the minimum radius I would bend without straps and end blocks is about 33 in. Bends made without straps are less stable and more springback can be expected. The bends are not as predictable for duplication because complete distortion of the fibers has not taken place and the "memory" of the wood cells will straighten it out. I seldom bend without a strap.

For shallow bends, or when stock is very thin, bending can be done without a strap. The steamed wood is clamped directly to a combination mold and drying jig such as the one shown above.

Complex curves

Bending a single piece of wood in a reverse, or S, curve or bending in two planes requires only a more complicated mold and strap. The principles remain the same: the strap must follow the convex side, or outside, of each portion of the curve, and end blocks must force the wood fibers on the inside of the curve to compress. Extensions of the end blocks, welded or bolted to the strap, provide handles to help in pulling the wood around the mold. Then it is clamped in place and left to set.

Bending off the corner

Table or stool legs can be bent off the corner by using a 1/2-in. x 1/2-in. x 1/8-in. angle iron as the bending strap. It fits over the outside corner of the steamed piece. Near the ends, the strap is fortified by welding on short lengths of a larger-size angle iron, to which is welded the solid steel end blocks. The small angle iron is flexible enough to bend around a gentle curve. The bending mold is made of two pieces of solid wood bandsawn to the desired curve, with the bandsaw table tilted 45°. The steamed stock is placed in the bending strap, the strap and stock are inserted under a shackle at the end of the bending mold and then the piece is simply forced around the mold and clamped.

Further Reading

Forest Products Laboratory, *Wood Handbook: Wood as an Engineering Material.* Agricultural Handbook No. 72, Washington, D.C.: U.S. Government Printing Office, 1974.

Forest Products Laboratory, *Wood Handbook. Basic Information on Wood as a Material of Construction with Data for Its Use in Design and Specification.* Agriculture Handbook No. 72, Washington, D.C.: U.S. Government Printing Office, 1955.

Peck, Edward C., *Bending Solid Wood to Form.* Agriculture Handbook No. 125, Washington, D.C.: U.S. Government Printing Office, 1968.

Stevens, W.C. and Turner, N., *Wood Bending Handbook.* London: Her Majesty's Stationery Office, 1970.

Wangaard, Frederick J., *The Steam-Bending of Beech.* Beech Utilization Series No. 3, Northeastern Forest Experiment Sta., 1952.

For a reverse curve in one plane, strap iron is fastened to each portion of mold where curve changes direction. Steamed wood is clamped at end blocks, then to mold, and quickly pulled around. End blocks are angle iron, backed up with hardwood fastened by bolts.

For a bend in two planes, ends of two pieces of strap iron are overlapped at right angles and welded edge-to-edge—in effect, forming a few inches of angle iron at point where curve changes direction. Three clamps hold overlapping iron and hot wood to mold; end blocks and handles are lengths of tee iron welded to straps.

Off-the-corner strap, left, is welded from two sizes of angle iron. Steamed wood fits tightly between end blocks, is tucked under shackle on mold, and forced into place, above. After 15 minutes it is removed, placed in drying jig, and clamped with the aid of blocks notched at 45°.

Hot-Pipe Bending

Coordination, concentration and practice ensure success

by William R. Cumpiano

Bending guitar sides on a hot pipe is the most dramatic and challenging of all instrument-making techniques. All your senses come into play in the "dance" in front of the bending iron. You feel the intense heat radiating onto your face and chest. You can smell the sweet aroma of hot wood and the quite different odor of a singed surface. You hear the creaking sound of straining wood fibers, and the change in sound that tells you the wood is about to break. In hot-pipe bending, one hand moves a thin, wet piece of wood over a hot pipe in short hops, while the other hand pushes down on the heated wood to bend it. The operation is tricky and requires coordination, concentration and practice. There is nothing quite as heart-stopping as watching a select Brazilian rosewood guitar side, with $10 market value, turn in an instant into scrap—accompanied, of course, by its unbent matching side.

Not surprisingly, many professional hand-builders resort to various molds and hydraulic/electric devices to circumvent hand-bending. But such devices limit their production to one or two body shapes. Those who have mastered the technique of hand-bending can custom-bend to the purchaser's specifications. One might also bend sides for boxes and trays, or to create sculpture.

The first step is to make a template of the curve to be bent. Stiff paper is fine for making other templates or for keeping a record of different body shapes, but for bending, something more durable and stiffer is needed. Tempered Masonite ⅛ in. thick is adequate; it does not get wrinkled and soggy when

---

William Cumpiano makes and repairs guitars in North Adams, Mass.

wet. The ideal material, albeit expensive, is ¹⁄₁₆-in. aluminum sheet. Score the outline from the paper original onto the aluminum. After cutting as close to the line as possible with a tinner's snips, mill-file to the scored line.

Study the template. Your success at capturing the outline in the bent wood depends on your familiarity with its shape. The two types of curves found most commonly are "fair" curves (sections of a circle) and accented curves. An accented curve is one that seems to have the force of a point straining to push it outwards. A fair curve has no accent. Mentally subdividing the template into straight-line segments, fair curves and accented curves will help you during bending.

Even with ideal facilities and the best guidance, your efforts will come to naught with poorly selected side blanks. Textbook-perfect side blank material is flawlessly quartersawn wood of perfectly even and homogenous consistency. Such material is indeed difficult to break accidentally. On the finished instrument it is superior for its stability and its ease of repair. But perfect side blanks are rare and one must often compromise. My criteria vary with the species. Maple can be used even if not well quartersawn, providing it is soaked a short time, because it is extremely tough and flexible in thin sheets. However, curly maple must be flawlessly surfaced, lest a small chip or dig allow a crack to start. Mahogany is the most forgiving of all: I select primarily for appearance and homogeneity. However, failure can occur along sap lines and pieces containing them must be avoided.

Because rosewood is often brittle, vitreous and non-uniform, it must be selected with the most care of all. What may appear to be fine, even material may actually hide long, fine cracks that render it useless. Gently flex and probe the entire

(please turn page)

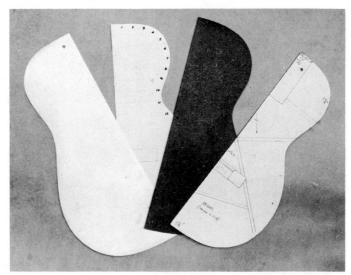

Typical guitar profiles include straight-line segments (S), fair curves, or sections of a circle (R indicates a radius to an imaginary center), and accented curves.

Templates may be made of (left to right) paper, cardboard, Masonite or aluminum. Beginners should start with gentle, large-radius bends, as in classical or 'dreadnaught' guitars.

Bending Irons

The simplest bending iron is made from a 2½-in.-diameter by 6-in. long pipe nipple, available in plumbing supply shops. Thread one end of the nipple into a flange. Screw the flange onto a sturdy board on which is mounted a ceramic bulb socket holding a heating coil. Bulb-socket heating coils can be obtained from an electric supply house; they may be difficult to find because they are the heating elements on infrared lamp fixtures and old-fashioned electric space heaters, which may be illegal in your state. A cylindrical coil is better than a cone-shaped one.

The round bending iron shown here is a beginner's apparatus. It is cheap, adequate and easy to throw together, but unsatisfactory in the long run, since the coils burn out frequently. A round bending iron offers only a line-contact source of heat. The pipe cannot bend a curve with a radius tighter than 1¼ in. Also, you must manually shut the iron on and off to maintain the correct temperature, a very troublesome and clumsy hindrance.

If you have started bending with a round pipe, you may be able to

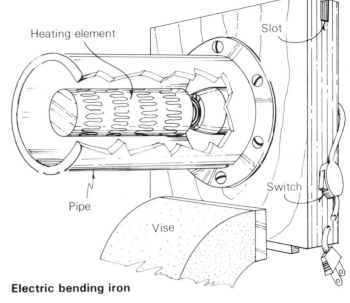

Electric bending iron

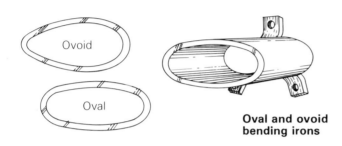

Oval and ovoid bending irons

become proficient, in time. However, bending is easier if you replace the pipe nipple with an oval, or even better, egg-shaped bending iron. Start with an 8-in. length of thick-walled, large-diameter (about 6 in.) pipe. It can be made egg-shaped in a large vise, beaten to shape with a sledge, or taken to a scrapyard and pressed by having the wrecker's magnet dropped on it from the height of a few inches. You can improve heat transfer by filing the contact surface flat. Iron

pipe is fine, but I've also used copper and aluminum. With a hacksaw, cut tabs that can be bent back and drilled for mounting. Asbestos "washers" at the tabs will prolong the life of the unit.

As with the round pipe, an electric heating coil may be used. The entire scheme can be greatly improved by hooking up a thermostatic device. I have seen various successful arrangements using lighting rheostats, electric-iron rheostats, and electric frying-pan controls. However, a heating coil may require as much as 1000 watts and whatever rheostat you use must operate within this capacity. You can purchase one of several electric bending irons, thermostatically controlled, that work very well but are frightfully expensive.

Bottled gas can be a heat source for the pipe. Build a small carriage behind the bending-iron platform to support the gas torch bottle valve upwards, with its nozzle inserted into a large opening in the platform. The nozzle controls heat effectively. Partially closing the oval opening at the end of the iron with a bent rectangular baffle of thin metal sheet will conserve heat that would otherwise be lost, protect your skin (which is usually directly in front of the opening) and reduce your gas bill. I use an ordinary propane torch. A refill costs less than $3 and lasts me about a month.

When installing a new torch, remember never to tighten the valve with force. One or two firm tightenings will ruin the valve seats and cause the torch to operate erratically. It will flare dramatically and unexpectedly, creep open or closed while in use, and make it impossible to maintain low settings.

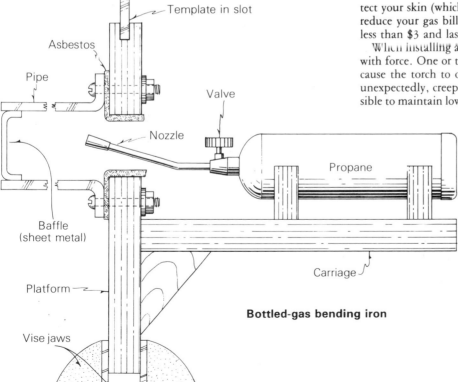

Bottled-gas bending iron

Author's bending iron, mounted on a table; note oval pipe and heat baffle. Slot on top can hold template.

surface. A small end check may cause the whole blank to split dramatically in twain when flexed during bending. Beware of uniformly textured rosewood that has a single, very black line running down its length. This is an interface between two varying densities, a line of stress that may split the blank. Start with material as straight and uniform as possible. If well-quartered yet dramatically grained material is used, its pattern should likewise be even and uniform. Do not use edge grain that wiggles and runs off quickly. Edge grain that runs off gently over a reasonable length of stock is acceptable.

The thin wood (1/16 in. to 1/8 in.) used in instrument making must be stored with fastidious care. Plates must be separated with dry spacers of uniform thickness placed accurately and neatly. The first slat in the pile must be similarly spaced from the supporting shelf, as must the last from the heavy weight above the entire pile. Rosewood and ebony blanks must have both ends parafinned or painted. Improperly stored material, however select and expensive, is liable to check or warp and will have to be discarded.

Various guitarmaking texts suggest that side blanks must first be treated vigorously and harshly to persuade them to bend, for example, by immersing them in boiling water for an hour, or soaking rosewood blanks in hot solvents and soapy water for days. I have observed that a great many problems in hand-bending in fact stem from overwetting and boiling thin slats. For example, maple falls apart under tension as the too-soft material simply separates away from itself under even the mildest pressure. Mahogany that has undergone too much soaking loses its "memory" and must be rebent time and again. Thin, waterlogged maple and mahogany will ripple across the grain after drying. Leaching out the resins by boiling leaves the wood lifeless and crack-prone.

Immersion time varies directly with blank thickness. Blanks of average thickness (.095 in. to .080 in.) need only be immersed in tepid water for a short time: rosewood for 30 to 40 minutes, mahogany for 15 to 20 minutes and maple for as little as 1 to 10 minutes. Side blanks thinner than .080 in. should be used on only the smallest guitars, although modern lute ribs may be as thin as .060 in. Marquetry strips should be immersed in very hot water for 60 to 90 seconds. No prebending is necessary for properly stored strips if the template curves are moderate; strips can be eased into place on the guitar immediately after wetting during the binding process. An ordinary 36-in. sheet metal window-box planter makes an excellent soaking trough.

You must remove all encumbrances and place the bending iron conveniently. You will be bending, taking the piece off the pipe at intervals and comparing it to your template. The template must be firmly secured; a slot in the platform that holds it snugly at eye level will minimize your movements. Another way is to clamp the template to an adjacent tabletop. Having it flat will help discourage the common tendency to bend a skew, or twist, into the blank. Keep handy a small dish with water and a sponge for wetting the wood, to minimize scorching.

Several reference marks in yellow crayon on your blanks will help ensure the proper bookmatch on right and left sides. I find the bookmatch, put the sides together and joint only the common edges, leaving the opposite edges rough or even wany. This helps prevent the mistake of accidentally bending two right or two left sides. The straight, true edge will be glued to the guitartop; the rough edge will be hand-planed

and sanded to the proper arch just before the instrument's back is assembled. Allow no less than 1/4-in. extra width.

I also find it helpful to mark the finished length on the blanks (allowing not less than a 1-in. overhang at each end) and to mark "outside" and "inside" on both pieces. If you choose to bend the waist first, a clear mark on the blank at the apex will keep you from running out of material while bending the upper and lower bouts. This point can be calculated by measuring with a string from the template centerline to the waist apex. Another way is to mark off 1-in. increments on the template perimeter with a compass and transfer the waist measurement directly to the side blank with a ruler.

While the iron is heating, take stock of yourself and your task. Choose a time when you will be at your most alert. Take your phone off the hook and lock your shop door.

If you have planned correctly your pipe heat should be just right by the time the blanks are sufficiently wet. If you are a slow bender remove both sides from the trough. As you get faster, you will find yourself leaving the second side in the water while you bend the first.

Pipe heat is critical. The pipe should be the hottest that will not burn the wood on immediate contact. Remember that you will be constantly moving a wet piece of wood over the pipe. If it burns in spite of this, your pipe is too hot. A good test for correct heat is to sprinkle a few drops of water on the pipe. If they sit calmly or boil on the surface, the pipe is too cold. If the drops hop about, sizzling loudly, it is hot enough. If they instantly pop or vaporize, the pipe is too hot.

Even at the right temperature, the pipe may burn the wood if you pause for more than several seconds while bending a tight curve, since the side sometimes must be stopped and wrapped tightly around the pipe. Here additional moisture and short lifting and pressing movements are called for. Some singeing is inevitable, and lightly singed wood can be scraped away later. A tight bend demands some experience, so a beginner should choose a template with only gentle, large-radius bends (such as classical or "dreadnaught" shapes).

The two common procedures are bending from one end to the other and bending the waist first, followed by the upper and lower bouts. The first is considered to be the more difficult, but both will give excellent results when mastered.

If you are right-handed, feed the blank horizontally over the pipe with your right hand in a rapid succession of short up-and-down movements, which will advance the side in short hopping increments. A tight curve will require a slower feed, with faster hopping movements. A broad, gentle curve will require a faster feed, with slower, longer hops. You should rarely, if ever, stop the blank on the pipe. This will cause a kink or lump in the curve. An educated right hand advances the blank at an even, machine-like pace.

Your left hand determines the amount of pressure to apply, and thus the tightness of the resulting curve, by the angle at which the hot blank leaves the pipe surface as it is advanced by the right hand. Apply pressure square to the pipe, and keep the blank square to the pipe. The tendency is to angle the blank as it advances, and to tip the blank surface toward you as you grasp and press it. This results in a complex, changing twist in the finished piece, which in turn results in an instrument with one shape when viewed from the front and a different shape when viewed from the back.

The most valuable "feel" that you should be anticipating is the feedback given you by the change in springiness of the material as heat is applied. As you advance the blank over the top surface of the oval pipe, the rate of feed must be matched to the rate at which the wood absorbs enough heat to become plastic, or "relax." You should attempt to feel this change in stiffness, for it is at this point where the best bending occurs. If you are not sensitive to this change you may be applying pressure ineffectively—at best, the blank will simply not take the bend; at worst, the blank may crack.

If you have mentally subdivided the template into simplified steps, deciding when and where to apply pressure is likewise simplified. At the end of each step, or even more frequently, you should compare the piece with the template. But unless you maintain tension as you take the blank to the template, the piece will not hold the desired shape. Hesitate momentarily and allow the piece to cool slightly under tension. This pause is critical: The wood is "curing" at this time and the fibers are returning to a rigid state in the new shape. If you relax tension here, the piece will return to a random shape, and there will be no bending progress.

Take advantage of this curing interval by flexing the piece to match the template segment, then holding it still for a few moments against the template. The piece will retain the correct shape with little springback. Springback can be remedied at this point (after letting go of the piece) by gently and rhythmically flexing the piece while it is still warm until it springs back to the desired shape.

Bending mistakes can be corrected by reverse bending, but if you unbend too frequently and guess poorly at the place to rectify your error, the piece will take on a tortured, lumpy shape that is impossible ever to correct.

Acceptable deviation from the template should not exceed the ability of the material to flex after bending. Your criteria should be the wood's ability to be coaxed to the template line with only the gentlest pressure. Some builders feel that all the parts of an instrument should be under moderate tension during and after assembly, the justification being that the stress adds energy to the acoustic vibrations rippling through the guitar. Others feel exactly the opposite. This is a moot point, because there is no practical way of testing these contradictory assumptions. I choose to approximate the template to the best of my ability and reduce the variation to a minimum for other reasons: ease of assembly and the resulting improvement in the final appearance of the instrument.

Occasionally cracks and surface tearing of fibers at tight bends can occur. Some can be repaired. Cracks that appear as straight lines along straight-grained material can be closed by gentle clamping with glue and reinforcement from the back with a strip of tightly woven fabric saturated in white glue and pressed behind the glued crack. If jagged cracks occur in flatsawn materials, discard the piece. Moderate tearing of the surface fibers on tight bends can be repaired by working glue into the fracture and pressing the fibers down with a clamp and a gently curved caul.

Wet material locked into a mold over extended periods may mildew. I let the pieces air-dry for several hours and then tape them tightly to each other until assembly. Springback can be corrected by touching up dry on a moderately heated iron just before assembly. □

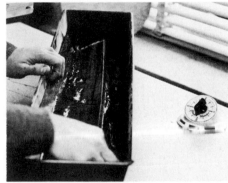

Gentle curves: less pressure, gentler blend.

Tight curves: greater pressure, tighter bend.

Amount of pressure and rate of feed determine tightness or curve. Fast feed with slow, long hops makes broad, gentle curve.

Side blanks are immersed in water in window-box planter; kitchen timer keeps track of minutes, prevents overwetting.

Right hand feeds evenly while the left fans rapidly (note blur) to advance the blank in small hops across the pipe.

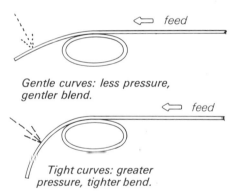

Waist-first bending: Mark at center of blank, where waist will be, ensures sufficient length for upper and lower bouts.

Neck-to-tail bending: Major curve section of upper bout is held in tension momentarily to permit wood to 'cure' in new shape.

Finished side is checked against template. Some deviation is acceptable; reverse bending, in moderation, can correct mistakes.

Hammer Veneering

Veneer the whole world, without clamps

by Tage Frid

Hammer veneering is the old way of applying veneers to solid wood or to a plywood ground. The main tool is a veneer hammer, which is not used for hammering at all, but for applying pressure. The hammer has a very narrow face, so you can transmit the strength of your arms and the weight of your body to a tiny area of veneer. The veneer is held down by hot hide glue, which sticks as soon as it cools. You spread the hot glue on the ground surface and the veneer, then you use the hammer to squeeze it down tight before it cools. You can reheat the glue, and soften it, with an iron. Hammer veneering is usually the easiest way to fix old furniture with missing or broken veneers, or air bubbles under the veneers.

Hammer veneering is very fast to do, but the big advantage is that you don't need a veneer press or cauls or clamps. In regular methods of veneering, the size of the work is limited by the size of the veneer press or of the clamps. But with hammer veneering you could veneer the whole world if you wanted to. The same rules apply, however: When you veneer one side of a piece of wood, you have to veneer the other side too, or else the piece will be pulled concave toward the veneered side as the glue dries.

When veneering plywood, always cross the grain direction of the face veneer and of the ground layer. You can use some angle other than 90°, as long as the grain of the veneer and the grain of the top layer of plywood don't run parallel. If they are parallel, the veneer will crack later on. If your veneer

is applied to solid wood, be sure the grain does run parallel so the two layers of wood can move together.

Equipment

You will need a veneer hammer, a veneer saw, a hot glue pot (or double boiler), animal glue, a brush and an iron.

Veneer hammers vary in design, but usually have a long handle and a hardwood wedge for a head, with an inset aluminum or brass strip, which is the working face. The face must be straight and about 3½ in. wide, with a rounded profile to squeeze the veneer along a thin line. If you make your own hammer, follow the dimensions in the sketch and use a hard, heavy wood such as maple. Don't use steel or iron for the face, because it would react with the tannic acid present in most woods and cause a stain. Before using a new hammer, soak it in raw linseed oil so the glue won't stick to it.

A veneer saw or knife is used to cut the veneer to size. It is called both a saw and a knife because it is filed as a saw and

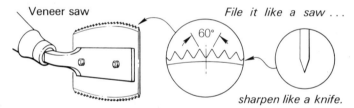

Veneer saw   *File it like a saw . . .*

60°

sharpen like a knife.

sharpened as a knife to make a smooth cut for edge-joining veneers. The curved blade of the saw is only about 3 in. long. Both sides of a veneer saw can be sharpened with a small triangular file. I file all the teeth at 90° to the surface of the blade, with no back or front, so that I can use the saw in either direction. This makes a slower but smoother cut.

After the teeth are filed sharp, the blade is sharpened so the cross section is like a knife, by rotating the saw along its curve against a stone. Hold the blade at a shallow angle, but be careful not to lose the points on the teeth.

A hot glue pot is a double boiler with a thermostat to prevent the glue from boiling. I don't use contact cement. I have seen too many failures, and it is just about impossible to repair. For large surfaces where veneers have to be edge-joined, contact cement could not be used. Contact cement has not been on the market very long, so nobody knows how long it will last. Hot glue is the oldest glue—it goes way back to the Egyptians. It is made from animal hides, bones and blood. It can be bought in dry sheets or as pearls. It must be soaked in water to soften it. Once it is soft, pour off any excess water. Then heat the glue in a glue pot or double boiler. Never put the pot directly on the heat source. It must always be over a pot of water. If hot glue boils it loses its strength, plus when it boils it doesn't smell like roses. When starting a new batch,

---

Tage Frid (the 'g' is silent, rhymes with 'hey, kid') teaches woodworking at Rhode Island School of Design in Providence.

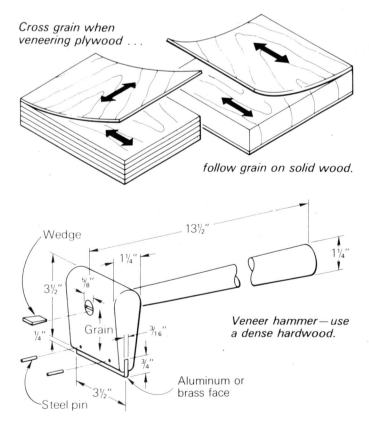

Cross grain when veneering plywood . . .

follow grain on solid wood.

Wedge

13½"

1¼"

3½"

⅝"

1¼"

Grain

¼"

³⁄₁₆"

¾"

Veneer hammer—use a dense hardwood.

Aluminum or brass face

3½"

Steel pin

melt the glue, let it cool and reheat it again and it will be ready to use. If the batch is already made up just heat it up and add water if it is too thick or let it heat for a while if it is too thin. Getting the right consistency is something you have to learn through experimenting. If the glue is hot all day its consistency changes constantly. If the consistency is right, the glue should drop from the brush like honey. You will know the glue is spoiled if it stays liquid after it cools.

To check that the glue is made correctly and is ready to use, put a drop between your fingers. Rub your fingers together, applying pressure. You should be able to squeeze out all the excess easily after about one minute if the room is around average temperature, 60° to 70° F. Your fingers should then start sticking together, because when hot glue gets cold it starts binding. The glue won't reach full strength until it dries completely, which takes about 24 hours.

Edge veneering

It is clumsy and time-consuming to veneer edges using clamps, but it is fast and easy to do it with the veneer hammer. It doesn't matter whether the edge is straight or curved. When you cut veneer, always have a flat piece of scrap wood underneath it to prevent cutting into the workbench, and use a straightedge to guide the saw. Cut strips of veneer only about ⅛ in. wider than the thickness of the work. If you cut them too wide, the excess sticking into the air will dry before the glue has cured and it will curl away from the wood.

When the veneer is cut, wet it on both sides to make it more flexible and also to see which way it naturally wants to arch. Glue it with the concave side toward the work, so the arch will keep it in place. If you do it the other way, it will be hard to keep the edges stuck down while the glue cures.

Begin by brushing glue onto the edge to be veneered, then turn the veneer over and lay what will be the outside surface right in the glue on the wood. Then brush glue onto the veneer. The glue that smears on the outside will help the hammer slide more easily. Later on you can scrape the veneer clean. Now flip the veneer over and hold it in place with one hand. Hot glue is very slippery. Hold the hammer in your other hand and press down hard to squeeze out the excess glue at one end. This will secure the veneer, and now you can put both hands on the hammer to squeeze out the excess glue all along the edge. You have to work fast to get all the veneer down while the glue is still hot. The minute the glue gets cold, the veneer will stick. Keep an old iron warmed up and handy. Then when you aren't fast enough, you can reheat the glue before going back with the hammer. Don't have the iron so hot that the glue burns, or you'll regret it. Burned glue makes an unpleasant stink that hangs around for a long time.

Use the veneer saw to clean off the extra glue and trim the veneer, while the glue is still soft. First dip the saw blade in hot water so it will be wet and warm and the glue won't stick to it. Then cut off the excess at both ends, holding the work up on an angle. After that, stand the work on edge and tilt it a little to apply pressure right at the corner, and saw off the excess veneer. Dip the blade in hot water after each cutting. Now put the piece aside to dry for about 24 hours.

It doesn't make any difference if the edge is curved or some other shape. Veneer it exactly as if it were straight. But when the work isn't straight, you must wait until the glue is hard and dry to remove the excess veneer and squeezed-out glue. Then use a block plane or a smooth plane to clean it off.

Wet the veneer to see which way it curls, then glue the concave side down, right, so the arch will help hold it in place.

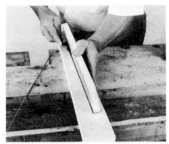

Use the veneer hammer to squeeze out the glue all along the edge.

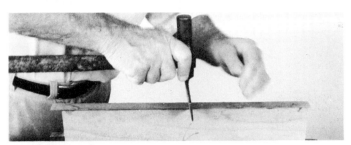

When trimming veneer, keep the saw warm and wet by dipping it in the glue-pot water. Stand the work on edge and tilt it a little to apply pressure, then draw the saw along the face of the board.

To trim a curved edge, let the glue dry hard, and plane.

Veneering large surfaces

To veneer a large surface, you will have to edge-join pieces of veneer either lengthwise or crosswise, or both. The edge joint must be very accurate. I ensure accuracy by overlapping the two pieces of veneer by about a half-inch at the joint, and after they are stuck down I cut through both pieces at the same time.

Begin by figuring out how you want the veneers to match and mark the location of each piece on the work. Then work on one section at a time. Wet the veneer and brush the hot glue onto the work. Place the moistened veneer upside down in the glue, exactly as when edge-veneering. Apply glue to the veneer itself, flip it over and put it in position, and use the hammer to secure it somewhere in the center.

Now use the warm iron to remelt the glue under a small section of the veneer. Push down with the veneer hammer as hard as you can, using the weight of your body, to squeeze out the excess glue. When that part is glued down, move to

Saw veneers to length with straightedge, backup board.

Lay veneer face down in glue. The glue that smears on it will help hammer slide easily.

With both sheets stuck and the seam trimmed, reheat with the iron and push hard with the hammer to squeeze the excess glue out through the line of the joint.

Lean your whole weight on the hammer, squeezing the glue toward the edges.

Saw through both veneers at once, carefully lift top sheet and peel away scrap beneath.

A hot iron remelts the glue in a troublesome spot. Then go over it with the hammer.

the next area. Heat the glue, press the veneer down, and proceed until the whole sheet is stuck tight. Work the hammer back and forth with the direction of the grain of the veneer, starting in the center of the width. But turn the face of the hammer at an angle so it will squeeze the excess glue toward the edges. Never work across the grain, as that would push the fibers apart and cause the veneer to crack when it dries.

Now apply glue to the next sheet of veneer and proceed in exactly the same way, making sure the edges to be joined overlap by about a half-inch. When they are both stuck, use a straightedge and a sharp, warm, wet veneer saw to cut through both sheets at once. Remove the scrap veneer from the top, then carefully lift up the top sheet and pull out the scrap from underneath. Then butt the edges together, heat with the iron, and push hard with the hammer to squeeze all the excess glue out through the line of the joint. When the joint is down tight, press a strip of heavy brown paper over the joint to prevent it from opening during drying. After the glue has dried, use a sharp scraper blade or a cabinet scraper to remove the paper and excess glue. But turn a heavier burr than normal on the blade ("The Scraper," Spring '77, p.29). A good seam should be invisible.

You must be sure there are no air bubbles under the veneer. If you can't find the bubbles when you push with the ham-

mer, tap the surface lightly with your fingernail and listen for hollow spots. If you don't get these hollow spots glued down, they will eventually crack. The veneer I used for these photographs was very curly in one spot in the center, and it would not stay down. So I heated the area to melt the glue, covered it with brown paper, and clamped a block of wood over the curly place to hold it down tight while the glue cooled and dried. If you don't notice the air bubbles until several days or months later, just apply water, heat and pressure to work the piece down. The glue will still hold. □

Block and clamp hold curly spot down while glue cools; strip of heavy paper along seam keeps it closed until glue dries. Then a sharp scraper cleans off paper and glue.

Leather on Wood
How to inlay it and tool it with gold

by Sandy Cohen

Inlaid and gold-tooled box top.

I love the feel and texture of fine leather. It is pliable, strong, and, with the proper care, enduring. In fact, I have written this article on an inlaid desk surface of fine grained olive-green morocco, richly tooled in gold and black, matched to fine English oak, a joy and a delight.

Creating such a surface is not that difficult, but it takes practice to get the feel. First the leather is cut and pasted into a recess as deep as the leather is thick. After the leather is inlaid, a design is stamped or rolled in with a heated brass tool. Gold tooling involves the further steps of sizing the impression with glair (an egg white/vinegar mordant to which gold adheres) and restamping the design over gold leaf. Some of the tools needed are quite specialized and a few are expensive, but they can be improvised with good results.

Combining wood, leather and gold is an ancient and honorable practice. This technique was introduced into Europe in the late 15th century by the Moors. Craftsmen who practiced this art were among the very first to come to America, and many of our founding fathers were directly involved in it. Benjamin Franklin, for example, sold leather to craftsmen. All over the world, palaces and cottages alike are richer because of the marriage of wood and leather on books, chairs, desk tops, tabletops and boxes. The 17th-century Dutch, among others, used gold-tooled leather wallpaper.

The first thing to do is to obtain the leather, because it must fit into a recess routed or paneled to a depth equal to its thickness. And because goats and cows, like woodworkers, come with hides of varying thickness, it's best to have the leather in your hand before doing any routing or grooving. Don't go by the supplier's sample cards because your hide will most likely be thicker or thinner. Goats and cows are the two best and most popular hides, but you can use anything from moose to shark. I would not recommend sealskin because it is too oily, or sheepskin (often called "roan") because it does not wear well. Avoid "skiver," which is sheep hide split very thin. While ideal for labels on books and covers for cameras, it is far too thin for the top of a desk or a card table.

Cowhide is a good choice. When it comes off the cow it is fairly smooth, a perfect surface for writing. Some manufacturers, however, roll it under big steel drums that emboss the leather with a grain that simulates the more expensive goatskins called "morocco." With cowhide, though, take care that no ferrous metal touches the leather when it is damp, or a dark and very permanent stain will result.

Goat is tougher than cow and easier to handle when wet, but considerably more expensive. The best goat is morocco; the best morocco, Niger. Since goats are small animals, you

Sandy Cohen, 30, is assistant professor of English at Albany (Georgia) State College. An avid amateur woodworker and leatherworker, he has demonstrated leather bookbinding for an educational television series.

will probably have to use cowhide if the area to be covered is more than two or three feet square.

Hides are usually sold by the whole skin or, in the case of large cows, by the side. Buy a side to avoid the spine, which is darker in color, rougher in texture and somewhat unsightly. Spines are good for book spines, but not secretary tops. When ordering your leather, send the dimensions of the area to be inlaid, and perhaps a rough diagram, to ensure that you get a large enough hide. You will need some extra for cutting and paring and will probably want the scraps to practice tooling before going on to the real thing.

If you want your handiwork to last, buy leather that is stamped "guaranteed to withstand the PIRA (Printers Industry Research Association) test." Technicians at the British Museum found that leather subjected to the modern tanning process decays because it creates sulfuric acid out of the sulfur spewed into the air by automobile exhaust, smoke, and so on, or absorbs free sulfuric acid already in the air from the same sources. They also found that treating leather with a potassium lactate solution interferes with acid absorption and hence prevents decay. Such PIRA-treated leather is considerably more expensive, not only because it has been treated but also because only the better grades are deemed worthy.

You can treat your own leather simply and inexpensively, both before and after tooling. Wipe the leather with a clean, dry flannel rag, then apply a generous amount of potassium lactate solution, available from leather suppliers, with a cotton ball. The next day, apply an even more generous amount of leather dressing and let it dry for three days, then wipe off the excess and polish gently with a flannel rag. The best leather dressing I know is Formula No. 6, a 2:3 mixture of anhydrous lanolin and neat's-foot oil. Buy it ready-made or mix your own. Potassium lactate prevents decay; dressing keeps the leather moist and supple. You should apply the potassium lactate solution and dressing to any valuable pieces of leather you have. PIRA-treated leather needs treatment only after tooling.

You will also need some paste to attach the leather to the wood. I recommend paste rather than glue because paste penetrates the pores better and makes for a longer-lasting bond. I know of leather pieces many hundreds of years old that are still sticking tightly, though they were pasted "only" with starch. My favorite formula is as follows: In a clean widemouthed jar, place 3 tablespoons of a gloss laundry starch such as Argo, ¼ teaspoon of powdered alum, ¾ tablespoon of powdered white chalk such as that used for chalk lines, 2 drops of oil of wintergreen, and enough cold water to stir into a mixture the thickness of cream. *Slowly* add boiling water, stirring constantly until it suddenly thickens. Then stop adding water, but stir until the mixture is smooth.

You will also need some newspaper for pasting up the leather. Get unprinted news (from art-supply stores) if the

175

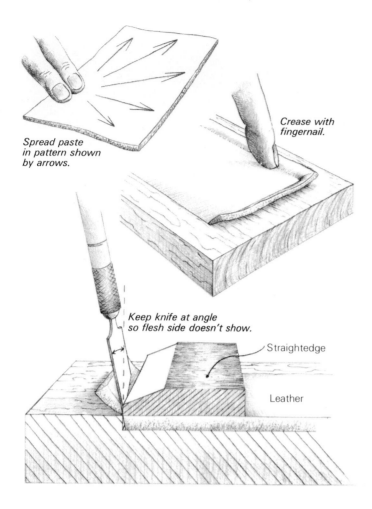

Spread paste
in pattern shown
by arrows.

Crease with
fingernail.

Keep knife at angle
so flesh side doesn't show.

Straightedge

Leather

leather is very light-colored, or "fair," that is, undyed.

Once the leather has arrived and you have routed or paneled the recess to receive it, cut a pattern out of light cardboard or heavy wrapping paper. This pattern should fit the recess exactly. Then place the pattern on the leather, flesh side up (the "fuzzy," undyed or "bad" side that will be pasted) and mark the leather. Before cutting, turn the leather over to be sure you are satisfied with the grain and texture on the good side. If not, reposition your pattern on the back. When the leather is marked, cut it slightly larger than pattern size with a sharp, small-bladed knife and straightedge.

Now place your leather, good side up, on a piece of newsprint and lightly sponge with water—only enough to dampen the leather. Use a cotton ball for all sponging, wiping and gold lifting. This dampening causes the leather to stretch out slightly and dry tight and flat. Now turn the leather over and

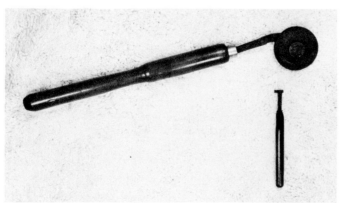

Gold can be tooled with either roll (top) or stamp.

apply the paste, spreading it with a round brush or with the fingers in the pattern shown. Spreading it this way ensures that the leather stretches evenly. Then fold the pasted side of the leather over on itself to "set" for a minute or so and spread paste on the wooden surface. Don't use too much paste—you don't want it to squeeze through the pores of the leather. Next, unfold the leather and spread it smooth in the recess, stretching it out with your fingertips in the same way you spread the paste. When it begins to stick, run your fingernail along the borders to crease the leather enough to see where to trim, then cut along the crease line with a knife and straightedge. Hold the knife with the handle angled away from the leather to ensure that no "white," or flesh, shows on the surface. If your leather is cowhide and your straightedge ferrous metal, put a piece of waxed paper between them to prevent unsightly staining.

With your fingertips, push the trimmed leather toward the borders for a good tight fit. The leather should be sticking by now. To be sure that it won't buckle or pull away from the borders, you might want to turn over the whole pasted-up piece and rest the leather on a few sheets of newspaper or unprinted news. The surface beneath the paper must be smooth; any imperfections will be transferred to the leather. Apply some light pressure with books and allow it to dry overnight. Do not apply too much pressure or the paste will seep through and give the leather a grey cast impossible to remove. The inlay should be perfect in the morning. But if any edge or corner has not stuck, dampen it with a small brush, lift slightly, repaste and work it into place.

There are two basic kinds of tools for tooling leather: rolls and stamps. Rolls are brass wheels with a continuous design engraved on their edges. One simply heats the tool on a stove and runs it along the leather. Rolls are quite expensive, and used ones are very hard to find. Even more expensive are the rolls with their own heating elements. The main advantage of rolls is that they save time, especially on long borders. But stamps, which have one design engraved into brass and are fitted with a wooden handle, can do an equally good job. They are much less expensive and can even be cut from brass scrap or bronze brazing rods.

Make sure the gold you buy is genuine. There are a lot of imitations on the market, many of them cleverly packaged. Genuine gold must by law say "genuine gold leaf" and give the gold content in carats. Real gold comes in books of 25 leaves, each 3¼ in. sq. Be wary of labels that read "gold metal leaf foil," or some such. Most phony gold leaf that I have tested tarnished completely within six months after application, some within two.

To cut your gold leaf you need a gold cushion and knife. The cushion is a piece of wood at least 6 in. sq., padded lightly with cotton, then covered with a soft leather, flesh side out. A new piece of chamois from your local auto supplier is perfect. This leather is sprinkled with rottenstone or very fine pumice to keep the gold leaf from sticking to it. You can use any thin-bladed, sharp, flexible knife, or buy one made specially for cutting gold.

Gold also comes in tooling rolls of Mylar atomized on one side with gold and presized. This is the easiest form of gold to use and gives excellent results. With Mylar rolls you don't need a gold cushion or glair. And they come in other metals and color pigments besides genuine gold.

If you are going to use gold leaf, you will need glair, the

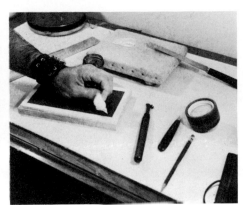

Special gold knife, lightly dusted with fine pumice, lifts sheet of genuine gold leaf. Beware of imitation gold, which tarnishes within months.

Lightly greased cotton ball transfers bit of gold leaf from gold cushion (in background) to glair-treated section of leather.

Heated stamp presses gold from Mylar roll into glair-coated impression.

mordant that makes the gold stick to the leather. Traditional glair is a preparation of egg white and vinegar. If you don't think eggs will make the gold stick as well as something more modern might, let me tell you that it has been used for well over 400 years. I have seen a number of books that were tooled with egg glair in the 16th century; the gold is still intact and bright. To make glair, beat up one egg white with ¼ teaspoon of vinegar until it froths. Let it sit overnight in a covered dish, then strain it into a jar with a funnel and a filter of clean cotton linen—a piece of an old bedsheet is fine. Keep the jar tightly covered. After a while the glair will smell horrible, but will still be usable.

If you don't want to make your own glair, you might want to try B. S. glair, a varnish formula based on French glairs first developed in the 18th century. It is much less troublesome to use, requires less heat, allows more time before it is ineffective and gives cleaner results.

If you are going to use gold leaf and traditional glair you must prepare the leather. Wash it over with a cotton ball slightly dampened with water, or water and vinegar. Some people like to put a little paste into the wash water, but I find that it dulls the leather. Old-time finishers often add some clear urine, I have never tried it. Now, with a good artist's brush, brush the glair only over the area to be tooled. Egg glair discolors the leather slightly, so neatness counts. When the glair is dry (when it looks dry and isn't sticky), apply a second coat, not as generously as the first. While it dries, prepare your gold leaf on the cushion. Open the book of gold to expose the first leaf. Slip your knife, which is free of grease and lightly dusted with rottenstone or fine pumice, under the gold, lift it, and transfer it to the cushion. If it does not lie flat, blow on it gently from directly above. Then cut the gold into appropriate strips with a very light back-and-forth motion. Cut only the gold, not the cushion.

As soon as the glair is dry, smear some light grease, such as petroleum jelly, onto the back of your hand, then rub a cotton ball in the grease to transfer a minute amount to the cotton. Rub the cotton gently on the leather wherever you intend to lay gold. This tiny amount of grease will hold the gold in place until it is tooled. Now lift a strip of gold with the lightly greased cotton ball and place the gold on the greased leather.

With the gold strip in place, heat the brass roll until it just sizzles when touched to a damp cotton ball or sponge. The etched surface of the tool should be shiny; if it isn't, buff it

on a piece of leather rubbed with red, or jeweler's, rouge. An etched surface that does not shine will mean a gold surface that does not shine.

The correct pressure and heat to apply are a matter of practice, since every piece of leather is different. But that is what your scrap leather is for. Cowhide needs less heat than goat, and for goat the tool should just sizzle.

Once the leather has been sized with egg glair, it must be tooled as soon as possible, certainly within two hours. With B. S. glair, once the second coat is dry (which takes an hour) the surface can be tooled anytime within two months, or longer. The tools can be cooler, with less chance of leather being burned, and there is no need to add moisture by sponging the leather with water, paste, urine or anything else.

If you don't have a roll, you can obtain excellent results with a stamp. Amateurs may get better results because one works with a paper pattern the exact size of the leather inlay. Any paper will do. After making the pattern, draw light pencil lines with a straightedge where you intend to make your border. Now, using your brass tool and an ink stamp pad, stamp in the border. When the pattern is to your liking, place tracing paper over the pattern and restamp the tracing paper in the same way you stamped the pattern. Tape the tracing paper to the wooden borders of the leather, clean the ink from your tool, heat it slightly (to the point where it is uncomfortable to touch) and impress through the tracing paper onto the leather. If needed, go over the impressions with the tool directly on the leather. Rock the tool in slightly in all directions to make sure the whole tool touches the leather, but be careful not to make a double or smeared impression. The impressions on the leather should be clear but not too deep. Then they are painted in with glair, greased and inlaid with gold leaf. The gold will stick only on the glair, where the heated tool touches it. The impressions should show through the gold; if they don't, pat the gold down with the cotton ball until they do.

If the gold cracks or tears, put another piece of leaf right over the first. In fact, it is probably a good idea to lay down double thicknesses of gold all over. When the gold is in place, re-impress the heated tool into the impression. The tool should barely sizzle when laid on the wet sponge. Hold it on the sponge until it just stops sizzling, then impress it on the leather. With B. S. glair, the tool can be a bit cooler.

With presized gold on Mylar rolls, simply tape the roll in place, shiny side up, then impress the heated tool. There

Full-sized paper pattern, right, has been traced, then imprinted in leather, before tooling border with presized Mylar roll.

is no glair, wash-up or fuss. You cannot do intricate patterns with a Mylar roll, but for borders it is perfect—the roll itself is a guide to straightness.

Once the gold is impressed, clean off the excess by wiping with a piece of flannel, then applying naphtha or benzine (not benzene, which is dangerous and will remove all the gold if you have used a Mylar roll). If the gold has not stuck properly, either the glair was too weak or dry, or the tools were too cool, or the tool failed to touch all corners. If the gold is dull, or "bleeds" over the impression, the tool was too hot or the glair too wet. Places that do not stick can sometimes be reworked if you are very careful.

Tooling in "blind," that is, without gold, is tricky, but correctly done, it leaves a rich, dark impression. Use a warm tool and slightly damp leather. If the tool is too hot, it will burn the leather, something much easier to do when the leather is moist. The tools should be just hot enough to be uncomfortable to hold for more than a second. Sponge over the section of the leather to be tooled just before the tool touches it. On light-colored leathers, sponge the entire piece, so as not to leave water marks. Touch the tool repeatedly to the same place until the desired darkness is achieved. Each time the tool touches the damp leather the leather is made drier, and the tool cooler, and each time, you must hold the tool in place longer. Some workers advocate holding the tool in a candle until it is sooty with lampblack, then impressing this soot to the leather. I don't recommend this method because the soot can smear. It is far less permanent and looks not as rich—like staining pine to make it look like oak.

A final treatment of potassium lactate solution and leather dressing completes the job. □

AUTHOR'S NOTE: Specialty shops carry leather and tooling supplies. Basic Crafts, 1201 Broadway, New York, N.Y. 10001 sells leather, stamps, adhesives and gold (free catalog). TALAS, 104 5th Ave., New York, N.Y. 10011 has leather, stamps, gold, adhesives, potassium lactate, Formula No. 6 and B.S. glair (catalog, $1). Amend Drugs, 117 E. 24th St., New York, N.Y. 10010 and Newberry Library, 60 W. Walton St., Chicago, Ill. 60610 both sell potassium lactate and Formula No. 6. A good general supplier is Tandy, 115 W. 45th St., New York, N.Y. 10036 (catalog, $1), though the leather I've tried was quite below par.

Cutting Corners

How to mount marquetry

by Peter L. Rose

Many marquetarians still use white glue and a press to mount their pictures, because they aren't sure how to use the modern contact glues. And many who have advanced to contact glue use a brown-paper slip-sheet to align the picture and the board. Either way, it is very difficult to make mitered border veneers meet precisely at the corners of the mounting board. The methods described here are the least complicated and most direct solutions to these problems.

Trimming veneer

Once the marquetry picture is complete, the edges must be trimmed square and clean so the border veneers can fit tightly against them. Use a carpenter's square to mark two adjacent sides, and continue around the picture by lining up one arm of the square with one of the lines previously drawn. With a single-edge razor blade, make several passes against each edge. Do not try to cut through in one pass as this may damage the veneers.

My $30 foreign-made veneer trimmer works well on straight-grained veneers but not on irregular-grained wood. This trimmer is difficult to operate because the blade has to be set at a fixed depth; it is awkward to control when going over the veneer in several passes. Used in one pass, its cut is not perfectly straight and either splits the wood or follows the grain. This trimmer is not to be confused with a veneer saw, which works well, but for a perfectly flush cut (in matching veneers or making borders) sawn veneer must have a final sanding or planing in a wood jig.

My own veneer trimmer costs almost nothing and for me it works better. The advantage is that several passes can be made, lowering the blade a little each time by a slight hand movement. Thus it is easier to trim irregular grains and hard

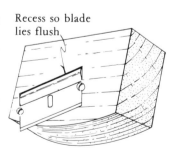

Inexpensive homemade veneer trimmer is fashioned from scrap block and single-edge razor blade, attached at an angle. Perfectly even bottom permits scoring, then successively deeper cuts. Metal straightedge can be held against back side of block, as shown here, or against razor-blade side.

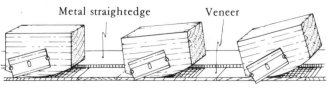

veneer. The 3/4-in. wide block of wood keeps the blade perpendicular. Because of the curved bottom, each pass can cut more deeply. The curved bottom can be cut with a sabre saw, or on a power jigsaw with the table perfectly flat. Medium sandpaper glued or attached with double-faced tape to the bottom of a metal ruler makes a guide that will not slide on the veneer. I change blades frequently—one blade can be used twice by turning it around. Dimensions of the trimmer aren't critical, but the bottom must be even, or it will stray away from the straightedge.

Borders

Four strips of veneer should be prepared for the borders, but a good inch wider than required and several inches longer. Lay them tightly along each side of the picture, front side up, with the corners overlapping, and tape to the front. Now turn the picture over, so the back side is facing up, as in the drawing at the bottom of this column. Put two small pencil marks on each border veneer an equal distance from the picture itself, cut the mounting board to size, and align it between these marks. Pencil a line around the board on the border veneers and write ''back'' on the board so you can replace it exactly the same way. Remove the board, and with straightedge and single-edge razor blade cut from each corner of the picture through the corners you just penciled on the borders. Do this very carefully, as you will be going through two layers of veneer. Remove the waste and the border miters should fit exactly together. Miters cut this way will always meet exactly at the corners of the board, even if the board is not cut quite to size or is a little out of square.

Turn the picture over again, tape the entire face with masking tape butt-to-butt, and remove the tape from the back side. In a paper cup mix crack filler (sanding dust) with white glue until it is creamy and press it into any cracks with a putty knife. Remove excess filler and lay a board over the picture for several hours. When the filler is dry, the picture is ready to glue. I prefer Constantine's veneer glue because it is thinner and easier to work with than other brands of contact cement. Do not use water-based contact glues for marquetry, because the water will cause the veneers to expand, and gaps will be created in the picture.

Back

To veneer the back of the mounting board, choose a piece of veneer about an inch too large on all sides. Lay the back side of the mounting board on the veneer and pencil a line around the board. Spread contact cement thinly on both sur-

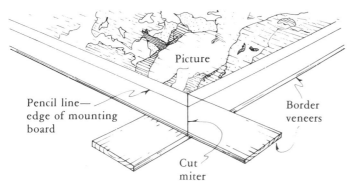

With reverse side up and oversize borders taped to picture, miters can now be cut through both borders at once to ensure perfect fit.

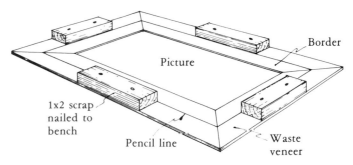

Scrap pieces nailed to waste veneer outside pencil lines form frame that aligns mounting board during glue-up with contact cement.

faces. If the wood is porous it is best to let the first coat dry and apply a second coat. Go beyond the pencil line to make sure the edges will adhere. When the glue is dry, nail four pieces of 1x2 or similar scrap wood to the veneer along the outside of the pencil lines. This creates a frame into which the mounting board can be dropped, to ensure perfect alignment. The scrap wood won't stick to the veneer because contact glue must be on both surfaces before it can make a bond.

Carefully lift the board by its edges and turn it over, glue side down. Hold it over the veneer, a fraction of an inch below the surface of the four pieces of scrap wood, and drop it squarely into place. Apply a little pressure with your hands, then remove the nails holding the scrap to the bench. Turn the board over and roll down the veneer to ensure contact. Now with your veneer saw trim off the overhanging veneer.

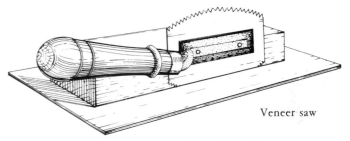

Veneer saw

Always triple-check everything before gluing, because veneers once glued cannot be moved.

Edges

The edges of the board should be veneered next. Apply glue to two opposite edges and to two oversized veneer strips. When the glue has dried (usually about 20 minutes), hold the mounting board over one of the veneers and slowly lower it into place. Roll to ensure good contact, then trim with the veneer saw. Do the opposite edge next, then the remaining two sides in the same manner.

At last the board is ready for the picture itself. Lightly sand the back side of the picture, to make sure it is smooth and free of lumps. Lay the mounting board on the picture, with the back sides of both facing up, to verify that the miters, corners and pencil marks line up properly. Mark an *X* on the top edge of the board and of the picture so there will be no guessing, apply glue to both surfaces, let it dry, and tack down the guide strips, as when veneering the back of the board. Drop the board into place, roll down tightly and trim the edges. Your picture is ready for sanding and finishing.

Pete Rose is a founder of the Marquetry Society of America and writes for the Society's newsletter.

Parsons Tables
Building and veneering them

by C. Edward Moore

Solid walnut table with recessed glass top. Exposed rail tenons are mitered.

The Parsons table came into existence during the 1930s as a result of a simple drafting technique. Students of John Michele Franc of the Paris division of the Parsons School of Design were taught to block out a cube or rectangular prism and then to design an object within it. At some point the students and Franc decided that such a block form itself could be a design solution. Consequently, the first Parsons table was produced and one of Franc's own designs is in the collection of the Cooper-Hewitt Museum in New York City.

A Parsons table is a rectangular table that appears to be made of stock of one thickness. Simplicity has made these tables a stock item with interior decorators (especially those besieged by clients with visions of "modern eclectic"). They are frequently placed behind a sofa to support a lamp. Large cities, where contemporary design is most likely to flourish, sometimes have small shops specializing in wooden Parsons tables. One also finds wicker, plastic, metal, glass-topped, painted and plastic-laminated Parsons tables. It is possible to adapt this style to obtain a wide variety of results.

It would appear that the easiest way to make such a simple item as a Parsons table would be with solid wood, with the skirt outside and around a beautiful solid wood top. I made such a table once, with a beautiful butcher-block walnut center, finished it with much elbow grease, and gave it as a wedding gift. Six months later there was a split (in the table, not the marriage). The violation of grain direction doomed it from the start, despite the valiant efforts of resorcinol glue. Consequently, I am convinced that it is virtually impossible

to make a true Parsons table with a solid top and solid rails that will withstand the test of time. A parquet top might be the exception.

Industry has produced a vast assortment of false or floating tops in this style of table to circumvent the problem. Many such tables are laminated or lacquered particle board, designed more for quick sale than for strength or durability. In general, Parsons tables are among the worst-made items available from any source. One eventually concludes that a Parsons table with wood as its visible surface should be veneered over a sturdy base.

Some early thought should be given to the veneer. If you are new to veneering, stick with mahogany, walnut, oriental-wood and other "strong" veneers, and avoid thinner veneers such as rosewood and the burls. If you aren't using any matching, some attention should be given to "loose" versus "tight" sides of the veneer. Flick your finger across the end of a piece of veneer and note from which side little pieces chip. This is the loose side and when possible it should be the glue side rather than the exposed side. Obviously this is of more concern with some veneers than others. I frequently maximize the randomness in the butcher-block patterns I use and violate the principle just stated. Some books ignore this subject and others seem to say little more.

Let's discuss an end table 21 in. wide, 31 in. long and 22 in. high, with stock thickness *a* 2⅜ in. These are arbitrary dimensions, provided only for ease of discussion. It is best to use a leveler or glide on the bottom of the legs, and to account for it in designing the height of the table. I start with 4/4 poplar, which I plane and laminate in three layers with Titebond glue. (I use Titebond glue for the entire project when making a table this size.) Then I rip, joint and plane the poplar to stock that is 2⅜ in. square. Suitable solid stock could be used for smaller tables.

For the legs, cut four pieces 5/16 in. shorter than the final height of the table, or 21 11/16 in. long. I try to add a touch of elegance by beveling the inside of the legs, but this is a matter of personal taste. The next step is to veneer the inside of the legs, before cutting the joints.

It is important that the beveled side of the leg be veneered first, then the two adjoining sides, because this sequence will yield the fewest visible seams. I apply the glue to the leg with a rubber roller or brayer, to get a uniform application. Then I place the veneer on the glue-covered wood and clamp the assembly against a suitable flat surface. Sometimes I roll the veneer with a dry rubber roller before clamping.

Glue spread with a roller seems to dry very quickly, so some haste is required. But use no more glue than is necessary. If

Parsons table appears to be made from stock of constant thickness, a, although it looks best when inside of leg is beveled as shown. Veneer the bevel first, clamping with V-block, then veneer adjoining sides.

2⅜"
1⅜"
45°

Ed Moore is an associate professor of mathematics at the U.S. Naval Academy in Annapolis, Md. His work is usually on display at Elizabeth Interiors in Annapolis.

you apply too much glue it will either seep through the porous veneer or form dry pockets, leaving you with either a sandwich of leg and clamping bench, or a lumpy surface. To avoid making a sandwich, cover the bench with a plastic film such as "Glad Wrap" (but not waxed paper, because it can mess up finishes). The plastic forms a moisture barrier, so the clamping time must be increased and after removing the clamps the wood should be allowed to sit undisturbed overnight, until the moisture dissipates.

It takes a little care to trim the veneer at the bevel. Place the veneered side down on a piece of scrap wood and insert a piece of waste veneer between the stock and cutting tool. I find a serrated veneer knife most convenient. Cut carefully and then plane or sand off the little lip of veneer that remains. A slip or split here can lead to a very ugly repair. Next veneer the adjacent inside faces in the same way.

With three of the five sides veneered, one may start cutting and fitting the joints at the top of the leg. Cut a ½-in. shoulder 2¹⁄₁₆ in. from the top of the leg on the inside faces, leaving a 1⅞-in. square cross section. Then cut open mortises ½ in. wide and ¾ in. long, and ½ in. from the outside. I use a router mounted under a table. This is a lot of wood to remove in a single pass, and it is best to drill out some of the waste first. Extreme care must be taken to have the fences fit snugly and to control the feed carefully.

The end and side rails are each 2¼ in. shorter than the respective outside dimensions of the table, so you need two pieces 18¾ in. long and two pieces 28¾ in. long. For the top I use ⅝-in. imported 11-ply birch plywood. To accommodate it, it is necessary to cut a rabbet ½ in. wide and ⅝ in. deep into the inner edge of the side and end rails. For balanced construction, you must completely veneer the rails. Cover the 1¾-in. inside face first, then the bottom of these four pieces. Each end of each rail gets a tenon ¾ in. long, ½ in. thick and ½ in. from the outside edge. I crosscut the shoulders on the radial arm saw (using a stop-block for uniformity) and rip the other cuts on a band saw, (using a rip fence). A dry fit of a rail and a leg shows two things: One, you need a ½-in. miter on the inside shoulder, so cut it; and two, the rail is ⁵⁄₁₆ in. plus the veneer thickness higher than the top of the leg. Cut a dado ⁵⁄₁₆ in. deep across the top of each end of each rail, 2 in. or 2½ in. from the end. Adjust this cut to make the resulting surface flush with the top of the leg when the joint is in place. This will accommodate a cap, to prevent end grain from telegraphing through the veneer.

When everything fits, glue up the two end assemblies. Then dry-clamp the two side rails in place to get a precise measurement for the plywood top. Be sure the plywood has no hollow spots, and veneer its bottom side to balance the construction. With 11-ply stock, as opposed to 5-ply or 7-ply, this balance may be more cosmetic than actual. Now glue up the two end assemblies, side rails and top. By breaking the gluing into these segments you are more likely to get square corners and parallel legs. Sometimes I glue a cross-rail to the underside of the top, between the long sides of the table. If the table is so large that the 5/8-ply seems too thin I glue another layer of plywood, of a size to fit tightly between the rails, to the underside. I always use glue blocks between the top and rails, as insurance, and a 3-in. mitered brace at each corner. The brace solidifies the leg construction when it is glued to the top and screwed into the adjoining rails.

I cap the corners with ⅜-in. poplar that is 2 in. wide and

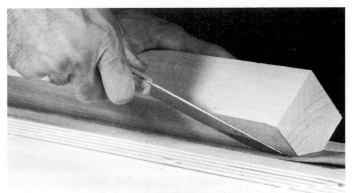

When the glue has set, use a serrated veneer knife, or a veneer saw, to trim the excess veneer and plane flush.

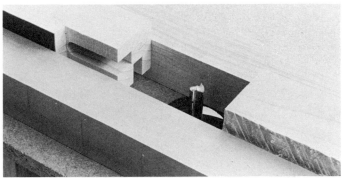

With some of the waste drilled out, a two-flute straight bit in the router table is used to mortise the legs.

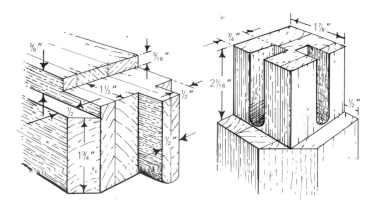

Typical leg-rail joint is dimensioned above, and fits together as shown below. End caps strengthen joint and keep grain from telegraphing through veneer.

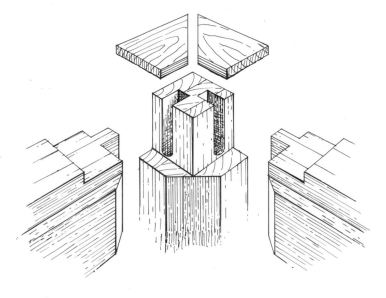

mitered to cross the corner. After these eight pieces are glued in place it is best to let the table sit idle for a day or so while the glue cures. Then hand-plane to true up the surfaces at the corners. Now the only exposed end grain is on the bottom of the legs. Capping avoids the telegraphing of end grain, which one can see on old pieces where uncapped dovetailed corners are veneered. This is the "ring around the collar" of veneer work and should be avoided. Also, running the caps back onto the rails strengthens the joints.

The outer surfaces of the table will be veneered in the order of end, side and top. Now the advantage gained by veneering the inside of the legs and the underside of the rails while they were accessible becomes apparent. Matching veneer patterns is the dominant consideration in determining the overall appearance of the table, but the details are best left up to each maker and the wood he is using. I like the crispness of

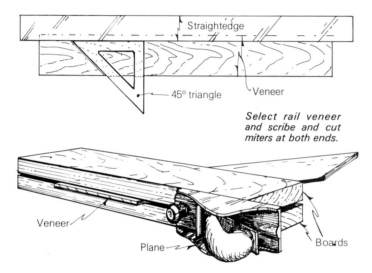

Select rail veneer and scribe and cut miters at both ends.

Sandwich the veneer between two boards to plane the miter clean and true.

mitered corners that meet exactly, and the drawings above show how I do it.

First, I veneer the ends of the table. Cut overlong strips for the rails and legs, at least a half-inch wider than dimension *a*. Choose a strip to cover an end rail and overlap ¼ in. of veneer with the long metal ruler. Find the finished length (21 in., at the 10-in. and 31-in. marks), and use a plastic drafting triangle to scribe the miters. Then cut them along a metal straightedge—I use a Stanley utility knife with a new blade, or a deluxe musical instrument maker's knife.

Sandwich each veneer between two boards with the mitered edge protruding 1/16 in., and use a shoulder or block plane to clean off the irregularities left by the knife. If you don't square up the cuts, the joints will open when you sand or scrape the finished surface.

Now cut a miter at one end of each leg piece, and join the three pieces of veneer together to form an overlarge *U*. Check each joint and get it perfect before taping tightly across the joints with several strips of masking tape. Then turn the veneer face down and apply a little glue with the joints cocked slightly open. Rub the glue into the joint with your finger, flatten out the veneer, and roll. Place a piece of tape across the glue line to equalize the tension of the tape on the other side. Avoid getting glue on the front. Place this veneer on a

flat surface and prevent the joint from buckling by applying a little weight (such as a plane) while the glue sets. The result should be a U-shaped piece that, when carefully placed, has joints crossing the interior and exterior corners exactly and appropriately.

Leave the tape on what will be the outside surface, but remove it from the inside and put the veneer face down on the bench, with the corresponding end of the table on top of it. Manipulate the arrangement until the corners do line up just right, and mark the position. Then turn the table over, remove all but one piece of tape from the veneer (take care not to break the joint), and apply glue to the table end.

When you glue, keep in mind that too much glue makes it difficult to clamp the veneer in place without drifting, and that clamping force applied even slightly askew can pull the joints apart. After spreading glue on the wood, place the veneer exactly in place and lay smooth 4/4 maple cauls across the rail and along the legs. First put bar clamps along the top side of the rail (anchoring them to the bench or to the other end of the table), and C-clamps along the bottom side of the rail. Then C-clamps with protective blocks go down both legs. Before tightening them down hard, I check and recheck the positioning to make sure nothing has drifted.

After removing the clamps and boards, carefully peel off the tape to avoid tearing up patches of veneer. Lacquer thinner will soften the tape and remove its traces. Trim, and repeat this process at the other end and on the sides. I clean up the edges of the veneer with a router and a three-flute carbide bit with ball-bearing guide. Be wary of grain directions. I pass the router in the opposite direction of normal feed so that it nibbles off the excess veneer. This prevents wholesale splitting, which can be disastrous if there is an area of nonadhesion at the edge. Trim the inside corners with a knife. Before moving on, feather (gently flick as if to lift) the trimmed edge with your finger to detect spots that did not adhere—the remedy is a little glue. Be very careful when you remove the clamp boards since there always seems to be a spot or two where glue comes through. Use a cabinet scraper to remove such debris from the clamping boards before using them again. And repeat the whole process on the other three sides

Tape and glue joints to get a U-shaped piece for end of table; repeat for the other end and both sides.

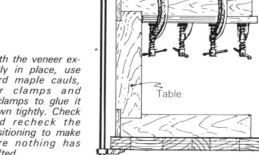

With the veneer exactly in place, use hard maple cauls, bar clamps and C-clamps to glue it down tightly. Check and recheck the positioning to make sure nothing has drifted.

Left, finished table in walnut veneer has butcher-block center field and crisply mitered corners. Veneered construction can be enhanced by geometric marquetry, center. Solid oak table, right, has ceramic-tile top and will be used for plants.

of the table. Now you are ready to veneer the top.

Although innumerable veneer patterns might be used, my most popular tabletop is walnut veneer in a butcher-block pattern, set inside a veneer border of width *a* (here 2⅜ in.) which adds to the illusion of constant dimension. Randomness and variety count more than pattern matching in achieving an attractive top.

Begin by laying out the border directly on the plywood tabletop and draw in the miters from the outside corner to the center field. Measure the center field—on this 21-in. by 31-in. table, it is 16¼-in. wide and 26¼-in. long. Use eight strips 2¹⁄₃₂ in. wide or ten strips 1⅝ in. wide. To obtain strips of uniform width and with good edges, pass the edge of a 30-in. piece of veneer across the jointer (or past a sharp router bit). Then cut a strip about ⅛ in. larger than needed. Cut a good second edge on the router table with a rip fence and a three-flute carbide bit. Tape and glue the joints one at a time, as before, cut the field to length and carefully plane across the edge to square it. The center field is done.

The four mitered joints of the border can be most difficult. Veneer matching, joint tightness and corner alignment are crucial. Start by jointing one edge of a 3-in. strip of veneer, and miter one end so the jointed edge is inside.

Fit this jointed edge and the mitered corner along one edge of the center field, tack it in place with tape, then scribe and cut the miter at the other end. Cut it the merest hair fat, so the knife-work can be planed clean, then tape tightly in place, turn over and rub glue into the joint.

Prepare the next strip the same way, with a jointed inside edge and a miter at one end, and fit it along an adjacent edge of the tabletop. Tuck the uncut end under the extended miter of the side already taped. Tack down with tape, then use the first miter as a guide to scribe and cut the new piece—again, allow a tiny bit extra and plane it clean. Tape and glue, and continue around the tabletop. If the miters drawn on the plywood table-

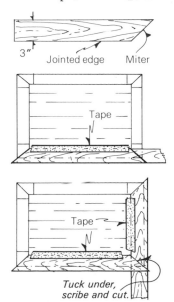

To fit the top border, scribe each miter from the real table, not from the drafting triangle.

top are not precisely 45°, prejudice your miter cuts in the veneer accordingly.

When the top is completely taped and glued together, remove the tape from the side that will be attached to the table. Remove all but a few strategic pieces from the exposed side, and place the veneers face down on the bench. Align the table on the veneer and mark the corner positions—a red pencil is easiest to see. Turn the table over again, roll a thin but uniform layer of Titebond glue onto it with a rubber roller (brayer), and move quickly because one side of the surface may dry before you finish spreading the glue. Carefully align the top on the table and clamp with care. I sometimes press the veneer down with a clean rubber roller before placing the clamping boards, and check the alignment again. Then cover with as many clamps as will fit. If the table is simply too big to be clamped, you will have to use contact cement—another problem altogether, and a course I do not recommend, whenever it can be avoided.

After trimming the edge, feather it with your finger to locate spots that didn't adhere and reglue them. Then pass your fingers lightly over the surface and listen carefully. At a bad spot it will sound almost as if you are passing over loose newspaper instead of solid material. When you suspect an area, tap it with your finger and again the sound will tell you if the veneer is not stuck down. Make a small slit with a razor blade, with the grain, inject a little glue with a syringe, and roll. Immediately wipe with a moist cloth to remove all exterior glue traces. The moisture in the glue and from the cloth will swell the slit back tight. Rub dry with a different cloth and roll again with a clean roller; clamp if necessary.

Don't use steel wool on bare veneer; it invariably snags and requires difficult repair. Never throw away any veneer scraps; you never know when a sliver will be needed for a repair. An oil finish, if necessary on, for example, rosewood, should not be allowed to saturate an area. If oils penetrate deeply, they may break down glues, especially contact cements. First test your finish on a sample. Satin urethane varnish over a light application and immediate rub-off of Watco oil have worked well on my walnut tables with butcher-block centers. Don't forget to stain the underside of the top if you used a dark veneer. Always apply finish to the underside to seal the wood and prevent warpage. The faint smile of surprise on the face of someone who runs a hand underneath a side or end rail and discovers a solid, finished surface is usually amplified when curiosity leads him to peek and discover that it is actually veneered. Somehow this justifies the extra effort and thorough approach we have taken. □

FINISHING

Stains, Dyes and Pigments
The wood grain should remain readable

by George Frank

We all love wood because of its endless variety of grain. To put the natural markings of the wood in evidence is the true task of anyone who tries to beautify it through finishing. Concerning beauty in woodfinishing, I have set up a rule for myself: The first requisite of a beautiful finish is that the wood must remain "readable." This means not only that the grain must be clearly visible after finishing—that is self-evident. It also means that from the grain of the wood, qualified people can read the whole history of the tree: its origins, age and environment, its fights for survival, its adventures.

Woodfinishing is the stepchild of the woodworking industry. Even its vocabulary is poor and misleading. We use the word "staining" when we refer to a chemical action that changes the color of the wood, to a process where a dye brings this change about, or to a process where we cover the wood with a colored film, or a thin layer of colored pigment. Only this last method should rightly be called staining. The first two should be called dyeing. The difference between dyeing and staining is like the difference between getting a deep suntan and using makeup to imitate one. While stains always reduce the readability of the wood, they have great merits, especially on the production line. Ease of application is one, but far more important is that stains help to achieve uniform coloring, and this, especially on the assembly line, is a fair compensation for the reduced readability.

Chemical action

Cuban mahogany has the color of raw steak. Sponge it with a solution of potassium dichromate, a yellow crystal, and its color deepens considerably. Not only does it become a dark rusty red, but the contrast between the light and dark markings becomes more accentuated. This chemical process, wrongly called staining, really enhances the beauty of the wood. Napoleon's craftsmen often used this process, and most French Empire furniture is "stained" by this method.

It is a well-known fact that wheat-colored oak becomes brownish-grey when sponged with ammonia. Here is a short story about another chemical action: In 1938, a Pennsylvania manufacturer imported a shipload of timber from Europe. To mystify the competition, he gave it a name—palazota. It looked like bird's-eye maple, but was whiter and had more eyes in it. He made bedroom suites of it and sold them successfully. By 1942, the market was saturated with white palazota bedrooms, and dealers asked for something new. Since he had over two-thirds of his lumber still in stock, he tried stains. His stains obliterated most of the delicate markings of the wood, and the stained palazota did not sell. That is when I was called in. After three weeks of experimenting, I found the answer. A weak solution of ferrous sulfate brought unbelievable changes to this wood. The miniature eyes opened

---

George Frank is a consulting editor of Fine Woodworking.

up considerably, while the flat areas remained almost unchanged. The wood seemed to acquire a third dimension, depth. When I added some coloring dyes to the ferrous chemical, I produced a whole new gamut of decorative effects. Regardless of whether the palazota was tinted grey, brown, gold or red, its markings always came out loud and clear. Three years later, the manufacturer did not have a single board left in his factory.

A simple example illustrates the possibilities: Apply potassium dichromate solution to a piece of birch or maple and the wood becomes pleasantly dyed a rich yellow color. Apply it to a piece of oak, and the wood becomes a dark rusty brown. So far so good. Now imagine that you can get somehow a cake of logwood extract, more scientifically called extract of campeche wood. Dissolve one ounce in a pint of water, and with this wine-like brew you sponge the three pieces of wood you are experimenting with. Let dry, sandpaper lightly and apply the potassium dichromate solution. After an hour you will find that the birch and the maple have become rusty brown, and the oak a rich chocolate color.

Potassium permanganate is a common chemical. One ounce dissolved in a pint of water will stain most hardwoods a pleasant brown. But the tint will fade and change color—from brown-violet to brown. If the color you get is too dark, wash down the wood with a fairly strong solution of sodium thiosulfate (available from photo-supply stores as hypo solution). You will get a nicely bleached wood.

Another woodfinishing concoction can be prepared by mixing equal amounts of ordinary vinegar and water, then throwing in all the rusty iron you can find—old nails, screws, hinges, tools and so on. Let sit for a week, then filter through a piece of cloth. The resulting liquid will produce a silvery grey color on oak. It won't be so effective, though, on woods lacking tannic acid. This can be remedied by prestaining with a mordant made of an ounce of tannic acid in a quart of water. Obviously the vinegar mixture is rather iffy, since its strength depends on the amount of iron the liquid will absorb. Ferrous sulfate dissolved in water (about 1½ oz. to one quart water) will produce a more positive and very pleasant grey color on oak.

Dyeing

Until about 1870, dyes for textiles or for wood were always extracted from plants, insects or animals, and rarely from minerals. For example, to obtain one pound of the dye called Tyrian purple, Mediterranean fishermen had to bring up close to four million mollusks (*Murex branderis*), break their shells individually and carve out a small sac from their bellies, which contained the coloring matter. The price of this dyestuff was so high that in ancient Rome, its use was reserved by law to royalty and to the princes of the church (hence its popular name, cardinal purple). Another red dye was brewed from a little bug, *Coccus cacti L.* Seventy thousand of these bugs had to give up their lives so that men could brew one pound of dye from their dried bodies. Only a hundred years ago, England imported seven million pounds of these dried insects annually. Tea is not only one of the most popular beverages in the world, it is also an excellent dye, used mostly on antique reproductions, since it conveys to the wood a pleasant golden hue, characteristic of many fine antiques. There are a few hundred of these natural dyes that can be used on wood, but progress has relegated them mercilessly to obsolescence.

A little over 100 years ago, W. H. Perkin accidentally came across the first aniline dye. Others were discovered in rapid succession and the era of synthetic dyes began. Between the two wars, a giant industry was born in Germany, the manufacturing of colors and dyes. A huge company, I.G. Farben, had almost a monopoly, and its subsidiary, Arti A.G., specialized in dyes for wood. There were no wood-coloring problems in Europe during the 1930s because Arti always had the answer. They had simple dyes that would give the selected color to nearly any wood. Other dyes involved two applications, a prestain, or mordant, which was followed by the dye, resulting in deeper penetration and more positive coloring. The most important tools in any woodfinishing shop during this period were a pharmacist's scale and a graduated glass to weigh and measure the proper amount of dye and water. All these dyes were properly numbered and matched a master color chart. Arti also supplied dyes to be dissolved in alcohol or in oils, for special needs. Before World War II, Arti tried to gain a foothold on the American market, evidently without success. I do not know of any manufacturer here that markets dyes for wood with proper color samples and reliable instructions. This does not mean that American-made dyes are inferior to European. I simply deplore that they are presented in a very haphazard way.

Pigments

Any solid substance that can be reduced to powder can become a pigment. With the proper carrier and a binder, it can become a pigmented stain. All pigmented stains have the same formula: pigment, carrier and binder. Again, let me give you an example from my past. The first person who ever sought my professional help was a small-town manufacturer of a line of children's furniture, such as playpens and high chairs. The local lumber he used varied so much in color that he simply could not obtain a uniform light finish. I mixed for him equal amounts of powdered chalk and French ochre powder, and stirred the mixture into a pail of lukewarm rabbit-skin glue solution. This simple stain not only solved his coloring problem, but also acted as a sealer on his wood. In this instance the chalk-ochre combination was the pigment, the water was the carrier and the glue was the binder.

The most popular and the best-known pigment-stains are the commercial oil colors. They contain very finely ground pigments mixed into the oil (the carrier), to which a drying agent is added (thus the oil becomes the binder, too). Almost always, the carrier in this mixture is extended with turpentine or other paint thinner. Pigment stains in general do not change the color of the wood. But even after the most thorough wiping off, some of the pigment remains on the wood and adds its own color to it.

There appears to be a clear-cut difference between the three ways of changing the color of wood. The reality is far

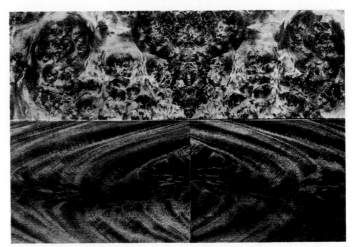

Top, ferrous sulfate brings out contrasting figure in 'palazota' maple, Bottom, mahogany treated with potassium dichromate gives illusion of great depth.

more complex. The three methods can be and very often are intermixed. My story about coloring the palazota illustrated how chemicals can be combined with dyes to create new horizons in changing the color of the wood. But that is just one story out of thousands. Chemicals can be mixed to dyes, dyes can be mixed to pigment-stains, and all three can be combined together to improve the quality of the finished products, this time correctly called "stains." Nearly any stain purchased in a paint store contains pigments, dyes and some chemicals (for deeper penetration), and all do an adequate job for the amateur, even for the average professional. The fine woodworker sticks to chemicals, natural dyes maybe, or accepts synthetic dyes to color the wood, but seldom uses pigment stains in spite of their great advantages and simplicity.

Application

Waterstains, dyes and chemicals should be generously applied with a sponge. The area to be dyed should be thoroughly soaked and then the excess should be taken off with the same sponge, squeezed out, to leave the wood uniformly moist. The stronger the concentration, the more potent the stain or dye. Chemical dyes, more than aniline dyes, should be used in weak concentration and applied repeatedly, since they show their final effect only after thorough drying, and it is far more difficult to lighten the wood than to darken it.

Some dyes can be dissolved in alcohol or lacquer thinner. Therefore, a liquid shellac can be further diluted and tinted with colored alcohol and the resulting colored shellac when applied would convey a tint to the surface. The same goes for the lacquer—if the thinner is colored, it becomes a tinting lacquer. Wax, varnish, shellac and lacquers can be tinted with dyes dissolved in their respective thinners. They can also be "loaded," that is, some finely ground coloring matter can be mixed into them—a fourth way of "staining" the wood. These four ways are very much like the four strings on a violin. The melodies one can play on these four strings are really endless, but the beauty of the melody depends on the person holding the bow. □

EDITOR'S NOTE: H. Behlen & Bros., Inc., Box 698, Amsterdam, N.Y. 12010 makes and sells a wide range of stains, pigments and dyes. Their products are also sold by Constantine, 2065 Eastchester Rd., Bronx, N.Y. 10461. For chemicals, check in the Yellow Pages under "Hobby Supplies" and "Chemicals."

Methods of Work

Staining curly maple

Curly maple—fiddleback, tiger-tail, or whatever you may call it—requires a staining technique all its own. Maple with a curl was the favorite wood for the stocks of the muzzle-loading rifles of yesteryear. The staining method described here has come down by word of mouth from the old gunsmiths.

Great-grandpa used two stains and he made both of them. For the first you must find a handful of rusty cut nails—very old and very rusty cut nails are best. Place about a dozen in a soup bowl and cover them with homemade apple-cider vinegar, the stronger the better. Do not use a metal dish and do not substitute synthetic vinegars or white vinegar. Cover to prevent evaporation and let stand for two weeks.

For the second stain, dissolve potassium dichromate crystals in water. It need not be a saturated solution but I use it fairly strong. You can buy these crystals, or you might try begging a few from your high-school chemistry teacher. This stain can be used immediately.

We will assume your curly maple stock is now in the white and you have it sanded smooth. Use a rag to coat the stock with the vinegar stain. When it dries it should be about the color of a slate roof—not very pretty. This stain will penetrate deeply into the soft spots, but it will only sit on the surface of the hard stripes. Allow an hour for drying, or speed it up a bit with some heat. Now with a good grade of 220 garnet paper, sand this stain off the hard stripes; you will be unable to sand it off the soft spots. Sand a bit more here and a bit less there to bring out all the figure. Be sure to use a sanding block. The stripes are very hard and the spaces are soft. Sanding without a block can result in a washboard effect.

Now, using a new swab, stain the stock with the potassium dichromate stain. This stain will penetrate those hard, white stripes and color them a rich orange-yellow. It will also change that slate color to a rich dark brown. When the second stain is dry, sand it off with a very fine paper. Now put several drops of boiled linseed oil in the palm of each hand and rub it in lovingly, lean back, and feast your eyes. The oil is only to bring out the color. Allow plenty of drying time before you apply your favorite finish.

If you prefer to stick to grandpap's methods, give it an oil finish. An old gunsmith put it this way: "...three drops of boiled linseed oil and then three weeks of rub." Use as little oil as possible to cover the stock.

—*Bob Winger, Montoursville, Pa.*

Removing mill marks

In order to achieve a good finish, the tiny ridges left by milling machines must be removed. The best method my students and I have found for removing mill marks is with the cabinet scraper (Stanley #80). The problem is being able to see these mill marks. By rubbing a piece of white chalk over the entire surface of a surfaced or jointed board, one can readily see these imperfections. The mill marks show up as white waves across the grain.

You can then scrape with a cabinet scraper until the chalk marks—and the mill marks—disappear. Drag the chalk across the stock again and it will hardly leave a mark. Using a cabinet scraper also reduces sanding time.

—*Dennis W. Kempf, Bellevue, Wash.*

Notes on Finishing
Avoid the unseemly rush to glue up

by Ian Kirby

Compared to the paucity of attention given to the preparation stages of woodworking, a plethora of technical data is available about various wood finishes. Despite this, many otherwise fine pieces of work are spoiled at this final stage. Finishing problems seem to create as many problems at the end of a job as bad preparation of wood creates at the start.

Everybody seems to understand the need for extreme care and discipline when cutting joints and fitting pieces together. Yet when it comes to the finishing work, the time needed is usually underestimated. Then the urge to get the piece put together for the last time often overrides the need to assemble and finish in a considered sequence and under careful conditions. Ironically, an undignified rush to glue up before everything is absolutely ready inevitably requires substantially more time for finishing than would otherwise have been the case, and the result can only be less than acceptable.

This is not another article about wood finishes as such. It is an attempt to make a few points, which in my experience seem often to be forgotten at the finishing stage.

Cleaning up, applying a finish and assembly are all related parts of the finishing stage. The most common error is not to see them as such, especially where assembly is concerned. People glue together full or part assemblies and forget that it is far easier to clean up a piece of wood when it is separate from any other than to clean it up when it is glued into an assembly. Where two or more pieces come together at right angles to each other as in, say, a frame, it is virtually impossible to plane the inside surfaces or even to sand them properly without considerable frustration and sometimes taking the skin off the knuckles. Even when one is prepared to make this sacrifice, it remains impossible to reach right into the corners and a good crisp result simply cannot be achieved. It is also difficult to apply finish, at least by hand methods, to inside surfaces.

In general, it is best to prepare the surface for finishing with a minimum amount of sanding. The best finish comes from wood that is carefully smooth-planed, then sanded lightly (if at all) with 220-grit paper. This is particularly true when working ring-porous hardwoods, which may have considerable variation in density between earlywood and latewood. Excessive sanding cuts down the harder tissues in each growth ring, and depresses the soft tissues. As soon as the finish hits the wood, the compressed soft tissue springs back and the surface may become quite rough.

Once the piece is ready to go together, a sequence has to be worked out for each particular job, along the following lines: All inside and subsequently inaccessible surfaces should be planed with a very sharp smoothing plane and sanded lightly with fine garnet paper. Then they need to be dusted and given their full, final finish. Great care must be taken not to contaminate the surfaces to be glued during assembly, since the finish would prevent adhesion. Nevertheless it is necessary to apply the finish right up to the part to be glued.

Doing it this way saves time and energy and ensures high quality. Other benefits also accrue. During assembly glue inevitably will squeeze out from the joints, leaving beads and dribbles on the work. If the surface of the wood is polished these can be, indeed should be, left strictly alone to cure. Resist the strong temptation to wash or scrape them off immediately. Once they have cured they will simply fly off when the edge of a chisel is eased gently under them, leaving no trace or mark. Had the work not been polished, the glue would have penetrated the wood. Even if an attempt had been made to wash it off immediately, some would have still entered the surface tissue of the wood, since washing only dilutes the glue and increases its rate of absorption. If the wood is cleaned up before assembly but not polished, the squeezed-out glue will have to be chiseled off. This can only result in damage to the surfaces, in precisely those places inaccessible to cleaning-up tools. Further, the residual glue on the surface of the wood forms a barrier to polish applied over it, and shows up as an unsightly mark about which little can be done.

These considerations don't matter with surfaces on the outside or accessible to planing after assembly, because they won't yet have been cleaned up. Indeed, it would be unwise to smooth-plane such surfaces before assembly, as they are often scuffed and dirtied while the piece is being put together.

Why finish?
Wood finishes have to cater to at least five requirements: 1) to keep dirt out of the wood; 2) to prevent degrade of the wood surface as a result of abrasion and heat; 3) to produce visual and tactile qualities; 4) to bring out the colors in the wood, and 5) to slow down moisture exchange with the air.

I don't intend to go into great detail about all the different finishes available nor to describe the merits or debilities of each, relative to these five requirements. Indeed, a full accounting would require a lengthy excursion into exotic chemical technology. The point I do want to emphasize is that no one finish can be regarded as best, separate from the specific requirements of the job at hand.

In all but the most stringently clean conditions, wood will be degraded through discoloration from dirt, unless the finish provides a barrier. If it were not for the fact that wood absorbs debris from the atmosphere and through direct contact, it would need no finish at all.

The second requirement, to prevent degrade of the surface, is related to the first. But here I have in mind potentially more harmful agents such as physical and chemical abrasion and wet and dry heat. The degree to which such degrade can be repaired is a factor to weigh against the longevity of any finish that is not easy to repair.

The available choices of visual and tactile qualities are determined primarily by whether the finish resides in the wood, such as waxes and oils, or on top of its surface, such as lacquers and varnishes. This is a decision about texture. Once this decision has been made, the maker must choose the degree of gloss the surface is to have. The range from gloss to matte is narrow with waxes and oils, but very broad with varnishes and lacquers, from totally matte to mirror glossy. However, the choice is determined by the manufacturer—there is little a maker can do to transform a glossy varnish into a matte finish, and vice versa.

It has to be stressed that in touching a piece that has been

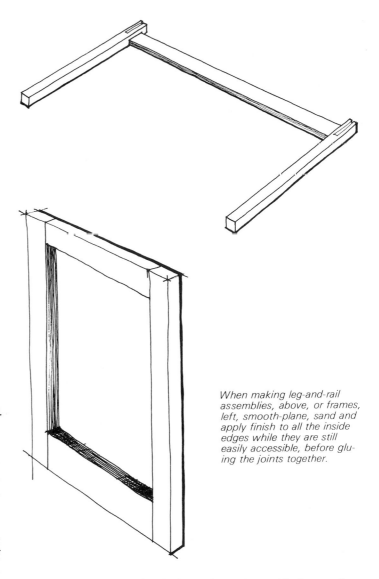

When making leg-and-rail assemblies, above, or frames, left, smooth-plane, sand and apply finish to all the inside edges while they are still easily accessible, before gluing the joints together.

lacquered or varnished, one is not in contact with the wood at all, but with the film lying over it. The number of coats of varnish or lacquer also affects visual and tactile qualities. Two light coats of varnish put directly onto the natural wood leave an open finish, in contrast to the full finish achieved by first filling the grain and then creating a build with a number of coats, each one being cut back before the next is applied, and the final one polished.

The fourth requirement, that of bringing out the colors in the wood, is often regarded more from an emotional point of view than from a practical one. For while some finishes do accentuate the visual characteristics, usually by differentiating light and dark features, others can discolor the wood far more than one might wish. Staining is a complete topic in itself, but it ought to be said that in the main it kills the visual qualities of wood, making it bland and lifeless. So much of the furniture one sees is adulterated in this way, and it's sad that so much beauty is stained away for spurious reasons.

The principal spurious reason for this state of affairs is usually given as economy. Manufacturers take wood randomly from the pile and cut whole sets of furniture "en suite," in whatever manner wastes the least, and then employ men to stain it all to uniformity. The public has come to expect walnut or maple always to have the same color it does in the furniture store. It probably would cost the industry less to employ a man to select the lumber at the start, as does a maker working alone, according to subtle variations in color and figure. The saving in finishing materials would offset any additional waste in cutting. And despite industry's perception of the public's expectations, most people—once they are given the chance—quickly come to relish the juxtaposition of heartwood and sapwood on a surface, and the beauty of the wood in all its color and variety. Indeed, this is a part of what gives custom furniture its quality. I never use stains, except when matching new parts to old in repair work.

Generally speaking, the visual qualities and certainly the tactile qualities of the wood are best brought out by the finishes that reside in the surface. However some light woods such as maple and sycamore tend to turn yellow, and lacquer or varnish inhibit this better than wax does. It is always a question of weighing one factor against the other.

Finally, no finish will prevent wood from taking up or losing moisture as the humidity of the atmosphere varies with the seasons, nor as a consequence from shrinking and expanding. Finishes do, however, provide an effective barrier against sudden changes in relative humidity and in this respect varnish or lacquer offers the most protection. This is also why all wood surfaces, both visible and invisible, should be finished in top-quality work.

Varnish and lacquer

Most people are aware of the advantages of varnish or lacquer over oils and waxes when it comes to protecting horizontal surfaces against wet and dry heat, and chemical abrasion. The tendency is, however, to think of on-the-surface finishes as entirely appropriate in all other situations, irrespective of whether the work is likely ever to meet harsh conditions, and in spite of the fact that varnish and lacquer have disadvantages in other directions, when compared to wax and oil. Also, there is no reason that one must apply the same type of finish to every part of a piece. For instance, a vertical surface rarely needs to be highly resistant to the wet and dry heat or chemical abrasion that a horizontal surface is liable to encounter. The tabletop clearly needs protection, while the apron and legs usually do not. Also, because of the way light and shadow work, we rarely see the same effect from a horizontal surface as from a vertical surface. There is no reason why they shouldn't be finished differently, to capitalize on the combined advantages of a variety of finishes.

I have used the terms varnish and lacquer together to refer to on-the-surface films. This is because there is tremendous confusion about just what each word means, aggravated by advances in chemical technology over the last 50 years. A century ago, each town or locality had its own paint maker who mixed varnish according to his own secret recipe. Usually the base was boiled linseed oil, with the addition of various gums, resins and dryers. The same preparation became paint with the addition of whitening and pigment. Such preparations were soluble in oil, turpentine and mineral spirits. The original lacquer, on the other hand, was shellac, prepared from the resinous deposits of the lac insect and soluble in alcohol. But things changed soon after the turn of the century with the development of nitro-cellulose lacquer, and since then with the creation of a veritable flood of synthetic resins.

Manufacturers first introduced these synthetic resins into existing varnish and lacquer mixtures. But chemists quickly developed more sophisticated, and more highly reactive, preparations that required new formulations. Most began as two-can products which the user had to mix, but people are

notorious about experimenting with directions and the resulting disastrous finishes forced the chemists to devise single-can preparations that polymerized upon contact with oxygen or moisture in the atmosphere or by internal catalysis. The result today is a profusion of clear wood finishes, marketed under the familiar old names of varnish and lacquer, but containing few of the original ingredients of these materials.

This is a case where big is better, since the research that goes into a modern finish is extraordinarily expensive, and so is the factory required to produce it. Indeed, most synthetic resins are made by a few large firms and sold in bulk to smaller producers of paint and varnish. These resins are vastly better than the products they have replaced, but they ought to be applied according to the directions on the can. Many furniture makers begin with commercial varnishes and mix their own oil-varnish preparations, according to experiment and intuition. It's possible to achieve good results this way ("Oil/Varnish Mix," Spring '76, pp. 46-47), but I never do it. I don't think I can match the research facilities of DuPont or Farben, especially when the label usually doesn't even tell precisely what is inside the can.

Most lacquers and varnishes may be sprayed on, but they can be applied with a brush or rag. If they are being applied to a veneered surface where the veneer has been bonded with white or yellow glue, it is always best to apply the first coat sparingly with a rag to form a seal, because an excess of lacquer may seep through the veneer and attack the glue line, resulting in blisters. I don't mean to dilute the preparation, but to rub a little of it over a large area. Once the grain has been sealed by the first coat, which must be abraded to denib the surface, subsequent coats should be applied sparingly and quickly without too much brushing in. Each coat should be allowed to flow out and left to cure.

One hazard to a glossy lacquer or varnish finish is floating dust from the air. The best way to avoid the problem is to work in a dust-free finishing room. Without such a room, one can guard against dust fall-out only by scrupulous cleanliness. Clear all the tools and debris from your bench, sweep well, and cover the bench top with a piece of clean plywood. Have nothing on the bench but the tools and materials you need for finishing. Apply finish to the furniture parts and lay them out flat on the plywood, then block up another piece of plywood over the work, as an umbrella against falling dust. If despite these precautions you do get dust in the finish, then you will have to sand out the offending spots with fine, worn paper and refinish.

Many makers attempt to turn a gloss finish into a matte finish by sanding or rubbing with steel wool. This scatters the incident light by abrading the top surface of the finish. The scratches are large at first, but the more rubbing the finer the scratches and the glossier the surface becomes. A glossy finish dulled with steel wool or pumice and oil will soon become shiny again under the normal abrasion of routine household cleaning. If you want a matte finish, buy a matte varnish or lacquer. These products contain stearates in suspension, which scatter the incident light by their presence throughout the film.

Wax and shellac

A wax finish gives, in the main, excellent visual and tactile results. It protects well against knocks and physical abrasion and is very easy and fast to apply and repair. It is entirely suitable for vertical surfaces in most situations. The quickest and easiest way to achieve a good finish is with a coat of shellac to seal the wood, followed by wax, for polish. An equally good method is to finish with oil, or with oil followed by wax, although the speed of drying and ultimate curing is considerably longer than with wax and shellac.

While lacquers and varnishes are bought as prepared products with full data sheets and instructions, the best furniture wax is made up in the workshop from beeswax. Beeswax is the basis of most commercial furniture waxes, although it is often adulterated with paraffin wax and other substances. I use the word "adulterated" advisedly, for often the proportion of beeswax to other substances is very small in name brands. A good mix can be made quite easily from a block of pure beeswax grated with an ordinary household grater or pared with a wide chisel. Put the chips into a wide-necked container, that is, wide enough to get your hands in, such as a large mayonnaise or peanut-butter jar. Pack them loosely and add pure turpentine to half the depth taken up by the chips and set aside to dissolve. This will take about 24 hours. The final consistency should be that of soft butter just before it melts into oil. If it is too thin add more wax, or if too thick, more turpentine. When stirring, take care not to splash because, while it won't damage the skin, it can be very painful in the eyes.

Store the mix in the same wide-necked vessel with a lid, to prevent evaporation of the turpentine and hardening of the wax (although if it does harden, it can always be softened

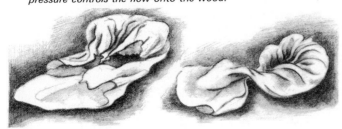

Left, a squirrel-hair 'mop' kept in a shellac bottle. Below, how to make a 'mouse.'

A square of cotton cloth is wrapped around a wad of cotton batting a little smaller than a tennis ball. Finishing material is poured in, and the cloth is folded and twisted around. Hand pressure controls the flow onto the wood.

again by the addition of a little more turpentine).

Additives can be used with this sort of preparation, but it is questionable whether it is worth it in the long run. Carnauba wax, which is added while heating the mix, results in a wax that finishes out harder than beeswax but becomes more difficult to use. Drying can be speeded by the addition of up to 25% gasoline, but the easiest and safest way is to use pure beeswax and pure turpentine. Incidentally, if you heat this wax up, you should use a hot water bath or double boiler.

Before waxing, apply an initial sealing coat of dilute shellac with a large, soft brush called a "mop" or with a "mouse" rubber. A mop is a round, squirrel-hair brush about 1½ in. in diameter, and it is best to keep it right in the shellac, suspended through a hole in the lid. The diagram shows how to make a mouse. Its advantage is that while it has a substantial reservoir of liquid, it allows fine flow control according to the amount of pressure exerted by the fingers. You can obtain a more even coat than with the brush. Only one application of shellac is necessary, to act as a barrier to inhibit the wax from penetrating the wood so deeply that it eventually disappears. If the ground of shellac were not there, it would take very much longer, and more wax, to finish the surface. The best is pure shellac dissolved in wood alcohol, rather than a commercial preparation that also contains polymerizing agents, rapid drying agents or gums. Shellac dries rapidly anyway, and you don't want to achieve a build.

Apply the wax with either a rag or brushes. The brushing method, all too infrequently used, is very similar to shining shoes or horse tack, in that two brushes are used, both of which need fairly soft bristles. Whether the brush or rag is used, apply the wax across the grain in circles to get an even, light spread, then make the final strokes with the grain.

A common mistake is to apply too much wax, leaving a deposit on the surface, on the false assumption that it will harden and disappear into the wood. The result is a sticky, uneven surface that is very difficult to level. Two or three light coats of wax are much better than one heavy one.

Oil finishes

Oil is also a sound finish in itself or as a base for subsequent waxing. Oils for furniture are usually based either on linseed oil to which polymerizing agents have been added, or on synthetic resins with hardeners added. These latter oils are often referred to as "teak" oils or "Danish" oils but this should not be taken to mean that they are used only on teak or by Danes. They can be used on any wood where the main concern is to protect and enhance the visual and tactile qualities.

Oils do, however, present more problems at the pre-gluing stages because they are highly fugitive—it is easy to contaminate gluing surfaces with oily fingers or with a touch or drip from the rag. Great care must be taken to avoid the risk of poor adhesion due to oil contamination. Also, because of its volatile nature, oil tends to creep along the grain, which makes working up to joint lines more of a risk.

It is the maker's responsibility to advise customers about the finish, its expected performance and daily care. For your own protection and reputation, this should not be merely verbal. A printed sheet giving all the information necessary should accompany the delivered furniture. □

Ian Kirby, 45, who was trained in England, directs the Hoosuck Design and Woodworking school in North Adams, Mass.

Methods of Work

Veneering cylinders

Paul Villiard in *A Manual of Veneering* makes two suggestions, among others, for veneering cylinders. (1) Use photographic print-flattening solution to make the veneer flexible; and (2) clamp the veneer by wrapping the veneered cylinder in several layers of friction tape. After veneering a large, tapered cylinder, I offer these comments: (1) The print-flattening solution produced good results on a wavy and brittle zebrano veneer ⅟₂₈ in. thick. (2) As an alternative to friction tape, I used strips of old rubber bicycle inner tube, cut about ½ in. to ¾ in. wide. The strips should be cut as long as possible in a continuous cut around the tube. Then the strips are stretched as tightly as possible around the veneered cylinder after gluing. I found I was able to get a much tighter wrap with one layer of rubber than with several of tape. And the rubber strips are reusable and virtually free if discard tubes are used. —*David J. Lutrick, Seattle, Wash.*

Repairing with glue

To reattach edge splinters on lumber or to reglue a glue void beneath the face veneer of plywood, spread the splinter open or lift the veneer up with a sewing needle, razor blade or palette knife. Then lay a fine glue bead next to the crack or

void. Force the glue into the void by blowing through a short length of flexible tubing that is narrow in diameter—windshield-washer hose or fine surgical tubing, for example. Then remove the spreaders and clamp.
—*Steve Voorheis, Missoula, Mont.*

Removing broken screws

I'm sure we have all broken off a screw head while twisting the screw into a tight hole. It is hard to remove the screw without damaging the piece. One remedy utilizes two simple plug cutters. With one plug cutter, bore out a hole around the broken screw shank. If the screw is large and runs deep and cannot be snapped out with the plug, you can chisel away the plug and grab the shank with pliers. Be careful, however, not to damage the rim of the hole. Once the screw and plug are removed, you can fill the hole with a plug made with a

cutter two sizes larger than the one used to cut the original hole. This method is better than using a dowel as a plug because the fit usually will be much tighter, the plug will be less visible since its grain will match that of the original piece, and the screw can be resunk across grain instead of into the end grain of a dowel. —*John Rocus, Ann Arbor, Mich.*

Marking tips

Old furniture that is to be taken apart, repaired and reassembled must be marked so that the pieces can be easily identified. Since surface marks will be obliterated by stripping and refinishing chemicals, it is best to use indentation marks. I mark all pieces before disassembly, and always on the underside. I mark only one end of the male/tenon member close to the female/mortise member. I use one set of chisel marks with the grain, then one set across the grain, then tiny nail-set marks. Next I use *X* marks or any combination of the above.
—*Price G. Schulte, St. Louis, Mo.*

Sanding small pieces

While doing some restoration work, I needed to inlay a patch in a veneered surface. The piece to be inlaid was a bit too thick. Ordinarily, one would sand it flush with the surface after gluing. In this case, sanding would have marred the surrounding finish. I had to devise a way to hold the patch so that it could be sanded evenly. I put coarse-grit sandpaper on the bench, then put the patch on it. This way it could be easily and evenly worked with a sanding block, using a finer grit. When a thin workpiece is sandwiched between two grits, it locks into the coarser grit as pressure is applied and is held firmly. —*Joseph T. Ponessa, Moorestown, N.J.*

Marquetry patching

Your marquetry picture is cut, mounted, sanded and with a coat of finish, but something seems wrong. This happens often, because no matter how carefully you select veneer, you don't notice until the end that a piece doesn't look right. Some people just cut out the section to be replaced, trace the opening and insert a new piece. With my method, the section is traced before cutting.

With tracing paper taped to the picture, draw the section you wish to replace. Tape the tracing paper with carbon paper and trace the pattern onto the new piece of veneer. Then cut out the piece. Lay it on top of the picture to see how it looks; if you don't like it, cut another piece.

With the new section positioned on the picture, secure half of it with tape and score around the other half with a knife, using the veneer as a guide. Then tape the scored side, remove the tape and cut very carefully along the marking through the veneer that is to be replaced. With a small chisel or square-bladed X-acto knife, stab this veneer in the center and pry it up, working carefully from the center to the edges. Now fit the new section into the gap. If it doesn't fit, sand or shave the edges until it does. Glue with white glue and press. Wipe off excess glue and sand just a little with fine sandpaper backed by a wood block to get dust into the cracks that are filled with wet glue. Put a small board and a heavy weight atop the piece and let dry overnight. Then sand until all is level, and finish. —*Peter L. Rose, Saddle Brook, N.J.*

Sanding
The basic tools and techniques

by Ben Green

Sanding equipment includes (left to right) a Merit Sand-O-Flex, a belt sander, a drum sander, an orbital sander and a sanding block.

Many woodworkers don't have a clear understanding of the role of sanding in finishing and refinishing. Commonly asked questions include: Does this need sanding? How much? What paper and what sander should I use? What is coarse grit? Should the final sanding always be done by hand? Almost everyone agrees that some sanding must be done, grabs the sandpaper and gives it a shot. If sanding is incorrectly or hastily done, however, the finish will never be as fine as it could be. Sanding is work and takes time, but the many recent improvements in equipment and abrasive papers make it possible for today's finisher or refinisher to surpass even the most meticulous craftsman of yesteryear.

Equipment needs depend on the job being done and the kind of shop being outfitted. A well-equipped shop would have a belt sander, an orbital (pad) sander, a Sand-O-Flex, drum sanders (attached to an electric drill), a sanding block and various pieces of stationary bench equipment. For those just starting out, however, about $20 will buy an orbital sander that will do an excellent job.

The belt sander, designed for fast sanding of large, flat surfaces, is ideally a part of the cabinet shop, though optional for the refinishing shop. It effectively sands new wood before it is assembled and sands down large surfaces that have been glued up from narrower stock. In the refinishing shop the belt sander is useful for sanding down tops that have been reglued, warped areas or pieces that were particularly rough to start with. Belt sanders should have a low center of gravity and a 4-in. belt. Vacuum pickup is a must. Belt sanders are heavy, powerful and quick-cutting. It is important to keep them flat to the work, which is why the 4-in. width and the low center of gravity are important. Make sure the belt size is standard, such as 4 in. by 24 in., or 4 in. by 36 in. Standard belts are more readily available and competitively priced.

The orbital sander removes stock quickly and smoothly by the circular motion of its sanding pad. In a typical shop, it probably does about 90% of the sanding. There are two popular sizes. The size that takes ⅓ of a sheet of sandpaper is best in a refinishing shop. If a cabinet shop has a belt sander, then the ⅓-sheet size is a good companion to it, otherwise the ½-sheet size is better, because it is large enough and heavy enough to cut down new wood before it is assembled. There are two popular orbit speeds, 4,000 and 10,000 rpm. The 10,000 speed doesn't work faster, but is somewhat easier to handle. Some pad sanders can be shifted from orbital to inline motion, and while this appears to be desirable, I do not find it very useful. Orbital motion cuts faster than inline motion, and in the 120 to 320-grit range will not leave swirl marks, as commonly thought. The price range of ⅓-sheet orbital sanders is from about $20 to $100. If you have extra

Ben Green, 40, works at Sears, Roebuck and Co., Chicago. He has been teaching furniture refinishing for four years.

money to spend on equipment, this is the place to spend it. Top-of-the-line sanders last longer and can be worked harder, accomplishing more in a given period of time.

The Sand-O-Flex (manufactured by Merit Abrasive Company) is useful in a refinishing shop but would be optional in a cabinet shop. It has six sanding surfaces backed by bristle brushes that contour the sandpaper to the surface being sanded. It can be attached to a ¼-in. or ⅜-in. electric drill or to a flexible shaft on an electric motor. It is one of the few methods of effectively sanding turned, carved or irregular surfaces. The Sand-O-Flex sells for less than $20, and sandpaper refills cost about $2. The sandpaper comes in coarse, medium and fine (fine is 150 grit). It is either scored or unscored, but scored is the best for irregular surfaces. The Sand-O-Flex should not be confused with tools called "flap sanders." Flap sanders are less expensive but cannot be refilled with sandpaper. I find they do not do as good a job as the Sand-O-Flex.

Small drum sanders attached to an electric drill are useful for irregular edges, such as those cut with a band saw or jigsaw. Several sizes are available. Something in the 1½-in. to 2½-in. diameter range is a useful size to have. A sanding block is a must for hand-sanding. It gives the hand something large to hold on to and apply pressure to, and it ensures that the abrasive paper is applied flat to the surface, avoiding the uneven pressure that would be applied by three or four fingers. A good sanding block uses ¼ of a sheet of sandpaper and has a rubber surface between the paper and its metal parts. Don't buy a block that must use special paper—the paper will be more expensive than cutting your own from regular sandpaper sheets.

Stationary bench sanding equipment includes belt sanders, disc sanders and drum sanders. Their usefulness is so limited in the small shop that the expense of owning them is usually not justified. The common disc sander that is attached to an electric drill can be used for fast cutting if nothing else is available, but use it with extreme care, with about 100-grit paper, and only as a preliminary step.

Modern abrasive papers allow the refinisher a quality that was not available even as recently as 50 years ago. They are somewhat confusing in their generic names and in the different methods of grading.

Silicon-carbide paper, either black or white in color, is the best available. Its features are hardness (resistance to wear), adhesion of the grit to the backing, and resistance to loading (filling up the grit with the abraded surface). Black silicon carbide is generally waterproof, for wet sanding with water or finishing liquids. There is no difference between the two when comparing equal grits of both. Silicon carbide is difficult to find but worth the effort and the price.

Aluminum-oxide paper, grey in color, is a good abrasive, readily available and close in quality to silicon carbide. Garnet paper, the most widely used good-quality abrasive paper, is the choice of many refinishers and cabinetmakers. Its popularity is probably due to the fact that it has been on the market longer than the other good abrasive papers. Flint, the original "sandpaper," is a waste of money and should be used only when absolutely nothing else is available.

Select an abrasive paper according to personal preference, price and availability. Papers can be purchased in large packages of 50 to 100 sheets at a considerable saving. Abrasive paper can be kept indefinitely if it is stored flat and wrapped in plastic to protect it from moisture.

Paper for orbital sanders and sanding blocks can be cut from regular sheets—cheaper than buying precut paper. A

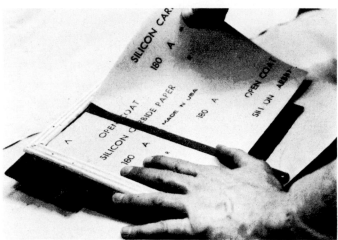

A simple jig for cutting standard sandpaper to fit an orbital sander is made by mitering and gluing two strips of wood to a base of Masonite or plywood. The hacksaw blade is glued only under the top strip. To use, slide the paper under the blade and against the side strip. Then rip, with the thumb holding the blade down.

Sandpaper grading

The most common gradings on sandpaper package labels are "fine," "medium," and "coarse," and degrees of these, such as "very fine." These terms are practically useless to the serious finisher, because their meaning is variable. Two accurate methods of describing sandpaper grading are the use of aughts and grit numbers. High grit numbers, such as 400, and many aughts, such as 10/0, represent very fine abrasive paper. Low grit numbers, such as 80, and few aughts, such as 2/0, represent coarse abrasive paper. At least one of these grading methods will be printed on the backing of most abrasive paper, although it may be necessary to open the package to find the grade.

Grit #		Aughts
400 320	Very fine	10/0 9/0
280 240 220	Fine	8/0 7/0 6/0
180 150 120	Medium	5/0 4/0 3/0
100 80	Coarse	2/0 1/0
60 50	Very coarse	1/2 1

cutting jig can be constructed from a piece of Masonite or plywood, a hacksaw blade and two strips of wood.

Sanding is a critical step in the total finishing/refinishing process. When refinishing, the proper application of paint and varnish remover may leave the work so clean and smooth that it is tempting to proceed directly to the final finish. Don't. When building a new piece, the wood may look so nice that the maker is tempted to skip sanding. Again, don't. Every piece of furniture that is being refinished or finished for the first time can be vastly improved by a good sanding.

The first rule is to sand with the grain. You must resist the natural tendency of the arm to work in an arc. Position the piece so that the grain of the wood runs with the body and not opposite it. On most jobs, sanding should start with 120-grit (3/0) abrasive paper. If the piece is already quite smooth, start with a finer grit, such as 150. On the other hand, if the piece is especially rough, begin with a coarser grit, such as 100. Coarse grit papers should always be used sparingly and carefully because the scratches they make are too deep and hard to remove at later stages.

All areas of the piece that are to be finished should receive the same amount of sanding. The initial sanding should correct any bad spots, such as burns or gouges that can't be filled, and when it is done all areas of the piece should be the same color and smoothness. Any crack filler that has been used in repairs should have been smoothed out. This step accomplishes most of the work and the next two steps will only lighten the color and smooth out the surface slightly.

Certain areas, such as depressions, warped boards and tool burns, will require the application of more pressure. In effect, these areas will become "dished out," but only slightly, and will not be noticeable unless closely inspected.

After initial sanding, the piece must be sanded twice more with finer paper. The second sanding should use 180-grit paper. Final sanding should use 280-grit paper or finer. These are suggested grits—use what is available. Don't skip the intermediate sanding; in particular, don't go from coarse paper to very fine without an intermediate paper. Sanding removes imperfections but if an intermediate grit is skipped, then the big scratches left by initial sanding will not be removed and will show through the finish. This is true for sanding by hand or with an orbital sander.

When trying to judge if a piece has been sanded enough, feel it as well as look at it. Stain and finish don't cover up a poor sanding job. In fact, they tend to amplify imperfections such as swirls left by an orbital sander.

Ideally, the final sanding with the finest paper should be done just before applying the first coat of finish or stain. In any case, the time between the final sanding and the first coat of finish or stain should not exceed 24 hours. It is too easy to soil or damage a project, and raw, unsealed wood can pick up moisture from the air. It may appear perfect after standing a week after the final sanding, but stain or finish will often show up dark areas, or an edge that might have been slightly bruised will show up dark. If some time has passed since the final sanding, a quick touch-up with the final paper will prevent a serious problem later.

Wet-sanding, feathering the grain after the final sanding and then sanding again, is an old but commonly used technique. Many people think this is the best way to get a smooth finish, but I think that modern abrasive papers and a good orbital sander have eliminated the need for it. To wet-sand, the wood should be slightly dampened with a rag or sponge after the final sanding. After the wood has dried, the grain will be slightly raised; these "feathers" are then cut off with fine paper. This step is necessary if the wood is going to be stained with a water-based stain, but not if you use modern penetrating oil or non-grain-raising stains.

Power equipment can speed up the sanding of any piece and make it a great deal easier. Most of the principles that apply to hand-sanding also apply to power sanding, but always remember that power-sanding cuts away more material than hand-sanding does. The use of coarse papers should therefore be restricted with power sanders. Never sand cross-grain with a power sander, and take care to avoid rounding off an edge, corner or the raised part of a carving.

Many pieces can be completely sanded with an orbital sander. As with hand-sanding, the starting grit should be 120, the intermediate 180 and the finish 280 or finer. There is no reason to hand-sand over an area that has been properly sanded with an orbital sander. Always move the orbital sander with the grain of the wood, in a natural swirling motion, allowing its weight and its motion to do the work. The sander can be held on areas that are particularly rough or discolored because it will cut even when standing still.

Belt sanding does not eliminate any hand or orbital sanding steps, but is only preliminary to initial sanding. Use nothing coarser than an 80 or 100-grit belt. If the belt sander has both a low and high speed, use the low speed.

Sanding new wood before assembly is advantageous because the parts can be worked on flat before they are connected. They are easier to get to and there are no inside corners. Plywood is generally smooth enough not to need any sanding before assembly. Regular mill stock should be sanded with a belt sander and a 100-grit belt, followed by an orbital sander with 120 or 150-grit paper. At this point paper finer than 150 should not be used, because assembling, handling and storing will soil or mar the piece to the point where the final sanding would only have to be repeated.

Turnings should be sanded to 280-grit or finer while still chucked in the lathe. Even though some sanding may have to be repeated after the piece is assembled, these pieces can be sanded effectively only while they are rotating in the lathe.

After the project is completely assembled, touch-up sanding with the initial paper will have to be done. Glue joints should be carefully sanded with coarse paper, followed by intermediate and fine sanding.

Irregular surfaces are difficult to sand because most power sanding equipment conforms only to a flat surface. This is a problem for the refinisher, because old pieces usually have intricate carving, spindles or applied decoration. Many times these irregular areas will stand out after the piece is finished, because they were not sanded as well as the flat surfaces. Start with an extra good job of cleaning with paint and varnish remover. After the top coats of paint or varnish have been removed, the paint remover should be applied again and carefully worked into corners and crevices with a pointed stick. After the last coat of paint remover has been removed with a coarse rag or fine steel wool, the surface should be scrubbed with a dry scrub brush. If a water-wash paint remover has been used, these areas can be scrubbed with a brush and soap and water. The grain will be raised but getting the wood completely clean is worth it.

Whenever water is used on wood, it should be immediately

Molded edges can be sanded with a wadded-up piece of used sandpaper. Start with 120 grit, follow with 180 grit, and finish with dry 4/0 steel wool.

Sand spindles by twisting some wadded sandpaper around them, or by twisting the paper with one hand and the turning with the other.

Places that are hard to reach can be sanded with a long, narrow strip of sandpaper worked like a shoeshine cloth.

and thoroughly dried, especially in cracks or crevices. Allow the piece to dry overnight before starting to sand.

The sanding of carved surfaces, applied decorations, pressed wood designs or intricately molded edges is best started by wadding up a used piece of 120-grit paper. Use a gentle scrubbing motion to work the wadded sandpaper into the intricacies of the design, but take care not to rub off the sharp corners that give the design its character. If deep or delicate areas of the design cannot be reached with the wadded sandpaper, they should be gently scraped with a small knife blade. Then follow with a wadded, used piece of 180-grit paper. The final step should be a gentle scrubbing with dry 4/0 steel wool.

Turnings can also be sanded with a wadded piece of sandpaper that is wrapped around the spindle. Either twist the paper around the turning, or if the piece is apart, twist the paper with one hand and the turning with the other. Follow with 180-grit paper and finish with dry 4/0 steel wool. Closely spaced spindles can be sanded with a long, narrow strip of sandpaper that is wrapped around the turning and worked like a shoeshine cloth. These narrow strips can be cut from paper-backed abrasive paper, but emery cloth or used sander belts are much stronger. The edges of the narrow strips are very sharp and can make a mark in the turning if they are not moved carefully. It may be necessary to cut strips of varying widths to reach all surfaces of the turning. This will be cross-grain sanding but it compares to the way such pieces were sanded while still on the lathe. The final sanding should be with a wadded piece of 280-grit paper, going with the grain.

No matter how good a building project or how fine an antique, a poor job of finishing results in only mediocre projects and so-so antiques. The proper equipment, good abrasive paper and a consistent approach to sanding will provide the basis for a fine finish.

□

Tung Oil
Quick-drying finish is handsome and tough

by William D. Woods

If you haven't used tung oil, and you're tired of worrying about stain and filler colors, primers, adhesion, drying time, runs and drips, checking and water marks, it may be time to give it a try. While there's probably no stage of woodworking easier to mess up than finishing, it's hard to go wrong with tung oil. It yields a finish with contrast and depth, and is readily available and easy to use. It also builds well, dries quickly, and is water and solvent-resistant.

Tung oil is an aromatic natural drying oil extracted from the nuts of the tung tree (*Aleurites montana* or *A. fordii*), which is native to the Orient but now cultivated in the Gulf States. The color of tung oil ranges from golden yellow to dark brown, depending on the amount of heat used during extraction. The oil takes its name from the Chinese word "tung," or stomach, because it has a purgative action when taken internally. The properties of the oil are almost proverbial, and the preservation of the Great Wall has been attributed in part to tung-oil treatment of the masonry. In modern varnishes, tung oil is often used as a drying oil, giving elasticity and durability to the film.

Tung oil (sometimes called tung-oil varnish) is commonly available in two forms: the "pure" or unthinned state, which has about the viscosity of glycerine, and the volatilized or thinned state, which is watery or sometimes a little thicker. Although manufacturers are loath to reveal their "trade secrets," the odor suggests that the vehicle is mineral spirits or something similar. Pure tung oil can be thinned with paint thinner or turpentine; however, the commercially thinned oil, which probably contains a drying agent, dries faster than tung oil mixed with paint thinner alone. In general, the commercially thinned oil is easier to use and more versatile than the pure oil. The pure oil is also becoming harder to find.

The characteristics of tung oil are unlike those of most "oil" finishes. In fact, the name "tung oil" is misleading, because it produces not only a soaking finish but also a building finish. If brushed on like any other surface finish and left to dry, it will harden into a glossy film much like varnish. If used as an oil finish, it will build quickly and effectively consolidate the wood surface; furthermore, it will yield a much better sheen than any other oil preparation I know of.

Cured tung oil is tough. When I first encountered this oil, I conducted some experiments to compare it to other finishes. I found that a dried tung-oil film is considerably more flexible than a lacquer or varnish film—it is possible to bend the film sharply double and then flatten it out again without breaking it. Although a tung-oil film is not as resistant to abrasion as urethane varnish, tung oil soaked into the wood is incredibly resistant to marring. It also shows good solvent resistance, even against a short exposure to acetone. To test tung oil's resistance to water, I made up a sample of Honduras mahogany with three soak coats of tung oil, drying it in the sun and overnight. I then applied a large drop of water to one

section of the sample and kept that area wet for an entire day. At the end of the day I dried the sample off, and with 4/0 steel wool burnished away the mineral ring left by the water. I couldn't detect any damage. My uncle, a gunsmith, claims similar results on gunstocks. He says that tung oil puts the more commonly used linseed oil "right out on the back porch." Tung oil is also often recommended for use on salad bowls, butcher blocks and other wood surfaces exposed to water, acids, oils and food residues. When used on eating utensils, however, the oil should be allowed to dry thoroughly before using. Because tung oil is not prone to checking, it is also suitable for certain outdoor applications.

In my experience, tung oil is easier to use than any other wood finish. It will prime any raw wood I have tried, including rosewood and vermilion, without delayed drying and without bleeding the color. The first coat is applied immediately after finish-sanding or scraping—use a brush, your fingers or a rag. I use thinned oil because it flows and soaks better without filling the pores, but for maximum build or a final coat pure oil is suitable. You can make thinned oil as thick as you want by exposing it to the air in a shallow pan. The oil should soak into the wood anywhere from 30 seconds to about 10 minutes, depending on weather conditions, the properties of the wood, and the particular oil being used. It may be beneficial to rub the oil into the wood with the hand or a pad. After soaking, wipe off all the excess with a clean rag. If the oil has become tacky, wipe it off with a rag moistened in fresh oil. Clean up brushes and spills with mineral spirits or lacquer thinner.

Each coat of oil should dry at least an hour, longer if it is very humid. I have sometimes recoated within 20 or 30 minutes on warm dry days with no trouble. To hasten the drying, the project may be set in the sun to cook. Tung oil does not seep out of the wood and "bead" on the surface, since it dries quickly, supposedly from the inside out. It usually does not raise the grain, and a quick rub with 4/0 steel wool after the first coat will ensure a smooth surface. Otherwise, it is not necessary to rub between coats.

The number of coats required depends on the porosity of the wood, the thickness of the oil, and the desired sheen. For protection, two coats of thin oil are often enough, although I would recommend three coats for the best durability and an

Burl bowls of ponderosa pine, 8 in. and 3½ in. in diameter, made by the author and finished with tung oil.

attractive satin sheen. After drying for a day, the surface may be burnished with 4/0 steel wool for a more even sheen. All subsequent cleaning and polishing of the finished surface should be done only with lemon-oil treatment. Although I have used tung oil as a surface finish in experiments, I do not recommend it as such, because it is not as durable as varnish or lacquer and poses the same application problems as any other surface finish.

Tung oil can also be used as a filler finish, because it will build with repeated applications. Apply the oil in the usual fashion, but let it dry until it becomes viscous (from 5 to 30 minutes). With the palm of the hand or with a rag, rub the gelled oil into the open pores of the wood much as you would a regular filler, then wipe off the excess. It will be necessary to dry the project for a day or more, because more than the usual amount of oil has been applied. Filling the pores completely may require five or more applications. Remember that the oil in the pores will shrink, so thorough drying is essential before any rubbing. This method is more laborious and time-consuming than the apply-and-wipe method.

Like many wood finishes, tung oil tends to skin over and finally to congeal if stored in a container less than about three-quarters full. If thickened tung oil is not too far gone, it can be reconstituted by adding mineral spirits and straining; however, always test such oil before using it. The problem of storage can be overcome by using a variable-volume container like a flexible polyethylene bottle. As the oil is used up, the bottle is squeezed to drive out all air before being capped. Better yet, obtain two or three of the refillable plastic food tubes made for hikers (they look like large toothpaste tubes). Cap the tube, then fill it with oil through the large open end, leaving enough room to fold the tube over and install the retaining clip. As you use the oil, squeeze the tube to eliminate the air. As for the storage life of tung oil, I have not had opportunity for a long-term experiment. It has a shelf life as good or better than traditional varnishes, if kept from temperature extremes and direct light in a nearly full, tightly sealed container.

Tung oil, because it soaks into the wood, heightens contrast and deepens color. Its finished sheen is warm, yet it permits easy view of the wood without any disturbing glare. And the disadvantages? Undoubtedly, the price of tung oil has been a deterrent to potential users—the unthinned extract is about $9 a pint, while the thinned variety is about $6 a quart—but a little goes a long way. One quart of thinned oil will easily finish three or four medium-size pieces of furniture. Considering the properties of tung oil, the price becomes rather insignificant. Because tung oil emphasizes most subtleties of graining, it may infrequently be found objectionable as a primer for light softwoods (spruce, for example) where the revelation of peculiar grain patterns may spoil the even, creamy color. With these woods, a test sample is in order. Personally, I think nothing looks better on wood than tung oil, because in finishing, I prefer to alter the wood as little as possible. I seldom use stains and usually make no attempt to fill the pores, which I feel are part of the wood's natural beauty. Above all, I want to see the wood, so I avoid glossy finishes. Tung oil agrees with my sense of esthetics. □

Bill Woods, 25, of Phoenix, Ariz., refinishes furniture part-time and makes guitars. He is now establishing himself as a professional woodworker.

INDEX

In this index, references to entire articles list only the first page of the article. Entries in small capitals are names of authors. For easy reference, many of the entries are grouped under the following general subject headings: design, finishing, joinery, saws, tools, wood. For example, look for dovetails under joinery.

ALEXANDER, JOHN D., JR., 28
ANDERSON, JOYCE and EDGAR, 7

Band saw, circle-cutting jig, 116
Bearings, machine, 65
Beeswax, 191
Belts, machine, 66
Bench, low, 28
Bending
  hot-pipe, 168
  irons, 169
  steam, 162
Blacksmithing tools, 32
BLANDFORD, PERCY W., 75
Boring, cylindrical, 142
Bottles, laminated, 134
Bowls
  finishing, 133
  laminated, 134, 140
  spalted, 128, 131
Bowsaw, how to make, 55
Boxes, clamping, 49
Boxes, turned, 125
BROOKS, JON, 148
BUTZ, RICK, 152
BUYER, ROBERT L., 146

Cabinet, tool, 26
Carving
  ball-and-claw feet, 156
  beginning, 146
  chain-saw, 148
  cockleshell, 158
  gouges, 152, 153
  relief, 152
  tools, 146
  workbench, 25
Chain
  ripping, 5
  roller, 67
  sharpening, 5
Chair, post-and-rung, 28
Chemicals, finishing, 186
CHILD, PETER, 120
Chisels, making, 60
Circles, cutting, 116
Clamping
  boxes, 49
  picture frames, 49
Clamps
  bedspring, 49
  bench, 31
  making, 42
  storing, 48
  wooden, 42
Cleaving, 13
Clocks, 110
COHEN, SANDY, 175
Cones, staved, 139
CUMPIANO, WILLIAM R., 168
Cutting-unit method, 11

DAVIES, BEN, 98
Design, 95, 151
  bowls, 131
  clocks, 110
  doors, 98, 104
  Fibonacci series, 101
  golden rectangle, 101
  scale models, 63
  table, dining extension, 106
  tambours, 88
  workbench, 25
Desks, cylinder, 95
Doors
  frame-and-panel, 98, 104
  hanging, 102, 103
  louvered, 96
  tamboured, 88
Dowel maker, 45
Drawer, 78
  assembly, 78
  bottoms, 83
  push, 82
Drilling, 62
Drum, Aztec, 144
Drying, microwave, 130
Dust-collection system, 22
Dust removal, 131

End boring, jig for, 62

Face edge, 70
Face side, 70
Feet, ball and claw, 156
Fibonacci series, 101
Finishing, 188
  beeswax, 191
  bowls, 133
  carving, 150
  chemicals, 186
  dyeing, 186
  lacquer, 190
  maple, curly, 188
  mill marks, removing, 188
  oil, 191
  oil and varnish, 133
  polyurethane, 133
  sanding, 193
  shellac, 190
  staining, 186, 188
    birch, 186
    mahogany, 186
    maple, 186
    oak, 186
    palazota, 186
    stains, 188
  steel-wool holder, 124
  tung oil, 196
  varnish, 190
  veneer, 183
  Watco oil, 183
  wax, 190
Flageolet, 142, 144
Forging tools, 32
Formulas, for cones, 137, 139
FORRESTER, KENT, 142
FRANK, GEORGE, 186
FRID, TAGE, 26, 52, 102, 106, 172
Froe, 13

Gauges
  marking, 51, 75
  pencil, 75
  saw-filing, 58
Glue
  blocks, 81
  hide, 92, 172
  hot animal, 92
  yellow, 92, 99
Gluing, 92
  bowls, 137, 140
  clamps, 46
  doors, 99
  frame, 49
  repairs, 192
  tambours, 91
  veneer, 172, 180
Gold inlay, 176
GOTTSHALL, FRANKLIN H., 158
Gouges
  carving, 152, 153
  turning, 120
Grading
  hardwood, 11
  softwood, 10
GRAVES, GARTH F., 134
GREEN, BEN, 193
Grinders, hand, 41
Grindstones, 120
  resurfacing, 40
Guitars, bending, 168

Hammer veneering, 172
HARRA, JOHN, 86
Hinges, two-way, 105
HOADLEY, R. BRUCE, 8, 17, 25
Holding devices, 28

Inlay, leather, 175
Inletting hardware, 96
Instruments, musical, 142, 144, 168
IRWIN, HARRY, 140

Jigs
  circle-cutting, 116
  end-boring, 62
  rings, 138
  router, 87, 96
  sandpaper-cutting, 194
  saw-sharpening, 5, 53
  tambour-gluing, 91
  tapering, 109
  veneer thicknesser, 152
JOHNSON, DOYLE, 22
Joinery,
  curved-edge, 82
  dovetail, 80
  dovetail, door-frame, 102
  doweled, blind, 99
  drawers, 80, 83
  frame-and-panel, 98
  miters, 139
  mortise-and-tenon, 99, 108, 181
  routed-edge, 86
  scarf, clamping, 49
Jointer, 71

KEYSER, WILLIAM A., JR., 162
KIRBY, IAN, 70, 188
KRAMER, HENRY J., 50

Lacquer, 190
Laminations, 134, 140
  bent, 162
  handles, 44
LANGSNER, DREW, 13
LARSEN, RAY, 32
Leather
  on wood, 175
  tooling, 176
Legs, cabriole, 156
LINDQUIST, MARK, 128
LORD, JOHN R., 110
Lubricants, 64
Lumber grading, 10
Lumbering, chain-saw, 2

Machinery maintenance, 64
MACKANESS, TIM 105
MARCH, BOB, 94
Marking, 75, 192
  triangle system, 76
MARKS, ALAN, 83
MARLOW, A. W., 156
Marquetry
  mounting, 178
  patching, 192
Mathematics, cones, 137, 139
MATTIA, ALPHONSE, 88
Mill, portable chain-saw, 2, 7
Models, scale, 63
Moisture meters, 8
Moldings, 50, 61
  door, 100
  ogee, 82
Molds, steam-bending, 164
MOORE, C. EDWARD, 180

NITTA, RAY, 144

Oil finish, 191
  tung, 196

Paste, for leather, 175
Planer, surface, 71
Planes
  jointer, 72
  mortising, 96
Planing
  hand, 72
  shooting board for, 74
Plywood, veneering, 172
Pulleys, machine, 66

Resawing, 55
REYNOLDS, WILLIAM F., 96
RICE, WILLIAM W., 10
RICHEY, JIM, 51
ROBINSON, TREVOR, 45
ROSE, PETER L., 178
ROTH, EUGENE, 56
Router, 86
Routing, tracking grooves, 89
RYAN, WILLIS N., III, 103